HEALTHY FOOD CHOICES

A PURE VEGETARIAN RECIPE BOOK

By

Leona R. Alderson

TEACH Services, Inc.
Brushton, New York 12916

Copyright © 1994 by Leona R. Alderson

ISBN 0-945383-98-3

Library of Congress Catalog Card Number 94-60900

Published by

TEACH Services, Inc.

Route 1, Box 182
Brushton, New York 12916

ACKNOWLEDGEMENTS:

I would like to thank all those who have helped with classes through the years by doing demonstrations, washing dishes, taking attendance, befriending the participants, and making suggestions (Lila Adams, Orville Bishop, Nina Chernipeski, Carol Couser, Linda Curtis, Zahwa Deeb, Barbara Dronan, Gladys Fenton, Gem Fitch, Victor Fitch Jr, Helen Fowlie, Tim Fowlie, Karen Halminen, Mary Jane Heilman, Mable & Herb Jeffery, Mona Karst, Iris McClair, Rosalie McClair-Nichol, Pharolyn Perk, Dian Perkins, Don Polishuk, Ella Saarinen, Esko Saarinen, Bill Slywka, Frances Straughan, Marjorie Thomas, Sandra Thomas, Beverley Thorne, Eleanor Von Gunten, Rosemarie Davidson-Welsh and any others who I may have forgotten).

I would especially like to thank Dr. Winston Craig and Dr. Hans Diehl for giving me permission to quote from their books.

I would also like to express appreciation to Dr. Elmia Buxton, Dr. Haskell Edwards, and David Higgins for their encouragement in this project.

Special thanks to Keith Rasmussen for his patient help with computer difficulties.

Thanks to Robin Carby for designing the cover.

I would also like to thank those who have attended the classes and invited friends to come, especially Susan Genge, a United Church Pastor, who attended six series and has encouraged her friends to attend and Bill Slywka who has attended every series since the fall of 1982 and faithfully tells his friends about the classes and helps with demonstrations.

Without the help of so many people and the blessing of God this book would never have become a reality.

INTRODUCTION:

This is a compilation of some of the best recipes used in HEALTHY CHOICES vegetarian nutrition classes conducted for the public since 1982 and is a result of requests from people who have attended. In each series I have tried to have some new recipes. Many of those who attend have come as a result of a friend's recommendation and some have attended up to six series, so there is a need to have new recipes, but the new people say things like, "My friend got a recipe for fruit soup. We didn't get that recipe." This book is to satisfy those people. Many longtime lacto-ovo vegetarians have expressed delighted surprise when they find the foods made from these recipes quite palatable.

Some of the recipes may seem complicated at first, but as in any other aspect of life, practice makes perfect. In some cases the list of ingredients is long because of a variety of seasonings. The extra effort involved in making them pays off when people in the family who may not be convinced at first on the value of a vegetarian diet accept the new foods.

It is not intended that the average person would eat only half cup servings of many of the dishes, but both the Canadian and United States recommended numbers of servings from the various food groups use half-cup servings, so most of the recipes have been calculated with this in mind.

If time is limited it is still possible to eat adequately without preparing several recipes per day. For example, plain beans with pasta, potatoes, or rice, another vegetable and a salad would be satisfying, but may become monotonous on a daily basis. Many of the recipes can be frozen in portions suitable for the family and used later.

An attempt is made to follow the advice given by Ellen White in *The Ministry of Healing* page 296 "Grains, fruits, nuts, and vegetables constitute the diet chosen for us by our Creator. These foods, prepared in as simple and natural a manner as possible, are the most healthful and nourishing. They impart a strength, a power of endurance, and a vigour of intellect that are not afforded by a more complex and stimulating diet." I have put very little emphasis on the obvious, that **more raw fruits, vegetables, and whole grains** should be included in the day's menu.

Attention should be paid to the appearance of the food, so garnishing and serving food attractively should become a habit.

The recipes: -are free of animal products and consequently free of cholesterol
-use a minimum of separated fat and refined sugars
-are free of: harmful spices
baking soda
baking powder
vinegar
-appeal to the palate of those who are trying to adopt a vegan
diet, but need help getting started

Leona R. Alderson

TABLE OF CONTENTS

FORWARD:

C. W. Ceran said, "Genius is the ability to reduce the complicated to the simple." I think that Leona Alderson has taken the complicated subject of nutrition and produced some very basic, simple, good tasting recipes. All of us, I think, know that we ought not to eat junk food and we ought to eat close to nature. But most times, we don't have the ability, skills or the knowledge to make it taste good. If it doesn't taste good, we probably won't stick with the diet, no matter how healthy it is.

Leona Alderson taught high school and college nutrition for 23 years. Since her retirement she has been teaching nutrition and cooking classes for more than 12 years. From her practical experience, she has culled out the very best recipes and tested them over and over again. I remember sitting in her kitchen and eating at her table. The food that she set before me was very attractive and so tasty that it was hard to believe that everything was so healthy.

There are several vegetarian recipe cookbooks out but few have been prepared by people who have as much knowledge and practical skill as Leona Alderson. I believe that a cholesterol-free diet was the original Edenic diet that God gave to us. I believe that when we once again dine in the earth made new it will be the same cholesterol-free diet (there'll be no killing of any animals, for the wolf and the lamb shall feed together, Isaiah 65:25. There'll be golden streets but no golden arches.) I especially like the food analysis, the calorie breakdown and the exchanges on each and every recipe. On many of the pages she has weaved in an encouraging thought and nutritional tidbits that I like to read as I am studying and preparing the recipes.

In all, I think Leona has prepared an excellent cholesterol-free cookbook with superb tasting recipes. This textbook proves that a vegan can get the recommended nutrients and a balanced diet without any meat products. Following these recipes, one will get adequate protein, calcium, iron and only about 15% of total calories will be from fat.

D. S. Williams, Ed.D., M. P. H., C.H.E.S.
Director, North American Division Health and Temperance Department
of the General Conference of the Seventh-day Adventist Church

ARMENIAN BULGUR (makes 8-10 servings)

15 mL	(1 Tbsp.)	oil (adjust amount according to how much you can afford)
250 mL	(1 cup)	chopped onion
2	(2)	garlic cloves, minced
375 mL	(1 1/2 cups)	tomatoes (fresh or canned)
5 mL	(1 tsp.)	salt
5 mL	(1 tsp.)	chicken style seasoning
500 mL	(2 cups)	coarse bulgur
1125 mL	(4 1/2 cups)	boiling water

Method:

SAUTE the onion and garlic in the oil. ADD tomatoes. Bring to a boil. MIX in salt, chicken style seasoning, bulgur and boiling water. BRING to a boil. TURN down heat. COVER and COOK until water is absorbed. REMOVE lid and COVER with a paper towel to absorb steam that accumulated on the lid. SERVE with lentils, broccoli, and a salad. (Recipe, courtesy of Mrs. Susan Doukmetzian)

```
-----------------------------------------------------------------------------
| Analysis: ARMENIAN BULGUR                         Divided by: 8           |
|           Wgt: 237 g (8.35 oz.)                   Water:      83%         |
-----------------------------------------------------------------------------
```

Calories	153		Vitamin C	8.31 mg
Protein	5.13 g		Vitamin D	0 mcg
Carbohydrates	30.6 g		Vit E-Alpha E	.521 mg
Fat - Total	2.3 g		Vitamin K	mcg
Saturated Fat	.334 g		Biotin	mcg
Mono Fat	1.33 g		Calcium	33.4 mg
Poly Fat	.393 g		Copper	.201 mg
Cholesterol	0 mg		Iodine	mcg
Dietary Fibre	7.46 g		Iron	1.28 mg
Soluble Fibre	1.46 g		Magnesium	67.5 mg
Total Vit A	27.8 RE		Manganese	1.17 mg
Thiamin-B1	.162 mg		Phosphorus	127 mg
Riboflavin-B2	.073 mg		Potassium	284 mg
Niacin-B3	2.28 mg		Selenium	8.23 mcg
Niacin Equiv.	2.15 mg		Sodium	364 mg
Vitamin B6	.212 mg		Zinc	.865 mg
Vitamin B12	0 mcg		Complex Carbs	20.2 g
Folate	29.4 mcg		Sugars	2.83 g
Pantothenic	.495 mg		Water	197 g

CALORIE BREAKDOWN		FAT		EXCHANGES	
Protein	13%	*Saturated :	1.8%	Bread	1.33
Carbohydrates	75%	Mono Unsat:	7.3%	Vegetables	.625
Fat-Total *	13%	Poly Unsat:	2.2%	Fat	.327

CHEERFULNESS:

The stomach is closely related to the brain; . . . . When demands are too frequent, the brain becomes congested. When there is lack of physical exercise, even plain food should be eaten sparingly. At mealtime cast off care and anxious thought; do not feel hurried, but eat slowly and with cheerfulness, with your heart filled with gratitude to God for His blessings. Ellen White: *Ministry of Healing*, page 306.

BAKED BEANS (makes 8 servings)

500 mL	(2 cups)	dry white beans
5 mL	(1 tsp.)	salt
500 mL	(2 cups)	Hunt's tomato sauce (or homemade)
500 mL	(2 cups)	sliced onions (steamed before adding to beans)
45 mL	(3 Tbsp.)	brown sugar or date butter
15 mL	(1 Tbsp.)	molasses
5 mL	(1 tsp.)	ground celery seed
1 mL	(1/4 tsp.)	ground cardamon

Method:

COOK beans. (REMEMBER they won't get any softer after acidic ingredients are added (page 15 and 21). STIR in remaining ingredients. POUR into casserole. BAKE covered at 300° F. for about 3 hours. UNCOVER for the last part of the baking. May be frozen.

```
-------------------------------------------------------------------
| Analysis: BAKED BEANS                 Divided by: 8             |
|           Wgt: 153 g (5.4 oz.)        Water:      8%            |
-------------------------------------------------------------------
```

Calories	117	Vitamin C	10.6 mg
Protein	5.36 g	Vitamin D	0 mcg
Carbohydrates	24.4 g	Vit E-Alpha E	.464 mg
Fat - Total	.523 g	Vitamin K	mcg
Saturated Fat	.106 g	Biotin	mcg
Mono Fat	.09 g	Calcium	78.9 mg
Poly Fat	.199 g	Copper	.277 mg
Cholesterol	0 mg	Iodine	mcg
Dietary Fibre	5.34 g	Iron	2.47 mg
Soluble Fibre	1.5 g	Magnesium	53.9 mg
Total Vit A	60 RE	Manganese	.532 mg
Thiamin-B1	.165 mg	Phosphorus	112 mg
Riboflavin-B2	.073 mg	Potassium	577 mg
Niacin-B3	.93 mg	Selenium	3.61 mcg
Niacin Equiv.	.93 mg	Sodium	286 mg
Vitamin B6	.217 mg	Zinc	.773 mg
Vitamin B12	0 mcg	Complex Carbs	8.96 g
Folate	74.7 mcg	Sugars	10.3 g
Pantothenic	.37 mg	Water	120 g

CALORIE BREAKDOWN		FAT		EXCHANGES	
Protein	17%	*Saturated :	.8%	Bread	1.9
Carbohydrates	79%	Mono Unsat:	.7%	Lean Meat	.945
Fat-Total *	4%	Poly Unsat:	1.4%	Fruit	.308
				Vegetables	1.25

TRUE REMEDIES:

Pure air, sunlight, abstemiousness (temperance), rest, exercise, proper diet, the use of water, trust in divine power--these are the true remedies. Ellen White, *Counsels on Diet and Foods*, page 301.

BREAD DRESSING (makes 8 servings)

15 mL	(1 Tbsp.)	olive oil
250 mL	(1 cup)	chopped onion
250 mL	(1 cup)	chopped celery
2	(2)	cloves minced garlic
15 mL	(1 Tbsp.)	chicken style seasoning
5 mL	(1 tsp.) EACH	sage, thyme, savory, **and** salt
2 L	(8 cups)	cubed whole wheat bread
		water to moisten

Method:
STEAM the onions, celery, and garlic in the oil in a large skillet. STIR in seasonings. MIX well. Then ADD cubed bread and MIX again. ADD water just to moisten to right consistency. COVER and BAKE at 350° for 45 minutes. SERVE with chicken style gravy (page 201). Note: For special occasions you may want to use Worthington frozen chicken style slices cut in half and stood on their sides with dressing between them in the baking dish.

```
-----------------------------------------------------------------------
| Analysis: BREAD DRESSING                    Divided by: 8           |
|           Wgt: 157 g (5.53 oz.)             Water:      76%         |
-----------------------------------------------------------------------
```

Calories	159		Vitamin C	4.29 mg
Protein	4.43 g		Vitamin D	.107 mcg
Carbohydrates	27 g		Vit E-Alpha E	.409 mg
Fat - Total	3.82 g		Vitamin K	mcg
Saturated Fat	.732 g		Biotin	mcg
Mono Fat	2.27 g		Calcium	45.5 mg
Poly Fat	.518 g		Copper	.131 mg
Cholesterol	0 mg		Iodine	mcg
Dietary Fibre	2.69 g		Iron	1.76 mg
Soluble Fibre	.226 g		Magnesium	17.7 mg
Total Vit A	3.12 RE		Manganese	.267 mg
Thiamin-B1	.224 mg		Phosphorus	62.7 mg
Riboflavin-B2	.138 mg		Potassium	182 mg
Niacin-B3	2.12 mg		Selenium	14.3 mcg
Niacin Equiv.	2.12 mg		Sodium	492 mg
Vitamin B6	.09 mg		Zinc	.476 mg
Vitamin B12	0 mcg		Complex Carbs	21.3 g
Folate	20.3 mcg		Sugars	3.56 g
Pantothenic	.399 mg		Water	120 g

CALORIE BREAKDOWN		FAT		EXCHANGES	
Protein	11%	*Saturated :	4.1%	Bread	1.48
Carbohydrates	68%	Mono Unsat:	12.7%	Vegetables	.666
Fat-Total *	21%	Poly Unsat:	2.9%	Fat	.426

CAUSES OF HYPERTENSION:
Three of the four major contributing factors of hypertension are diet-linked. We are committing suicide by the fork. (salt, arterial placque, obesity.) With the reduction of salt to no more than 5 grams of salt a day hypertension could be prevented. Hans Diehl, Dr. HSc, MPH in *To Your Health*, page 75.

BREAKFAST TOFU AND RICE (makes 6 servings)

250 mL	(1 cup - 2 blocks)	tofu
125 mL	(1/2 cup)	celery, diced or sliced thinly
250 mL	(1 cup)	diced eggplant
125 mL	(1/2 cup)	green onions
1 mL	(1/4 tsp.)	salt
15 mL	(1 Tbsp.)	Maggi seasoning **or** Bragg Liquid Aminos
15 mL	(1 Tbsp.)	chicken style seasoning
1 mL	(1/8 tsp.)	turmeric
1 L	(4 cups)	cooked brown rice
45 mL	(3 Tbsp.)	minced parsley

Method:

DRAIN and **CUBE** tofu. **STEAM** celery in small amount of water until nearly done. **ADD** onions and eggplant. **MIX** tofu and seasonings together. **COMBINE** all ingredients and **SIMMER** a few minutes in a Teflon or Pam-sprayed pan to combine flavours. **SERVE** with crackers.

```
Analysis: BREAKFAST TOFU AND RICE          Divided by: 6
          Wgt: 208 g (7.35 oz.)            Water:     77%
```

Calories	191	Vitamin C	5.22	mg
Protein	7.4 g	Vitamin D	0	mcg
Carbohydrates	33.7 g	Vit E-Alpha Eq	1.4	mg
Fat - Total	3.31 g	Vitamin K		mcg
Saturated Fat	.536 g	Biotin		mcg
Mono Fat	.874 g	Calcium	70.2	mg
Poly Fat	1.57 g	Copper	.284	mg
Cholesterol	0 mg	Iodine		mcg
Dietary Fibre	3.31 g	Iron	3.27	mg
Soluble Fibre	.327 g	Magnesium	104	mg
Total Vit A	18 RE	Manganese	1.48	mg
Thiamin-B1	.183 mg	Phosphorus	170	mg
Riboflavin-B2	.123 mg	Potassium	218	mg
Niacin-B3	2.75 mg	Selenium	19.5	mcg
Niacin Equiv.	2.75 mg	Sodium	281	mg
Vitamin B6	.24 mg	Zinc	1.32	mg
Vitamin B12	0 mcg	Complex Carbs	27.9	g
Folate	25.3 mcg	Sugars	1.39	g
Pantothenic	.698 mg	Water	161	g

CALORIE BREAKDOWN		FAT		EXCHANGES	
Protein	15%	*Saturated :	2.5%	Vegetables	.443
Carbohydrates	69%	Mono Unsat:	4%	Fat	.167
Fat-Total	15%	Poly Unsat:	7.3%		

PEANUT BUTTER FOR A GOOD NIGHT'S SLEEP:

Dr. Yang Ceming of Nuclear Industry Hospital 416 China says that just one teaspoon of peanut butter after the evening meal can improve your sleep. In a two year study with 300 insomniacs, 89% were sleeping like babies within three weeks.

BULGUR RISOTTO (makes 8 servings)

250 mL	(1 cup)	bulgur
250 mL	(1 cup)	boiling water
250 mL	(1 cup)	finely chopped onion
250 mL	(1 cup)	finely chopped celery
10 mL	(2 tsp.)	crushed garlic
5 mL	(1 tsp.)	olive or canola oil
125 mL	(1/2 cup)	chopped sweet red pepper
125 mL	(1/2 cup)	chopped sweet green pepper
125 mL	(1/2 cup)	chopped unsalted, dry roasted peanuts
3 mL	(1/2 tsp.)	Italian seasoning
5 mL	(1 tsp.)	Marmite or Savorex, dissolved in 1/4 cup water
10 mL	(2 tsp.)	soy sauce
125 mL	(1/2 cup) **EACH**	corn **and** peas
30 mL	(2 Tbsp.)	fresh lemon juice

Method:

PUT the bulgur and boiling water into a bowl. LEAVE for about 10 minutes. Meanwhile, STEAM the onion, celery, and garlic in the oil in a large saucepan. ADD the peppers, peanuts, bulgur, corn, peas, and seasoning. MIX together well. CONTINUE cooking for 5 more minutes. MIX in the lemon juice and transfer to a heated serving dish. SERVE immediately. (If the risotto is too dry ADD a little more water.)

```
Analysis: BULGUR RISOTTO (makes 8 servings)        Divided by: 8
          Wgt: 131 g (4.62 oz.)                    Water:     73%
```

Calories	151		Vitamin C	23.1 mg
Protein	5.88 g		Vitamin D	0 mcg
Carbohydrates	22.7 g		Vit E-Alpha E	1.01 mg
Fat - Total	5.47 g		Vitamin K	mcg
Saturated Fat	.773 g		Biotin	mcg
Mono Fat	2.72 g		Calcium	32.3 mg
Poly Fat	1.64 g		Copper	.172 mg
Cholesterol	0 mg		Iodine	mcg
Dietary Fibre	5.57 g		Iron	1.21 mg
Soluble Fibre	.816 g		Magnesium	56.3 mg
Total Vit A	52.4 RE		Manganese	.867 mg
Thiamin-B1	.147 mg		Phosphorus	115 mg
Riboflavin-B2	.082 mg		Potassium	274 mg
Niacin-B3	2.74 mg		Selenium	5.78 mcg
Niacin Equiv.	2.62 mg		Sodium	113 mg
Vitamin B6	.194 mg		Zinc	.878 mg
Vitamin B12	0 mcg		Complex Carbs	13.5 g
Folate	37.7 mcg		Sugars	3.6 g
Pantothenic	.435 mg		Water	95.7 g

CALORIE BREAKDOWN		FAT		EXCHANGES	
Protein	14%	* Saturated :	4.3%	Bread	.885
Carbohydrates	55%	Mono Unsat:	15%	Lean Meat	.312
Fat-Total *	30%	Poly Unsat:	9%	Vegetables	.468
		Fat	.753--->	Fruit	.141

CHILI BEANS (10 one-cup servings)

1250 mL	(5 cups)	cooked pinto and/or red kidney beans
1000 mL	(4 cups)	tomatoes
375 mL	(1 1/2 cups)	chopped onion
1	(1)	large garlic clove, minced
180 mL	(3/4 cup)	chopped sweet green pepper
15 mL	(1 Tbsp.)	cumin
3 mL	(1/2 tsp.)	paprika
3 mL	(1/2 tsp.)	salt (or to taste)
2 mL	(1/4 tsp.)	basil
2 mL	(1/4 tsp.)	oregano

Method:

STEAM onions, garlic, and green pepper a few minutes. ADD remaining ingredients and BAKE or SIMMER for 30-60 minutes at 350°F. (May be frozen.)

```
Analysis: CHILI BEANS                          Divided by: 10
          Wgt: 217 g (7.66 oz.)               Water:      81%
```

Calories	153		Vitamin C	31.4 mg
Protein	9.18 g		Vitamin D	0 mcg
Carbohydrates	28.8 g		Vit E-Alpha E	.634 mg
Fat - Total	1.04 g		Vitamin K	mcg
Saturated Fat	.131 g		Biotin	mcg
Mono Fat	.103 g		Calcium	43.8 mg
Poly Fat	.441 g		Copper	.33 mg
Cholesterol	0 mg		Iodine	mcg
Dietary Fibre	9.83 g		Iron	3.69 mg
Soluble Fibre	3.83 g		Magnesium	59.2 mg
Total Vit A	84.8 RE		Manganese	.619 mg
Thiamin-B1	.229 mg		Phosphorus	169 mg
Riboflavin-B2	.118 mg		Potassium	692 mg
Niacin-B3	1.36 mg		Selenium	3.02 mcg
Niacin Equiv.	1.36 mg		Sodium	67.6 mg
Vitamin B6	.247 mg		Zinc	1.15 mg
Vitamin B12	0 mcg		Complex Carbs	12.2 g
Folate	133 mcg		Sugars	6.8 g
Pantothenic	.511 mg		Water	177 g

CALORIE BREAKDOWN		FAT		EXCHANGES	
Protein	23%	* Saturated :	.7%	Bread	1.36
Carbohydrates	71%	Mono Unsat:	.6%	Vegetables	1.38
Fat-Total *	6%	Poly Unsat:	2.5%		

EATING TO MUSIC:

The atmosphere at a meal influences the amount of food eaten. Playing lively, fast-tempo music can move one to eat more, while slow, soothing music will help to cut down on the amount eaten. The speed of the music also influences the speed with which the food is eaten. Winston J. Craig, Ph.D., R.D., *Nutrition for the Nineties*, page 247.

CHILI BEANS WITH BULGUR (makes 12 servings)

125 mL	(1/2 cup)	bulgur wheat
125 mL	(1/2 cup)	boiling water
250 mL	(1 cup)	chopped onions
250 mL	(1 cup)	finely chopped celery
1	(1)	garlic clove, minced
125 mL	(1/2 cup)	finely chopped green pepper
250 mL	(1 cup)	tomato sauce (homemade or Hunts)
5 mL	(1 tsp.)	salt (Use less if on a low sodium diet)
3 mL	(1/2 tsp).	oregano
3 mL	(1/2 tsp.)	ground cumin
1 mL	(1/4 tsp.)	celery seed
750 mL	(3 cups)	cooked red kidney or pinto beans

Method:

   SOAK the bulgur wheat in boiling water for 15 minutes. **STEAM** onions, celery, and pepper in a small amount of water. **ADD** tomato sauce and seasonings. **SIMMER** 15 minutes. **ADD** cooked beans and bulgur, **STIR. SIMMER** 10 minutes to blend flavours. **SERVE** hot with rice, another vegetable and a green salad.

```
-----------------------------------------------------------------------
| Analysis: CHILI BEANS WITH BULGUR              Divided by: 12        |
|           Wgt: 109 g (3.84 oz.)                Water:      77%       |
-----------------------------------------------------------------------
```

Calories	91.6		Vitamin C	8.75 mg
Protein	5.15 g		Vitamin D	0 mcg
Carbohydrates	18.1 g		Vit E-Alpha E	.213 mg
Fat - Total	.438 g		Vitamin K	mcg
Saturated Fat	.065 g		Biotin	mcg
Mono Fat	.048 g		Calcium	28 mg
Poly Fat	.208 g		Copper	.185 mg
Cholesterol	0 mg		Iodine	mcg
Dietary Fibre	5.77 g		Iron	1.84 mg
Soluble Fibre	2.01 g		Magnesium	37.6 mg
Total Vit A	36.3 RE		Manganese	.482 mg
Thiamin-B1	.113 mg		Phosphorus	96.3 mg
Riboflavin-B2	.057 mg		Potassium	343 mg
Niacin-B3	.902 mg		Selenium	2.87 mcg
Niacin Equiv.	.902 mg		Sodium	194 mg
Vitamin B6	.142 mg		Zinc	.704 mg
Vitamin B12	0 mcg		Complex Carbs	9.48 g
Folate	66.7 mcg		Sugars	2.84 g
Pantothenic	.259 mg		Water	83.7 g

CALORIE BREAKDOWN		FAT		EXCHANGES	
Protein	21%	Saturated :	.6%	Bread	.9
Carbohydrates	75%	Mono Unsat:	.4%	Vegetables	.51
Fat - Total *	4%	Poly Unsat:	1.9%		

CHILIRONI (makes 8 servings)

375 mL	(1 1/2 cups)	water
375 mL	(1 1/2 cups)	macaroni elbows
375 mL	(1 1/2 cups)	chopped onion
250 mL	(1 cup)	chopped celery
180 mL	(3/4 cup)	chopped sweet green pepper
2	(2)	large garlic cloves, minced
250 mL	(1 cup)	tomato sauce
5 mL	(1 tsp.)	salt, oregano, **and** basil
4 mL	(3/4 tsp.)	cumin
1 L	(4 cups)	cooked pinto or red kidney beans

Method:

   BRING the water to a boil. **ADD** macaroni, onions, celery, chopped pepper, garlic, tomato sauce, and seasonings. **RETURN** pot to a boil. **REDUCE** heat and **COOK** 10 minutes. **REMOVE** from heat, but do **NOT DRAIN**. **STIR** in beans. **HEAT** thoroughly. **SERVE** hot with something crunchy. (May be frozen.)

```
Analysis: CHILIRONI (makes 8 cups)          Divided by: 8
          Wgt: 262 g (9.23 oz.)             Water:    79%
```

Calories	203		Vitamin C	21.6 mg
Protein	9.44 g		Vitamin D	0 mcg
Carbohydrates	40.4 g		Vit E-Alpha E	.605 mg
Fat - Total	1.04 g		Vitamin K	mcg
Saturated Fat	.172 g		Biotin	mcg
Mono Fat	.156 g		Calcium	79.4 mg
Poly Fat	.391 g		Copper	.384 mg
Cholesterol	0 mg		Iodine	mcg
Dietary Fibre	3.97 g		Iron	3.8 mg
Soluble Fibre	1.08 g		Magnesium	61.1 mg
Total Vit A	63.7 RE		Manganese	.624 mg
Thiamin-B1	.386 mg		Phosphorus	175 mg
Riboflavin-B2	.221 mg		Potassium	714 mg
Niacin-B3	2.69 mg		Selenium	12.5 mcg
Niacin Equiv.	2.69 mg		Sodium	951 mg
Vitamin B6	.271 mg		Zinc	1.38 mg
Vitamin B12	0 mcg		Complex Carbs	17 g
Folate	92.3 mcg		Sugars	3.54 g
Pantothenic	.48 mg		Water	207 g

CALORIE BREAKDOWN		FAT		EXCHANGES	
Protein	18%	* Saturated:	.7%	Bread	2.13
Carbohydrates	77%	Mono Unsat:	.7%	Lean Meat	.25
Fat-Total *	4%	Poly Unsat:	1.7%	Fruit	.162
				Vegetables	.898

CONFETTI RICE (Makes 10 servings)

1750 mL	(7 cups)	hot, cooked brown rice (preferably Uncle Ben's whole grain)
500 mL	(2 cups)	peas, cooked one minute
45 mL	(3 Tbsp)	chopped and steamed red pepper

Method:

COMBINE all ingredients and PRESS into a ring mould. UNMOULD at once onto a 12-inch round serving plate. GARNISH with parsley and cherry tomatoes.

```
Analysis: CONFETTI RICE                          Divided by: 10
          Wgt: 171 g (6.03 oz.)                  Water:       75%
```

Calories	177	Vitamin C	7.52 mg
Protein	5.19 g	Vitamin D	0 mcg
Carbohydrates	36.2 g	Vit E-Alpha E	1.51 mg
Fat - Total	1.32 g	Vitamin K	mcg
Saturated Fat	.262 g	Biotin	mcg
Mono Fat	.455 g	Calcium	21.6 mg
Poly Fat	.485 g	Copper	.183 mg
Cholesterol	0 mg	Iodine	mcg
Dietary Fibre	3.8 g	Iron	1.09 mg
Soluble Fibre	.417 g	Magnesium	68.3 mg
Total Vit A	31 RE	Manganese	1.37 mg
Thiamin-B1	.223 mg	Phosphorus	142 mg
Riboflavin-B2	.067 mg	Potassium	117 mg
Niacin-B3	2.57 mg	Selenium	19.4 mcg
Niacin Equiv.	2.57 mg	Sodium	34.7 mg
Vitamin B6	.24 mg	Zinc	1.16 mg
Vitamin B12	0 mcg	Complex Carbs	30 g
Folate	24.6 mcg	Sugars	2.39 g
Pantothenic	.437 mg	Water	128 g

CALORIE BREAKDOWN		FAT		EXCHANGES	
Protein	12%	*Saturated :	1.3%	Bread	2.18
Carbohydrates	82%	Mono Unsat:	2.3%	Vegetables	.037
Fat-Total *	7%	Poly Unsat:	2.5%		

RICE:

In its natural state, rice has good nutritional value. It is better than corn and approximately as good as wheat. BROWN RICE -- rice with the hulls removed, but with the bran left on -- has about the same caloric, vitamin, and mineral content as whole wheat, less protein, but better quality proteins and more carbohydrates and fats. MILLED RICE -- the kernels after the milling is completed and the hulls, bran layers, and the germ are removed. WHITE RICE (polished rice) -- brown rice that has been milled and polished to remove the bran and germ loses a portion of its best protein and most of its fat, vitamins, and minerals. PARBOILED (converted rice) -- rice in the hull soaked in warm water, steamed under pressure, and dried before milling. This treatment gelatinizes the starch and diffuses the soluble vitamins from the exterior to the interior of the grain. RICE POLISHINGS are the inner white bran, protein-rich aleurone layers, and starchy endosperm obtained in the milling operation by brushing the grain to polish the kernel.

CORN-TOFU CASSEROLE (makes about 8 servings)

1	(1)	green pepper, chopped
250 mL	(1 cup)	sliced onion
125 mL	(1/2 cup)	water
1	(1)	garlic clove, minced
125 mL	(1/2 cup)	cornmeal
30 mL	(2 Tbsp.)	sunflower seeds or nuts
1 L	(4 cups)	frozen or fresh corn
250 mL	(1 cup)	tofu
60 mL	(1/4 cup)	lemon juice
15 mL	(1 Tbsp.)	flake food yeast
5 mL	(1 tsp.)	sage
3 mL	(1/2 tsp.)	salt
3 mL	(1/2 tsp.)	turmeric
2 mL	(1/4 tsp.)	ground cumin

Method:

STEAM pepper, onion, and garlic in the water until it is limp. MASH tofu and MIX in corn meal and steamed ingredients. BLEND sunflower seeds or nuts with the lemon juice and a little water if needed. ADD seasonings and corn. STIR well. BAKE at 375° for 30 minutes.

```
--------------------------------------------------------------------------
| Analysis: CORN-TOFU CASSEROLE              Divided by: 8                |
|            Wgt: 178 g (6.29 oz)            Water:     75%               |
--------------------------------------------------------------------------
```

Calories	173		Vitamin B6	.242 mg
Protein	9.59 g		Vitamin B12	0 mcg
Carbohydrates	28.8 g		Folate	81.3 mg
Complex Carbs	20.2 g		Pantothenic	.574 mcg
Sugars	3.57 g		Vitamin C	13.8 mg
Dietary Fiber	3.41 g		Vitamin D	0 mg
Soluble Fiber	.535 g		Vit E-Alpha E	1.31 mg
Fat - Total	4.19 g		Calcium	83.4 mg
Saturated Fat	.562 g		Copper	.217 mg
Mono Fat	.885 g		Iron	4.52 mg
Poly Fat	2.41 g		Magnesium	62.4 mg
Omega 3 FA	.192 g		Manganese	.637 mg
Cholesterol	0 mg		Phosphorus	153 mg
Trans FA	0 g		Potassium	307 mg
Total Vit A	35.8 RE		Selenium	2.92 mcg
Thiamin-B1	.415 mg		Sodium	145 mg
Riboflavin-B2	.205 mg		Water	134 g
Niacin Equiv.	1.79 mg		Zinc	1.06 mg

CALORIE BREAKDOWN		FAT	EXCHANGES	
Protein	20%	*Saturated : 2.7%	Bread	1.45
Carbohydrates	60%	Mono Unsat: 4.2%	Lean Meat	.033
Fat-Total *	20%	Poly Unsat: 11.4%	Fruit	.281
			Vegetables	.342
			Fat	.156

COUSCOUS, FAST AND HOT (makes 6 servings)

310 mL	(1 1/4 cups)	water
15 mL	(1 Tbsp.)	chicken style seasoning
5 mL	(1 tsp.)	olive or canola oil
5 mL	(1 tsp.)	soy sauce or Bragg liquid aminos
2 mL	(1/4 tsp.)	salt
375 mL	(1 1/2 cups)	couscous
30 mL	(2 Tbsp.)	chopped fresh parsley

Method:

In a heavy saucepan with a tight-fitting lid, **COMBINE** water, chicken style seasoning, oil, soy sauce, and salt, **BRING** to a boil. **STIR** in couscous and **REMOVE** from heat. **COVER** and **LET** stand for 5 minutes. **UNCOVER** and **FLUFF** the grains with a fork to separate. **STIR** in parsley and **SERVE** hot as you would rice or quinoa.

```
-----------------------------------------------------------------------
| Analysis: COUSCOUS, FAT AND HOT (6 SERVINGS)      Divided by: 6      |
|           Wgt: 204 g (7.18 oz.)                   Water:     78%     |
-----------------------------------------------------------------------
```

Calories	180		Vitamin C	1.66 mg
Protein	5.77 g		Vitamin D	0 mcg
Carbohydrates	35.8 g		Vit E-Alpha E	.127 mg
Fat - Total	1.06 g		Vitamin K	mcg
Saturated Fat	.147 g		Biotin	mcg
Mono Fat	.59 g		Calcium	14.9 mg
Poly Fat	.162 g		Copper	.067 mg
Cholesterol	0 mg		Iodine	mcg
Dietary Fibre	4.21 g		Iron	.672 mg
Soluble Fibre	1.1 g		Magnesium	13.5 mg
Total Vit A	6.5 RE		Manganese	.132 mg
Thiamin-B1	.096 mg		Phosphorus	34.7 mg
Riboflavin-B2	.042 mg		Potassium	94.6 mg
Niacin-B3	1.52 mg		Selenium	.023 mcg
Niacin Equiv.	1.52 mg		Sodium	156 mg
Vitamin B6	.079 mg		Zinc	.421 mg
Vitamin B12	0 mcg		Complex Carbs	.047 g
Folate	24.5 mcg		Sugars	.062 g
Pantothenic	.562 mg		Water	159 g

CALORIE BREAKDOWN		FAT		EXCHANGES	
Protein	13%	* Saturated :	.7%	Bread	.09
Carbohydrates	81%	Mono Unsat:	3%	Vegetables	.018
Fat-Total *	5%	Poly Unsat:	.8%	Fat	.145

COUSCOUS:

Any of several North African dishes made either with steamed semolina (the gritty or grainlike portions of wheat retained in the bolting machine after the fine flour has been sifted through. This hard wheat is used for making pastas, such as macaroni), crushed rice, cracked wheat or other starch. Couscous can be eaten alone as a kind of porridge, it can be put into a savory stew, or it can be sweetened, mixed with fruits and nuts and eaten as a dessert. *Cook's and Diner's Dictionary*, page 63.

CUBAN BLACK BEANS (makes 6 servings)

250 mL	(1 cup)	dry black beans (**SOAK** overnight or quick soak, **DRAIN**)
1 L	(4 cups)	water
250 mL	(1 cup)	chopped onion
125 mL	(1/2 cup)	chopped green sweet pepper
3	(3)	large garlic cloves, minced
5 mL	(1 tsp.)	salt
5 mL	(1 tsp.)	oregano

Method:

ADD cold water to drained soaked beans. **BRING** to a boil. **REDUCE** heat. **SIMMER** until done. Then **ADD** remaining ingredients. **CONTINUE** to simmer until vegetables are done. **SERVE** with something colourful such as carrots and peas. May be frozen.

```
Analysis: CUBAN BLACK BEANS                 Divided by: 6
          Wgt: 123 g (4.33 oz.)             Water:    75%
```

Calories	115	Vitamin C	10.6	mg
Protein	7 g	Vitamin D	0	mcg
Carbohydrates	21.6 g	Vit E-Alpha E	.167	mg
Fat - Total	.5 g	Vitamin K		mcg
Saturated Fat	.121 g	Biotin		mcg
Mono Fat	.046 g	Calcium	35.1	mg
Poly Fat	.215 g	Copper	.186	mg
Dietary Fibre	5.11 g	Iron	1.77	mg
Soluble Fibre	1.39 g	Magnesium	56.2	mg
Total Vit A	7.69 RE	Manganese	.421	mg
Thiamin-B1	.201 mg	Phosphorus	118	mg
Riboflavin-B2	.054 mg	Potassium	342	mg
Niacin-B3	.49 mg	Selenium	6.84	mcg
Niacin Equiv.	.491 mg	Sodium	358	mg
Vitamin B6	.135 mg	Zinc	.922	mg
Vitamin B12	0 mcg	Complex Carbs	12.2	g
Folate	116 mcg	Sugars	4.36	g
Pantothenic	.231 mg	Water	91.5	g

CALORIE BREAKDOWN		FAT		EXCHANGES	
Protein	24%	*Saturated :	.9%	Bread	1.07
Carbohydrates	73%	Mono Unsat:	.3%	Lean Meat	.179
Fat-Total *	4%	Poly Unsat:	1.6%	Vegetables	.583

HINTS FOR ALWAYS HAVING TENDER BEANS:

Legumes will cook faster in distilled water than in hard water because the calcium and magnesium in hard water combine with the pectin in the beans to make them tough. When beans are going to be used in a dish that requires tomatoes, lemon juice, or any other acidic food, be sure they are cooked as tender as you want them to be in the finished product before adding the acidic food. They will not get any softer after the acid is added. **ADD** 3/4 tsp. of salt per cup of dry beans after the beans are cooked (Also, see page 21).

EGGPLANT AND KIDNEY BEANS (makes 10 servings)

180 mL	(3/4 cup)	green pepper, washed and chopped
15 mL	(1 Tbsp.)	olive oil
1 L	(4 cups)	canned or frozen tomatoes
1 L	(4 cups)	cubed eggplant
30 mL	(2 Tbsp.)	food yeast flakes
8 mL	(1 1/2 tsp.)	salt
5 mL	(1 tsp.)	onion powder
5 mL	(1 tsp.)	basil
3 mL	(1/2 tsp.)	oregano
3 mL	(1/2 tsp.)	celery seed
3 mL	(1/2 tsp.)	garlic powder
500 mL	(2 cups)	cooked red kidney beans

Method:

SAUTE pepper in the oil. WASH and CUBE eggplant. LEAVE skin on. ADD tomatoes, eggplant, yeast flakes, salt, onion powder, basil, oregano, celery seed, and garlic powder. COOK until just done, about 5 minutes. ADD the kidney beans. (If using canned kidney beans use less salt.)

```
Analysis: EGGPLANT AND KIDNEY BEANS          Divided by: 10
          Wgt: 171 g (6.04 oz.)              Water:     86%
```

Calories	87		Vitamin C	27.5 mg
Protein	4.59 g		Vitamin D	0 mcg
Carbohydrates	16.5 g		Vit E-Alpha E	.607 mg
Fat - Total	1.11 g		Vitamin K	mcg
Saturated Fat	.154 g		Biotin	mcg
Mono Fat	.426 g		Calcium	35.3 mg
Poly Fat	.326 g		Copper	.22 mg
Cholesterol	0 mg		Iodine	mcg
Dietary Fibre	5.63 g		Iron	1.93 mg
Soluble Fibre	2.06 g		Magnesium	35.4 mg
Total Vit A	78.8 RE		Manganese	.366 mg
Thiamin-B1	.159 mg		Phosphorus	94.5 mg
Riboflavin-B2	.085 mg		Potassium	503 mg
Niacin-B3	1.17 mg		Selenium	1.85 mcg
Niacin Equiv.	1.17 mg		Sodium	333 mg
Vitamin B6	.208 mg		Zinc	.57 mg
Vitamin B12	0 mcg		Complex Carbs	5.59 g
Folate	65.5 mcg		Sugars	5.27 g
Pantothenic	.409 mg		Water	147 g

CALORIE BREAKDOWN		FAT	EXCHANGES	
Protein	19%	*Saturated : 1.5%	Bread	.532
Carbohydrates	70%	Mono Unsat: 4.1%	Vegetables	1.47
Fat-Total *	11%	Poly Unsat: 3.1%	Fat	.087

FETTUCCINE ALFREDO (makes 5 servings)

300 gm	(10.7 oz)	fettucini
250 mL	(1 cup)	sliced celery
250 mL	(1 cup)	chopped onions
4	(4)	large garlic cloves, minced
250 mL	(1 cup)	diced eggplant
15 mL	(1 Tbsp.)	chicken style seasoning
500 mL	(2 cups)	SUNFLOWER-PIMENTO "CHEESE"
250 mL	(1 cup)	tofu, blended until smooth
45 mL	(3 Tbsp.)	chopped green pepper (optional)
45 mL	(3 Tbsp.)	finely chopped parsley

Method:

COOK fettuccine. COMBINE celery, onions, garlic, and eggplant with sufficient liquid to steam in a large pot. COVER and STEAM until vegetables are tender. STIR in chicken style seasoning, blended tofu, and SUNFLOWER-PIMENTO "CHEESE". ADD cooked fettuccine and parsley. SERVE. May be made a day ahead and reheated.

```
--------------------------------------------------------------------
| Analysis: FETTUCCINE ALFREDO                Divided by: 8         |
|           Wgt: 197 g (6.96 oz.)             Water:    70%         |
--------------------------------------------------------------------
```

Calories	246		Vitamin C	16.8 mg
Protein	12.4 g		Vitamin D	0 mcg
Carbohydrates	38.7 g		Vit E-Alpha E	1.44 mg
Fat - Total	5.26 g		Vitamin K	mcg
Saturated Fat	.704 g		Biotin	mcg
Mono Fat	1.05 g		Calcium	104 mg
Poly Fat	2.96 g		Copper	.402 mg
Cholesterol	0 mg		Iodine	mcg
Dietary Fibre	3.48 g		Iron	5.93 mg
Soluble Fibre	.427 g		Magnesium	74.7 mg
Total Vit A	46.4 RE		Manganese	.727 mg
Thiamin-B1	.907 mg		Phosphorus	207 mg
Riboflavin-B2	.328 mg		Potassium	352 mg
Niacin-B3	4.22 mg		Selenium	26.4 mcg
Niacin Equiv.	3.15 mg		Sodium	177 mg
Vitamin B6	.321 mg		Zinc	1.49 mg
Vitamin B12	0 mcg		Complex Carbs	26.6 g
Folate	125 mcg		Sugars	3.31 g
Pantothenic	.72 mg		Water	138 g

CALORIE BREAKDOWN		FAT		EXCHANGES	
Protein	20%	* Saturated:	2.5%	Bread	2.21
Carbohydrates	61%	Mono Unsat:	3.7%	Lean Meat	.75
Fat-Total *	19%	Poly Unsat:	10.6%	Vegetables	.564

PASTA:

The milling of durum wheat into semolina is different from that used to make flour because a granular product is desired. The durum wheat is moistened before milling to toughen the outer layers of the wheat kernels so that they may be removed readily from the inner portion which yields the semolina. Then the wheat is broken into coarse particles. To make pasta dough, semolina, durum flour, farina, or non durum flour may be used.

FETTUCCINE WITH EGGPLANT AND ZUCCHINI (12 servings)

300 gm	(12 oz.)	fettuccine
15 mL	(1 Tbsp.)	olive oil
250 mL	(1 cup)	chopped onions
1	(1)	garlic clove, minced
1	(1)	small eggplant (about 1 pound) cut into 1/2" cubes
2	(2)	small zucchini (about 6 oz each, cut into strips)
796 mL	(28 oz.)	Italian plum tomatoes
8 mL	(1 1/2 tsp.)	salt
5 mL	(1 tsp.)	basil

Method:

PREPARE fettuccine as label directs. DRAIN; KEEP warm. Meanwhile, in 12" skillet over medium heat, in hot olive oil, COOK eggplant, zucchini, onions, and garlic until tender and golden, stirring occasionally. To vegetable mixture, ADD tomatoes, salt, and basil. HEAT to boiling. REDUCE heat to low, COVER and SIMMER 10 minutes.

```
Analysis: FETTUCCINE-EGGPLANT-ZUCCHINI        Divided by: 12
          Wgt: 169 g (5.98 oz.)               Water:      78%
```

Calories	146		Vitamin C	14.5 mg
Protein	5.08 g		Vitamin D	0 mcg
Carbohydrates	28 g		Vit E-Alpha E	.489 mg
Fat - Total	1.83 g		Vitamin K	mcg
Saturated Fat	.258 g		Biotin	mcg
Mono Fat	.915 g		Calcium	42.1 mg
Poly Fat	.386 g		Copper	.206 mg
Cholesterol	0 mg		Iodine	mcg
Dietary Fibre	2.87 g		Iron	1.85 mg
Soluble Fibre	.899 g		Magnesium	33.1 mg
Total Vit A	54.1 RE		Manganese	.385 mg
Thiamin-B1	.374 mg		Phosphorus	79.2 mg
Riboflavin-B2	.164 mg		Potassium	355 mg
Niacin-B3	2.94 mg		Selenium	17.5 mcg
Niacin Equiv.	2.94 mg		Sodium	385 mg
Vitamin B6	.163 mg		Zinc	.588 mg
Vitamin B12	0 mcg		Complex Carbs	20 g
Folate	24.3 mcg		Sugars	5.16 g
Pantothenic	.3 mg		Water	133 g

CALORIE BREAKDOWN		FAT		EXCHANGES	
Protein	14%	* Saturated :	1.6%	Bread	1.62
Carbohydrates	75%	Mono Unsat:	5.5%	Vegetables	1.31
Fat-Total *	11%	Poly Unsat:	2.3%	Fat	.218

1 Corinthians 9:25
And every man that striveth for the mastery is temperate in all things. Now they do it to obtain a corruptible crown; but we are incorrutible.

GARBANZO-RICE CASSEROLE (makes 12 one and a half cup servings)

375 mL	(1 1/2 cups)	chopped onion
4	(4)	large garlic cloves, minced
180 mL	(3/4 cup)	diced green pepper
180 mL	(3/4 cup)	thinly sliced celery
1 L	(4 cups)	water
796 mL	(28 oz.)	canned tomatoes
500 mL	(2 cups)	long-grain brown rice (uncooked)
250 mL	(1 cup)	cooked garbanzos
30 mL	(2 Tbsp.)	Bragg liquid aminos, soy sauce, **or** Maggi seasoning
10 mL	(2 tsp.)	SAVOREX or MARMITE
5 mL	(1 tsp.)	dried sweet basil,
5 mL	(1 tsp.)	oregano
5 mL	(1 tsp.)	celery seed

Method:

STEAM onion, garlic, pepper, and celery in a small amount of water. ADD remaining ingredients. With lid slightly ajar, BRING to boil, then COVER and LET simmer until water is absorbed (about 45 minutes) ADJUST seasonings to taste. Serve with a vegetable and a green salad.

```
-------------------------------------------------------------------------------
| Analysis: GARBANZO-RICE CASSEROLE (12 SERVINGS)     Divided by: 12          |
|           Wgt: 232 g (8.19 oz.)                     Water:       82%        |
-------------------------------------------------------------------------------
```

Calories	166		Vitamin C	18.6 mg
Protein	5.1 g		Vitamin D	0 mcg
Carbohydrates	33.7 g		Vit E-Alpha E	.418 mg
Fat - Total	1.54 g		Vitamin K	mcg
Saturated Fat	.259 g		Biotin	mcg
Mono Fat	.468 g		Calcium	53.2 mg
Poly Fat	.588 g		Copper	.245 mg
Cholesterol	0 mg		Iodine	mcg
Dietary Fibre	3.57 g		Iron	1.77 mg
Soluble Fibre	.927 g		Magnesium	66.2 mg
Total Vit A	49.4 RE		Manganese	1.48 mg
Thiamin-B1	.197 mg		Phosphorus	155 mg
Riboflavin-B2	.098 mg		Potassium	345 mg
Niacin-B3	2.54 mg		Selenium	13.6 mcg
Niacin Equiv.	2.37 mg		Sodium	298 mg
Vitamin B6	.313 mg		Zinc	1.07 mg
Vitamin B12	0 mcg		Complex Carbs	26 g
Folate	42.9 mcg		Sugars	4.03 g
Pantothenic	.694 mg		Water	190 g

CALORIE BREAKDOWN		FAT		EXCHANGES	
Protein	12%	* Saturated :	1.4%	Bread	1.66
Carbohydrates	80%	Mono Unsat:	2.5%	Lean Meat	.068
Fat-Total *	8%	Poly Unsat:	3.1%	Vegetables	.951

GLUTEN STEAKS (makes about 64 steaks)

250 mL	(1 cup)		soaked garbanzos (measured after soaking)
180 mL	(3/4 cup)	EACH	walnuts and rolled oats
125 mL	(1/2 cup)		food yeast flakes
60 mL	(1/4 cup)		Maggi seasoning, Bragg Liquid Aminos, or soy sauce
5 mL	(1 tsp.)		salt
625 mL	(2 1/2 cups)		water
875 mL	(3 1/2 cups)		gluten flour (may not need that much)

GLUTEN STEAK BROTH:

4.5 L	(18 cups)		water
125 mL	(1/2 cup)		Maggi seasoning, Bragg Liquid Aminos, or soy sauce
750 mL	(3 cups)	EACH	chopped onions and chopped celery (Use leaves)
4	(4)		large cloves of fresh garlic
90 mL	(6 Tbsp.)		chicken-style seasoning (if available)

Method:

BLEND garbanzos, walnuts, rolled oats, food yeast flakes, Maggi sauce and salt together in food processor until smooth. ADD water a little at a time blending after each addition and saving a little to rinse the food processor. POUR into a bowl. ADD gluten flour, one cup at a time, mixing and kneading thoroughly. FORM a sausage-like roll, COVER. REFRIGERATE overnight. CUT into 1/2 inch slices, ROLL with a rolling pin on a floured surface or SQUEEZE into a flat round. For broth: In a very large pot PUT all the ingredients. BRING all this to a boil and ADD prepared gluten steaks. BOIL in BROTH about two hours.

```
-------------------------------------------------------------------------------
| Analysis: GLUTEN STEAK                           Divided by: 64             |
|            Wgt: 39.7 g (1.4 oz.)                 Water:      64%            |
-------------------------------------------------------------------------------
```

Calories	57.9	Vitamin C	1.01 mg
Protein	4.51 g	Vitamin D	0 mcg
Carbohydrates	7.38 g	Vit E-Alpha E	.084 mg
Fat - Total	1.21 g	Vitamin K	mcg
Saturated Fat	.101 g	Biotin	mcg
Mono Fat	.236 g	Calcium	16.1 mg
Poly Fat	.612 g	Copper	.042 mg
Dietary Fibre	.65 g	Iron	.509 mg
Soluble Fibre	.161 g	Magnesium	9.37 mg
Total Vit A	1.08 RE	Manganese	.131 mg
Thiamin-B1	.2 mg	Phosphorus	52 mg
Riboflavin-B2	.078 mg	Potassium	80.7 mg
Niacin-B3	.735 mg	Selenium	.733 mcg
Niacin Equiv.	.181 mg	Sodium	168 mg
Vitamin B6	.07 mg	Zinc	.166 mg
Vitamin B12	0 mcg	Complex Carbs	4.92 g
Folate	48.1 mcg	Sugars	.779 g
Pantothenic	.192 mg	Water	25.4 g

CALORIE BREAKDOWN		FAT	EXCHANGES	
Protein	31%	Saturated : 1.5%	Bread	.45
Carbohydrates	50%	Mono Unsat: 3.6%	Lean Meat	.02
Fat - Total *	19%	Poly Unsat: 9.4%	Vegetables	.125

GNOCCHI (makes 6-8 servings)

4	(2 lbs.)	russet potatoes
325 mL	(1 1/3 cups)	unbleached flour
		salt to taste

Method:

PEEL the potatoes, CUT into large chunks and COOK until tender. DRAIN and MASH with a potato masher. MIX in the flour and KNEAD until the mixture is smooth. SHAPE the dough into long rolls about 1 inch in diameter. CUT dough into 2 inch pieces, now called gnocchi. DROP the gnocchi into boiling water a few at a time. When they rise to the surface REMOVE with a slotted spoon. PLACE in a casserole dish with a lid to keep warm. SERVE with a tomato sauce to cover them. May also add sauteed onions. (Recipe courtesy of Theresa Dreosi)

```
-----------------------------------------------------------------------
| Analysis: GNOCCHI                          Divided by: 10            |
|           Wgt: 70.4 g (2.48 oz.)           Water:      62%           |
-----------------------------------------------------------------------
```

Calories	106		Vitamin C	4 mg
Protein	2.6 g		Vitamin D	0 mcg
Carbohydrates	23.2 g		Vit E-Alpha E	.087 mg
Fat - Total	.214 g		Vitamin K	mcg
Saturated Fat	.039 g		Biotin	mcg
Mono Fat	.015 g		Calcium	6.83 mg
Poly Fat	.09 g		Copper	.113 mg
Cholesterol	0 mg		Iodine	mcg
Dietary Fibre	1.25 g		Iron	.922 mg
Soluble Fibre	.334 g		Magnesium	14.4 mg
Total Vit A	0 RE		Manganese	.187 mg
Thiamin-B1	.18 mg		Phosphorus	39.2 mg
Riboflavin-B2	.091 mg		Potassium	194 mg
Niacin-B3	1.67 mg		Selenium	5.43 mcg
Niacin Equiv.	1.67 mg		Sodium	56.3 mg
Vitamin B6	.152 mg		Zinc	.26 mg
Vitamin B12	0 mcg		Complex Carbs	21.4 g
Folate	9.03 mcg		Sugars	.525 g
Pantothenic	.346 mg		Water	43.8 g

CALORIE BREAKDOWN		FAT		EXCHANGE	
Protein	10%	*Saturated:	.3%	Bread	1.34
Carbohydrates	88%	Mono Unsat:	.1%		
Fat-Total *	2%	Poly Unsat:	.8%		

BEAN COOKING UPDATED:

SORT beans; WASH well; BRING to a boil; SIMMER for 2 minutes; COVER tightly; TURN off heat; SOAK for an hour or longer. Then COOK as you would if they had been soaked overnight. (Lentils and split peas do not require soaking.) DRAIN and ADD fresh distilled water. BRING to a boil, REDUCE heat. SIMMER until tender (Also see page 15).

JAMBALAYA (makes 10 servings - 1 litre)

250 mL	(1 cup)	EACH	chopped onion **and** sliced celery
1	(1)		large clove of garlic, minced
625 mL	(2 1/2 cups)		cubed GLUTEN STEAKS (see recipe on page 20 or 41)
796 mL	(28 oz.)		tomato sauce (Hunts, Heinz or homemade)
5 mL	(1 tsp.)		ground cumin
1	(1)		medium green pepper, cut in strips
15 mL	(1 Tbsp.)	EACH	soy sauce **and** corn starch

Method:

STEAM onions, celery, and garlic in a small amount of water for two minutes. **ADD** GLUTEN STEAKS, tomato sauce, and cumin. **SIMMER** 10 minutes. **ADD** the pepper strips and **SIMMER** for 5 minutes. **MIX** soy sauce and cornstarch. **ADD** to tomato mixture. **STIR** until thickened (about 2 minutes). **SERVE** with CONFETTI RICE, another vegetable and a salad. May be frozen.

```
------------------------------------------------------------------
| Analysis: JAMBALAYA                        Divided by: 10      |
|           Wgt: 191 g (6.73 oz.)            Water:      79%     |
------------------------------------------------------------------
```

Calories	146	Vitamin C	20.4 mg
Protein	9.23 g	Vitamin D	0 mcg
Carbohydrates	24 g	Vit E-Alpha E	.587 mg
Fat - Total	2.21 g	Vitamin K	mcg
Saturated Fat	.198 g	Biotin	mcg
Mono Fat	.411 g	Calcium	52.3 mg
Poly Fat	1.07 g	Copper	.249 mg
Cholesterol	0 mg	Iodine	mcg
Dietary Fibre	1.66 g	Iron	1.98 mg
Soluble Fibre	.382 g	Magnesium	37.5 mg
Total Vit A	80.5 RE	Manganese	.544 mg
Thiamin-B1	.404 mg	Phosphorus	134 mg
Riboflavin-B2	.258 mg	Potassium	569 mg
Niacin-B3	2.53 mg	Selenium	1.89 mcg
Niacin Equiv.	1.64 mg	Sodium	1060 mg
Vitamin B6	.399 mg	Zinc	.55 mg
Vitamin B12	0 mcg	Complex Carbs	9.32 g
Folate	105 mcg	Sugars	2.8 g
Pantothenic	.688 mg	Water	150 g

CALORIE BREAKDOWN		FAT		EXCHANGES	
Protein	24%	*Saturated :	1.2%	Bread	.997
Carbohydrates	63%	Mono Unsat:	2.4%	Lean Meat	.021
Fat-Total *	13%	Poly Unsat:	6.3%	Vegetables	1.22

GLUTEN FLOUR:

Gluten is the protein in wheat, and also the part that traps the gases produced by yeast and thus allows bread to rise. It is especially useful when baking with buckwheat, millet, or rice, which by themselves don't have great rising potential. Kneading is what develops the gluten so it can work when the baking begins. It is not a complete protein, so it is wise to combine it with a legume when using as an entree.

KASHA AND ONIONS (makes 4 servings)

250 mL	(1 cup)	whole or coarse-ground roasted kasha
5 mL	(1 tsp.)	olive oil
375 mL	(1 1/2 cups)	finely chopped onions
4	(4)	scallions (optional)
1	(1)	large garlic clove, minced
2 mL	(1/4 tsp.)	dried thyme
500 mL	(2 cups)	water
3 mL	(1/2 tsp.)	salt

Method:

WASH the kasha. Then PUT it into a non-stick pan over medium heat. STIR with a fork until the kasha grains are separated and slightly brown. Meanwhile PLACE oil in another pan that has a lid, and ADD the onion, scallion bulbs, and garlic. COOK over medium-low heat until onions are soft (about 5 minutes.) ADD a small amount of water if necessary to prevent burning or sticking. ADD the thyme and salt. REMOVE from heat. ADD the remaining water gradually to the kasha stirring constantly. Don't let it get sticky. When kasha is soft STIR in the steamed onions and scallion tops (optional). LET stand, covered, 10 minutes. SPRINKLE with parsley and SERVE with a vegetable and green salad.

```
---------------------------------------------------------------
| Analysis: BASIC KASHA AND ONIONS          Divided by: 4     |
|           Wgt: 218 g (7.69 oz.)           Water:      84%    |
---------------------------------------------------------------
```

Calories	129		Vitamin C	10.5 mg
Protein	4.18 g		Vitamin D	0 mcg
Carbohydrates	24.6 g		Vit E-Alpha Eq	.29 mg
Fat - Total	1.88 g		Vitamin K	mcg
Saturated Fat	.179 g		Biotin	mcg
Mono Fat	.856 g		Calcium	60.1 mg
Poly Fat	.371 g		Copper	.059 mg
Cholesterol	0 mg		Iodine	mcg
Dietary Fibre	3.86 g		Iron	1.57 mg
Soluble Fibre	.391 g		Magnesium	74.4 mg
Total Vit A	22.8 RE		Manganese	.122 mg
Thiamin-B1	.192 mg		Phosphorus	96.6 mg
Riboflavin-B2	.059 mg		Potassium	251 mg
Niacin-B3	1.54 mg		Selenium	1.28 mcg
Niacin Equiv.	.187 mg		Sodium	275 mg
Vitamin B6	.104 mg		Zinc	.241 mg
Vitamin B12	0 mcg		Complex Carbs	.835 g
Folate	21.9 mcg		Sugars	4.05 g
Pantothenic	.122 mg		Water	183 g

CALORIE BREAKDOWN		FAT	EXCHANGE	
Protein	13%	Saturated : 1.2%	Bread	.003
Carbohydrates	75%	Mono Unsat: 5.8%	Vegetables	.88
Fat - Total *	13%	Poly Unsat: 2.5%	Fat	.22

KASHA ORIENTAL (makes 8 servings)

1.5 L	(6 cups)	cooked kasha (2 cups before cooking) Cook in 3 cups of water
250 mL	(1 cup)	onion, minced
500 mL	(2 cups)	carrots, cut into match sticks
30 mL	(2 Tbsp.)	Maggi seasoning **or** Bragg liquid aminos **or** soy sauce
375 mL	(1 1/2 cups)	tofu, cut into pieces
250 mL	(1 cup)	peas, fresh or frozen (If frozen thaw before adding.)

Method:

STEAM onions and carrots in a small amount of water for 5 minutes. ADD seasoning and tofu. SIMMER 15 minutes, stirring occasionally. ADD peas and cooked kasha. MIX thoroughly.

```
------------------------------------------------------------------------------
| Analysis: KASHA ORIENTAL (makes 8 servings)      Divided by: 8             |
|           Wgt: 167 g (5.9 oz.)                   Water:      62%           |
------------------------------------------------------------------------------
```

Calories	256		Vitamin C	4.24 mg
Protein	12.4 g		Vitamin D	0 mcg
Carbohydrates	156 g		Vit E-Alpha E	.279 mg
Fat - Total	4.28 g		Vitamin K	mcg
Saturated Fat	.625 g		Biotin	mcg
Mono Fat	.925 g		Calcium	118 mg
Poly Fat	2.4 g		Copper	.276 mg
Cholesterol	0 mg		Iodine	mcg
Dietary Fibre	2.54 g		Iron	7.08 mg
Soluble Fibre	.713 g		Magnesium	58.6 mg
Total Vit A	978 RE		Manganese	.981 mg
Thiamin-B1	1.36 mg		Phosphorus	131 mg
Riboflavin-B2	.151 mg		Potassium	274 mg
Niacin-B3	1.65 mg		Selenium	1.6 mcg
Niacin Equiv.	.855 mg		Sodium	307 mg
Vitamin B6	.193 mg		Zinc	1.1 mg
Vitamin B12	0 mcg		Complex Carbs	2.45 g
Folate	35.5 mcg		Sugars	4.13 g
Pantothenic	.246 mg		Water	104 g

CALORIE BREAKDOWN		FAT	EXCHANGES	
Protein	7%	*Saturated : .8%	Bread	.749
Carbohydrates	88%	Mono Unsat: 1.2%	Lean Meat	1.12
Fat-Total *	5%	Poly Unsat: 3 %	Vegetables	.749

BUCKWHEAT - KASHA:

Buckwheat is the staple grain of Russia and Poland. The familiar Russian and Polish name for cooked buckwheat is **KASHA**. Jewish cookery uses buckwheat extensively and also uses the term **KASHA**. Roasted hulled buckwheat kernels are also called **KASHA**. **KASHA** can be purchased in three ways; whole or coarse, medium, and fine ground. The whole form is best for most dishes. In North America buckwheat is used mainly as flour for pancakes. Buckwheat contains a high proportion of all eight essential amino acids. Buckwheat is closer to being a complete protein than any other plant source--even soy beans and has much less fat. Bert Green, *The Grains Cookbook*, Workman Publishing NY, 1988.

KIBBEE (A Middle Eastern Dish) (makes 8 half-cup servings)

250 mL	(1 cup)		bulgur wheat
900 mL	(3 2/3 cups)		water
8 mL	(1 3/4 tsp.)		salt
125 mL	(1/2 cup)		large flake rolled oats
5 mL	(1 tsp.)		olive oil
2	(2)		garlic cloves, minced
125 mL	(1/2 cup)	**EACH**	chopped onions **and** chopped green peppers
125 mL	(1/2 cup)		chopped roasted pimentos **or** red sweet peppers
125 mL	(1/2 cup)		chopped celery
30 mL	(3 Tbsp.)		dried parsley
10 mL	(2 tsp.)		onion powder
3 mL	(1/2 tsp.)	**EACH**	sage **and** oregano
3 mL	(1/2 tsp.)		garlic powder
3 mL	(1/2 tsp.)		thyme

Method:

SOAK bulgur in 3 cups water overnight. In saucepan, **BRING** 2/3 cup of water and the salt to a boil. **ADD** oats and **REDUCE** heat. **COVER** and **SIMMER** 15-20 minutes. **REMOVE** from heat and **PUT** into bowl. **ADD** bulgur and any remaining water from soaking. In skillet **STEAM** garlic, onions, peppers, and celery until soft. **PUT** into bowl with remaining ingredients. **MIX** well. **PUT** into lecithin oiled baking dish. **BAKE** at 350° for one hour.

```
Analysis: KIBBEE                                    Divided by: 8
          Wgt: 159 g (5.61 oz)                      Water:    83%
```

Calories	97.4		Vitamin C	7.27 mg
Protein	3.45 g		Vitamin D	0 mcg
Carbohydrates	19.7 g		Vit E-Alpha E	.239 mg
Fat - Total	1.25 g		Vitamin K	mcg
Saturated Fat	.213 g		Biotin	mcg
Mono Fat	.556 g		Calcium	39.7 mg
Poly Fat	.3 g		Copper	.108 mg
Cholesterol	0 mg		Iodine	mcg
Dietary Fibre	4.63 g		Iron	1.97 mg
Soluble Fibre	.87 g		Magnesium	43.8 mg
Total Vit A	15.2 RE		Manganese	.841 mg
Thiamin-B1	.1 mg		Phosphorus	89 mg
Riboflavin-B2	.042 mg		Potassium	163 mg
Niacin-B3	1.08 mg		Selenium	5.84 mcg
Niacin Equiv.	1.08 mg		Sodium	481 mg
Vitamin B6	.154 mg		Zinc	.66 mg
Vitamin B12	0 mcg		Complex Carbs	13.6 g
Folate	13.9 mcg		Sugars	1.48 g
Pantothenic	.308 mg		Water	133 g

CALORIE BREAKDOWN		FAT		EXCHANGES	
Protein	13%	Saturated :	1.8%	Bread	.876
Carbohydrates	76%	Mono Unsat:	4.8	Vegetables	.23
Fat	11%	Poly Unsat:	2.6	Fat	.1

LASAGNA (makes 12 servings)

1 L	(4 cups)	TOMATO SAUCE (homemade, Hunts or Heinz)
12	(12)	lasagna strips (uncooked)
1	(1)	batch TOFU COTTAGE "CHEESE" (page 196)
500 mL	(2 cups)	chopped onions, steamed
2	(2)	garlic cloves, minced and steamed
500 mL	(2 cups)	diced eggplant, steamed
250 mL	(1 cup)	SUNFLOWER-PIMENTO "CHEESE" (page 195)
5 mL	(1 tsp.)	oregano
5 mL	(1 tsp.)	basil

Method:

PLACE the above ingredients by layers in a 13" x 9" x 2" pyrex dish, starting with a layer of tomato sauce, then lasagna strips, mixed TOFU COTTAGE "CHEESE", onions, garlic, eggplant, oregano, and basil. REPEAT these layers and END with frozen and grated SUNFLOWER-PIMENTO "CHEESE". Note: Since the lasagna strips are not cooked, be sure to add extra sauce because it will be soaked up as pasta cooks. BAKE at 350° for one hour. This dish is best made ahead and reheated. (If time is limited COOK lasagna strips first.)

```
Analysis: TOFU LASAGNA (12 servings)        Divided by: 12
          Wgt: 222 g (7.82 oz.)             Water:      81%
```

Calories	161		Vitamin C	15.7 mg
Protein	8.65 g		Vitamin D	0 mcg
Carbohydrates	25.9 g		Vit E-Alpha E	1.03 mg
Fat - Total	3.51 g		Vitamin K	mcg
Saturated Fat	.482 g		Biotin	mcg
Mono Fat	.701 g		Calcium	84.4 mg
Poly Fat	1.94 g		Copper	.354 mg
Cholesterol	0 mg		Iodine	mcg
Dietary Fibre	3.75 g		Iron	4.54 mg
Soluble Fibre	.676 g		Magnesium	84.4 mg
Total Vit A	99.5 RE		Manganese	.718 mg
Thiamin-B1	.413 mg		Phosphorus	142 mg
Riboflavin-B2	.193 mg		Potassium	465 mg
Niacin-B3	2.65 mg		Selenium	17.6 mcg
Niacin Equiv.	2.15 mg		Sodium	767 mg
Vitamin B6	.277 mg		Zinc	1.05 mg
Vitamin B12	0 mcg		Complex Carbs	17 g
Folate	59 mcg		Sugars	4.84 g
Pantothenic	.605 mg		Water	180 g

CALORIE BREAKDOWN		FAT		EXCHANGES	
Protein	20%	*Saturated: 2.6%		Bread	1.05
Carbohydrates	61%	Mono Unsat: 3.7%		Lean Meat	.424
Fat-Total *	19%	Poly Unsat: 10.3%		Fruit	.157
				Vegetables	1.4
				Fat	.28

LENTIL-POTATO CASSEROLE (makes 3 cups - 12 quarter-cup servings)

75 mL	(1/3 cup)	chopped onion (steamed)
75 mL	(1/3 cup)	chopped bell pepper (steamed)
75 mL	(1/3 cup)	walnuts, chopped
310 mL	(1 1/4 cups)	cooked green lentils, mashed
310 mL	(1 1/4 cups)	cooked potatoes, mashed
2 mL	(1/4 tsp.)	sage
3 mL	(1/2 tsp.)	salt

Method:

MIX well. PACK into a small casserole and BAKE at 350°F. SERVE plain or with gravy.

```
Analysis: LENTIL-POTATO CASSEROLE              Divided by: 12
          Wgt: 43.5 g (1.53 oz.)              Water:    72%
```

Calories	53		Vitamin C	4.16 mg
Protein	2.53 g		Vitamin D	0 mcg
Carbohydrates	7.62 g		Vit E-Alpha E	.117 mg
Fat - Total	1.65 g		Vitamin K	mcg
Saturated Fat	.157 g		Biotin	mcg
Mono Fat	.37 g		Calcium	8.69 mg
Poly Fat	1.03 g		Copper	.113 mg
Cholesterol	0 mg		Iodine	mcg
Dietary Fibre	1.48 g		Iron	.811 mg
Soluble Fibre	.501 g		Magnesium	15.2 mg
Total Vit A	1.91 RE		Manganese	.203 mg
Thiamin-B1	.061 mg		Phosphorus	52.6 mg
Riboflavin-B2	.023 mg		Potassium	146 mg
Niacin-B3	.429 mg		Selenium	1.05 mcg
Niacin Equiv.	.429 mg		Sodium	90.2 mg
Vitamin B6	.097 mg		Zinc	.38 mg
Vitamin B12	0 mcg		Complex Carbs	5.12 g
Folate	41.6 mcg		Sugars	1.01 g
Pantothenic	.215 mg		Water	31.1 g

CALORIE BREAKDOWN		FAT		Exchanges	
Protein	18%	* Saturated :	2.5%	Bread	.356
Carbohydrates	55%	Mono Unsat:	6%	Lean Meat	.103
Fat-Total *	27%	Poly Unsat:	16.7%	Vegetables	.104

HAZARDS OF CAFFEINE USE:

Coffee causes dizziness, unsteadiness on the feet, restlessness, depression, anxiety, hostility, circulatory problems, irritability, bladder and ovary cancer, birth defects, and peptic ulcers. **IT IS NO FRIEND.** Coffee drinkers, as compared to non-coffee drinkers, have a greater incidence of overweight, consume more alcohol and smoke more cigarettes, and have lower occupational status. Coffee is the principle source of caffeine consumed, but there is also caffeine in colas, tea, and chocolate. Abstracted from Agatha Thrash, M.D., *Poison with a Capital C.*

LIMA BEAN AND TOMATO CASSEROLE (makes 8 one-cup servings)

500 mL	(2 cups - 1 lb.)	dry lima beans (large ones)
750 mL	(3 cups)	sliced onions
125 mL	(1/2 cup)	diced celery
8 mL	(1 1/2 tsp.)	salt
5 mL	(1 tsp.)	savory
500 mL	(2 cups)	canned or frozen tomatoes

Method:

    SOAK limas overnight or **USE** the quick-soak method. **COOK** until tender. **STEAM** onions and celery until tender. **COMBINE** all ingredients. **PLACE** in a casserole and **BAKE** slowly for one hour at 325° F.

```
------------------------------------------------------------------------
| Analysis: LIMA BEAN AND TOMATO CASSEROLE           Divided by: 16     |
|           Wgt: 78.2 g (2.76 oz.)                   Water:      68%    |
------------------------------------------------------------------------
```

Calories	90.3		Vitamin C	6.16 mg
Protein	5.35 g		Vitamin D	0 mcg
Carbohydrates	17.3 g		Vit E-Alpha E	.222 mg
Fat - Total	.271 g		Vitamin K	mcg
Saturated Fat	.054 g		Biotin	mcg
Mono Fat	.031 g		Calcium	33.8 mg
Poly Fat	.115 g		Copper	.213 mg
Cholesterol	0 mg		Iodine	mcg
Dietary Fibre	7.56 g		Iron	1.96 mg
Soluble Fibre	2.07 g		Magnesium	56.6 mg
Total Vit A	19 RE		Manganese	.449 mg
Thiamin-B1	.137 mg		Phosphorus	99.5 mg
Riboflavin-B2	.06 mg		Potassium	495 mg
Niacin-B3	.61 mg		Selenium	1.83 mcg
Niacin Equiv.	.611 mg		Sodium	257 mg
Vitamin B6	.169 mg		Zinc	.73 mg
Vitamin B12	0 mcg		Complex Carbs	5.66 g
Folate	95.4 mcg		Sugars	4.12 g
Pantothenic	.38 mg		Water	53.3 g

CALORIE BREAKDOWN		FAT		EXCHANGES	
Protein	23%	*Saturated :	.5%	Bread	.89
Carbohydrates	74%	Mono Unsat:	.3%	Lean Meat	.056
Fat-Total	3%	Poly Unsat:	1.1%	Vegetables	.541

NOT ALL CALORIES ARE CREATED EQUAL:

    It used to be that people who needed to lose weight were told to count calories. There were warnings against empty calories, but no reference was made to the type of food to eat, so carbohydrate calories were considered just as bad as fat calories. In fact people who wanted to lose weight always cut down on potatoes and bread. Generally they did lose, but were not aware that it was not the cutting out of bread and potatoes, but the margarine, butter, gravy, and sour cream that usually accompanied these foods that were being eliminated. Now it is known that fat calories, especially animal fat calories, help to make you fat. Dr. John McDougall has good success with people eating a high complex carbohydrate diet with a consciously reduced fat intake even of vegetables fats.

MACARONI AND "CHEESE" (makes 10 servings)

500 mL	(2 cups)	elbow or small shell macaroni
1	(1)	large garlic clove, minced
250 mL	(1 cup)	**EACH** chopped onions **and** chopped celery
125 mL	(1/2 cup)	chopped green pepper
250 mL	(1 cup)	SUNFLOWER-PIMENTO "CHEESE"
60 mL	(1/4 cup)	fine whole wheat bread crumbs (optional)

Method:

   MAKE SUNFLOWER-PIMENTO "CHEESE". **COOK** macaroni. **STEAM** garlic, onions, celery, and peppers in a small amount of water until tender. **STIR** vegetables into cooked macaroni and ADD enough of the "cheese" to make the mixture the consistency you like. May **SERVE** as is or **PLACE** in casserole and **TOP** with bread crumbs. **PLACE** in 350° F oven and **BAKE** until golden brown. Just before serving **SPRINKLE** some grated (frozen) SUNFLOWER-PIMENTO "CHEESE" on top. **GARNISH** with parsley and cherry tomatoes. **SERVE** with peas or broccoli and a tossed salad. (May be frozen.)

```
Analysis: Macaroni and "Cheese"              Divided by: 10
     Wgt: 73.8 g (2.5 oz.)                        Water: 64%
```

Calories	109		Vitamin C	9.16 mg
Protein	3.98 g		Vitamin D	.009 mcg
Carbohydrates	20.7 g		Vit E-Alpha E	.596 mg
Fat - Total	1.21 g		Vitamin K	mcg
Saturated Fat	.166 g		Biotin	mcg
Mono Fat	.237 g		Calcium	19.3 mg
Poly Fat	.642 g		Copper	.124 mg
Cholesterol	0 mg		Iodine	mcg
Dietary Fibre	1.51 g		Iron	1.39 mg
Soluble Fibre	.164 g		Magnesium	21.3 mg
Total Vit A	15.9 RE		Manganese	.191 mg
Thiamin-B1	.419 mg		Phosphorus	68.9 mg
Riboflavin-B2	.156 mg		Potassium	114 mg
Niacin-B3	2.24 mg		Selenium	14.5 mcg
Niacin Equiv.	1.81 mg		Sodium	91.3 mg
Vitamin B6	.124 mg		Zinc	.481 mg
Vitamin B12	.001 mcg		Complex Carbs	16.4 g
Folate	46.9 mcg		Sugars	1.42 g
Pantothenic	.301 mg		Water	47.2 g

CALORIE BREAKDOWN		FAT		EXCHANGES	
Protein	15%	* Saturated :	1.4%	Bread	1.32
Carbohydrates	76%	Mono Unsat:	1.9%	Vegetables	.183
Fat-Total *	10%	Poly Unsat:	5.3%	Fat	.006

MACARONI WITH BLACK-EYED PEAS (makes 6 servings)

5 mL	(1 tsp.)		olive oil
375 mL	(1 1/2 cups)		chopped onions
250 mL	(1 cup)		thinly sliced celery
3	(3)		large garlic cloves, finely minced
500 mL	(2 cups)	**EACH**	cooked tomatoes **and** water
5 mL	(1 tsp.)		salt
3 mL	(1/2 tsp.)		oregano
250 mL	(1 cup)		uncooked macaroni
500 mL	(2 cups)		cooked black-eyed peas
30 mL	(2 Tbsp.)		fresh parsley, finely chopped

Method:

Using a pan with a tight-fitting lid, **SAUTE** the onions, celery and garlic in the oil with a little water. **ADD** tomatoes, water, salt, oregano, and macaroni. **COOK** until macaroni is tender. **STIR** in cooked beans. **SIMMER** to blend flavours. **ADD** parsley just before serving.

```
Analysis: MACARONI W BLACK-EYED PEAS (6 SERVINGS)   Divided by: 6
          Wgt: 296 g (10.4 oz.)                           Water: 86%
```

Calories	162	Vitamin C	19.4 mg
Protein	5.48 g	Vitamin D	0 mcg
Carbohydrates	32.5 g	Vit E-Alpha E	.613 mg
Fat - Total	1.55 g	Vitamin K	mcg
Saturated Fat	.246 g	Biotin	mcg
Mono Fat	.652 g	Calcium	119 mg
Poly Fat	.395 g	Copper	.249 mg
Cholesterol	0 mg	Iodine	mcg
Dietary Fibre	6.68 g	Iron	2.12 mg
Soluble Fibre	1.3 g	Magnesium	55.2 mg
Total Vit A	101 RE	Manganese	.648 mg
Thiamin-B1	.302 mg	Phosphorus	91.1 mg
Riboflavin-B2	.204 mg	Potassium	570 mg
Niacin-B3	2.83 mg	Selenium	22.2 mcg
Niacin Equiv.	2.83 mg	Sodium	511 mg
Vitamin B6	.21 mg	Zinc	1.07 mg
Vitamin B12	0 mcg	Complex Carbs	18.5 g
Folate	94.5 mcg	Sugars	7.35 g
Pantothenic	.388 mg	Water	254 g

CALORIE BREAKDOWN		FAT	EXCHANGES	
Protein	13%	* Saturated : 1.3%	Bread	1.67
Carbohydrates	78%	Mono Unsat: 3.5%	Vegetables	1.29
Fat-Total *	8%	Poly Unsat: 2.1%	Fat	.145

BORON FOR THE BONES:

In addition to vigorous exercise, a diet rich in calcium, low in sodium, modest in protein, adequate in Vitamin D, and free of caffeine and alcoholic beverages, and an adequate intake of the trace mineral boron may help to reduce the risk of osteoporosis. Fruits, vegetables, nuts, soy beans, almonds, peanuts, raisins, prunes, and hazel nuts have high levels of boron. Winston Craig, PhD., R.D. *Nutrition for the Nineties*, page 143.

MILLET V-8 CASSEROLE (makes 8 servings)

180 mL	(3/4 cup)	dry millet
500 mL	(2 cups)	water
4 mL	(3/4 tsp.)	salt
1	(1)	large garlic clove, minced
250 mL	(1 cup)	chopped onion
125 mL	(1/2 cup)	chopped celery
125 mL	(1/2 cup)	sliced black olives
60 mL	(1/4 cup)	slivered almonds
3 mL	(1/2 tsp.)	savory
15 mL	(1 Tbsp.)	basil
750 mL	(3 cups)	V-8 juice
500 mL	(2 cups)	frozen or fresh green peas

Method:

BOIL millet in salted water for 3 minutes; **TURN** heat to low; **COVER** tightly and **SIMMER** 20 minutes. **STIR** in remaining ingredients. **PUT** into prepared baking dish. **COVER** and **BAKE** at 350°F. for 45 minutes. **TURN** off heat and **LET** stand for 10 minutes. **SERVE** hot. Variation: **OMIT** nuts and **ADD** 2 cups garbanzos. May be frozen.

```
Analysis: MILLET-V8 CASSEROLE (T) (8)       Divided by: 8
          Wgt: 285 g (10 oz.)               Water:      81%
```

Calories	205	Vitamin C	35 mg
Protein	8.77 g	Vitamin D	0 mcg
Carbohydrates	37.7 g	Vit E-Alpha E	.884 mg
Fat - Total	3.45 g	Vitamin K	mcg
Saturated Fat	.326 g	Biotin	mcg
Mono Fat	1.08 g	Calcium	83 mg
Poly Fat	.922 g	Copper	.476 mg
Cholesterol	0 mg	Iodine	mcg
Dietary Fibre	6.26 g	Iron	3.07 mg
Soluble Fibre	1.52 g	Magnesium	50.9 mg
Total Vit A	124 RE	Manganese	.879 mg
Thiamin-B1	.185 mg	Phosphorus	190 mg
Riboflavin-B2	.117 mg	Potassium	481 mg
Niacin-B3	1.45 mg	Selenium	3.68 mcg
Niacin Equiv.	1.18 mg	Sodium	606 mg
Vitamin B6	.282 mg	Zinc	1.36 mg
Vitamin B12	0 mcg	Complex Carbs	14.8 g
Folate	144 mcg	Sugars	5.77 g
Pantothenic	.494 mg	Water	232 g

CALORIE BREAKDOWN		FAT	EXCHANGES	
Protein	16%	*Saturated : 1.4%	Bread	1.18
Carbohydrates	70%	Mono Unsat: 4.5%	Lean Meat	.337
Fat-Total *	14%	Poly Unsat: 3.8%	Vegetables	1.21
			Fat	.187

ONE-DISH MEAL (makes 8 servings)

5 mL	(1 tsp.)	olive oil
250 mL	(1 cup)	chopped onion
250 mL	(1 cup)	thinly sliced celery
2	(2)	large cloves of garlic, minced
3 mL	(1/2 tsp.)	thyme
5 mL	(1 tsp.)	Marmite
625 mL	(2 1/2 cups)	GLUTEN STEAKS cut in cubes (page 20 or 41)
250 mL	(1 cup)	hot water
500 mL	(2 cups)	cooked or canned tomatoes
125 mL	(1/2 cup)	green pepper, cut in narrow strips
45 mL	(3 Tbsp.)	cornstarch
30 mL	(2 Tbsp.)	soy sauce
750 mL	(3 cups)	hot cooked brown rice

Method:

SAUTE the onion, celery, and garlic in the oil. ADD thyme, Marmite, and hot water. ADD GLUTEN STEAKS and tomatoes. BRING to a boil. MIX cornstarch and soy sauce with a little of the liquid from the pot, STIR into hot mixture and ALLOW to boil. ADD green peppers and SIMMER until peppers are tender crisp. SERVE over brown rice.

```
-----------------------------------------------------------------------
| Analysis: ONE-DISH MEAL (8 servings)          Divided by: 8         |
|           Wgt: 297 g (10.5 oz.)               Water: 79%            |
-----------------------------------------------------------------------
```

Calories	248		Vitamin C	23.8 mg
Protein	12.6 g		Vitamin D	0 mcg
Carbohydrates	41.6 g		Vit E-Alpha E	1.39 mg
Fat - Total	3.97 g		Vitamin K	mcg
Saturated Fat	.46 g		Biotin	mcg
Mono Fat	1.18 g		Calcium	60.6 mg
Poly Fat	1.65 g		Copper	.251 mg
Cholesterol	0 mg		Iodine	mcg
Dietary Fibre	4.32 g		Iron	2.21 mg
Soluble Fibre	.837 g		Magnesium	66.7 mg
Total Vit A	52.9 RE		Manganese	1.11 mg
Thiamin-B1	.541 mg		Phosphorus	206 mg
Riboflavin-B2	.252 mg		Potassium	466 mg
Niacin-B3	3.58 mg		Selenium	12.5 mcg
Niacin Equiv.	2.35 mg		Sodium	875 mg
Vitamin B6	.388 mg		Zinc	.985 mg
Vitamin B12	0 mcg		Complex Carbs	29.4 g
Folate	118 mcg		Sugars	5.79 g
Pantothenic	.875 mg		Water	234 g

CALORIE BREAKDOWN		FAT		EXCHANGES	
Protein	20%	*Saturated :	1.6%	Bread	2.1
Carbohydrates	66%	Mono Unsat:	4.2%	Lean Meat	.026
Fat-Total *	14%	Poly Unsat:	5.9%	Vegetables	1.27
				Fat	.109

ORIENTAL RICE (12 half-cup servings)

250 mL	(1 cup)	**EACH**	chopped celery, minced onion, **and** cubed eggplant
284 mL	(10 oz.)		sliced water chestnuts
60 mL	(1/4 cup)		chopped nuts
3 mL	(1/2 tsp.)		salt
15 mL	(1 Tbsp.)		soy sauce, Maggi seasoning, or Bragg liquid aminos
750 mL	(3 cups)		thawed frozen peas
1 L	(4 cups)		hot cooked brown rice

Method:

STEAM onions and celery until tender. ADD eggplant, water chestnuts, nuts, and seasonings. SIMMER for 3 minutes. ADD peas. COMBINE with rice. May be used for stuffing for cabbage, eggplant, peppers, or tomatoes. May also be served with mixed vegetables and TOFU FU YUNG.

```
Analysis: ORIENTAL RICE (12 servings)        Divided by: 12
          Wgt: 113 g (4 oz.)                 Water:      78%
```

Calories	101		Vitamin C	1.91 mg
Protein	2.46 g		Vitamin D	0 mcg
Carbohydrates	19.2 g		Vit E-Alpha E	.827 mg
Fat - Total	1.8 g		Vitamin K	mcg
Saturated Fat	.233 g		Biotin	mcg
Mono Fat	.486 g		Calcium	18.3 mg
Poly Fat	.967 g		Copper	.126 mg
Cholesterol	0 mg		Iodine	mcg
Dietary Fibre	2.06 g		Iron	.583 mg
Soluble Fibre	.257 g		Magnesium	35.6 mg
Total Vit A	2.06 RE		Manganese	.709 mg
Thiamin-B1	.088 mg		Phosphorus	73.2 mg
Riboflavin-B2	.033 mg		Potassium	122 mg
Niacin-B3	1.21 mg		Selenium	9.25 mcg
Niacin Equiv.	1.21 mg		Sodium	188 mg
Vitamin B6	.161 mg		Zinc	.572 mg
Vitamin B12	0 mcg		Complex Carbs	14.1 g
Folate	11.5 mcg		Sugars	1.52 g
Pantothenic	.273 mg		Water	88.9 g

CALORIE BREAKDOWN		FAT	EXCHANGES
Protein	10%	*Saturated : 2 %	Bread .915
Carbohydrates	75%	Mono Unsat: 4.3%	Vegetables .561
Fat-Total *	16%	Poly Unsat: 8.5%	

IDEAL DIET:

Grains, fruits, nuts, and vegetables constitute the diet chosen for us by our Creator. These foods, prepared in as simple and natural a manner as possible, are the most healthful and nourishing. They impart a strength, a power of endurance, and a vigour of intellect that are not afforded by a more complex and stimulating diet. Ellen White, *Ministry of Healing*, page 296.

ORIENTAL VERMICELLI DELIGHT (makes about 15 servings)

500 gm	(1 lb.)		vermicelli (broken in 3 pieces)
5 mL	(1 tsp.)		olive oil
500 mL	(2 cups)	EACH	sliced onions and sliced celery
500 mL	(2 cups)		cubed eggplant
125 mL	(1/2 cup)	EACH	chopped red pepper and green sweet pepper
2	(2)		large garlic cloves, minced
500 mL	(2 cups)		diced tofu, frozen and thawed
125 mL	(1/2 cup)		wheat germ
60 mL	(1/4 cup)		soy sauce, Maggi seasoning, or Bragg liquid aminos
30 mL	(2 Tbsp.)		chicken style seasoning
5 mL	(1 tsp.)		salt
500 mL	(2 cups)		water (less if mixture seems moist enough)
250 mL	(1 cup)		whole wheat bread crumbs (optional)

Method:

COOK vermicelli. SAUTE onions, celery, eggplant, peppers, and garlic in the oil and a small amount of water in a covered pot. ADD tofu and STIR. ADD wheat germ, soy sauce, seasoning, and water as needed. COMBINE the steamed mixture with the vermicelli. PLACE in baking dish and SPRINKLE with crumbs if baking. This dish may be eaten without baking or BAKE at 350° F. for 45 minutes. (It freezes very well.)

```
--------------------------------------------------------------------------
| Analysis: ORIENTAL VERMICELLI                      Divided by: 15       |
|           Wgt: 164 g (5.79 oz.)                    Water:       69%     |
--------------------------------------------------------------------------
```

Calories	211		Vitamin C	11.7 mg
Protein	9.3 g		Vitamin D	.024 mcg
Carbohydrates	36.5 g		Vit E-Alpha E	.951 mg
Fat - Total	3.22 g		Vitamin K	mcg
Saturated Fat	.499 g		Biotin	mcg
Mono Fat	.827 g		Calcium	73.4 mg
Poly Fat	1.47 g		Copper	.226 mg
Cholesterol	0 mg		Iodine	mcg
Dietary Fibre	2.82 g		Iron	3.97 mg
Soluble Fibre	.387 g		Magnesium	68 mg
Total Vit A	26.9 RE		Manganese	1.02 mg
Thiamin-B1	.515 mg		Phosphorus	140 mg
Riboflavin-B2	.232 mg		Potassium	255 mg
Niacin-B3	3.59 mg		Selenium	24.5 mcg
Niacin Equiv.	3.59 mg		Sodium	495 mg
Vitamin B6	.172 mg		Zinc	1.27 mg
Vitamin B12	.001 mcg		Complex Carbs	29 g
Folate	33.6 mcg		Sugars	3.79 g
Pantothenic	.34 mg		Water	113 g

CALORIE BREAKDOWN		FAT	EXCHANGES	
Protein	18%	*Saturated : 2.1%	Bread	2.34
Carbohydrates	69%	Mono Unsat: 3.5%	Lean Meat	.288
Fat-Total *	14%	Poly Unsat: 6.2%	Vegetables	.613
			Fat	.242

PASTA-VEGETABLE CASSEROLE (makes about 10 servings)

500 gm	(1 lb.)		pasta (elbows or shells)
500 mL	(2 cups)	**EACH**	sliced or chopped onions **and** cubed eggplant
4	(4)		large cloves of garlic, minced
60 mL	(1/4 cup)		chopped green **or** red pepper
60 mL	(1/4 cup)		chopped parsley
250 mL	(1 cup)		tofu

"CHEESE" SAUCE

75 mL	(1/3 cup)	**EACH**	raw cashews **and** pimentos
75 mL	(1/3 cup)		food yeast flakes
5 mL	(1 tsp.)		salt
3 mL	(1/2 tsp.)		onion powder
3 mL	(1/2 tsp.)		garlic powder
625 mL	(2 1/2 cups)		water

Method:

COOK pasta. STEAM onions, eggplant, garlic, pepper, and tofu. MIX pasta and vegetables and PLACE in large casserole. WHIZ cashews in blender or food processor until almost a paste. ADD pimentos, food yeast, salt, onion powder, garlic powder, and part of the water. WHIZ until well blended. ADD remaining water. POUR "Cheese" over casserole contents. BAKE for 45 minutes at 325° F. SERVE with tossed salad, and peas or green beans.

```
Analysis: PASTA-VEGETABLE CASSEROLE          Divided by: 10
          Wgt: 205 g (7.24 oz.)              Water:      67%
```

Calories	289	Vitamin C	10.4 mg
Protein	12 g	Vitamin D	0 mcg
Carbohydrates	47.1 g	Vit E-Alpha E	.218 mg
Fat - Total	6.38 g	Vitamin K	mcg
Saturated Fat	1.16 g	Biotin	mcg
Mono Fat	2.89 g	Calcium	66.2 mg
Poly Fat	1.75 g	Copper	.555 mg
Cholesterol	0 mg	Iodine	mcg
Dietary Fibre	4.55 g	Iron	4.8 mg
Soluble Fibre	.543 g	Magnesium	89.5 mg
Total Vit A	18.1 RE	Manganese	.671 mg
Thiamin-B1	1.19 mg	Phosphorus	232 mg
Riboflavin-B2	.432 mg	Potassium	348 mg
Niacin-B3	5.59 mg	Selenium	33.8 mcg
Niacin Equiv.	5.59 mg	Sodium	229 mg
Vitamin B6	.382 mg	Zinc	1.77 mg
Vitamin B12	.001 mcg	Complex Carbs	37.3 g
Folate	182 mcg	Sugars	5.27 g
Pantothenic	.742 mg	Water	137 g

CALORIE BREAKDOWN		FAT		EXCHANGES	
Protein	16%	*Saturated : 3.5%		Bread	2.98
Carbohydrates	64%	Mono Unsat: 8.9%		Lean Meat	.334
Fat-Total *	20%	Poly Unsat: 5.4%		Vegetables	.784
				Fat	.636

POLENTA SUPPER (makes 6 servings)

250 mL	(1 cup)	yellow cornmeal
3 mL	(1/2 tsp.)	salt
1 L	(4 cups)	water
500 mL	(2 cups)	tomato sauce
150 mL	(2/3 cup)	SUNFLOWER-PIMENTO "CHEESE"
75 mL	(1/3 cup)	frozen, grated SUNFLOWER-PIMENTO "CHEESE"

Method:

MIX the corn meal with one cup of the cold water until blended. BRING the remaining water to a boil in a heavy saucepan. ADD salt, then STIR in the cornmeal paste. RETURN to a boil, stirring constantly. REDUCE heat to low. SIMMER, stirring occasionally until the mixture is very thick. COOK 10 to 15 minutes. When ready to serve, stir in the "CHEESE". SPOON into bowls or one large bowl. TOP with hot tomato sauce and SPRINKLE with grated "CHEESE". SERVE with green salad and warm bread, hot CHILI BEANS, or stir-fried vegetables. VARIATION: PLACE polenta in a loaf pan. CHILL and SLICE. REHEAT. TOP each slice with beans, tomato sauce, or any combination of vegetables.

```
Analysis: POLENTA SUPPER                        Divided by: 6
          Wgt: 333 g (11.7 oz.)                 Water:      88%
```

Calories	144		Vitamin C	20.5 mg
Protein	4.81 g		Vitamin D	0 mcg
Carbohydrates	29.3 g		Vit E-Alpha E	1.43 mg
Fat - Total	1.57 g		Vitamin K	mcg
Saturated Fat	.189 g		Biotin	mcg
Mono Fat	.316 g		Calcium	31.7 mg
Poly Fat	.864 g		Copper	.307 mg
Cholesterol	0 mg		Iodine	mcg
Dietary Fibre	3.84 g		Iron	2.46 mg
Soluble Fibre	.957 g		Magnesium	45.2 mg
Total Vit A	143 RE		Manganese	.373 mg
Thiamin-B1	.504 mg		Phosphorus	103 mg
Riboflavin-B2	.25 mg		Potassium	549 mg
Niacin-B3	3.35 mg		Selenium	3.91 mcg
Niacin Equiv.	2.69 mg		Sodium	938 mg
Vitamin B6	.332 mg		Zinc	.69 mg
Vitamin B12	0 mcg		Complex Carbs	20.1 g
Folate	72.2 mcg		Sugars	4.86 g
Pantothenic	.755 mg		Water	293 g

CALORIE BREAKDOWN		FAT	EXCHANGES	
Protein	13%	*Saturated : 1.1%	Lean Meat	.066
Carbohydrates	78%	Mono Unsat: 1.9%	Fruit	.203
Fat-Total *	9%	Poly Unsat: 5.2%	Vegetables	1.54
			Fat	.124

POLYNESIAN DINNER (makes 12 servings)

500 gm	(1 lb.)	firm tofu, cubed
		Maggi **or** soy sauce to cover tofu
15 mL	(1 Tbsp.)	olive oil and a little water
540 mL	(19 oz.)	unsweetened pineapple chunks (Do not drain)
125 mL	(1/2 cup)	water
30 mL	(2 Tbsp.)	cornstarch or arrowroot powder
15 mL	(1 Tbsp.)	chicken style seasoning
750 mL	(3 cups)	celery cut diagonally into 1 inch lengths
500 mL	(2 cups)	carrots cut diagonally into thin strips
1	(1)	large red onion, thinly sliced
2	(2)	large green sweet peppers cut into long strips
1	(1)	large red sweet pepper cut into strips
		thyme and Maggi or soy sauce (to taste)

Method:

SPRINKLE Maggi on the tofu. PLACE on a cookie sheet and TOAST in a 350° F. oven for 20 minutes, turning once. HEAT the pineapple to boiling. STIR in the cornstarch mixed with the water. CONTINUE stirring until mixture boils again and is clear. ADD seasonings. PREPARE the vegetables. STIR-FRY the vegetables and tofu in the oil. ADD a little water, COVER. STEAM until vegetables are tender-crisp. POUR pineapple mixture over vegetables. SERVE on brown rice.

```
Analysis: POLYNESIAN DINNER              Divided by: 12
          Wgt: 278 g (9.82 oz.)          Water:      81%
```

Calories	214	Vitamin C	23.6 mg
Protein	10 g	Vitamin D	0 mcg
Carbohydrates	35.9 g	Vit E-Alpha E	1.19 mg
Fat - Total	4.62 g	Vitamin K	mcg
Saturated Fat	.709 g	Biotin	mcg
Mono Fat	1.1 g	Calcium	127 mg
Poly Fat	2.41 g	Copper	.349 mg
Cholesterol	0 mg	Iodine	mcg
Dietary Fibre	3.49 g	Iron	5.46 mg
Soluble Fibre	.697 g	Magnesium	92.5 mg
Total Vit A	680 RE	Manganese	2.07 mg
Thiamin-B1	.231 mg	Phosphorus	177 mg
Riboflavin-B2	.114 mg	Potassium	388 mg
Niacin-B3	2.05 mg	Selenium	12.3 mcg
Niacin Equiv.	2.05 mg	Sodium	397 mg
Vitamin B6	.339 mg	Zinc	1.4 mg
Vitamin B12	0 mcg	Complex Carbs	19.8 g
Folate	35.4 mcg	Sugars	10.3 g
Pantothenic	.512 mg	Water	225 g

CALORIE BREAKDOWN		FAT		EXCHANGES	
Protein	18%	*Saturated :	2.8%	Bread	1.29
Carbohydrates	64%	Mono Unsat:	4.4%	Lean Meat	1
Fat-Total *	18%	Poly Unsat:	9.6%	Fruit	.495
				Vegetables	.749

PUERTO RICAN RICE (makes about 12 servings)

500 mL	(2 cups)	**UNCOOKED** brown rice (Uncle Ben's)
1250 mL	(5 cups)	boiling water
10 mL	(2 tsp.)	salt
5 mL	(1 tsp.)	oregano
2 mL	(1/4 tsp.)	basil
2 mL	(1/4 tsp.)	cumin
2 mL	(1/4 tsp.	turmeric
60 mL	(1/4 cup)	water
250 mL	(1 cup)	minced onion
2	(2)	large garlic cloves, minced
1	(1)	medium green pepper, diced
2	(2)	large stalks celery
30 mL	(2 Tbsp.)	chopped, ripe black olives
625 mL	(2 1/2 cups)	canned tomatoes

Method:

PLACE boiling water, salt, oregano, basil, cumin, and turmeric in pot with a tight-fitting lid. **ADD** rice, **BRING** to a boil and **COVER**. **LOWER** heat and cook for 25 minutes. **STEAM** onions and garlic in a heavy saucepan with a tight cover. **ADD** peppers, celery, olives, and tomatoes. **SIMMER**. **ADD** to cooked rice; **MIX** well. **SIMMER** to blend flavours.

```
-------------------------------------------------------------------
| Analysis:  PUERTO RICAN RICE              Divided by: 12        |
|            Wgt: 247 g (8.71 oz.)          Water:      84%       |
-------------------------------------------------------------------
```

Calories	149	Vitamin C	17.8 mg
Protein	3.75 g	Vitamin D	0 mcg
Carbohydrates	31.2 g	Vit E-Alpha E	.417 mg
Fat - Total	1.35 g	Vitamin K	mcg
Saturated Fat	.245 g	Biotin	mcg
Mono Fat	.484 g	Calcium	45.2 mg
Poly Fat	.447 g	Copper	.205 mg
Dietary Fibre	3 g	Iron	1.21 mg
Soluble Fibre	.76 g	Magnesium	60.2 mg
Total Vit A	47.7 RE	Manganese	1.33 mg
Thiamin-B1	.181 mg	Phosphorus	134 mg
Riboflavin-B2	.065 mg	Potassium	329 mg
Niacin-B3	2.21 mg	Selenium	13.4 mcg
Niacin Equiv.	2.21 mg	Sodium	494 mg
Vitamin B6	.292 mg	Zinc	.88 mg
Vitamin B12	0 mcg	Complex Carbs	23.2 g
Folate	23 mcg	Sugars	4.97 g
Pantothenic	.645 mg	Water	208 g

CALORIE BREAKDOWN		FAT		EXCHANGES	
Protein	10%	* Saturated:	1.5%	Bread	1.42
Carbohydrates	82%	Mono Unsat:	2.9%	Vegetables	1.18
Fat-Total *	8%	Poly Unsat:	2.6%	Fat	.033

QUINOA PILAFF (makes 6-8 servings)

250 mL	(1 cup)		quinoa (before cooking)
500 mL	(2 cups)		water (for cooking quinoa)
15 mL	(1 Tbsp.)		chicken style seasoning
5 mL	(1 tsp.)		olive oil
250 mL	(1 cup)		diced or sliced carrots
125 mL	(1/2 cup)	**EACH**	sliced green onion **and** thinly sliced celery
125 mL	(1/2 cup)		diced mixed green and red pepper
2	(2)		garlic cloves, crushed
3 mL	(1/2 tsp.)		oregano
125 mL	(1/2 cup)		toasted sliced almonds
			salt to taste

Method:
Thoroughly **RINSE** quinoa, either by using a strainer or by running fresh water over the quinoa in a pot. **DRAIN** excess water. **PLACE** water, chicken style seasoning, and quinoa in a 1 1/2 qt. sauce pan and **BRING** to a boil. **REDUCE** to a simmer, **COVER**, and **COOK** until all the water is absorbed (about 15 minutes.) **SAUTE** the chopped vegetables in the oil and a little water in a covered pot until clear, yet crisp. **STIR** in oregano. **ADD** sauteed vegetables to cooked, hot quinoa, mixing well. **ADD** salt to taste. **STIR** in almonds.

```
------------------------------------------------------------------
| Analysis: QUINOA PILAFF                    Divided by: 6        |
|           Wgt: 72 g (2.54 oz.)             Water:     43%       |
------------------------------------------------------------------
```

Calories	172	Vitamin C	9.6 mg
Protein	5.92 g	Vitamin D	0 mcg
Carbohydrates	24.7 g	Vit E-Alpha E	.561 mg
Fat - Total	5.94 g	Vitamin K	mcg
Saturated Fat	.401 g	Biotin	mcg
Mono Fat	2.67 g	Calcium	54.4 mg
Poly Fat	.89 g	Copper	.096 mg
Cholesterol	0 mg	Iodine	mcg
Dietary Fibre	1.7 g	Iron	2.97 mg
Soluble Fibre	.304 g	Magnesium	28.3 mg
Total Vit A	272 RE	Manganese	.24 mg
Thiamin-B1	.094 mg	Phosphorus	186 mg
Riboflavin-B2	.201 mg	Potassium	153 mg
Niacin-B3	1.17 mg	Selenium	1.12 mcg
Niacin Equiv.	.464 mg	Sodium	14.4 mg
Vitamin B6	.062 mg	Zinc	1.38 mg
Vitamin B12	0 mcg	Complex Carbs	.924 g
Folate	15.2 mcg	Sugars	1.59 g
Pantothenic	.09 mg	Water	30.9 g

CALORIE BREAKDOWN		FAT		EXCHANGES	
Protein	13%	*Saturated :	2.1%	Lean Meat	.221
Carbohydrates	56%	Mono Unsat:	13.6%	Fruit	.111
Fat-Total *	30%	Poly Unsat:	4.6%	Vegetables	.324
				Fat	.607

RICE-GLUTEN CASSEROLE (makes 8 servings)

1.5 L	(6 cups)	cooked brown rice
500 mL	(2 cups)	GLUTEN STEAK chunks
375 mL	(1 1/2 cups)	onion slices (steamed in microwave)
250 mL	(1 cup)	chopped celery (steamed in microwave)
500 mL	(2 cups)	SUNFLOWER-PIMENTO "CHEESE"
180 mL	(3/4 cup)	water

Method:

ARRANGE in a casserole dish, layers of rice, gluten chunks, onion and celery. **DILUTE** SUNFLOWER-PIMENTO "CHEESE" with the water. **POUR** over the ingredients in casserole. **BAKE** at 350° F. for 45 minutes.

```
-----------------------------------------------------------------------------
| Analysis: RICE-GLUTEN CASSEROLE              Divided by: 10               |
|           Wgt: 287 g (10.1 oz.)              Water:        79%            |
-----------------------------------------------------------------------------
```

Calories	248	Vitamin C	11.6	mg
Protein	10.9 g	Vitamin D	0	mcg
Carbohydrates	42.9 g	Vit E-Alpha E	2.36	mg
Fat - Total	4.09 g	Vitamin K		mcg
Saturated Fat	.514 g	Biotin		mcg
Mono Fat	.978 g	Calcium	53.3	mg
Poly Fat	2.09 g	Copper	.311	mg
Cholesterol	0 mg	Iodine		mcg
Dietary Fibre	4.54 g	Iron	2.01	mg
Soluble Fibre	.531 g	Magnesium	83.7	mg
Total Vit A	26.3 RE	Manganese	1.29	mg
Thiamin-B1	.735 mg	Phosphorus	235	mg
Riboflavin-B2	.233 mg	Potassium	305	mg
Niacin-B3	3.76 mg	Selenium	20.3	mcg
Niacin Equiv.	2.19 mg	Sodium	520	mg
Vitamin B6	.449 mg	Zinc	1.38	mg
Vitamin B12	0 mcg	Complex Carbs	31.4	g
Folate	151 mcg	Sugars	3.15	g
Pantothenic	.99 mg	Water	226	g

CALORIE BREAKDOWN		FAT		EXCHANGES	
Protein	17%	Saturated : 1.8%		Bread	2.2
Carbohydrates	68%	Mono Unsat: 3.5%		Lean Meat	.02
Fat - Total *	15%	Poly Unsat: 7.5%		Vegetables	.5

CALORIES IN NUTRIENTS (PER GRAM):

Carbohydrates 4
Protein 4
Fat 9
Alcohol (not really a nutrient) 7

ROSANN'S GLUTEN STEAKS (makes 10 servings)

375 mL	(1 1/2 cups)	gluten flour
125 mL	(1/2 cup)	whole wheat flour
8 mL	(5 tsp.)	minute tapioca
375 mL	(1 1/2 cups)	water

Broth:

4.5 L	(18 cups)	water
125 mL	(1/2 cup)	soy sauce, Bragg liquid aminos, or Maggi seasoning
750 mL	(3 cups)	chopped onion
750 mL	(3 cups)	chopped celery with leaves
4	(4)	large cloves garlic
90 mL	(6 Tbsp.)	chicken style seasoning

Method:

MIX all ingredients. MAKE into long rolls. CUT into wedges or slices. BOIL in broth for two hours. These steaks can be used as is or in casseroles as commercial gluten would be used or ground and used as burger in loaves or patties. Recipe, courtesy of Rosann Hunt.

```
Analysis: ROSANN'S GLUTEN STEAKS          Divided by: 10
          Wgt: 594 g (20.9 oz.)           Water:    93%
```

Calories	149	Vitamin C	5.95	mg
Protein	11.3 g	Vitamin D	0	mcg
Carbohydrates	24.7 g	Vit E-Alpha E	.266	mg
Fat - Total	.727 g	Vitamin K		mcg
Saturated Fat	.048 g	Biotin		mcg
Mono Fat	.036 g	Calcium	49.9	mg
Poly Fat	.109 g	Copper	.113	mg
Cholesterol	0 mg	Iodine		mcg
Dietary Fibre	2.36 g	Iron	1.01	mg
Soluble Fibre	.461 g	Magnesium	26.9	mg
Total Vit A	4.68 RE	Manganese	.415	mg
Thiamin-B1	.083 mg	Phosphorus	92.9	mg
Riboflavin-B2	.079 mg	Potassium	247	mg
Niacin-B3	1.27 mg	Selenium	6.77	mcg
Niacin Equiv.	1.17 mg	Sodium	869	mg
Vitamin B6	.154 mg	Zinc	.522	mg
Vitamin B12	0 mcg	Complex Carbs	14.7	g
Folate	28.6 mcg	Sugars	4.32	g
Pantothenic	.246 mg	Water	552	g

CALORIE BREAKDOWN		FAT		EXCHANGES	
Protein	30%	*Saturated :	.3%	Bread	1.24
Carbohydrates	66%	Mono Unsat:	.2%	Vegetables	.798
Fat-Total *	4%	Poly Unsat:	.6%		

ADULT ONSET DIABETES:

"Ninety-five percent of adult onset diabetics on oral drugs could be off of such drugs in less than eight weeks, and 50 to 75 percent could normalize their blood sugar and get off insulin within weeks." Prof. James Anderson, M.D.

SCRAMBLED TOFU WITH QUINOA, RICE, OR MILLET (makes 10 servings)

60 mL	(1/4 cup)	**EACH**	chopped green onions **and** thinly sliced celery
45 mL	(3 Tbsp.)	**EACH**	finely chopped green **and** red sweet pepper, mixed
15 mL	(1 Tbsp.)		parsley flakes
15 mL	(1 Tbsp.)		soy sauce, Maggi seasoning, or Bragg liquid aminos
5 mL	(1 tsp.)		chicken style seasoning
1 mL	(1/4 tsp.)		turmeric
500 mL	(2 cups)		mashed tofu

Method:

STEAM the onions, celery, and peppers in a small amount of water in a non-stick pan with a lid. STIR in remaining ingredients and CONTINUE to cook. (SERVE on quinoa, rice, millet, couscous, or on whole grain toast)

```
Analysis: SCRAMBLED TOFU (without quinoa)        Divided by: 10
          Wgt: 60.1 g (2.12 oz.)                 Water:      72%
```

Calories	76.9	Vitamin C	3.26	mg
Protein	8.18 g	Vitamin D	0	mcg
Carbohydrates	3.04 g	Vit E-Alpha E	.047	mg
Fat - Total	4.44 g	Vitamin K		mcg
Saturated Fat	.639 g	Biotin		mcg
Mono Fat	.974 g	Calcium	109	mg
Poly Fat	2.49 g	Copper	.198	mg
Cholesterol	0 mg	Iodine		mcg
Dietary Fibre	.26 g	Iron	5.52	mg
Soluble Fibre	.04 g	Magnesium	49.3	mg
Total Vit A	17.3 RE	Manganese	.631	mg
Thiamin-B1	.085 mg	Phosphorus	100	mg
Riboflavin-B2	.06 mg	Potassium	148	mg
Niacin-B3	.298 mg	Selenium	.13	mcg
Niacin Equiv.	.3 mg	Sodium	113	mg
Vitamin B6	.06 mg	Zinc	.823	mg
Vitamin B12	0 mcg	Complex Carbs	.193	g
Folate	19.7 mcg	Sugars	.265	g
Pantothenic	.085 mg	Water	43.3	g

CALORIE BREAKDOWN		FAT		EXCHANGES	
Protein	39%	*Saturated :	6.8%	Bread	.102
Carbohydrate	14%	Mono Unsat:	10.3%	Lean Meat	1.2
Fat-Total *	47%	Poly unsat:	26.4%	Vegetables	.075

QUINOA:

Quinoa (pronounced keen-wa) is a complete protein grain. It supplies all the essential amino acids in a balanced pattern. It contains more protein than any other grain - an average of 16.2%, compared with 7.5% for rice, 9.9% for millet and 14% for wheat. It is light, delicious, and easy to digest. It is quick and easy to prepare. It can be served like rice. Quinoa is an ancient South American grain. Quinoa needs to be thoroughly rinsed to remove a naturally occurring bitter coating on each grain, before cooking. This coating is removed prior to sale. However there may a small amount of bitter residue left on the grain. This can be removed simply by rinsing before cooking.

SLOPPY JOES (makes about 4 servings)

5 mL	(1 tsp.)		olive oil
125 mL	(1/2 cup)	**EACH**	chopped green pepper **and** chopped onion
500 mL	(2 cups)		GRANBURGER or ground gluten
375 mL	(1 1/2 cups)		boiling water (omit if using ground gluten)
156 mL	(5 1/2 oz.)		tomato paste
1 mL	(1/4 tsp.)		salt
3 mL	(1/2 tsp.)	**EACH**	oregano **and** garlic powder
5 mL	(1 tsp.)		parsley flakes
15 mL	(1 Tbsp.)		Maggi seasoning, soy sauce, or Bragg liquid aminos

Method:

SAUTE peppers and onions in oil and a little water. **REHYDRATE** the granburger in boiling water. **ADD** to onions and peppers or **USE** 3 cups of ground gluten. **ADD** remaining ingredients. **SIMMER** 10 minutes. **ADD** more water if mixture seems too thick. **SERVE** on whole wheat buns, rice, pasta, couscous, or quinoa.

```
Analysis: SLOPPY JOES WITH GRANBURGER (4 servings) Divided by: 4
          Wgt: 185 g (6.52 oz.)                    Water:    78%
```

Calories	139	Vitamin C	39.7 mg
Protein	16.3 g	Vitamin D	0 mcg
Carbohydrates	18.6 g	Vit E-Alpha Eq	.99 mg
Fat - Total	1 g	Vitamin K	mcg
Saturated Fat	.082 g	Biotin	mcg
Mono Fat	.078 g	Calcium	94.7 mg
Poly Fat	.229 g	Copper	.334 mg
Cholesterol	0 mg	Iodine	mcg
Dietary Fibre	3.02 g	Iron	7.24 mg
Soluble Fibre	.774 g	Magnesium	32.9 mg
Total Vit A	136 RE	Manganese	.359 mg
Thiamin-B1	.282 mg	Phosphorus	58.7 mg
Riboflavin-B2	.414 mg	Potassium	777 mg
Niacin-B3	6.47 mg	Selenium	1.18 mcg
Niacin Equiv.	1.89 mg	Sodium	914 mg
Vitamin B6	.609 mg	Zinc	.528 mg
Vitamin B12	1.29 mcg	Complex Carbs	7 g
Folate	22 mcg	Sugars	3.79 g
Pantothenic	.837 mg	Water	144 g

CALORIE BREAKDOWN		FAT		EXCHANGES
Protein	44%	*Saturated : .5%		Vegetables 2.21
Carbohydrates	50%	Mono Unsat: .5%		
Fat-Total *	6%	Poly Unsat: 1.4%		

MEAT ANALOGUES:

These are vegetarian products made from plant sources such as soy beans and gluten with flavourings to make them simulate animal products. Many of them are high in sodium and fat and are a very concentrated source of protein. If choosing to use them they should be used **SPARINGLY** to add flavour and/or texture to a vegetarian dish.

SPINACH-STUFFED MANICOTTI (makes 24)

24	(24)	jumbo pasta shells
500 mL	(2 cups)	tofu
350 mL	(12 oz.)	frozen spinach
2	(2)	large garlic cloves, minced
250 mL	(1 cup)	hot cooked millet
3 mL	(1/2 tsp.)	salt
15 mL	(1 Tbsp.)	flake food yeast (not active)
15 mL	(1 Tbsp.)	lemon juice
375 mL	(1 1/2 cups)	Hunt's tomato sauce or homemade

Method:

COOK the millet. (1/4 cup millet and 1 cup water for about 40 minutes.) DRAIN tofu well. STEAM spinach with garlic. Do not overcook. CHOP fine. DRAIN. COOK shells just until they will bend without breaking. MIX tofu, spinach, millet, salt, and lemon juice. POUR tomato sauce on bottom of large pyrex baking dish. FILL each shell with 30 mL (2 Tbsp) spinach mixture. BAKE at 350° F. for 45 minutes.

```
Analysis:  SPINACH-STUFFED MANICOTTI           Divided by: 12
           Wgt: 133 g (4.68 oz.)               Water:      76%
```

Calories	125		Vitamin C	11.1 mg
Protein	7.29 g		Vitamin D	0 mcg
Carbohydrates	19.7 g		Vit E-Alpha E	.655 mg
Fat - Total	2.55 g		Vitamin K	mcg
Saturated Fat	.373 g		Biotin	mcg
Mono Fat	.51 g		Calcium	78.8 mg
Poly Fat	1.37 g		Copper	.241 mg
Cholesterol	0 mg		Iodine	mcg
Dietary Fibre	2.28 g		Iron	3.94 mg
Soluble Fibre	.464 g		Magnesium	83.8 mg
Total Vit A	192 RE		Manganese	.691 mg
Thiamin-B1	.357 mg		Phosphorus	118 mg
Riboflavin-B2	.206 mg		Potassium	351 mg
Niacin-B3	2.31 mg		Selenium	9.36 mcg
Niacin Equiv.	1.94 mg		Sodium	119 mg
Vitamin B6	.181 mg		Zinc	.909 mg
Vitamin B12	0 mcg		Complex Carbs	15.3 g
Folate	86.1 mcg		Sugars	1.93 g
Pantothenic	.329 mg		Water	101 g

CALORIE BREAKDOWN		FAT		EXCHANGES	
Protein	22%	*Saturated :	2.6%	Bread	1.1
Carbohydrates	60%	Mono Unsat:	3.5%	Lean Meat	.333
Fat-Total *	18%	Poly Unsat:	9.4%	Fruit	.005
				Vegetables	.751
				Fat	.167

THIRD JOHN 2:

"Beloved, I wish above all things that thou mayest prosper and be in health, even as thy soul prospereth."

STROGANOFF (makes 10 half-cup servings)

500 mL	(2 cups)	diced onions
250 mL	(1 cup)	chopped celery
125 mL	(1/2 cup)	chopped sweet green pepper
1	(1)	large garlic clove, minced
60 mL	(1/4 cup)	unbleached all-purpose flour
250 mL	(1 cup)	tomato sauce
10 mL	(2 tsp.)	Savorex, Vegex, **or** Marmite
2 mL	(1/2 tsp.)	marjoram
15 mL	(1 Tbsp.)	chicken style seasoning
500 mL	(2 cups)	GLUTEN STEAKS (page 20 or 41), cut into spoon-size pieces
250 mL	(1 cup)	water
250 mL	(1 cup)	fresh tofu, blended **or** GARLIC-DILL DRESSING (page 112)

Method:

SIMMER onions, celery, pepper, and garlic until vegetables are tender. **MIX** flour and tomato sauce. **STIR** into vegetable mixture. **ADD** Marmite, marjoram, chicken style seasoning, GLUTEN STEAKS, and water. **BRING** to a boil. **ADD** tofu just before serving. **HEAT**, but do not boil. **SERVE** with brown rice, pasta, or potatoes.

```
-----------------------------------------------------------------------
| Analysis: STROGANOFF (8 half-cup servings)       Divided by: 8      |
|           Wgt: 226 g (7.99 oz.)                  Water:      79%    |
-----------------------------------------------------------------------
```

Calories	189		Vitamin C	15 mg
Protein	14.1 g		Vitamin D	0 mcg
Carbohydrates	24.1 g		Vit E-Alpha Eq	.42 mg
Fat - Total	4.93 g		Vitamin K	mcg
Saturated Fat	.591 g		Biotin	mcg
Mono Fat	1.01 g		Calcium	116 mg
Poly Fat	2.61 g		Copper	.292 mg
Cholesterol	0 mg		Iodine	mcg
Dietary Fibre	2.76 g		Iron	5 mg
Soluble Fibre	.676 g		Magnesium	59.2 mg
Total Vit A	43.2 RE		Manganese	.776 mg
Thiamin-B1	.458 mg		Phosphorus	180 mg
Riboflavin-B2	.252 mg		Potassium	447 mg
Niacin-B3	2.39 mg		Selenium	3.7 mcg
Niacin Equiv.	1.26 mg		Sodium	679 mg
Vitamin B6	.293 mg		Zinc	.999 mg
Vitamin B12	0 mcg		Complex Carbs	12 g
Folate	104 mcg		Sugars	5.44 g
Pantothenic	.584 mg		Water	179 g

CALORIE BREAKDOWN		FAT		EXCHANGES	
Protein	29%	Saturated :	2.7%	Bread	1
Carbohydrates	49%	Mono Unsat:	.78%	Lean Meat	.78
Fat - Total	22%	Poly Unsat:	1.2%	Vegetables	1.2

SWEET AND SOUR GLUTEN STEAKS (makes 8 servings)

5 mL	(1 tsp.)	olive oil
125 mL	(1/2 cup)	sweet green pepper strips
125 mL	(1/2 cup)	sliced celery
125 mL	(1/2 cup)	onions (cut in 1-inch squares and separated)
1	(1)	large garlic clove, minced
625 mL	(2 1/2 cups)	cubed GLUTEN STEAKS (page 20 or 41)
10 mL	(2 tsp.)	corn starch
30 mL	(2 Tbsp.)	date butter
45 mL	(3 Tbsp.)	lemon juice
75 mL	(1/3 cup)	tomato paste
125 mL	(1/2 cup)	pineapple juice
250 mL	(1 cup)	pineapple tidbits (do not drain)
15 mL	(1 Tbsp.)	soy sauce, Maggi seasoning, or Bragg liquid aminos

Method:

   SAUTE peppers, celery, onions, and garlic in the oil until the onion is transparent. **ADD** cubed gluten steaks. **COMBINE** the remaining ingredients in a large sauce pan; **SIMMER**, stirring constantly until thickened; **ADD** sauteed ingredients; **SIMMER** a few minutes. **SERVE** hot over brown rice.

```
--------------------------------------------------------------------------
| Analysis: SWEET AND SOUR GLUTEN STEAKS          Divided by: 8          |
|           Wgt: 175 g (6.18 oz.)                 Water:     74%         |
--------------------------------------------------------------------------
```

Calories	176		Vitamin C	18.9 mg
Protein	10.2 g		Vitamin D	0 mcg
Carbohydrates	28.1 g		Vit E-Alpha Eq	.51 mg
Fat - Total	3.18 g		Vitamin K	mcg
Saturated Fat	.305 g		Biotin	mcg
Mono Fat	.913 g		Calcium	50.2 mg
Poly Fat	1.35 g		Copper	.212 mg
Cholesterol	0 mg		Iodine	mcg
Dietary Fibre	2.49 g		Iron	1.69 mg
Soluble Fibre	.58 g		Magnesium	35.8 mg
Total Vit A	32.5 RE		Manganese	.879 mg
Thiamin-B1	.472 mg		Phosphorus	130 mg
Riboflavin-B2	.202 mg		Potassium	383 mg
Niacin-B3	2.26 mg		Selenium	2.3 mcg
Niacin Equiv.	1.11 mg		Sodium	805 mg
Vitamin B6	.268 mg		Zinc	.531 mg
Vitamin B12	0 mcg		Complex Carbs	12.3 g
Folate	110 mcg		Sugars	10.1 g
Pantothenic	.573 mg		Water	130 g

CALORIE BREAKDOWN		FAT		EXCHANGES	
Protein	22%	*Saturated :	1.5%	Bread	.946
Carbohydrates	62%	Mono Unsat:	4.5%	Fruit	.536
Fat-Total *	16%	Poly Unsat:	6.6%	Vegetables	.612
				Fat	.109

TOFU QUICHE (makes 8 servings)

125 mL	(1/2 cup)	raw cashews
250 mL	(1 cup)	water
500 mL	(2 cups)	well-drained tofu
45 mL	(3 Tbsp.)	cornstarch or arrowroot powder
125 mL	(1/2 cup)	chopped onion
15 mL	(1 Tbsp.)	lemon juice
10 mL	(2 tsp.)	salt
5 mL	(1 tsp.) **EACH**	basil **and** oregano
1	(1)	garlic clove, minced
250 mL	(1 cup)	diced eggplant
500 mL	(2 cups)	steamed broccoli, onions, **or** spinach
4	(4)	thinly sliced unpeeled Russet potatoes

Method:

   WHIZ cashews in a dry food processor until very fine. **ADD** part of the water and **WHIZ** some more. **ADD** remaining water, tofu, cornstarch, onion, lemon juice, salt, basil, and oregano. **STEAM** the garlic, eggplant, and broccoli flowerlets. **STIR** into the tofu mixture. **POUR** into a quiche dish that has been lined petal fashion with potatoes that have been dipped in diluted lemon juice and partially baked to prevent discolouration. **BAKE** at 350° F. for one hour or until set. **COVER** edges with foil part way through baking. **SPRINKLE** top with paprika and parsley. This is also good reheated and eaten the day following preparation.

```
--------------------------------------------------------------------
| Analysis: TOFU QUICHE                     Divided by: 8          |
|           Wgt: 162 g (5.7 oz.)            Water:     83%         |
--------------------------------------------------------------------
```

Calories	124		Vitamin C	31.8 mg
Protein	7.71 g		Vitamin D	0 mcg
Carbohydrates	10.1 g		Vit E-Alpha E	.248 mg
Fat - Total	7.12 g		Vitamin K	mcg
Saturated Fat	1.24 g		Biotin	mcg
Mono Fat	3.01 g		Calcium	100 mg
Poly Fat	2.43 g		Copper	.353 mg
Cholesterol	0 mg		Iodine	mcg
Dietary Fibre	2.96 g		Iron	4.41 mg
Soluble Fibre	.644 g		Magnesium	98.7 mg
Total Vit A	66 RE		Manganese	.574 mg
Thiamin-B1	.106 mg		Phosphorus	135 mg
Riboflavin-B2	.097 mg		Potassium	294 mg
Niacin-B3	.594 mg		Selenium	3.23 mcg
Niacin Equiv.	.597 mg		Sodium	551 mg
Vitamin B6	.127 mg		Zinc	1.19 mg
Vitamin B12	0 mcg		Complex Carbs	4.84 g
Folate	41.7 mcg		Sugars	2.33 g
Pantothenic	.361 mg		Water	134 g

CALORIE BREAKDOWN		FAT		EXCHANGES	
Protein	23%	*Saturated :	8.2%	Bread	.187
Carbohydrates	30%	Mono Unsat:	20 %	Lean Meat	.624
Fat-Total *	47%	Poly Unsat:	16.1%	Fruit	.008
		Fat	.75 --->	Vegetables	.891

TOMATO-LENTIL DELIGHT (makes 10 one-cup servings)

500 mL	(2 cups)	uncooked green lentils
250 mL	(1 cup)	chopped onion
125 mL	(1/2 cup)	sliced celery
125 mL	(1/2 cup)	diced carrot
2	(2)	garlic cloves, minced
15 mL	(1 Tbsp.)	dried parsley or 1/4 cup fresh
1 L	(4 cups)	tomato juice or canned tomatoes
3 mL	(1/2 tsp.)	cumin
3 mL	(1/2 tsp.)	oregano
3 mL	(1/2 tsp.)	sweet basil
5 mL	(1 tsp.)	salt

Method:

COOK lentils, onion, celery, carrots, and garlic together in 4 cups water until lentils are cooked. ADD other ingredients and SIMMER until flavours are blended. SERVE over whole wheat toast or brown rice.

```
Analysis: TOMATO-LENTIL DELIGHT (1 cup servings)   Divided by: 10
          Wgt: 166 g (5.85 oz.)                    Water:      73%
```

Calories	161		Vitamin C	18.9 mg
Protein	12.1 g		Vitamin D	0 mcg
Carbohydrates	28.7 g		Vit E-Alpha E	.555 mg
Fat - Total	.669 g		Vitamin K	mcg
Saturated Fat	.097 g		Biotin	mcg
Mono Fat	.105 g		Calcium	56.3 mg
Poly Fat	.293 g		Copper	.46 mg
Cholesterol	0 mg		Iodine	mcg
Dietary Fibre	6.56 g		Iron	4.25 mg
Soluble Fibre	1.8 g		Magnesium	56.8 mg
Total Vit A	254 RE		Manganese	.78 mg
Thiamin-B1	.24 mg		Phosphorus	204 mg
Riboflavin-B2	.136 mg		Potassium	628 mg
Niacin-B3	1.81 mg		Selenium	5.34 mcg
Niacin Equiv.	1.81 mg		Sodium	385 mg
Vitamin B6	.347 mg		Zinc	1.62 mg
Vitamin B12	0 mcg		Complex Carbs	16 g
Folate	180 mcg		Sugars	6.18 g
Pantothenic	.929 mg		Water	122 g

CALORIE BREAKDOWN		FAT		EXCHANGES	
Protein	29%	*Saturated :	.5%	Bread	1.54
Carbohydrates	68%	Mono Unsat:	.6%	Lean Meat	.096
Fat-Total *	4%	Poly Unsat:	1.6%	Vegetables	1.14

BEAN LOAF (makes 10 servings)

1250 mL	(5 cups)		cooked beans (any kind)
250 mL	(1 cup)		cooked brown rice
250 mL	(1 cup)	**EACH**	chopped onion, **and** thinly sliced celery
125 mL	(1/2 cup)		chopped green pepper
1	(1)		large clove of garlic, minced
75 mL	(1/3 cup)		water
250 mL	(1 cup)		dry whole wheat bread crumbs
30 mL	(2 Tbsp.)		raw wheat bran
15 mL	(1 Tbsp.)	**EACH**	parsley flakes **and** soy sauce
5 mL	(1 tsp.)	**EACH**	basil, oregano, **and** cumin
375 mL	(1 1/2 cups)		tomato sauce (Hunts, Heinz or homemade)
15 mL	(1 Tbsp.)		corn meal

Method:

MASH the beans and **COMBINE** them with the rice. **SET** aside. **STEAM** the onions, celery, pepper and garlic in the water in a covered pot for 5 minutes. **ADD** to the rice-bean mixture. **ADD** all of the remaining ingredients except the corn meal, and **MIX** well. **SPRINKLE** the corn meal over the bottom of a 9"x 5"x 3" non-stick loaf pan. **PLACE** the bean mixture in the pan, smoothing out the top. **BAKE** in a 350° F. oven for 45 minutes. This makes a delicious sandwich spread when cold or serve hot with gravy.

```
Analysis: BEAN LOAF                    Divided by: 10
          Wgt: 239 g (8.41 oz.)        Water:      78%
```

Calories	197	Vitamin C	12.9 mg
Protein	9.64 g	Vitamin D	.036 mcg
Carbohydrates	38.1 g	Vit E-Alpha E	.618 mg
Fat - Total	1.4 g	Vitamin K	mcg
Saturated Fat	.257 g	Biotin	mcg
Mono Fat	.337 g	Calcium	78 mg
Poly Fat	.547 g	Copper	.335 mg
Cholesterol	0 mg	Iodine	mcg
Dietary Fibre	10.1 g	Iron	3.13 mg
Soluble Fibre	3.62 g	Magnesium	67.4 mg
Total Vit A	46 RE	Manganese	.806 mg
Thiamin-B1	.28 mg	Phosphorus	186 mg
Riboflavin-B2	.202 mg	Potassium	593 mg
Niacin-B3	2.29 mg	Selenium	8.14 mcg
Niacin Equiv.	2.28 mg	Sodium	647 mg
Vitamin B6	.184 mg	Zinc	1.2 mg
Vitamin B12	.002 mcg	Complex Carbs	22.7 g
Folate	80.3 mcg	Sugars	4.96 g
Pantothenic	.463 mg	Water	186 g

CALORIE BREAKDOWN		FAT	EXCHANGES	
Protein	19%	*Saturated : 1.1%	Bread	2.1
Carbohydrates	75%	Mono Unsat: 1.5%	Vegetables	.8
Fat-Total *	6%	Poly Unsat: 2.4%		

BLACK-EYE "PEA" LOAF (makes 8 servings)

250 mL	(1 cup)	dry black-eye peas (use quick soak method)
250 mL	(1 cup)	bean liquid and water to make 1 cup
250 mL	(1 cup)	chopped onions
250 mL	(1 cup)	finely chopped celery
2	(2)	large cloves garlic, minced
125 mL	(1/2 cup)	water
5 mL	(1 tsp.)	Savorex or Marmite
5 mL	(1 tsp.)	salt
30 mL	(2 Tbsp.)	Bisto or cornstarch
3 mL	(1/2 tsp.) EACH	thyme and sage
500 mL	(2 cups)	rolled oats
125 mL	(1/2 cup)	finely chopped walnuts

Method:

COOK the black-eye peas. BLEND in blender with part of the bean liquid. STEAM the onions, celery, and garlic in the rest of the water. ADD Savorex, Bisto, thyme, sage, and salt and BLEND. EMPTY contents of blender into a bowl. RINSE blender with water. STIR in steamed vegetables, oats, and walnuts. POUR into a greased loaf pan and BAKE, covered for 45 minutes at 350° F. REMOVE cover for last 15 minutes of baking. LET stand for 10 minutes before turning out onto a platter. SERVE with tomato sauce. (This is good on sandwiches.)

```
Analysis: BLACK-EYE "PEA" LOAF (COW)          Divided by: 10
          Wgt: 110 g (3.88 oz.)               Water:      64%
```

Calories	172		Vitamin C	3.11 mg
Protein	6.77 g		Vitamin D	0 mcg
Carbohydrates	25.8 g		Vit E-Alpha E	.529 mg
Fat - Total	5.15 g		Vitamin K	mcg
Saturated Fat	.587 g		Biotin	mcg
Mono Fat	1.22 g		Calcium	81 mg
Poly Fat	2.88 g		Copper	.222 mg
Cholesterol	0 mg		Iodine	mcg
Dietary Fibre	5.6 g		Iron	1.6 mg
Soluble Fibre	1.26 g		Magnesium	60.9 mg
Total Vit A	36.9 RE		Manganese	1.05 mg
Thiamin-B1	.203 mg		Phosphorus	135 mg
Riboflavin-B2	.109 mg		Potassium	335 mg
Niacin-B3	.865 mg		Selenium	13.1 mcg
Niacin Equiv.	.855 mg		Sodium	241 mg
Vitamin B6	.115 mg		Zinc	1.18 mg
Vitamin B12	0 mcg		Complex Carbs	17 g
Folate	71.3 mcg		Sugars	2.91 g
Pantothenic	.35 mg		Water	70.6 g

CALORIE BREAKDOWN		FAT		EXCHANGES	
Protein	15%	* Saturated	3%	Bread	1.4
Carbohydrates	58%	Mono Unsat:	6.2%	Vegetables	.266
Fat-Total *	26%	Poly Unsat:	14.7%		

CASHEW RICE LOAF (makes 8 servings)

500 mL	(2 cups)	raw cashews, finely chopped or ground
500 mL	(2 cups)	cooked brown rice
500 mL	(2 cups)	chopped onions
60 mL	(1/4 cup)	minced fresh parsley
500 mL	(2 cups)	water
4	(4)	slices whole grain bread made into crumbs
5 mL	(1 tsp.)	salt
4 mL	(3/4 tsp.)	sage

Method:
COMBINE all ingredients. **PLACE** in a covered dish and put the dish in a pan of water. **BAKE** at 350° F. for one hour. Recipe: Courtesy of Sadie Brown

```
Analysis: CASHEW-RICE LOAF              Divided by: 8
          Wgt: 199 g (7.02 oz.)         Water :    70%
```

Calories	302	Vitamin C	5.06 mg
Protein	8.53 g	Vitamin D	0 mcg
Carbohydrates	32.4 g	Vit E-Alpha E	.901 mg
Fat - Total	17 g	Vitamin K	mcg
Saturated Fat	3.41 g	Biotin	mcg
Mono Fat	9.74 g	Calcium	43.4 mg
Poly Fat	3.02 g	Copper	.888 mg
Cholesterol	0 mg	Iodine	mcg
Dietary Fibre	4.99 g	Iron	2.97 mg
Soluble Fibre	.301 g	Magnesium	129 mg
Total Vit A	10.1 RE	Manganese	.784 mg
Thiamin-B1	.184 mg	Phosphorus	259 mg
Riboflavin-B2	.12 mg	Potassium	313 mg
Niacin-B3	1.86 mg	Selenium	23 mcg
Niacin Equiv.	1.31 mg	Sodium	368 mg
Vitamin B6	.233 mg	Zinc	2.59 mg
Vitamin B12	0 mcg	Complex Carbs	16.9 g
Folate	43.9 mcg	Sugars	5.14 g
Pantothenic	.709 mg	Water	138 g

CALORIE BREAKDOWN		FAT		EXCHANGES	
Protein	11%	*Saturated :	9.7%	Bread	.673
Carbohydrates	41%	Mono Unsat:	27.6%	Lean Meat	.5
Fat-Total *	48%	Poly Unsat:	8.6%	Vegetables	.527
				Fat	2

DIET REFORM:
The diet reform should be progressive. As disease in animals increases, the use of milk and eggs will become more and more unsafe. An effort should be made to supply their place with other things that are healthful and inexpensive. The people everywhere should be taught how to cook without milk and eggs, so far as possible, and yet have their food wholesome and palatable. Ellen White, *Ministry of Healing*, page 320 - 321.

LENTIL-RICE ROAST (makes 8 servings)

250 mL	(1 cup)	chopped onion
125 mL	(1/2 cup) **EACH**	chopped celery **and** stewed tomatoes
500 mL	(2 cups)	cooked lentils
375 mL	(1 1/2 cups)	cooked brown rice or bread crumbs
125 mL	(1/2 cup)	chopped walnuts
5 mL	(1 tsp.)	salt

Method:

       SIMMER the onions and celery in the tomatoes until soft. **COMBINE** all the ingredients and **MIX** thoroughly. **PLACE** in a sprayed baking dish and **BAKE** at 350° F. for approximately one hour.

```
------------------------------------------------------------------
| Analysis: LENTIL-RICE ROAST (8 servings)        Divided by: 8   |
|           Wgt: 135 g (4.75 oz.)                 Water:     75%  |
------------------------------------------------------------------
```

Calories	140		Vitamin C	4.81 mg
Protein	6.51 g		Vitamin D	0 mcg
Carbohydrates	22.3 g		Vit E-Alpha E	.653 mg
Fat - Total	3.38 g		Vitamin K	mcg
Saturated Fat	.357 g		Biotin	mcg
Mono Fat	.799 g		Calcium	31.6 mg
Poly Fat	2 g		Copper	.257 mg
Cholesterol	0 mg		Iodine	mcg
Dietary Fibre	4.06 g		Iron	2.21 mg
Soluble Fibre	1.33 g		Magnesium	46.3 mg
Total Vit A	11.1 RE		Manganese	.758 mg
Thiamin-B1	.156 mg		Phosphorus	145 mg
Riboflavin-B2	.065 mg		Potassium	313 mg
Niacin-B3	1.3 mg		Selenium	7.32 mcg
Niacin Equiv.	1.3 mg		Sodium	317 mg
Vitamin B6	.199 mg		Zinc	1.06 mg
Vitamin B12	0 mcg		Complex Carbs	15.2 g
Folate	100 mcg		Sugars	3.02 g
Pantothenic	.501 mg		Water	101 g

CALORIE BREAKDOWN		FAT		EXCHANGES	
Protein	18%	* Saturated:	2.2%	Bread	1.05
Carbohydrates	61%	Mono Unsat:	4.9%	Lean Meat	.247
Fat-Total *	21%	Poly Unsat:	12.3%	Vegetables	.451

CALCULATING PERCENTAGE OF CALORIES FROM THE ENERGY NUTRIENTS:

       If the food has 307 calories;

11 grams of fat;	11 x 9 = 99 calories from fat
12 grams of protein,	12 x 4 = 48 calories from protein
40 grams of carbohydrates	40 x 4 = 160 calories from carbohydrates

              99 divided by 307 = 32.2% of calories from fat
              48 divided by 307 = 15.6% of calories from protein
              160 divided by 307 = 52.1% of calories from carbohydrates
                         99.9% total

LENTIL-TOMATO LOAF (makes 10 servings)

750 mL	(3 cups)	cooked lentils
375 mL	(1 1/2 cups)	chopped onions
3	(3)	large cloves of garlic, minced
15 mL	(1 Tbsp.)	Savorex or Marmite
375 mL	(1 1/2 cups)	cooked tomatoes
375 mL	(1 1/2 cups)	whole grain bread crumbs or cubes
60 mL	(1/4 cup)	rolled oats
125 mL	(1/2 cup)	pecan meal

Method:
   COOK lentils. (1 1/2 cups before cooking) **STEAM** onions and garlic until tender.
STIR in Marmite to dissolve. **ADD** remaining ingredients and **MIX** well. **PLACE** in Lecithin oil
treated pan (page 110) or ring mould. **BAKE** at 375° F. 45 minutes. **LET** set for 10 minutes
before unmoulding. **GARNISH** with cherry tomatoes or red pepper slices and parsley.
Menu suggestion: **SERVE** with mashed potatoes, brown gravy, and a green or yellow
vegetable.

```
Analysis: LENTIL-TOMATO LOAF            Divided by: 10
          Wgt: 144 g (5.08 oz.)         Water:      69%
```

Calories	195		Vitamin C	8.25 mg
Protein	9 g		Vitamin D	.054 mcg
Carbohydrates	29.3 g		Vit E-Alpha E	.473 mg
Fat - Total	5.32 g		Vitamin K	mcg
Saturated Fat	.585 g		Biotin	mcg
Mono Fat	2.92 g		Calcium	68.3 mg
Poly Fat	1.44 g		Copper	.309 mg
Cholesterol	0 mg		Iodine	mcg
Dietary Fibre	5.14 g		Iron	3.62 mg
Soluble Fibre	1.79 g		Magnesium	45.8 mg
Total Vit A	23.2 RE		Manganese	.852 mg
Thiamin-B1	.318 mg		Phosphorus	172 mg
Riboflavin-B2	.179 mg		Potassium	404 mg
Niacin-B3	2.33 mg		Selenium	7.75 mcg
Niacin Equiv.	2.03 mg		Sodium	190 mg
Vitamin B6	.226 mg		Zinc	1.44 mg
Vitamin B12	.003 mcg		Complex Carbs	19.8 g
Folate	121 mcg		Sugars	4.27 g
Pantothenic	.681 mg		Water	98.8 g

CALORIE BREAKDOWN		FAT		EXCHANGES	
Protein	18%	* Saturated :	2.6%	Bread	1.39
Carbohydrates	58%	Mono Unsat:	13 %	Lean Meat	.352
Fat-Total *	24%	Poly Unsat:	6.4%	Fruit	.069
				Vegetables	.6
				Fat	.753

A ONE SENTENCE COURSE IN NUTRITION:
   Eat at proper times, a variety of natural foods in quantities to maintain proper
weight! John Scharffenberg, M.D.

OAT-BEAN LOAF (makes 8 servings)

5 mL	(1 tsp.)	olive oil
250 mL	(1 cup)	chopped onion
250 mL	(1 cup)	chopped celery
3	(3)	garlic cloves, minced
5 mL	(1 tsp.)	Savorex or Marmite
3 mL	(1/2 tsp.)	sage
7 mL	(1 1/2 tsp.)	salt
125 mL	(1/2 cup)	chopped walnuts
125 mL	(1/2 cup)	tomato paste
30 mL	(2 Tbsp.)	soy flour
250 mL	(1 cup)	cooked beans (soy, navy, or pinto)
500 mL	(2 cups)	rolled oats

Method:

SAUTE the onions, celery, and garlic in the oil. ADD a little water. ALLOW them to cook until soft. MIX in Marmite, sage, salt, chopped walnuts, tomato paste, and soy flour. WHIZ beans in food processor and ADD to other ingredients. STIR in rolled oats. PRESS into treated loaf pan. COVER, and BAKE at 325° F for about 45 minutes. UNCOVER and BAKE 15 minutes more. UNMOULD and SERVE with gravy.

```
Analysis: OAT-BEAN LOAF                         Divided by: 8
          Wgt: 106 g (3.75 oz.)                 Water:     58%
```

Calories	194	Vitamin C	10 mg
Protein	8.16 g	Vitamin D	0 mcg
Carbohydrates	27.2 g	Vit E-Alpha E	.828 mg
Fat - Total	6.91 g	Vitamin K	mcg
Saturated Fat	.803 g	Biotin	mcg
Mono Fat	1.94 g	Calcium	56.6 mg
Poly Fat	3.64 g	Copper	.429 mg
Cholesterol	0 mg	Iodine	mcg
Dietary Fibre	5.81 g	Iron	2.4 mg
Soluble Fibre	1.83 g	Magnesium	71.7 mg
Total Vit A	45.7 RE	Manganese	1.27 mg
Thiamin-B1	.275 mg	Phosphorus	188 mg
Riboflavin-B2	.118 mg	Potassium	459 mg
Niacin-B3	1.13 mg	Selenium	7.65 mcg
Niacin Equiv.	1 mg	Sodium	545 mg
Vitamin B6	.231 mg	Zinc	1.3 mg
Vitamin B12	0 mcg	Complex Carbs	18.2 g
Folate	60.6 mcg	Sugars	3.16 g
Pantothenic	.579 mg	Water	61.5 g

CALORIE BREAKDOWN		FAT		EXCHANGES	
Protein	16%	*Saturated:	3.5%	Bread	1.13
Carbohydrates	53%	Mono Unsat:	8.6%	Lean Meat	.187
Fat-Total *	31%	Poly Unsat:	16.1%	Fruit	.125
		Fat	------->	Vegetables	.583

TOFU WALNUT LOAF (makes 8 servings)

250 mL	(1 cup)		finely chopped onions
2	(2)		large cloves of garlic, minced
250 mL	(1 cup)	**EACH**	dry whole wheat bread crumbs **and** rolled oats
125 mL	(1/2 cup)		gluten flour
375 mL	(1 1/2 cups)		cubed tofu
125 mL	(1/2 cup)		finely chopped walnuts
30 mL	(2 Tbsp.)		flake food yeast
30 mL	(2 Tbsp.)		Maggi seasoning, soy sauce, **or** Bragg liquid aminos
5 mL	(1 tsp.)		salt or less
5 mL	(1 tsp.)	**EACH**	Italian seasoning **and** paprika
3 mL	(1/2 tsp.)		sage
250 mL	(1 cup)		hot water
10 mL	(2 tsp.)		Savorex, Vegex, **or** Marmite

Method:

COMBINE all ingredients except hot water and Marmite. **DISSOLVE** the Marmite in the hot water. **ADD** to dry mixture and **MIX** well. **SPRAY** all inside surfaces of pan (loaf or ring mould) with a thin layer of Pam or rub with a mixture of 1 part lecithin and 3 parts corn oil. **PRESS** mixture into pan. **BAKE** at 350° F for approximately one hour or until set in the middle. **SERVE** sliced or turned out of the pan for a platter arrangement with parsley and cherry tomatoes. Good with mashed potatoes, gravy, peas, and salad.

```
Analysis: TOFU WALNUT LOAF              Divided by: 8
         Wgt: 140 g (4.93 oz.)         Water:    65%
```

Calories	221	Vitamin C	2.01 mg
Protein	12.9 g	Vitamin D	.045 mcg
Carbohydrates	25.2 g	Vit E-Alpha E	.331 mg
Fat - Total	8.44 g	Vitamin K	mcg
Saturated Fat	1.04 g	Biotin	mcg
Mono Fat	2.03 g	Calcium	107 mg
Poly Fat	4.66 g	Copper	.333 mg
Cholesterol	0 mg	Iodine	mcg
Dietary Fibre	3.7 g	Iron	4.48 mg
Soluble Fibre	.612 g	Magnesium	88.8 mg
Total Vit A	23.8 RE	Manganese	1.01 mg
Thiamin-B1	.567 mg	Phosphorus	191 mg
Riboflavin-B2	.22 mg	Potassium	242 mg
Niacin-B3	2.11 mg	Selenium	8.33 mcg
Niacin Equiv.	1.99 mg	Sodium	649 mg
Vitamin B6	.23 mg	Zinc	1.28 mg
Vitamin B12	.003 mcg	Complex Carbs	19.2 g
Folate	102 mcg	Sugars	2.24 g
Pantothenic	.455 mg	Water	90.2 g

CALORIE BREAKDOWN		FAT		EXCHANGES	
Protein	23%	* Saturated :	4.1%	Bread	1.52
Carbohydrates	44%	Mono Unsat:	8 %	Lean Meat	.375
Fat-Total *	33%	Poly Unsat:	18.4%	Vegetables	.437
				Fat	.219

BARLEY BALLS (makes 46 two-tablespoon balls)

500 mL	(2 cups)	EACH	cooked barley flakes or pot barley
500 mL	(2 cups)	EACH	minced onions (steamed) **and** grated raw potatoes
500 mL	(2 cups)		whole grain bread crumbs
125 mL	(1/2 cup)		finely chopped walnuts
60 mL	(1/4 cup)		soy flour
250 mL	(1 cup)		water
5 mL	(1 tsp.)	EACH	onion powder **and** salt (less if on a low sodium diet)
3 mL	(1/2 tsp.)	EACH	thyme **and** sage

Method:

BRING 1 3/4 cups of water to a boil. **STIR** in 1 1/3 cups barley flakes, **COVER, REDUCE** heat and **LET** cook undisturbed for about 15 minutes. **PLACE** in a bowl. **ADD** remaining ingredients. **WAIT** 15 minutes. **FORM** into 2 Tbsp sized balls. **PLACE** on sprayed cookie sheet. **BAKE** in 400° oven for 30 minutes. **TURN** once with a spatula after 15 minutes. **SERVE** with gravy or tomato sauce.

Menu suggestion: **SERVE** with cauliflower, potatoes, gravy, green beans, and salad.

```
| Analysis: BARLEY BALLS (46)              Divided by: 46  |
|           Wgt: 30.6 g (1.08 oz.)         Water:     64%  |
```

Calories	46.3	Vitamin C	.722 mg
Protein	1.46 g	Vitamin D	.016 mcg
Carbohydrates	7.82 g	Vit E-Alpha E	.066 mg
Fat - Total	1.18 g	Vitamin K	mcg
Saturated Fat	.153 g	Biotin	mcg
Mono Fat	.296 g	Calcium	15.1 mg
Poly Fat	.655 g	Copper	.091 mg
Cholesterol	0 mg	Iodine	mcg
Dietary Fibre	.973 g	Iron	.459 mg
Soluble Fibre	.154 g	Magnesium	9.09 mg
Total Vit A	.232 RE	Manganese	.131 mg
Thiamin-B1	.055 mg	Phosphorus	27.5 mg
Riboflavin-B2	.027 mg	Potassium	65.7 mg
Niacin-B3	.531 mg	Selenium	2.9 mcg
Niacin Equiv.	.531 mg	Sodium	84.7 mg
Vitamin B6	.045 mg	Zinc	.192 mg
Vitamin B12	.001 mcg	Complex Carbs	6.12 g
Folate	5.88 mcg	Sugars	.721 g
Pantothenic	.088 mg	Water	19.7 g

CALORIE BREAKDOWN		FAT		EXCHANGES	
Protein	12%	Saturated :	2.9%	Bread	.4
Carbohydrates	65%	Mono Unsat:	5.6%	Vegetables	.1
Fat-Total *	22%	Poly Unsat:	12.3%		

SOY FLOUR:

Soy flour is useful because of its high protein value and the fact that so many people are allergic to wheat. It can be purchased in de-fatted or full-fat forms. It acts as a binder. Products containing soy flour should be well-cooked because the soy bean contains certain toxic elements which interfere with protein digestion if it is not well cooked.

BARLEY-GARBANZO PATTIES (makes 10 patties, 1/3 cup each)

250 mL	(1 cup)		cooked barley (1/4 cup before cooking)
250 mL	(1 cup)		cooked garbanzos, mashed
125 mL	(1/2 cup)		uncooked rolled oats
250 mL	(1 cup)	**EACH**	finely chopped celery **and** finely chopped onions
1	(1)		large garlic clove, minced
1 mL	(1/4 tsp.)		salt
5 mL	(1 tsp.)		paprika
30 mL	(2 Tbsp.)		soy sauce
3 mL	(1/2 tsp.)		sage

Method:
STEAM celery, onions, and garlic. MIX all ingredients well together. LET stand a few minutes. SHAPE into patties by pressing into a mason jar lid. TURN out onto a prepared silver stone cookie sheet. BAKE at 350° F. COVER with another cookie sheet for the first 15 minutes of the baking time. UNCOVER, TURN and FINISH baking. SERVE in a burger bun with lettuce, tomato, cucumber, and KETCHUP, or with gravy.

```
---------------------------------------------------------------------
| Analysis: BARLEY-GARBANZO PATTIES              Divided by: 8      |
|           Wgt: 90.9 g (3.21 oz.)               Water:      71%    |
---------------------------------------------------------------------
```

Calories	100		Vitamin C	2.93 mg
Protein	4.2 g		Vitamin D	0 mcg
Carbohydrates	19.4 g		Vit E-Alpha E	.232 mg
Fat - Total	1.22 g		Vitamin K	mcg
Saturated Fat	.183 g		Biotin	mcg
Mono Fat	.267 g		Calcium	28.6 mg
Poly Fat	.555 g		Copper	.194 mg
Cholesterol	0 mg		Iodine	mcg
Dietary Fibre	4.22 g		Iron	1.35 mg
Soluble Fibre	1.09 g		Magnesium	28.9 mg
Total Vit A	20.7 RE		Manganese	.544 mg
Thiamin-B1	.101 mg		Phosphorus	104 mg
Riboflavin-B2	.049 mg		Potassium	197 mg
Niacin-B3	.781 mg		Selenium	7.5 mcg
Niacin Equiv.	.781 mg		Sodium	339 mg
Vitamin B6	.107 mg		Zinc	.757 mg
Vitamin B12	0 mcg		Complex Carbs	13.1 g
Folate	47.6 mcg		Sugars	2.13 g
Pantothenic	.251 mg		Water	64.7 g

CALORIE BREAKDOWN		FAT		EXCHANGES	
Protein	16%	*Saturated :	1.6%	Bread	.885
Carbohydrates	74%	Mono Unsat:	2.3%	Lean Meat	.103
Fat-Total *	10%	Poly Unsat:	4.7%	Vegetables	.333

NUTRIENT VALUE OF BARLEY:
In comparison with corn, barley contains approximately the same percentage of carbohydrates, about 3% more protein and slightly less fat. Barley is good in soups and stews and barley flour may be used for breads, pies, and pancakes. (Condensed from *Foods and Nutrition Encyclopedia - Volume 1* - pages 161-164. Also see page 93.)

BARLEY BURGERS (makes 12 1/4-cup patties)

250 mL	(1 cup)		dry raw garbanzos (soak overnight)
5 mL	(1 tsp)		olive oil (for cookie sheet)
125 mL	(1/2 cup)	**EACH**	finely chopped onion **and** finely chopped celery
1	(1)		large clove of garlic, minced
250 mL	(1 cup)		cooked barley (1/3 raw makes 1 cup cooked)
125 mL	(1/2 cup)		dry rolled oats
2 mL	(1/4 tsp.)		salt
5 mL	(1 tsp.)		paprika
15 mL	(1 Tbsp.)		flake food yeast or torula
3 mL	(1/2 tsp.)		sage
30 mL	(2 Tbsp.)		Bragg liquid aminos, soy sauce **or** Maggi seasoning

Method:

   SOAK garbanzos. **DRAIN**. **WHIZ** soaked garbanzos in food processor until well chopped. **STEAM** onions, celery, and garlic in a little water. **COVER** and **LET** steam until soft. **PLACE** cooked barley, rolled oats, salt, paprika, yeast, sage, and soy sauce in a bowl. **ADD** garbanzos and steamed vegetables and **MIX** well. **STIR** into mixture in bowl. **LET** set a few minutes. **USE** a 1/4 cup measure or a mason jar ring and lid to shape each patty. **DROP** onto a prepared cookie sheet. **BAKE** until brown on one side. **TURN** and brown the other side. **COVER** and **FINISH** baking at 350° F. for about 20 more minutes. **SERVE** on a bun or with gravy as a casserole.

```
-----------------------------------------------------------------
| Analysis: BARLEY BURGERS                    Divided by: 12     |
|           Wgt: 53.2 g (1.88 oz.)            Water:      49%    |
-----------------------------------------------------------------
```

Calories	108		Vitamin C	1.66 mg
Protein	5.02 g		Vitamin D	0 mcg
Carbohydrates	18.8 g		Vit E-Alpha E	.617 mg
Fat - Total	1.83 g		Vitamin K	mcg
Saturated Fat	.236 g		Biotin	mcg
Mono Fat	.598 g		Calcium	30.1 mg
Poly Fat	.686 g		Copper	.217 mg
Cholesterol	0 mg		Iodine	mcg
Dietary Fibre	4.97 g		Iron	1.67 mg
Soluble Fibre	1.4 g		Magnesium	32 mg
Total Vit A	13.9 RE		Manganese	.576 mg
Thiamin-B1	.243 mg		Phosphorus	118 mg
Riboflavin-B2	.098 mg		Potassium	230 mg
Niacin-B3	1.05 mg		Selenium	5.77 mcg
Niacin Equiv.	.68 mg		Sodium	225 mg
Vitamin B6	.154 mg		Zinc	.864 mg
Vitamin B12	0 mcg		Complex Carbs	11 g
Folate	123 mcg		Sugars	2.57 g
Pantothenic	.468 mg		Water	26.1 g

CALORIE BREAKDOWN		FAT		EXCHANGES	
Protein	18%	* Saturated :	1.9%	Bread	.939
Carbohydrates	67%	Mono Unsat:	4.8%	Lean Meat	.295
Fat-Total *	15%	Poly Unsat:	5.5%	Vegetables	.111
				Fat	.073

FALAFEL (makes 20 two-tablespoon falafels)

250 mL	(1 cup)	dry garbanzos (Soak overnight and drain))
75 mL	(1/3 cup)	water or less
150 mL	(2/3 cup)	chopped onions
1	(1)	large garlic clove, minced
30 mL	(2 Tbsp.)	fresh parsley
1 mL	(1/4 tsp.)	ground cumin
1 mL	(1/4 tsp.)	coriander
10 mL	(2 tsp.)	onion salt

Method:

COMBINE all ingredients in food processor and blend until smooth. DROP by two-tablespoon amounts on lecithin-treated cookie sheets. BAKE at 350° for 15 minutes. TURN and finish cooking.

```
-------------------------------------------------------------------------
| Analysis: FALAFELS                              Divided by: 20        |
|           Wgt: 20.2 g (.714 oz.)                Water:      51%       |
-------------------------------------------------------------------------
```

Calories	39.3	Vitamin C	1.3 mg
Protein	2.03 g	Vitamin D	0 mcg
Carbohydrates	6.69 g	Vit E-Alpha E	.314 mg
Fat - Total	.628 g	Vitamin K	mcg
Saturated Fat	.065 g	Biotin	mcg
Mono Fat	.141 g	Calcium	13.3 mg
Poly Fat	.275 g	Copper	.09 mg
Cholesterol	0 mg	Iodine	mcg
Dietary Fibre	2.04 g	Iron	.686 mg
Soluble Fibre	.615 g	Magnesium	12.7 mg
Total Vit A	2.68 RE	Manganese	.233 mg
Thiamin-B1	.051 mg	Phosphorus	39.4 mg
Riboflavin-B2	.023 mg	Potassium	100 mg
Niacin-B3	.17 mg	Selenium	1.03 mcg
Niacin Equiv.	.171 mg	Sodium	110 mg
Vitamin B6	.064 mg	Zinc	.366 mg
Vitamin B12	0 mcg	Complex Carbs	3.2 g
Folate	57.4 mcg	Sugars	1.45 g
Pantothenic	.169 mg	Water	10.3 g

CALORIE BREAKDOWN		FAT		EXCHANGES	
Protein	20%	*Saturated :	1.4%	Bread	.355
Carbohydrates	66%	Mono Unsat:	3.1%	Lean Meat	.177
Fat-Total *	14%	Poly Unsat:	6.1%	Vegetables	.072

HOME-STYLE OAT PATTIES (makes 12 servings)

250 mL	(1 cup)	chopped onion
1	(1)	large garlic clove, minced
30 mL	(2 Tbsp.)	food yeast flakes
125 mL	(1/2 cup)	chopped walnuts
90 mL	(6 Tbsp.)	soy flour
22 mL	(1 1/2 Tbsp.)	soy sauce, Maggi seasoning, Bragg liquid aminos
5 mL	(1 tsp.)	salt
3 mL	(1/2 tsp.)	sage
375 mL	(1 1/2 cups)	rolled oats
180 mL	(3/4 cup)	wheat germ
500 mL	(2 cups)	water

Method:

   STEAM onions and garlic until soft. **COMBINE** all ingredients. Mixture thickens on standing for 10 or 15 minutes and is easier to handle. **MEASURE** 1/4 cup amounts and **PRESS** into a standard-size Mason jar lid. **DROP** onto a greased cookie sheet. **COVER** with foil or another cookie sheet, and **BAKE** in a 350° F. oven for 15 minutes. **TURN** and **BAKE** on other side. May be prepared a day ahead and reheated. After cooking, put into a casserole; cover with gravy and bake until well heated. May also be used in hamburger bun. May be frozen, preferably without the gravy.

```
Analysis: HOME-STYLE OAT PATTIES                    Divided by: 12
          Wgt: 65.2 g (2.3 oz.)                     Water:      60%
```

Calories	112		Vitamin C	1.41 mg
Protein	6.43 g		Vitamin D	0 mcg
Carbohydrates	14.4 g		Vit E-Alpha E	1.59 mg
Fat - Total	3.91 g		Vitamin K	mcg
Saturated Fat	.564 g		Biotin	mcg
Mono Fat	1.07 g		Calcium	46.8 mg
Poly Fat	1.98 g		Copper	.375 mg
Cholesterol	0 mg		Iodine	mcg
Dietary Fibre	3.12 g		Iron	1.89 mg
Soluble Fibre	.613 g		Magnesium	53.2 mg
Total Vit A	8.5 RE		Manganese	1.46 mg
Thiamin-B1	.448 mg		Phosphorus	161 mg
Riboflavin-B2	.16 mg		Potassium	260 mg
Niacin-B3	1.46 mg		Selenium	8.52 mcg
Niacin Equiv.	1.21 mg		Sodium	183 mg
Vitamin B6	.232 mg		Zinc	1.41 mg
Vitamin B12	0 mcg		Complex Carbs	8.34 g
Folate	92.5 mcg		Sugars	2.81 g
Pantothenic	.515 mg		Water	38.9 g

CALORIE BREAKDOWN		FAT		EXCHANGES	
Protein	22%	* Saturated :	4.3%	Bread	.731
Carbohydrates	49%	Mono Unsat:	8.2%	Lean Meat	.207
Fat-Total *	30%	Poly Unsat:	15.1%	Vegetables	.167
				Fat	.135

LENTIL-RICE BURGERS (makes 16 1/4-cup burgers)

250 mL	(1 cup)	dried green lentils
125 mL	(1/2 cup)	uncooked brown rice
750 mL	(3 cups)	water
15 mL	(1 Tbsp.)	salt
250 mL	(1 cup)	fine, whole wheat bread crumbs
250 mL	(1 cup)	finely chopped onions, steamed
3 mL	(1/2 tsp.)	celery seed
3 mL	(1/2 tsp.)	thyme
3 mL	(1/2 tsp.)	marjoram
125 mL	(1/2 cup)	wheat germ

Method:

COMBINE lentils, rice, water, and salt in a medium-sized saucepan. BRING to boiling point, LOWER heat, COVER and SIMMER for about 45 minutes until lentils and rice are tender. REMOVE from heat. LET stand for 10 minutes. STIR in remaining ingredients, except wheat germ. SHAPE into patties (1/4 cup each). COAT each patty with wheat germ. PLACE patties on treated cookie sheet and BAKE at 350° F. for 15 minutes on each side. SERVE with onion gravy or tomato sauce.

```
-------------------------------------------------------------------
| Analysis: LENTIL-RICE BURGERS              Divided by: 16        |
|           Wgt: 82 g (2.89 oz.)             Water:      68%       |
-------------------------------------------------------------------
```

Calories	99.3	Vitamin C	1.4 mg
Protein	5.29 g	Vitamin D	.022 mcg
Carbohydrates	17.9 g	Vit E-Alpha E	.582 mg
Fat - Total	.885 g	Vitamin K	mcg
Saturated Fat	.173 g	Biotin	mcg
Mono Fat	.256 g	Calcium	28.2 mg
Poly Fat	.36 g	Copper	.158 mg
Cholesterol	0 mg	Iodine	mcg
Dietary Fibre	2.45 g	Iron	1.82 mg
Soluble Fibre	.394 g	Magnesium	31.8 mg
Total Vit A	.796 RE	Manganese	.776 mg
Thiamin-B1	.168 mg	Phosphorus	106 mg
Riboflavin-B2	.075 mg	Potassium	173 mg
Niacin-B3	1.2 mg	Selenium	7.54 mcg
Niacin Equiv.	1.2 mg	Sodium	457 mg
Vitamin B6	.139 mg	Zinc	.959 mg
Vitamin B12	.001 mcg	Complex Carbs	13.7 g
Folate	61.1 mcg	Sugars	1.77 g
Pantothenic	.371 mg	Water	56 g

CALORIE BREAKDOWN		FAT		EXCHANGES	
Protein	21%	*Saturated :	1.5%	Bread	1.13
Carbohydrates	71%	Mono Unsat:	2.3%	Lean Meat	.045
Fat-Total *	8%	Poly Unsat:	3.2%	Vegetables	.125
				Fat	.039

OAT BURGERS (makes 16 patties)

750 mL	(3 cups)		water
60 mL	(1/4 cup)		soy sauce
250 mL	(1 cup)	**EACH**	finely chopped onion **and** finely chopped celery
5 mL	(1 tsp)		sweet basil
5 mL	1 tsp)		Marmite or Savorex or Vegex
75 mL	(1/3 cup)		chopped walnuts
750 mL	(3 cups)		large flake rolled oats

Method:

PLACE the water, soy sauce, onion, celery, basil, and Marmite in a saucepan. **BRING** to a boil and **SIMMER** for 5 minutes. **ADD** walnuts and rolled oats. **RETURN** the mixture to a boil. **REMOVE** from heat and **ALLOW** to set 5 minutes. While mixture is still warm **FORM** into burgers by spooning mixture into a standard-size canning jar ring on an oiled cookie sheet. **BAKE** at 350° F. on first side. **FLIP** and **BAKE** 15 minutes on second side. **SERVE** topped with gravy or in a burger bun. (These burgers freeze very well.)

```
Analysis: OAT BURGERS (16 patties - jar lid size)  Divided by: 16
          Wgt: 84.1 g (2.97 oz.)                   Water:      77%
```

Calories	80.7		Vitamin C	1.29 mg
Protein	3.24 g		Vitamin D	0 mcg
Carbohydrates	12.2 g		Vit E-Alpha E	.205 mg
Fat - Total	2.38 g		Vitamin K	mcg
Saturated Fat	.3 g		Biotin	mcg
Mono Fat	.624 g		Calcium	19.5 mg
Poly Fat	1.24 g		Copper	.101 mg
Cholesterol	0 mg		Iodine	mcg
Dietary Fibre	1.99 g		Iron	.925 mg
Soluble Fibre	.774 g		Magnesium	30.3 mg
Total Vit A	3.65 RE		Manganese	.66 mg
Thiamin-B1	.131 mg		Phosphorus	89.5 mg
Riboflavin-B2	.045 mg		Potassium	113 mg
Niacin-B3	.401 mg		Selenium	4.58 mcg
Niacin Equiv.	.339 mg		Sodium	266 mg
Vitamin B6	.061 mg		Zinc	.594 mg
Vitamin B12	0 mcg		Complex Carbs	8.97 g
Folate	11 mcg		Sugars	1.22 g
Pantothenic	.251 mg		Water	65.1 g

CALORIE BREAKDOWN		FAT		EXCHANGES	
Protein	16%	*Saturated:	3.2%	Bread	.559
Carbohydrates	59%	Mono Unsat:	6.7%	Vegetables	.177
Fat-Total *	26%	Poly unsat:	13.4%		

OATMEAL-SUNFLOWER SEED PATTIES (makes 12 three-tablespoon patties)

250 mL	(1 cup)	chopped onion
125 mL	(1/2 cup)	ground sunflower seeds
60 mL	(1/4 cup)	soy flour
30 mL	(2 Tbsp.)	gluten flour
30 mL	(2 Tbsp.)	flake food yeast
15 mL	(1 Tbsp.)	soy sauce
5 mL	(1 tsp.)	salt
3 mL	(1/2 tsp.) **EACH**	sage, thyme, **and** marjoram,
3 mL	(1/2 tsp.) **EACH**	garlic powder, **and** onion powder
310 mL	(1 1/4 cups)	water
500 mL	(2 cups)	dry large flake rolled oats

Method:

STEAM onions in small amount of the water. **MIX** all ingredients together. **LET** stand at least 15 minutes. **USE** a standard size mason jar lid to shape patties. **PLACE** on treated teflon cookie sheet. **BAKE** until brown on one side. **TURN** and **BROWN** on the other side. **SERVE** with gravy.

```
Analysis: OATMEAL-SUNFLOWER SEED PATTIES          Divided by: 12
          Wgt: 65 g (2.29 oz.)                    Water:      61%
```

Calories	110		Vitamin C	1.11 mg
Protein	6 g		Vitamin D	0 mcg
Carbohydrates	13.6 g		Vit E-Alpha E	3.13 mg
Fat - Total	4.02 g		Vitamin K	mcg
Saturated Fat	.487 g		Biotin	mcg
Mono Fat	.866 g		Calcium	31.7 mg
Poly Fat	2.36 g		Copper	.258 mg
Cholesterol	0 mg		Iodine	mcg
Dietary Fibre	2.17 g		Iron	1.58 mg
Soluble Fibre	.707 g		Magnesium	50.6 mg
Total Vit A	2.3 RE		Manganese	.708 mg
Thiamin-B1	.484 mg		Phosphorus	154 mg
Riboflavin-B2	.13 mg		Potassium	197 mg
Niacin-B3	1.24 mg		Selenium	8.48 mcg
Niacin Equiv.	.502 mg		Sodium	266 mg
Vitamin B6	.146 mg		Zinc	.823 mg
Vitamin B12	0 mcg		Complex Carbs	9.1 g
Folate	78.6 mcg		Sugars	1.78 g
Pantothenic	.812 mg		Water	39.8 g

CALORIE BREAKDOWN		FAT		EXCHANGES	
Protein	21%	*Saturated :	3.8%	Bread	.59
Carbohydrates	48%	Mono Unsat:	6.8%	Lean Meat	.305
Fat-Total *	32%	Poly Unsat:	18.5%	Fruit	.667
		Fat .417----->		Vegetables	.167

OATMEAL-WALNUT PATTIES (makes 18 two-tablespoon patties)

500 mL	(2 cups	oatmeal
125 mL	(1/2 cup)	ground walnuts
250 mL	(1 cup)	chopped onion
60 mL	(1/4 cup)	soy flour
15 mL	(1 Tbsp.)	soy sauce
5 mL	(1 tsp.)	salt (Use less if on a low sodium diet)
3 mL	(1/2 tsp.) **EACH**	sage, thyme, marjoram, **and** garlic powder
3 mL	(1/2 tsp.)	onion powder
310 mL	(1 1/4 cups)	water

Method:

STEAM onions in small amount of water. **MIX** all ingredients together. **LET** stand at least 15 minutes. **DROP** in 2 Tbsp. amount on treated teflon cookie sheet. **BAKE** until brown on one side. **TURN** and **BROWN** on other side. **SERVE** with gravy.

```
Analysis: OATMEAL-WALNUT PATTIES                    Divided by: 18
          Wgt: 40.6 g (1.43 oz.)                    Water:       65%
```

Calories	65.3		Vitamin C	.748 mg
Protein	2.74 g		Vitamin D	0 mcg
Carbohydrates	8.11 g		Vit E-Alpha E	.162 mg
Fat - Total	2.74 g		Vitamin K	mcg
Saturated Fat	.304 g		Biotin	mcg
Mono Fat	.671 g		Calcium	14.5 mg
Poly Fat	1.57 g		Copper	.148 mg
Cholesterol	0 mg		Iodine	mcg
Dietary Fibre	1.29 g		Iron	.648 mg
Soluble Fibre	.473 g		Magnesium	23.5 mg
Total Vit A	1.75 RE		Manganese	.486 mg
Thiamin-B1	.089 mg		Phosphorus	65.3 mg
Riboflavin-B2	.025 mg		Potassium	98.2 mg
Niacin-B3	.184 mg		Selenium	2.96 mcg
Niacin Equiv.	.184 mg		Sodium	177 mg
Vitamin B6	.067 mg		Zinc	.418 mg
Vitamin B12	0 mcg		Complex Carbs	5.69 g
Folate	12.1 mcg		Sugars	1.13 g
Pantothenic	.178 mg		Water	26.2 g

CALORIE BREAKDOWN		FAT		EXCHANGES	
Protein	16%	Saturated :	4%	Bread	.381
Carbohydrates	48%	Mono Unsat:	8.9%	Lean Meat	.06
Fat - Total *	36%	Poly Unsat:	20.7%	Vegetables	.11

WALNUTS:

Walnuts contain moderately high quantities of linolenic acid, an omega-3 fatty acid, very similar to fish oils. Nuts, in general, mainly have mono-unsaturated fat, but walnuts contain a high amount of polyunsaturated fat. Nuts also contain fibre and are a relatively good source of Vitamin E, an antioxidant vitamin.

RED RIVER CEREAL PATTIES (makes 16 small patties)

750 ml	(3 cups)	boiling water
4 mL	(3/4 tsp.)	salt
5 mL	(1 tsp.)	thyme
15 mL	(1 Tbsp.)	Marmite, Vegex, or Savorex
375 mL	(1 1/2 cups)	Red River cereal (dry) May use 7-grain cereal
250 mL	(1 cup)	finely chopped onions
2	(2)	garlic cloves, minced
5 mL	(1 tsp.)	onion powder
60 mL	(1/4 cup)	sunflower seed meal
30 mL	(2 Tbsp.) **EACH**	walnut meal **and** gluten flour
60 mL	(1/4 cup)	soy flour

Method:

ADD first six ingredients to boiling water. **SIMMER** for 20 minutes. **ADD** remaining ingredients. **MIX** well, **COOL** enough to handle. **SHAPE** into patties using a jar-ring or a 1/4 cup measuring cup. **PLACE** on prepared baking sheet. **BAKE** at 350° F. for 35 minutes. **SERVE** with gravy.

```
-----------------------------------------------------------------------
| Analysis: RED RIVER CEREAL PATTIES (16 1/4 CUP PAT   Divided by: 16  |
|           Wgt: 72.3 g (2.55 oz.)                     Water:   75%    |
-----------------------------------------------------------------------
```

Calories	64.8		Vitamin C	.836 mg
Protein	3.28 g		Vitamin D	0 mcg
Carbohydrates	8.79 g		Vit E-Alpha E	1.17 mg
Fat - Total	1.83 g		Vitamin K	mcg
Saturated Fat	.188 g		Biotin	mcg
Mono Fat	.369 g		Calcium	14.9 mg
Poly Fat	1.17 g		Copper	.133 mg
Cholesterol	0 mg		Iodine	mcg
Dietary Fibre	1.36 g		Iron	.696 mg
Soluble Fibre	.055 g		Magnesium	14.6 mg
Total Vit A	.623 RE		Manganese	.143 mg
Thiamin-B1	.087 mg		Phosphorus	33 mg
Riboflavin-B2	.041 mg		Potassium	75.4 mg
Niacin-B3	.769 mg		Selenium	2.05 mcg
Niacin Equiv.	.169 mg		Sodium	105 mg
Vitamin B6	.061 mg		Zinc	.205 mg
Vitamin B12	0 mcg		Complex Carbs	1.17 g
Folate	18.6 mcg		Sugars	1.1 g
Pantothenic	.223 mg		Water	54 g

CALORIE BREAKDOWN		FAT		EXCHANGES	
Protein	20%	* Saturated : 2.6%		Bread	.47
Carbohydrates	54%	Mono Unsat: 5.1%		Lean Meat	.146
Fat-Total *	25%	Poly Unsat: 16.2%		Fruit	.25
P : S ratio	6.19 : 1	Potassium : Sodium .72 : 1		Vegetables	.125
				Fat	.156

SHAMBURGERS (makes 15 1/4-cup patties)

250 mL	(1 cup)		raw sunflower seeds
625 mL	(2 1/2 cups)		rolled oats
75 mL	(1/3 cup)		gluten flour
15 mL	(1 Tbsp.)	**EACH**	low fat soy flour **and** flake food yeast
1	(1)		large garlic clove, minced and steamed
250 mL	(1 cup)		onion, minced and steamed
3 mL	(1/2 tsp.)	**EACH**	thyme **and** savory
375 mL	(1 1/2 cups)		hot water

Broth:

1250 mL	(5 cups)	hot water
75 mL	(1/3 cup)	soy sauce, Bragg liquid aminos, or Maggi seasoning
30 mL	(2 Tbsp.)	parsley flakes

Method:

WHIZ the sunflower seeds in the blender. **COMBINE** with remaining ingredients. Let stand for 30 minutes. **PREPARE** broth in a large pot. **DIVIDE** burger mixture into 15 1/4-cup portions. Using a standard mason jar lid and ring mould the patties and **DROP** onto a lightly-sprayed cookie sheet. **BROWN** slightly on both sides. **DROP** patties into boiling broth and **SIMMER** for about an hour. **SERVE** on burger buns or in a gravy.

```
--------------------------------------------------------------------
| Analysis: SHAMBURGERS                         Divided by: 15      |
|           Wgt: 147 g (5.17 oz.)               Water:      81%     |
--------------------------------------------------------------------
```

Calories	129		Vitamin C	.946 mg
Protein	6.55 g		Vitamin D	0 mcg
Carbohydrates	14.3 g		Vit E-Alpha E	4.94 mg
Fat - Total	5.72 g		Vitamin K	mcg
Saturated Fat	.657 g		Biotin	mcg
Mono Fat	1.18 g		Calcium	30.4 mg
Poly Fat	3.48 g		Copper	.253 mg
Cholesterol	0 mg		Iodine	mcg
Trans FAT	0 g		Iron	1.64 mg
Dietary Fibre	2.31 g		Magnesium	60.2 mg
Soluble Fibre	.698 g		Manganese	.743 mg
Total Vit A	4.98 RE		Phosphorus	160 mg
Thiamin-B1	.422 mg		Potassium	170 mg
Riboflavin-B2	.09 mg		Selenium	10.8 mcg
Niacin-B3	1.08 mg		Sodium	333 mg
Niacin Equiv.	.78 mg		Zinc	1 mg
Vitamin B6	.137 mg		Complex Carbs	10.1 g
Vitamin B12	0 mcg		Sugars	1.59 g
Folate	52 mcg		Water	118 g
Pantothenic	.929 mg			

CALORIE BREAKDOWN		FAT	EXCHANGES	
Protein	19%	*Saturated: 3.4%	Bread	.673
Carbohydrates	42%	Mono Unsat: 8.9%	Lean Meat	.062
Fats-Total *	38%	Poly Unsat: 3.4%	Fruit	.854
			Fat	.274

SOY SIZZLERS (makes about 18 quarter-cup patties)

310 mL	(1 1/4 cups)		soaked, raw soybeans (3/4 cup before soaking)
375 mL	(1 1/2 cups)		water
3 mL	(1/2 tsp.)		salt
30 mL	(2 Tbsp.)		food yeast flakes **or** Engevita yeast
15 mL	(1 Tbsp.)		parsley flakes
15 mL	(1 Tbsp.)		Maggi seasoning **or** soy sauce
3 mL	(1/2 tsp.)	**EACH**	celery seed **and** thyme
2 mL	(1/4 tsp.)	**EACH**	marjoram **and** savory
310 mL	(1 1/4 cups)		finely chopped onion
250 mL	(1 cup)		finely chopped celery
1	(1)		large clove of garlic, minced
375 mL	(1 1/2 cups)		large flake oats
125 mL	(1/2 cup)		ground walnuts

Method:

SOAK soybeans overnight. BLEND soaked soybeans with the water until creamy. ADD salt, yeast, parsley, Maggi, celery seed, thyme, marjoram, and savory. BLEND well. STEAM onions, celery, and garlic until onions are soft. POUR contents of blender into a bowl. STIR in steamed vegetables, rolled oats, and nuts. LET stand for 5 minutes for oats to absorb liquid. Using a jar lid SHAPE patties and DROP on a treated cookie sheet. BAKE at 350° F. for 15 minutes. TURN and BAKE 10 minutes more. SERVE with tomato sauce or gravy.

```
------------------------------------------------------------------------
| Analysis: SOY SIZZLERS                     Divided by: 15            |
|           Wgt: 66.5 g (2.34 oz.)           Water:     68%            |
------------------------------------------------------------------------
```

Calories	99	Vitamin B6	.14 mg
Protein	5.37 g	Vitamin B12	0 mcg
Carbohydrates	10.5 g	Folate	81.2 mcg
Complex Carbs	5.75g	Pantothenic	.309 mg
Sugars	1.77 g	Vitamin C	2.12 mg
Dietary Fiber	2.98 g	Vitamin D	0 mcg
Soluble Fiber	.46 g	Vit E-Alpha E	.541 mg
Fat - Total	4.59 g	Clacium	40.8 mg
Saturated Fat	.553 g	Copper	.261 mg
Mono Fat	1.09 g	Iron	2.01 mg
Poly Fat	2.65 g	Magnesium	45.9 mg
Omega 3 FA	.384 g	Manganese	.646 mg
Cholesterol	0 mg	Phosphorus	131 mg
Trans FA	0 g	Potassium	255 mg
Total Vit A	4.24 RE	Selenium	3.73 mcg
Thiamin-B1	.32 mg	Sodium	81.6 mg
Riboflavin-B2	.138 mg	Water	44.9 g
Niacin Equiv.	.691 mg	Zinc	.877 mg

CALORIE BREAKDOWN		FAT	EXCHANGES	
Protein	20%	* Saturated : 4.7%	Bread	.516
Carbohydrates	40%	Mono Unsat: 9.4%	Lean Meat	.349
Fat-Total *	39%	Poly Unsat: 22.7%	Vegetables	.211

SUNBURGERS (makes ten 1/4-cup servings)

250 mL	(1 cup)	finely chopped onion
250 mL	(1 cup)	finely chopped celery
250 mL	(1 cup)	sunflower seeds, ground
750 mL	(3 cups)	grated carrots
5 mL	(1 tsp.)	parsley
125 mL	(1/2 cup)	rolled oats
125 mL	(1/2 cup)	tomato juice
60 mL	(1/4 cup)	barley or wheat flakes
3 mL	(1/2 tsp.)	salt
3 mL	(1/2 tsp.)	basil

Method:

STEAM onions and celery until onions are transparent. COMBINE all ingredients. FORM patties. Place on prepared cookie sheet. BAKE 15 minutes on each side at 350° F.

```
-----------------------------------------------------------------
| Analysis: SUNBURGERS                      Divided by: 10       |
|           Wgt: 86.9 g (3.07 oz.)          Water:      77%      |
-----------------------------------------------------------------
```

Calories	88.3		Vitamin C	7.33 mg
Protein	3.25 g		Vitamin D	0 mcg
Carbohydrates	11.4 g		Vit E-Alpha E	3.92 mg
Fat - Total	3.97 g		Vitamin K	mcg
Saturated Fat	.445 g		Biotin	mcg
Mono Fat	.779 g		Calcium	31
Poly Fat	2.51 g		Copper	.192 mg
Cholesterol	0 mg		Iodine	mcg
Dietary Fibre	2.8 g		Iron	1.09 mg
Soluble Fibre	.76 g		Magnesium	43.6 mg
Total Vit A	938 RE		Manganese	.454 mg
Thiamin-B1	.253 mg		Phosphorus	103 mg
Riboflavin-B2	.062 mg		Potassium	268 mg
Niacin-B3	.917 mg		Selenium	8.33 mcg
Niacin Equiv.	.917 mg		Sodium	174 mg
Vitamin B6	.16 mg		Zinc	.68 mg
Vitamin B12	0 mcg		Complex Carbs	4.55 g
Folate	33 mcg		Sugars	4.04 g
Pantothenic	.691 mg		Water	67.1 g

CALORIE BREAKDOWN		FAT		EXCHANGES	
Protein	14%	*Saturated :	4.2%	Bread	.235
Carbohydrates	48%	Mono Unsat:	7.4%	Lean Meat	.266
Fat-Total *	38%	Poly UNsat:	24 %	Fruit	.8
		Fat---->		Vegetables	.833

SUNFLOWER SEED PATTIES (makes 24 two-tablespoon patties)

5 mL	(1 tsp.)	oil
250 mL	(1 cup)	chopped onion
250 mL	(1 cup)	chopped celery (may use leaves)
1	(1)	large garlic clove, minced
125 mL	(1/2 cup)	sunflower seeds (ground)
75 mL	(1/3 cup)	walnuts (ground)
310 mL	(1 1/4 cups)	grated raw potato
310 mL	(1 1/4 cups)	quick cooking rolled oats
180 mL	(3/4 cup)	soy milk, rice milk, or water
30 mL	(2 Tbsp.)	Bisto or cornstarch
5 mL	(1 tsp.)	Maggi seasoning, Marmite, or Savorex
2 mL	(1/4 tsp.)	celery seed
2 mL	(1/4 tsp.)	sage

Method:

STEAM onions, celery, and garlic in the oil and part of the liquid. MIX all ingredients together. LET stand 5 minutes. SHAPE into patties. PLACE on treated cookie sheet. BAKE in a 350° F. oven for 15 minutes on a side..

```
Analysis: SUNFLOWER SEED PATTIES (24 patties)      Divided by: 24
          Wgt: 37.3 g (1.32 oz.)                   Water:      67%
```

Calories	60.1	Vitamin C	2 mg
Protein	1.94 g	Vitamin D	0 mcg
Carbohydrates	7.22 g	Vit E-Alpha E	1.63 mg
Fat - Total	2.9 g	Vitamin K	mcg
Saturated Fat	.319 g	Biotin	mcg
Mono Fat	.725 g	Calcium	12.7 mg
Poly Fat	1.7 g	Copper	.121 mg
Cholesterol	0 mg	Iodine	mcg
Dietary Fibre	1.09 g	Iron	.615 mg
Soluble Fibre	.28 g	Magnesium	23.1 mg
Total Vit A	1.45 RE	Manganese	.295 mg
Thiamin-B1	.121 mg	Phosphorus	54.4 mg
Riboflavin-B2	.028 mg	Potassium	104 mg
Niacin-B3	.391 mg	Selenium	3.69 mcg
Niacin Equiv.	.35 mg	Sodium	5.97 mg
Vitamin B6	.082 mg	Zinc	.375 mg
Vitamin B12	0 mcg	Complex Carbs	5.31 g
Folate	12.8 mcg	Sugars	.811 g
Pantothenic	.334 mg	Water	24.9 g

CALORIE BREAKDOWN		FAT		EXCHANGES	
Protein	12%	*Saturated :	4.6%	Bread	.331
Carbohydrates	46%	Mono Unsat:	10.4%	Lean Meat	.111
Fat-Total *	42%	Poly Unsat:	24.3	Fruit	.333
				Vegetables	.111
				Fat	.245

TOFU CHESTNUT BALLS - (makes 8 servings)

500 gm	(1 lb.)	well-drained tofu
500 mL	(2 cups)	cooked brown rice
250 mL	(1 cup)	shredded raw carrots
125 mL	(1/2 cup)	thinly-sliced green onions
125 mL	(1/2 cup)	finely chopped celery
60 mL	(1/4 cup)	chopped green pepper
250 mL	(1 cup)	chopped water chestnuts
1	(1)	large garlic clove, finely chopped
30 mL	(2 Tbsp.)	food yeast flakes
7 mL	(1 1/2 tsp.)	salt
60 mL	(1/4 cup)	cashew pieces (optional)

Method:

MASH tofu. COMBINE all ingredients. MIX well. FORM into balls. BAKE in lecithin-treated baking dish 30 minutes at 350° F. SERVE with tomato or tartar sauce.

```
-------------------------------------------------------------------
| Analysis: TOFU CHESTNUT BALLS              Divided by: 8         |
|           Wgt: 160 g (5.65 oz.)            Water :    73%        |
-------------------------------------------------------------------
```

Calories	184	Vitamin C	6.23	mg
Protein	12.1 g	Vitamin D	0	mcg
Carbohydrates	20.5 g	Vit E-Alpha Eq	.73	mg
Fat - Total	7.33 g	Vitamin K		mcg
Saturated Fat	1.19 g	Biotin		mcg
Mono Fat	2.4 g	Calcium	144	mg
Poly Fat	3.23 g	Copper	.387	mg
Cholesterol	0 mg	Iodine		mcg
Dietary Fibre	2.45 g	Iron	7.08	mg
Soluble Fibre	.342 g	Magnesium	93.6	mg
Total Vit A	401 RE	Manganese	1.2	mg
Thiamin-B1	.517 mg	Phosphorus	223	mg
Riboflavin-B2	.227 mg	Potassium	338	mg
Niacin-B3	2.39 mg	Selenium	7.94	mcg
Niacin Equiv.	1.28 mg	Sodium	451	mg
Vitamin B6	.278 mg	Zinc	1.6	mg
Vitamin B12	0 mcg	Complex Carbs	11.4	g
Folate	106 mcg	Sugars	1.78	g
Pantothenic	.629 mg	Water	117	g

CALORIE BREAKDOWN		FAT		EXCHANGES	
Protein	25%	*Saturated :	5.4%	Bread	.781
Carbohydrates	42%	Mono Unsat:	11 %	Lean Meat	1.41
Fat-Total *	34%	Poly Unsat:	14.8%	Fruit	.094
				Vegetables	.634
				Fat	.305

TOFU FU YUNG (makes 16 patties)

500 mL	(2 cups)	**EACH**	tofu, packed into a cup **and** water
250 mL	(1 cup)		quick oats
30 mL	(2 Tbsp.)		cornstarch
10 mL	(2 tsp.)		salt
125 mL	(1/2 cup)		food yeast flakes
60 mL	(1/4 cup)		cooked carrots
15 mL	(1 Tbsp.)	**EACH**	dried parsley **and** onion powder
5 mL	(1 tsp.)		thyme
3 mL	(1/2 tsp.)		garlic powder
250 mL	(1 cup)		slivered snow peas or grated zucchini
750 mL	(3 cups)		very thinly sliced cabbage strips
500 mL	(2 cups)	**EACH**	cubed eggplant **and** very thinly sliced onions
125 mL	(1/2 cup)		finely chopped parsley

Method:
   RINSE, DRAIN and MEASURE tofu. PUT into blender and ADD next 10 ingredients. BLEND on high until creamy. PUT into a bowl. ADD remaining ingredients and MIX together. DROP 1/2 cup portions on lecithin-oiled cookie sheet leaving 2 inches between patties. BAKE at 350° F. for 30 minutes. REMOVE from oven and ALLOW to sit for 5 minutes before removing from cookie sheet. SERVE with gravy, brown rice, and stir-fry vegetables.

```
Analysis: TOFU FU YUNG (1/16)          Divided by: 16
          Wgt: 110 g (3.88 oz.)        Water:      83%
```

Calories	72.2		Vitamin C	11.9 mg
Protein	5.65 g		Vitamin D	0 mcg
Carbohydrates	9.36 g		Vit E-Alpha E	.344 mg
Fat - Total	1.94 g		Vitamin K	mcg
Saturated Fat	.308 g		Biotin	mcg
Mono Fat	.46 g		Calcium	65.2 mg
Poly Fat	.993 g		Copper	.24 mg
Cholesterol	0 mg		Iodine	mcg
Dietary Fibre	3.19 g		Iron	3.17 mg
Soluble Fibre	.617 g		Magnesium	56.6 mg
Total Vit A	78.3 RE		Manganese	.456 mg
Thiamin-B1	.721 mg		Phosphorus	140 mg
Riboflavin-B2	.213 mg		Potassium	233 mg
Niacin-B3	1.82 mg		Selenium	4.26 mcg
Niacin Equiv.	1.82 mg		Sodium	281 mg
Vitamin B6	.292 mg		Zinc	.855 mg
Vitamin B12	.001 mcg		Complex Carbs	4.42 g
Folate	177 mcg		Sugars	1.75 g
Pantothenic	.547 mg		Water	91.1 g

CALORIE BREAKDOWN		FAT		EXCHANGES	
Protein	29%	* Saturated:	3.6%	Bread	.369
Carbohydrates	48%	Mono Unsat:	5.3%	Lean Meat	.25
Fat	23%	Poly Unsat:	11.5%	Vegetables	.622
				Fat	.125

VEGETARIAN "BIG MACS" (makes 18 patties)

250 mL	(1 cup)	dry garbanzos (Makes 2 1/2 cups when soaked.)
375 mL	(1 1/2 cups)	water
250 mL	(1 cup)	finely chopped onion
30 mL	(2 Tbsp.)	low-fat soy flour
125 mL	(1/2 cup)	finely chopped walnuts
500 mL	(2 cups)	dry large flake rolled oats
10 mL	(2 tsp.)	sage
4 mL	(3/4 tsp.)	salt
10 mL	(2 tsp.)	Savorex or Marmite
15 mL	(1 Tbsp.)	flake food yeast

Method:

SOAK garbanzos overnight. DRAIN. (May be soaked and frozen and thawed as needed.) WHIZ soaked garbanzos in water in food processor or blender. The remaining ingredients may be added and whizzed or if you prefer more texture REMOVE garbanzos and PLACE in a mixing bowl. ADD remaining ingredients and MIX well. DROP in 50 mL portions on a lightly oiled cookie sheet. To assure uniformity of size and shape USE a regular-size mason jar ring and snap lid to shape patties. BROWN on both sides. COVER and FINISH cooking. SERVE in a bun with lettuce, onion, and KETCHUP (page 207) or ARRANGE in a casserole and COVER with gravy or tomato sauce. BAKE for 30 minutes at 350° F.

```
Analysis: VEGETARIAN "BIG MACS"              Divided by: 18
          Wgt: 53.8 g (1.9 oz.)              Water:      56%
```

Calories	104		Vitamin C	1.14 mg
Protein	4.82 g		Vitamin D	0 mcg
Carbohydrates	14.6 g		Vit E-Alpha E	.495 mg
Fat - Total	3.37 g		Vitamin K	mcg
Saturated Fat	.369 g		Biotin	mcg
Mono Fat	.814 g		Calcium	28 mg
Poly Fat	1.84 g		Copper	.209 mg
Cholesterol	0 mg		Iodine	mcg
Dietary Fibre	3.39 g		Iron	1.42 mg
Soluble Fibre	1.12 g		Magnesium	35.4 mg
Total Vit A	2.55 RE		Manganese	.703 mg
Thiamin-B1	.219 mg		Phosphorus	110 mg
Riboflavin-B2	.089 mg		Potassium	187 mg
Niacin-B3	.664 mg		Selenium	3.8 mcg
Niacin Equiv.	.308 mg		Sodium	93.2 mg
Vitamin B6	.126 mg		Zinc	.796 mg
Vitamin B12	0 mcg		Complex Carbs	8.89 g
Folate	87.8 mcg		Sugars	2.12 g
Pantothenic	.406 mg		Water	30 g

CALORIE BREAKDOWN		FAT		EXCHANGES	
Protein	18%	*Saturated :	3.1%	Bread	.757
Carbohydrates	54%	Mono Unsat:	6.8%	Lean Meat	.224
Fat-Total *	28%	Poly Unsat:	15.3%	Vegetables	.111

BISCUITS FOR SHORT-CAKE (makes 7 1/4 cup biscuits)

180 mL	(3/4 cup)	warm water
5 mL	(1 tsp.)	sugar
15 mL	(1 Tbsp.)	yeast
500 mL	(2 cups)	flour (1 all-purpose + 1 whole wheat pastry)
3 mL	(1/2 tsp.)	salt
60 mL	(1/4 cup)	oil

Method:

COMBINE water, sugar and yeast. While the yeast is bubbling WORK together with your fingers the flour, salt, and oil. MIX dry and liquid ingredients together. TURN out on a PAM treated pan and SPREAD out evenly. LET rise 1/4" (about 20 minutes.) BAKE at 350° F. for approximately 25 minutes until golden.

```
Analysis: SHORT-CAKE (Seven 1/4 cup biscuits)      Divided by: 7
          Wgt: 69.5 g (2.45 oz.)                   Water:     42%
```

Calories	185		Vitamin C	.003 mg
Protein	4.6 g		Vitamin D	0 mcg
Carbohydrates	28.3 g		Vit E-Alpha E	1.51 mg
Fat - Total	6.38 g		Vitamin K	mcg
Saturated Fat	.831 g		Biotin	mcg
Mono Fat	1.5 g		Calcium	9.9 mg
Poly Fat	3.61 g		Copper	.099 mg
Cholesterol	0 mg		Iodine	mcg
Dietary Fibre	2.98 g		Iron	1.68 mg
Soluble Fibre	.524 g		Magnesium	29.1 mg
Total Vit A	0 RE		Manganese	.78 mg
Thiamin-B1	.242 mg		Phosphorus	92.5 mg
Riboflavin-B2	.184 mg		Potassium	110 mg
Niacin-B3	2.57 mg		Selenium	19.3 mcg
Niacin Equiv.	2.57 mg		Sodium	155 mg
Vitamin B6	.083 mg		Zinc	.707 mg
Vitamin B12	0 mcg		Complex Carbs	22.9 g
Folate	37.3 mcg		Sugars	2.42 g
Pantothenic	.372 mg		Water	29.3 g

CALORIE BREAKDOWN		FAT	EXCHANGES	
Protein	10%	*Saturated : 4 %	Bread	1.52
Carbohydrates	60%	Mono Unsat: 7.1%	Fruit	.116
Fat-Total *	30%	Poly Unsat: 17.2%	Vegetables	.121
			Fat	1.14

BLUEBERRY MUFFINS (makes 12 large muffins)

500 mL	(2 cups)	whole wheat pastry flour (soft wheat)
500 mL	(2 cups)	whole grain hard wheat flour
5 mL	(1 tsp.)	salt
60 mL	(1/4 cup)	wheat germ
15 mL	(1 Tbsp.)	instant blending yeast
500 mL	(2 cups)	blueberries
500 mL	(2 cups)	warm water (distilled if possible)
60 mL	(1/4 cup)	olive oil
125 mL	(1/2 cup)	honey

Method:

COMBINE dry ingredients in a bowl. **STIR** in blueberries. (If using frozen berries do not thaw.) **MIX** water, oil, and honey together thoroughly. Quickly **STIR** into dry ingredients. **SPOON** into muffin tins. **PLACE** in cold oven. **TURN** on oven just until light comes on. **LET** rise until double. **TURN** up temperature to 350° F. **BAKE** for 25-30 minutes.

```
----------------------------------------------------------------------
| Analysis: BLUEBERRY MUFFINS (12 LARGE)        Divided by: 12        |
|           Wgt: 127 g (4.47 oz.)               Water:      54%       |
----------------------------------------------------------------------
```

Calories	239	Vitamin C	.79 mg
Protein	6.22 g	Vitamin D	0 mcg
Carbohydrates	44.9 g	Vit E-Alpha E	1.64 mg
Fat - Total	5.59 g	Vitamin K	mcg
Saturated Fat	.797 g	Biotin	mcg
Mono Fat	3.49 g	Calcium	18.5 mg
Poly Fat	.876 g	Copper	.187 mg
Cholesterol	0 mg	Iodine	mcg
Dietary Fibre	6.08 g	Iron	1.88 mg
Soluble Fibre	1.01 g	Magnesium	61.8 mg
Total Vit A	2.07 RE	Manganese	1.78 mg
Thiamin-B1	.225 mg	Phosphorus	163 mg
Riboflavin-B2	.142 mg	Potassium	210 mg
Niacin-B3	3.04 mg	Selenium	33.7 mcg
Niacin Equiv.	3.04 mg	Sodium	182 mg
Vitamin B6	.183 mg	Zinc	1.47 mg
Vitamin B12	0 mcg	Complex Carbs	23.6 g
Folate	37.3 mcg	Sugars	15.1 g
Pantothenic	.538 mg	Water	68.6 g

CALORIE BREAKDOWN		FAT		EXCHANGES	
Protein	10%	*Saturated :	2.8%	Bread	1.72
Carbohydrates	70%	Mono Unsat:	12.3%	Lean Meat	.01
Fat-Total *	20%	Poly Unsat:	3.1%	Fruit	.833
				Vegetables	.071
				Fat	.889

DOUBLE BRAN APPLE MUFFINS (makes 12 muffins)

750 mL	(3 cups)		warm apple or orange juice
30 mL	(2 Tbsp.)		dry yeast
200 mL	(2/3 cup)		dates (blended with the hot juice)
30 mL	(2 Tbsp.)		PREPARED FLAX (see note on page 81)
5 mL	(1 tsp.)		vanilla or maple flavouring
125 mL	(1/2 cup)		tofu
250 mL	(1 cup)		grated raw apple
500 mL	(2 cups)		whole wheat flour
250 mL	(1 cup)	**EACH**	wheat bran **and** oat bran
15 mL	(1 Tbsp.)		gluten flour
3 mL	(1/2 tsp.)	**EACH**	salt **and** coriander
60 mL	(1/4 cup)		raisins

Method:

     PLACE a 1/2 cup of juice with the yeast in a bowl. **LET** rise for about 10 minutes. **WHIZ** the dates and part of the juice in the blender until mixture is smooth. **ADD** more juice, flax mixture, vanilla, and tofu. **WHIZ** until smooth. **POUR** into bowl with yeast. **RINSE** blender with remaining juice. **ADD** to contents of bowl. **ADD** remaining ingredients. **MIX** well. **PUT** into a PAM-coated muffin tin. **LET** rise for 7-10 minutes. **BAKE** at 350° F. for 25 minutes. **LOWER** oven temperature to 325° F. **BAKE** 15 minutes longer.

```
-----------------------------------------------------------------
| Analysis: DOUBLE-BRAN-APPLE MUFFINS          Divided by: 12  |
|       Wgt: 129 g (4.55 oz.)                     Water: 60%   |
-----------------------------------------------------------------
```

Calories	178	Vitamin C	16.8 mg
Protein	7.14 g	Vitamin D	0 mcg
Carbohydrates	40.6 g	Vit E-Alpha E	.644 mg
Fat - Total	1.94 g	Vitamin K	mcg
Saturated Fat	.316 g	Biotin	mcg
Mono Fat	.435 g	Calcium	38.5 mg
Poly Fat	.793 g	Copper	.25 mg
Cholesterol	0 mg	Iodine	mcg
Dietary Fibre	8.01 g	Iron	2.87 mg
Soluble Fibre	1.55 g	Magnesium	98.1 mg
Total Vit A	5.52 RE	Manganese	1.9 mg
Thiamin-B1	.294 mg	Phosphorus	219 mg
Riboflavin-B2	.186 mg	Potassium	406 mg
Niacin-B3	2.89 mg	Selenium	19.9 mcg
Niacin Equiv.	2.88 mg	Sodium	93.9 mg
Vitamin B6	.223 mg	Zinc	1.44 mg
Vitamin B12	0 mcg	Complex Carbs	16.5 g
Folate	67.2 mcg	Sugars	16 g
Pantothenic	.728 mg	Water	77.6 g

CALORIE BREAKDOWN		FAT		EXCHANGES	
Protein	14%	*Saturated :	1.4%	Bread	1.26
Carbohydrates	78%	Mono Unsat:	1.9%	Lean Meat	.083
Fat-Total *	8%	Poly Unsat:	3.4%	Fruit	1.1
		Fat .042 ----->		Vegetables	.183

CORN-OAT CRACKERS (54 crackers)

15 mL	(1 Tbsp.)	coconut
15 mL	(1 Tbsp.)	sesame seeds
60 mL	(1/4 cup)	raw unsalted cashews
30 mL	(2 Tbsp.)	flake food yeast
3 mL	(1/2 tsp.)	salt
3 mL	(1/2 tsp.)	onion powder
3 mL	(1/2 tsp.)	garlic powder
435 mL	(1 3/4 cups)	water
180 mL	(3/4 cup)	rolled oats
180 mL	(3/4 cup)	corn meal

Method:

WHIZ the first 3 ingredients in the blender or food processor until very fine. ADD 1/4 cup of water and WHIZ until smooth. ADD remaining ingredients and blend again. POUR onto two small cookie sheets or one large cookie sheet which has been treated with (lecithin-oil mixture - proportion 1-3). BAKE in a 350° F. oven for 10 minutes. REMOVE from oven. CUT into squares. RETURN to oven and CONTINUE to bake 40 minutes more. CHECK frequently and REMOVE the ones around the edges that bake first. The thinner the cracker the more crisp it will be.

```
Analysis: CORN-OAT CRACKERS                    Divided by: 54
         Wgt: 11.7 g (.413 oz.)                Water:      69%
```

Calories	16.7		Vitamin C	.004 mg
Protein	.496 g		Vitamin D	0 mcg
Carbohydrates	2.51 g		Vit E-Alpha Eq	.02 mg
Fat - Total	.55 g		Vitamin K	mcg
Saturated Fat	.14 g		Biotin	mcg
Mono Fat	.242 g		Calcium	1.48 mg
Poly Fat	.131 g		Copper	.023 mg
Cholesterol	0 mg		Iodine	mcg
Dietary Fibre	.327 g		Iron	.182 mg
Soluble Fibre	.095 g		Magnesium	4.87 mg
Total Vit A	.819 RE		Manganese	.053 mg
Thiamin-B1	.02 mg		Phosphorus	11.7 mg
Riboflavin-B2	.01 mg		Potassium	12.3 mg
Niacin-B3	.112 mg		Selenium	.647 mcg
Niacin Equiv.	.113 mg		Sodium	20.3 mg
Vitamin B6	.013 mg		Zinc	.107 mg
Vitamin B12	0 mcg		Complex Carbs	2.1 g
Folate	1.55 mcg		Sugars	.088 g
Pantothenic	.028 mg		Water	8.02 g

CALORIE BREAKDOWN		FAT		EXCHANGES	
Protein	12%	* Saturated:	7.4%	Bread	.136
Carbohydrates	59%	Mono Unsat:	2.4%	Lean Meat	.009
Fat-Total *	29%	Poly Unsat:	7 %	Fat	.065

BONNIE'S WHOLE GRAIN BREAD (makes 5 loaves)

1750 mL	(7 cups)		very warm water
1 L	(4 cups)		whole wheat flour
125 mL	(1/2 cup)		DATE BUTTER (page 137)
125 mL	(1/2 cup)		gluten flour
20 mL	(4 tsps.)		salt
75 mL	(1/3 cup)	**EACH**	flax seed **and** oat bran
125 mL	(1/2 cup)		raw sunflower seeds
250 mL	(1 cup)	**EACH**	large flake rolled oats, barley flakes, **and** rye flakes
60 mL	(1/4 cup)		dry yeast
2 L	(8 cups)		whole wheat flour (approximately)

Method:

COMBINE the first 5 ingredients and **MIX** well. **ADD** the flax seed, sunflower seeds, rolled oats, barley flakes, rye flakes, oat bran, and yeast. **MIX** another minute or two and then **LET** sit for 7 minutes. **ADD** 4 cups of whole wheat flour and **MIX** again. **ADD** remaining flour as needed and **KNEAD** for 10 minutes. **SHAPE** into 5 loaves and **PLACE** in pans which have been prepared with lecithin-oil. **PLACE** pans in oven at very lowest setting (that is as soon as the light comes on - not to the first numbers on the dial) Let rise about 25 minutes (until doubled). **TURN** oven to 350° F. and **BAKE** for 55-60 minutes. **TURN** out of pans onto wire racks, **LET** cool, **SLICE** and **FREEZE**. Bread without preservatives moulds very quickly.

```
Analysis: BONNIE'S WHOLE GRAIN BREAD           Divided by: 110
          Wgt: 34.8 g (1.23 oz.)               Water:      52%
```

Calories	64.3	Vitamin B6	.064 mg
Protein	2.81 g	Vitamin B12	0 mcg
Carbohydrates	12.6 g	Folate	15 mcg
Complex Carbs	9.62 g	Pantothenic	.24 mcg
Sugars	.634 g	Vitamin C	.01 mg
Dietary Fiber	2.29 g	Vitamin D	0 mcg
Soluble Fiber	.402 g	Vit E-Alpha E	.504 mg
Fat - Total	.791 g	Calcium	8.26 mg
Saturated Fat	.099 g	Copper	.081 mg
Mono Fat	.128 g	Iron	.856 mg
Poly Fat	.366 g	Magnesium	26.6 mg
Omega 3 FA	.009 g	Maganese	.64 mg
Cholesterol	0 mg	Phosphorus	68.8 mg
Trans FA	0 g	Potassium	82.2 mg
Total Vit A	.152 RE	Selenium	12.1 mcg
Thianmin-B1	.1 mg	Sodium	79 mg
Riboflavin-B2	.053 mg	Water	18 g
Niacin Equiv.	1.09 mg	Zinc	.557 mg

CALORIE BREAKDOWN		FAT		EXCHANGES	
Protein	16%	*Saturated :	1.3%	Bread	.696
Carbohydrates	73%	Mono Unsat:	1.7%	Fruit	.091
Fat-Total *	10%	Poly Unsat:	4.8%	Vegetables	.031
				Fat	.045

MULTIGRAIN BREAD (makes 4 loaves)

125 mL	(1/2 cup)		blackstrap molasses
1500 mL	(6 cups)		warm water
60 mL	(1/4 cup)		lemon juice
20 mL	(4 tsp.)		salt
185 mL	(3/4 cup)	**EACH**	soy flour, wheat germ, **and** rye flour
185 mL	(3/4 cup)	**EACH**	rolled oats **and** gluten flour
2250 mL	(8-9 cups)		hard wheat whole wheat flour
40 mL	(8 tsp.)		instant blending yeast

Method:

      PLACE molasses, water, lemon juice, and salt in large bowl or Bosch bowl. **ADD** the soy flour, wheat germ, rye flour, rolled oats, gluten flour, 3 cups of the whole wheat flour, and yeast. **BEAT** about 3 minutes to develop the gluten. Gradually **WORK** in as much more flour as is needed to make a soft dough. **KNEAD** for 10 minutes. **DIVIDE** into loaves and **PLACE** in greased pans. **PLACE** in oven that has been turned on just until the light comes on (before the numbers) **LET** rise until double in bulk. When a finger poked into the end of the loaf leaves a print it has doubled. **LEAVE** the bread in the oven **TURN** the temperature to 375° F. for 20 minutes. **REDUCE** heat to 350° and **BAKE** 20-25 minutes more or until it sounds hollow when tapped on the bottom.

```
------------------------------------------------------------------------
| Analysis: MULTIGRAIN BREAD                      Divided by:  88       |
|           Wgt: 39.8 g (1.4 oz.)                 Water:       55%      |
------------------------------------------------------------------------
```

Calories	63.3		Vitamin B6	.075 mg
Protein	3.11 g		Vitamin B12	0 mcg
Carbohydrates	12.6 g		Folate	15.8 mcg
Complex Carbs	9.25 g		Pantothenic	.193 mg
Sugars	1.43 g		Vitamin C	.173 mg
Dietary Fiber	1.96 g		Vitamin D	0 mcg
Soluble Fibre	.326 g		Vit E-Alpha E	.344 mg
Fat - Total	.47 g		Calcium	24.6 mg
Saturated Fat	.074 g		Copper	.143 mg
Mono Fat	.074 g		Iron	1.05 mg
Poly Fat	.205 g		Magnesium	29.3 mg
Omega 3 FA	.017 g		Manganese	.753 mg
Cholesterol	0 mg		Phosphorus	69.6 mg
Trans FA	0 g		Potassium	139 mg
Total Vit A	.113 RE		Selenium	12.3 mcg
Thiamin-B1	.078 mg		Sodium	502 mg
Riboflavin-B2	.048 mg		Water	21.7 g
Niacin Equiv.	.948 mg		Zinc	.6 mg

CALORIE BREAKDOWN		FAT	EXCHANGES	
Protein	18%	* Saturated : 1 %	Bread	.697
Carbohydrates	75%	Mono Unsat: 1 %	Lean Meat	.042
Fat-Total *	6%	Poly Unsat: 2.7%	Fruit	.073
		Fat .009 --->	Vegetables	.026

PITA BREAD (makes 12 medium pitas)

5 mL	(1 tsp.)	sugar
15 mL	(1 Tbsp.)	active dry yeast (instant blending)
10 mL	(1 tsp.)	salt (less if on a low sodium diet)
1 L	(4 cups)	whole wheat flour (may need more or less)
500 mL	(2 cups)	warm water

Method:

COMBINE sugar, yeast, salt, and half of the flour. ADD water. Gradually ADD more flour as needed. KNEAD until smooth and elastic, FORM dough into a long roll; CUT into 12 equal pieces. FORM each into a ball. COVER and LET rise about 5 minutes. ROLL each ball into 1/4-inch-thick circles. PLACE circles of dough on cookie sheets. COVER and LET rise. HEAT oven to 475° F. or hotter. BAKE 2-5 minutes until puffed and lightly browned. (WATCH as it bakes.) STUFF with any combination of chopped tomatoes, cabbage, lettuce, tahini, FALAFELS, and parsley or place in plastic bags and freeze.

```
Analysis: PITA                          Divided by: 12
          Wgt: 81.3 g (2.87 oz.)        Water:      54%
```

Calories	138		Vitamin C	.002 mg
Protein	5.71 g		Vitamin D	0 mcg
Carbohydrates	29.5 g		Vit E-Alpha E	.493 mg
Fat - Total	.775 g		Vitamin K	mcg
Saturated Fat	.132 g		Biotin	mcg
Mono Fat	.109 g		Calcium	15.4 mg
Poly Fat	.312 g		Copper	.159 mg
Cholesterol	0 mg		Iodine	mcg
Dietary Fibre	5.23 g		Iron	1.67 mg
Soluble Fibre	.837 g		Magnesium	56.7 mg
Total Vit A	0 RE		Manganese	1.53 mg
Thiamin-B1	.158 mg		Phosphorus	146 mg
Riboflavin-B2	.112 mg		Potassium	175 mg
Niacin-B3	2.54 mg		Selenium	32.1 mcg
Niacin Equiv.	2.54 mg		Sodium	359 mg
Vitamin B6	.132 mg		Zinc	1.23 mg
Vitamin B12	0 mcg		Complex Carbs	23.2 g
Folate	27 mcg		Sugars	1.05 g
Pantothenic	.374 mg		Water	43.6 g

CALORIE BREAKDOWN		FAT		EXCHANGES	
Protein	15%	*Saturated :	.8%	Bread	1.67
Carbohydrates	80%	Mono Unsat:	.7%	Fruit	.016
Fat-Total *	5%	Poly Unsat:	1.9%	Vegetables	.071

HOW TO TELL WHEN YEAST DOUGH HAS DOUBLED:

Cover the panned dough with wax paper and a clean damp towel. Let dough rise ONLY until it has doubled in bulk. You can tell that bread dough has doubled when the impression stays when you press gently in an inconspicuous place. The centre of the panned dough will have risen about 1 3/4 inches (4 cm) higher than the edges of the pan and the corners will be well filled. Care should be taken not to let yeast dough rise too much to avoid a split on top or dough collapsing.

RYE BREAD (makes 2 loaves)

500 mL	(2 cups)	warm apple juice (110° F)
625 mL	(2 1/2 cups)	warm water
15 mL	(1 Tbsp.)	salt
750 mL	(3 cups)	rye flour
125 mL	(1/2 cup)	gluten flour
37 mL	(2 1/2 Tbsp.)	caraway seeds
2 L	(6-8 cups)	whole wheat flour
45 mL	(3 Tbsp.)	yeast (instant blending)

Method:

COMBINE water and apple juice. ADD salt, rye flour, gluten flour, caraway seeds, 3 1/2 cups of whole wheat flour and yeast. BEAT for about 5 minutes. (May use mixer for this stage.) CONTINUE adding whole wheat flour as you knead dough. KEEP ADDING until the mix pulls away from the bowl or stops sticking to your hands if mixing by hand. This is quite a stiff mix compared with whole-wheat bread. (Don't ADD remaining flour all at once because you may not need it all.) SHAPE into loaves. PLACE in cold oven. TURN on the heat just until the light comes on. LET rise until double in bulk (about 25 minutes). ADJUST oven temperature up to 400° F. BAKE at 400° for about 10 minutes. REDUCE heat to 350° and BAKE about 20 minutes or until done. SLICE very thin.

```
Analysis: RYE BREAD                        Divided by: 46
          Wgt: 55.2 g (1.95 oz.)           Water:      46%
```

Calories	111		Vitamin C	.064 mg
Protein	4.93 g		Vitamin D	0 mcg
Carbohydrates	23.2 g		Vit E-Alpha E	.258 mg
Fat - Total	.729 g		Vitamin K	mcg
Saturated Fat	.1 g		Biotin	mcg
Mono Fat	.114 g		Calcium	16.2 mg
Poly Fat	.278 g		Copper	.15 mg
Cholesterol	0 mg		Iodine	mcg
Dietary Fibre	3.96 g		Iron	1.52 mg
Soluble Fibre	.627 g		Magnesium	51.7 mg
Total Vit A	.14 RE		Manganese	1.37 mg
Thiamin-B1	.133 mg		Phosphorus	136 mg
Riboflavin-B2	.096 mg		Potassium	174 mg
Niacin-B3	1.9 mg		Selenium	19.7 mcg
Niacin Equiv.	1.9 mg		Sodium	142 mg
Vitamin B6	.119 mg		Zinc	1.14 mg
Vitamin B12	0 mcg		Complex Carbs	17.2 g
Folate	26 mcg		Sugars	2.05 g
Pantothenic	.394 mg		Water	25.3 g

CALORIE BREAKDOWN		FAT		EXCHANGES	
Protein	17%	*Saturated : .8%		Bread	1.35
Carbohydrates	78%	Mono Unsat: .9%		Fruit	.087
Fat-Total *	6%	Poly Unsat: 2.1%		Vegetables	.055

CORN FRITTERS (makes 10)

310 mL	(1 1/4 cups)	water
125 mL	(1/2 cup)	tofu
250 mL	(1 cup)	cornmeal
5 mL	(1 tsp.)	Marmite, Savorex, **or** Vegex
250 mL	(1 cup)	kernel corn

Method:

PLACE water, tofu, cornmeal, and Marmite in the food processor or blender and **BLEND** well. **TRANSFER** to a large measuring cup and **ADD** the corn. **USE** 3 Tbsp of batter for each fritter. **SPREAD** evenly, but not too thinly. **BAKE** in hot teflon or lecithin treated skillet. Do not try to turn until nearly dry on top and **BROWN** on the bottom. If fritters do not turn easily it is because they are not sufficiently baked.

```
-----------------------------------------------------------------------
| Analysis: CORN FRITTERS                         Divided by: 10       |
|            Wgt: 72.6 g (2.56 oz.)               Water:      75%      |
-----------------------------------------------------------------------
```

Calories	73.7	Vitamin C	.438 mg
Protein	2.76 g	Vitamin D	0 mcg
Carbohydrates	14.3 g	Vit E-Alpha E	.037 mg
Fat - Total	.832 g	Vitamin K	mcg
Saturated Fat	.119 g	Biotin	mcg
Mono Fat	.191 g	Calcium	16 mg
Poly Fat	.439 g	Copper	.042 mg
Cholesterol	0 mg	Iodine	mcg
Dietary Fibre	1.36 g	Iron	1.36 mg
Soluble Fibre	.24 g	Magnesium	21.4 mg
Total Vit A	10.9 RE	Manganese	.12 mg
Thiamin-B1	.123 mg	Phosphorus	31.2 mg
Riboflavin-B2	.089 mg	Potassium	60 mg
Niacin-B3	1.03 mg	Selenium	1.21 mcg
Niacin Equiv.	.93 mg	Sodium	56.3 mg
Vitamin B6	.064 mg	Zinc	.267 mg
Vitamin B12	0 mcg	Complex Carbs	12.6 g
Folate	12.2 mcg	Sugars	.36 g
Pantothenic	.1 mg	Water	54.2 g

CALORIE BREAKDOWN		FAT		EXCHANGES	
Protein	15%	*Saturated : 1.4%		Bread	.8
Carbohydrates	76%	Mono Unsat: 2.3%		Vegetables	.05
Fat-Total *	10%	Poly Unsat: 5.2%		Fat	.05

FLAX AS AN EGG REPLACER:

BOIL 1 cup of water with 1/3 cup of ground flax for 3 minutes. **USE** 1 Tbsp. for each egg called for in recipe.

BEST-EVER CORN-OAT PANCAKES or WAFFLES

875 mL	(3 1/2 cups)	rolled oats
125 mL	(1/2 cup)	cornmeal
875 mL	(3 1/2 cups)	water
75 mL	(1/3 cup)	soy milk powder
5 mL	(1 tsp.)	salt
5	(5)	dates, finely chopped
15 mL	(1 Tbsp.)	vanilla

Method:

PUT all ingredients into the food processor or blender and BLEND until smooth. If mixture seems too thick ADD more water. (If the container is not big enough to hold all of the ingredients at once, DO half a batch at a time and TRANSFER to another container.) COAT surface of a frying pan with PAM or lecithin mixture. HEAT pan. DROP batter in 1/4 cup amounts onto hot pan. SPREAD it evenly. COVER and COOK until golden brown on the bottom. TURN and COOK on the other side. SERVE with Pineapple Marmalade, Berried Pleasure, peanut butter and applesauce, or other fruit.

```
------------------------------------------------------------------------
| Analysis: BEST-EVER PANCAKES                    Divided by:  12       |
|           Wgt: 106 g (3.73 oz.)                 Water:       69%      |
------------------------------------------------------------------------
```

Calories	133		Vitamin C	0 mg
Protein	5.47 g		Vitamin D	0 mcg
Carbohydrates	23.9 g		Vit E-Alpha E	.177 mg
Fat - Total	1.75 g		Vitamin K	mcg
Saturated Fat	.303 g		Biotin	mcg
Mono Fat	.527 g		Calcium	19.4 mg
Poly Fat	.668 g		Copper	.211 mg
Cholesterol	0 mg		Iodine	mcg
Dietary Fibre	3.18 g		Iron	1.41 mg
Soluble Fibre	1.31 g		Magnesium	44.1 mg
Total Vit A	4.74 RE		Manganese	.943 mg
Thiamin-B1	.217 mg		Phosphorus	131 mg
Riboflavin-B2	.064 mg		Potassium	171 mg
Niacin-B3	.568 mg		Selenium	7.05 mcg
Niacin Equiv.	.57 mg		Sodium	181 mg
Vitamin B6	.06 mg		Zinc	.826 mg
Vitamin B12	0 mcg		Complex Carbs	17.2 g
Folate	18.9 mcg		Sugars	3.14 g
Pantothenic	.375 mg		Water	73.1 g

CALORIE BREAKDOWN		FAT		EXCHANGES	
Protein	16%	* Saturated : 2 %		Bread	1.13
Carbohydrates	72%	Mono Unsat: 3.6%		Lean Meat	.1
Fat-Total *	12%	Poly Unsat: 4.5%		Fruit	.179
				Fat	.048

POTATO-TOFU PANCAKES (makes 7 six-inch pancakes)

8	(8)	medium potatoes, grated
250 mL	(1 cup)	tofu, blended
250 mL	(1 cup)	finely chopped onion
60 mL	(1/4 cup)	finely chopped fresh parsley
5 mL	(1 tsp.)	salt
3 mL	(1/2 tsp.)	garlic powder
45 mL	(3 Tbsp.)	whole wheat flour

Method:

MIX all ingredients together. For each pancake, BRUSH a cookie sheet with oil or spray and HEAT oven to 350° F. SPOON about 3/4 cup of the potato mixture into mounds on the cookie sheet and FLATTEN to 1/2 inch thick. BAKE until done enough to turn and then BAKE on the other side. SERVE hot with applesauce or creamed peas.

```
Analysis: POTATO-TOFU PANCAKES                    Divided by: 8
          Wgt: 192 g (6.77 oz.)                   Water:    76%
```

Calories	180	Vitamin C	13.8 mg
Protein	7.99 g	Vitamin D	0 mcg
Carbohydrates	32.4 g	Vit E-Alpha E	.169 mg
Fat - Total	2.99 g	Vitamin K	mcg
Saturated Fat	.45 g	Biotin	mcg
Mono Fat	.627 g	Calcium	83.3 mg
Poly Fat	1.65 g	Copper	.37 mg
Cholesterol	0 mg	Iodine	mcg
Dietary Fibre	2.84 g	Iron	3.99 mg
Soluble Fibre	.635 g	Magnesium	63.7 mg
Total Vit A	15.1 RE	Manganese	.701 mg
Thiamin-B1	.205 mg	Phosphorus	132 mg
Riboflavin-B2	.07 mg	Potassium	571 mg
Niacin-B3	2.12 mg	Selenium	3.92 mcg
Niacin Equiv.	2.13 mg	Sodium	279 mg
Vitamin B6	.462 mg	Zinc	1.01 mg
Vitamin B12	0 mcg	Complex Carbs	26.2 g
Folate	29.2 mcg	Sugars	1.96 g
Pantothenic	.804 mg	Water	146 g

CALORIE BREAKDOWN		FAT		EXCHANGES	
Protein	17%	*Saturated:	2.2%	Lean Meat	.75
Carbohydrates	69%	Mono Unsat:	3 %	Vegetables	.277
Fat-Total *	14%	Poly Unsat:	7.9%		

GAME OF LIFE:

In the game of life, you are the coach. Your are ultimately responsible for your health. Hans Diehl, *To Your Health*, page 65.

WAFFLES PERFECT (makes 4 large waffles)

250 mL	(1 cup)		water
10 mL	(2 tsp.)		vanilla
5	(5)		pitted dates
45 mL	(3 Tbsp.)		almond meal
500 mL	(2 cups)		rolled oats
180 mL	(3/4 cup)	**EACH**	millet flour **and** corn meal
5 mL	(1 tsp.)		salt
750 mL	(3 cups)		water

Method:

If the dates are hard, **SOAK** them in one cup of water until they are soft. **WHIZ** in the blender or food processor until well blended. **ADD** remaining ingredients (if all the water will fit) and **BLEND** again. **COAT** waffle iron with lecithin-oil mixture and **HEAT**. **POUR** batter in, being sure to go all the way to the edges. **BAKE** for 12 minutes or until it stops steaming. If batter gets too thick **ADD** more water and **BLEND** before pouring the next waffle. May be frozen and reheated in toaster or oven. **SERVE** with apple sauce and peanut butter, apple or pineapple marmalade, strawberry jam, sliced bananas, or other fruit.

```
------------------------------------------------------------------
| Analysis: WAFFLES PERFECT                   Divided by:  8      |
|           Wgt: 88.5 g (3.12 oz.)            Water:      41%     |
------------------------------------------------------------------
```

Calories	215		Vitamin C	.491 mg
Protein	6.69 g		Vitamin D	0 mcg
Carbohydrates	39.6 g		Vit E-Alpha E	.336 mg
Fat - Total	3.72 g		Vitamin K	mcg
Saturated Fat	.415 g		Biotin	mcg
Mono Fat	1.49 g		Calcium	25.3 mg
Poly Fat	.893 g		Copper	.125 mg
Cholesterol	0 mg		Iodine	mcg
Dietary Fibre	3.82 g		Iron	1.56 mg
Soluble Fibre	1.29 g		Magnesium	46.2 mg
Total Vit A	7.59 RE		Manganese	.834 mg
Thiamin-B1	.296 mg		Phosphorus	169 mg
Riboflavin-B2	.144 mg		Potassium	148 mg
Niacin-B3	1.3 mg		Selenium	6.62 mcg
Niacin Equiv.	1.03 mg		Sodium	202 mg
Vitamin B6	.071 mg		Zinc	.831 mg
Vitamin B12	0 mcg		Complex Carbs	20.6 g
Folate	15.1 mcg		Sugars	3.89 g
Pantothenic	.348 mg		Water	36.6 g

CALORIE BREAKDOWN		FAT		EXCHANGES	
Protein	12%	*Saturated :	1.7%	Bread	1.28
Carbohydrates	72%	Mono Unsat:	6.1%	Lean Meat	.086
Fat-Total *	15%	Poly Unsat:	3.7%	Fruit	.3
				Fat	.285

ALMOND CRUNCH GRANOLA (makes 12 cups - 24 half-cup servings)

250 mL	(1 cup)		boiling water
250 mL	(1 cup)		chopped dates
750 mL	(3 cups)		cored and shredded apples
5 mL	(1 tsp.)		vanilla
3 mL	(1/2 tsp.)		salt
125 mL	(1/2 cup)	**EACH**	almond meal, slivered almonds, **and** corn meal
250 mL	(1 cup)		chopped walnuts or sunflower seeds
250 mL	(1 cup)		barley flakes
2 L	(8 cups)		large flake oats

Method:
SIMMER dates and apples in the water until tender. **WHIZ** date mixture with salt and vanilla in blender. **PLACE** remaining ingredients in a large bowl. **MIX** all ingredients well. **SPREAD** on cookie sheets and **PLACE** in oven. **TURN** temperature control just until light comes on (less than 150° F.) **LEAVE** overnight. The next morning the granola will be cooked.

```
Analysis: Almond Crunch Granola              Divided by: 24
          Wgt: 75.4 g (2.66 oz.)             Water:      35%
```

Calories	222	Vitamin C	.977 mg
Protein	7.13 g	Vitamin D	0 mcg
Carbohydrates	32.3 g	Vit E-Alpha E	.748 mg
Fat - Total	8.08 g	Vitamin K	mcg
Saturated Fat	.924 g	Biotin	mcg
Mono Fat	3.24 g	Calcium	39.2 mg
Poly Fat	3.31 g	Copper	.257 mg
Cholesterol	0 mg	Iodine	mcg
Dietary Fibre	5.06 g	Iron	1.83 mg
Soluble Fibre	1.8 g	Magnesium	74.3 mg
Total Vit A	5.9 RE	Manganese	1.41 mg
Thiamin-B1	.282 mg	Phosphorus	195 mg
Riboflavin-B2	.115 mg	Potassium	241 mg
Niacin-B3	.797 mg	Selenium	9.12 mcg
Niacin Equiv.	.799 mg	Sodium	47.3 mg
Vitamin B6	.099 mg	Zinc	1.29 mg
Vitamin B12	0 mcg	Complex Carbs	19.5 g
Folate	19 mcg	Sugars	7.56 g
Pantothenic	.512 mg	Water	26.7 g

CALORIE BREAKDOWN		FATS		EXCHANGES	
Protein	12%	*Saturated :	3.6%	Bread	1.25
Carbohydrates	56%	Mono Unsat:	12.7%	Lean Meat	.159
Fat-Total *	32%	Poly Unsat:	12.9%	Fat	.454

MALT GRANOLA (makes 14 half-cup servings)

125 mL	(1/2 cup)		sesame seeds (whizzed to butter)
125 mL	(1/2 cup)		peanut butter
60 mL	(1/4 cup)		liquid barley malt (available at health food stores)
125 mL	(1/2 cup)		date butter (equal amounts of water and dates, softened)
15 mL	(1 Tbsp.)		vanilla
7 mL	(1 1/4 tsp.)		salt
250 mL	(1 cup)	EACH	boiling water and wheat germ
1250 mL	(5 cups)		large flake rolled oats
750 mL	(3 cups)		barley flakes
500 mL	(2 cups)		dry whole wheat bread crumbs
125 mL	(1/2 cup)	EACH	unsweetened dry coconut and slivered almonds
60 mL	(1/4 cup)		sunflower seeds

Method:

WHIZ sesame seeds in the food processor until a smooth paste. ADD peanut butter, malt, date butter, vanilla, salt, and boiling water. BLEND well. PLACE remaining ingredients in a large bowl. MIX well. ADD contents of food processor. RINSE food processor with a little water. ADD to mixture in the bowl. MIX well with your hands. SPREAD onto cookie sheets. BAKE by placing in oven that has the heat turned on at a very low setting. LEAVE overnight. In the morning it will be done.

```
-------------------------------------------------------------------
| Analysis: MALT GRANOLA                      Divided by: 24       |
|           Wgt: 68.4 g (2.41 oz.)            Water:      27%      |
-------------------------------------------------------------------
```

Calories	223		Vitamin C	.087 mg
Protein	8.27 g		Vitamin D	.03 mcg
Carbohydrates	32.4 g		Vit E-Alpha Eq	2.1 mg
Fat - Total	7.42 g		Vitamin K	mcg
Saturated Fat	1.46 g		Biotin	mcg
Mono Fat	2.8 g		Calcium	43.4 mg
Poly Fat	2.62 g		Copper	.227 mg
Cholesterol	0 mg		Iodine	mcg
Dietary Fibre	4.52 g		Iron	2.2 mg
Soluble Fibre	1.27 g		Magnesium	70.6 mg
Total Vit A	2.7 RE		Manganese	1.64 mg
Thiamin-B1	.291 mg		Phosphorus	216 mg
Riboflavin-B2	.106 mg		Potassium	225 mg
Niacin-B3	1.94 mg		Selenium	13.7 mcg
Niacin Equiv.	1.89 mg		Sodium	278 mg
Vitamin B6	.118 mg		Zinc	1.75 mg
Vitamin B12	.002 mcg		Complex Carbs	21.5 g
Folate	24.9 mcg		Sugars	4.56 g
Pantothenic	.506 mg		Water	18.4 g

CALORIE BREAKDOWN		FAT	EXCHANGES	
Protein	14%	*Saturated : 5.7%	Bread	1.79
Carbohydrates	56%	Mono Unsat: 11 %	Lean Meat	.23
Fat-Total *	29%	Poly Unsat: 10.3%	Fruit	.289
			Fat	.867

YUMMY GRANOLA (makes 15 cups)

250 mL	(1 cup)	pitted dates
250 mL	(1 cup)	water
3	(3)	ripe bananas
2250 mL	(9 cups)	rolled oats (may use partly rolled barley or rolled rye)
250 mL	(1 cup)	wheat bran
125 mL	(1/2 cup)	sunflower seeds
60 mL	(1/4 cup)	unsweetened coconut
60 mL	(1/4 cup)	walnuts
60 mL	(1/4 cup)	sesame seeds
7 mL	(1 1/2 tsp.)	salt

Method:

COMBINE dry ingredients in large bowl. SOFTEN dates by soaking in the water or by putting in microwave oven for a minute. WHIZ dates with the water and bananas in blender or food processor. STIR liquid ingredients into dry ingredients and MIX well. SPREAD on cookie sheets. PLACE pan in oven on lowest setting (less than 175° F.). LEAVE overnight. In the morning the granola is perfect with no stirring needed. STORE in an airtight container.

```
Analysis: YUMMY GRANOLA                    Divided by: 24
          Wgt: 66.1 g (2.33 oz.)           Water:      31%
```

Calories	194		Vitamin C	1.39 mg
Protein	6.81 g		Vitamin D	0 mcg
Carbohydrates	31.6 g		Vit E-Alpha Eq	1.9 mg
Fat - Total	5.74 g		Vitamin K	mcg
Saturated Fat	1.2 g		Biotin	mcg
Mono Fat	1.43 g		Calcium	27.8 mg
Poly Fat	2.61 g		Copper	.263 mg
Cholesterol	0 mg		Iodine	mcg
Dietary Fibre	5.53 g		Iron	2.04 mg
Soluble Fibre	1.71 g		Magnesium	85.3 mg
Total Vit A	4.63 RE		Manganese	1.56 mg
Thiamin-B1	.286 mg		Phosphorus	212 mg
Riboflavin-B2	.085 mg		Potassium	277 mg
Niacin-B3	1.02 mg		Selenium	12.6 mcg
Niacin Equiv.	1.02 mg		Sodium	136 mg
Vitamin B6	.196 mg		Zinc	1.51 mg
Vitamin B12	0 mcg		Complex Carbs	17.7 g
Folate	21.6 mcg		Sugars	8.34 g
Pantothenic	.66 mg		Water	20.4 g

CALORIE BREAKDOWN		FAT		EXCHANGES	
Protein	13%	*Saturated :	5.3%	Bread	1.51
Carbohydrates	62%	Mono Unsat:	6.3%	Lean Meat	.111
Fat-Total *	25%	Poly Unsat:	11.5%	Fruit	.886
				Fat	.46

BEAN-RICE SALAD (makes 12 half-cup servings)

500 mL	(2 cups)	cooked brown rice
500 mL	(2 cups)	cooked kidney beans **or** pinto beans
250 mL	(1 cup)	cooked fresh **or** frozen corn
125 mL	(1/2 cup)	sliced onions
75 mL	(1/3 cup)	red sweet pepper, cut into strips
3 mL	(1/2 tsp.)	salt or to taste
5 mL	(1 tsp.)	cumin
125 mL	(1/2 cup)	tomato sauce
15 mL	(1 Tbsp.)	lemon juice

Method:
     TOSS all ingredients together and **CHILL.**
Serving Suggestion: **SERVE** for lunch or supper with whole grain bread.

```
Analysis: BEAN-RICE SALAD                      Divided by: 12
          Wgt: 96.7 g (3.41 oz.)               Water:      74%
```

Calories	95.5		Vitamin C	5.79 mg
Protein	4.11 g		Vitamin D	0 mcg
Carbohydrates	19.3 g		Vit E-Alpha E	.427 mg
Fat - Total	.688 g		Vitamin K	mcg
Saturated Fat	.112 g		Biotin	mcg
Mono Fat	.174 g		Calcium	16.5 mg
Poly Fat	.283 g		Copper	.139 mg
Cholesterol	0 mg		Iodine	mcg
Dietary Fibre	4.1 g		Iron	1.3 mg
Soluble Fibre	1.27 g		Magnesium	35.3 mg
Total Vit A	15 RE		Manganese	.501 mg
Thiamin-B1	.12 mg		Phosphorus	89.6 mg
Riboflavin-B2	.044 mg		Potassium	224 mg
Niacin-B3	1.04 mg		Selenium	5.21 mcg
Niacin Equiv.	1.04 mg		Sodium	96.3 mg
Vitamin B6	.121 mg		Zinc	.636 mg
Vitamin B12	0 mcg		Complex Carbs	13.1 g
Folate	48.6 mcg		Sugars	2.1 g
Pantothenic	.319 mg		Water	71.6 g

CALORIE BREAKDOWN		FAT		EXCHANGES	
Protein	16%	*Saturated :	1 %	Bread	1.07
Carbohydrates	77%	Mono Unsat:	1.6%	Fruit	.005
Fat-Total *	6%	Poly Unsat:	2.6%	Vegetables	.233

BEAN-ZUCCHINI SALAD (makes 4 one-cup servings)

500 mL	(2 cups)	sliced yellow beans
500 mL	(2 cups)	sliced green beans
250 mL	(1 cup)	chopped celery
250 mL	(1 cup)	chopped zucchini
60 mL	(1/4 cup)	finely chopped green onions
15 mL	(1 Tbsp.)	chopped green or red sweet pepper
60 mL	(1/4 cup)	chopped tomato
1	(1)	small garlic clove, minced
3 mL	(1/2 tsp.)	salt
75 mL	(1/3 cup)	lemon juice
30 mL	(2 Tbsp.)	olive oil
10 mL	(2 tsp.)	honey
1 mL	(1/4 tsp.)	oregano
1 mL	(1/4 tsp.)	basil

Method:

BLANCH beans for one minute in boiling water; DRAIN and RINSE with cold water. In serving bowl COMBINE all ingredients and TOSS to mix. REFRIGERATE 1 hour or until serving. (Will keep up to a week)

```
----------------------------------------------------------------------
| Analysis: BEAN-ZUCCHINI SALAD                    Divided by: 6      |
|           Wgt: 148 g (5.21 oz.)                  Water:      88%    |
----------------------------------------------------------------------
```

Calories	82.9		Vitamin C	24.2 mg
Protein	1.97 g		Vitamin D	0 mcg
Carbohydrates	10.5 g		Vit E-Alpha E	.877 mg
Fat - Total	4.71 g		Vitamin K	mcg
Saturated Fat	.653 g		Biotin	mcg
Mono Fat	3.33 g		Calcium	45.8 mg
Poly Fat	.482 g		Copper	.089 mg
Cholesterol	0 mg		Iodine	mcg
Dietary Fibre	2.86 g		Iron	1.12 mg
Soluble Fibre	.795 g		Magnesium	28.5 mg
Total Vit A	46.8 RE		Manganese	.233 mg
Thiamin-B1	.098 mg		Phosphorus	45 mg
Riboflavin-B2	.103 mg		Potassium	314 mg
Niacin-B3	.802 mg		Selenium	1.43 mcg
Niacin Equiv.	.802 mg		Sodium	202 mg
Vitamin B6	.112 mg		Zinc	.295 mg
Vitamin B12	0 mcg		Complex Carbs	1.79 g
Folate	42.8 mcg		Sugars	5.82 g
Pantothenic	.162 mg		Water	129 g

CALORIE BREAKDOWN		FAT		EXCHANGES	
Protein	9%	*Saturated :	6.4%	Fruit	.161
Carbohydrates	45%	Mono Unsat:	32.5%	Vegetables	1.06
Fat-Total *	46%	Poly Unsat:	4.7%	Fat	.873

BEET SALAD- 1 (Makes 4 servings)

1 L	(4 cups)	coarsely shredded raw beets
60 mL	(1/4 cup)	water
3 mL	(1/2 tsp.)	salt
60 mL	(1/4 cup)	orange juice concentrate
125 mL	(1/2 cup)	finely chopped green onion
125 mL	(1/2 cup)	finely sliced celery

Method:

PEEL beets and SHRED. (Wear gloves so you won't stain your hands) BRING water to boil. ADD beets to boiling water. REDUCE heat and SIMMER about 10 minutes. STIR in salt orange juice, onion, and celery. SERVE hot or cold. (May use carrots or turnips the same way.)

```
-----------------------------------------------------------------
| Analysis: BEET SALAD -1                    Divided by: 8      |
|           Wgt: 115 g (4.04 oz.)            Water:     87%     |
-----------------------------------------------------------------
```

Calories	49.2	Vitamin C	10.1 mg
Protein	1.71 g	Vitamin D	0 mcg
Carbohydrates	11.2 g	Vit E-Alpha E	.309 mg
Fat - Total	.188 g	Vitamin K	mcg
Saturated Fat	.03 g	Biotin	mcg
Mono Fat	.036 g	Calcium	20.3 mg
Poly Fat	.067 g	Copper	.079 mg
Cholesterol	0 mg	Iodine	mcg
Dietary Fibre	2.35 g	Iron	.74 mg
Soluble Fibre	.746 g	Magnesium	23.1 mg
Total Vit A	5.57 RE	Manganese	.301 mg
Thiamin-B1	.043 mg	Phosphorus	39.9 mg
Riboflavin-B2	.042 mg	Potassium	325 mg
Niacin-B3	.351 mg	Selenium	.705 mcg
Niacin Equiv.	.351 mg	Sodium	206 mg
Vitamin B6	.082 mg	Zinc	.338 mg
Vitamin B12	0 mcg	Complex Carbs	.417 g
Folate	78.6 mcg	Sugars	8.47 g
Pantothenic	.171 mg	Water	100 g

CALORIE BREAKDOWN		FAT		EXCHANGES
Protein	13%	*Saturated :	.5%	Vegetables 1.7
Carbohydrates	84%	Mono Unsat:	.6%	P:S ratio 2.2 : 1
Fat-Total *	3%	Poly Unsat:	1.1%	

BEET SALAD- 2 (makes 10 servings)

1 L	(4 cups)	cooked beets (shredded or cubed)
125 mL	(1/2 cup)	finely chopped green onion
125 mL	(1/2 cup)	finely sliced celery
3 mL	(1/2 tsp.)	salt
180 mL	(3/4 cup)	GARLIC-DILL DRESSING

Method:

COMBINE all ingredients and CHILL.

```
Analysis: BEET SALAD -2                    Divided by: 10
          Wgt: 96.2 g (3.39 oz.)           Water:      87%
```

Calories	43.3		Vitamin C	4 mg
Protein	2.23 g		Vitamin D	0 mcg
Carbohydrates	8.11 g		Vit E-Alpha E	.625 mg
Fat - Total	.694 g		Vitamin K	mcg
Saturated Fat	.103 g		Biotin	mcg
Mono Fat	.147 g		Calcium	28 mg
Poly Fat	.361 g		Copper	.081 mg
Cholesterol	0 mg		Iodine	mcg
Dietary Fibre	2 g		Iron	1.2 mg
Soluble Fibre	.589 g		Magnesium	29.2 mg
Total Vit A	4.57 RE		Manganese	.239 mg
Thiamin-B1	.035 mg		Phosphorus	41.6 mg
Riboflavin-B2	.038 mg		Potassium	254 mg
Niacin-B3	.284 mg		Selenium	.75 mcg
Niacin Equiv.	.256 mg		Sodium	219 mg
Vitamin B6	.069 mg		Zinc	.358 mg
Vitamin B12	0 mcg		Complex Carbs	.333 g
Folate	59.5 mcg		Sugars	5.5 g
Pantothenic	.129 mg		Water	83.9 g

CALORIE BREAKDOWN		FAT		EXCHANGES
Protein	19%	*Saturated :	1.9%	Vegetables 1.36
Carbohydrates	68%	Mono Unsat:	2.8%	
Fat-Total *	13%	Poly Unsat:	6.8%	

THE NEW FOUR FOOD GROUPS (Physicians Committee for Responsible Medicine)

FOOD GROUP	NUMBER OF SERVINGS	SERVING SIZE
WHOLE GRAINS	5 or more	1/2 cup hot cereal
		1 oz. dry cereal
		1 slice whole grain bread
VEGETABLES	3 or more	1 cup raw
		1/2 cup cooked
LEGUMES	2 to 3	1/2 cup cooked beans
		4 oz. tofu
		8 oz. soy milk
FRUITS	3 or more	1 medium piece of fruit
		1/2 cup cooked fruit
		1/2 cup fruit juice

BULGUR AND SPLIT PEA SALAD (makes 8 half-cup servings)

200 mL	(3/4 cup)	dry, yellow, split peas
1	(1)	large garlic clove, minced
5 mL	(1 tsp.)	salt
500 mL	(2 cups)	water
180 mL	(3/4 cup)	bulgur wheat
180 mL	(3/4 cup)	tofu, well-drained and cut into small cubes
250 mL	(1 cup)	alfalfa sprouts
125 mL	(1/2 cup)	chopped green pepper
60 mL	(1/4 cup)	lemon juice, preferably fresh
5 mL	(1 tsp.)	crushed, dried basil
10 mL	(2 tsp.)	chicken style seasoning

Method:

RINSE peas and ADD water. BRING to a boil and SIMMER 25 to 30 minutes or until peas are tender. ADD garlic and salt (May need to add a little water.) COVER bulgur with hot water and LET stand until water is absorbed. COMBINE cooked peas, bulgur, and remaining ingredients. COVER and CHILL. MOUND the chilled salad on a large glass plate. DECORATE with cherry tomatoes, and green pepper strips.

```
------------------------------------------------------------------------
| Analysis: BULGUR  AND SPLIT PEA SALAD            Divided by: 8       |
|           Wgt: 134 g (4.74 oz.)                  Water:     74%      |
------------------------------------------------------------------------
```

Calories	134		Vitamin C	10 mg
Protein	8.35 g		Vitamin D	0 mcg
Carbohydrates	23.4 g		Vit E-Alpha E	.307 mg
Fat - Total	1.59 g		Vitamin K	mcg
Saturated Fat	.229 g		Biotin	mcg
Mono Fat	.317 g		Calcium	47.7 mg
Poly Fat	.821 g		Copper	.269 mg
Cholesterol	0 mg		Iodine	mcg
Dietary Fibre	5.63 g		Iron	2.55 mg
Soluble Fibre	1.36 g		Magnesium	70.4 mg
Total Vit A	11.4 RE		Manganese	.827 mg
Thiamin-B1	.194 mg		Phosphorus	135 mg
Riboflavin-B2	.076 mg		Potassium	295 mg
Niacin-B3	1.32 mg		Selenium	8.35 mcg
Niacin Equiv.	1.33 mg		Sodium	275 mg
Vitamin B6	.113 mg		Zinc	1.08 mg
Vitamin B12	0 mcg		Complex Carbs	14.7 g
Folate	61.5 mcg		Sugars	2.55 g
Pantothenic	.516 mg		Water	98.8 g

CALORIE BREAKDOWN		FAT		EXCHANGES	
Protein	24%	*Saturated :	1.5%	Bread	1.15
Carbohydrates	66%	Mono Unsat:	2 %	Lean Meat	.418
Fat-Total *	10%	Poly Unsat:	5.2%	Fruit	.031
				Vegetables	.24
				Fat	.094

CARROT SALAD (makes 4 cups - 6 two-third-cup servings)

750 mL	(3 cups)	grated raw carrots
125 mL	(1/2 cup)	thinly sliced celery
125 mL	(1/2 cup)	unsweetened pineapple chunks
60 mL	(1/4 cup)	raisins
45 mL	(3 Tbsp.)	orange juice
1 mL	(1/4 tsp.)	salt

Method:

    MIX all ingredients. **CHILL**. (It is better the next day.)

```
-----------------------------------------------------------------
| Analysis: CARROT SALAD                        Divided by:  6   |
|       Wgt: 96.4 g (3.4 oz.)                   Water: 82%       |
-----------------------------------------------------------------
```

Calories	62.7		Vitamin C	13.9 mg
Protein	1.03 g		Vitamin D	0 mcg
Carbohydrates	15.6 g		Vit E-Alpha E	.366 mg
Fat - Total	.172 g		Vitamin K	mcg
Saturated Fat	.032 g		Biotin	mcg
Mono Fat	.011 g		Calcium	26.1 mg
Poly Fat	.065 g		Copper	.073 mg
Cholesterol	0 mg		Iodine	mcg
Dietary Fibre	2.42 g		Iron	.514 mg
Soluble Fibre	.889 g		Magnesium	15.8 mg
Total Vit A	1549 RE		Manganese	.342 mg
Thiamin-B1	.099 mg		Phosphorus	36.2 mg
Riboflavin-B2	.049 mg		Potassium	305 mg
Niacin-B3	.682 mg		Selenium	1.56 mcg
Niacin Equiv.	.682 mg		Sodium	118 mg
Vitamin B6	.127 mg		Zinc	.169 mg
Vitamin B12	0 mcg		Complex Carbs	.27 g
Folate	18.3 mcg		Sugars	12.9 g
Pantothenic	.174 mg		Water	78.5 g

CALORIE BREAKDOWN		FAT	EXCHANGES	
Protein	6%	Saturated : .4%	Fruit	.62
Carbohydrates	92%	Mono Unsat: .2%	Vegetables	.82
Fat - Total *	2%	Poly Unsat: .9%		

BARLEY, POT AND PEARL:

    Most of the barley used for human food in North America is in the form of whole kernel from which the outer hull or husk and part of the aleurone layer (the bran layer) have been removed. Different types of machines provide scouring or abrasive actions, called pealing, to remove the indigestible hull and all or part of the bran layer. After three successive pearlings, all of the hull and most of the bran are removed; the remaining kernel part is known as **POT BARLEY.** The remaining kernel after 2 to 3 additional pearlings beyond the pot barley stage, followed by sizing--small round, white grains of uniform size, from which most of the embryo has been removed is **PEARL BARLEY.** (*Foods and Nutrition Encyclopedia Vol 1*, p. 161-164.)

COLD PEA SALAD (makes six 3/4-cup servings)

500 mL	(2 cups)	frozen peas, partially thawed
75 mL	(1/3 cup)	finely sliced celery
60 mL	(1/4 cup)	finely minced onion
250 mL	(1 cup)	diced tomatoes
2 mL	(1/4 tsp.)	salt
30 mL	(2 Tbsp.)	GARLIC-DILL DRESSING (page 112)

Method:

MAY thaw peas by placing them in a sieve and running warm water over them briefly.
ADD remaining ingredients. **MIX** and **SERVE.**

```
-----------------------------------------------------------------------
| Analysis: COLD PEA SALAD (6 SERVINGS)          Divided by: 6        |
|           Wgt: 102 g (3.61 oz.)                Water:      86%      |
-----------------------------------------------------------------------
```

Calories	50.5		Vitamin C	15.9	mg
Protein	3.19	g	Vitamin D	0	mcg
Carbohydrates	9.15	g	Vit E-Alpha E	.519	mg
Fat - Total	.459	g	Vitamin K		mcg
Saturated Fat	.075	g	Biotin		mcg
Mono Fat	.07	g	Calcium	22.5	mg
Poly Fat	.223	g	Copper	.096	mg
Cholesterol	0	mg	Iodine		mcg
Dietary Fibre	3.15	g	Iron	1.11	mg
Soluble Fibre	.431	g	Magnesium	20.9	mg
Total Vit A	55.8	RE	Manganese	.217	mg
Thiamin-B1	.154	mg	Phosphorus	54.4	mg
Riboflavin-B2	.071	mg	Potassium	192	mg
Niacin-B3	1.07	mg	Selenium	5.95	mcg
Niacin Equiv.	1.06	mg	Sodium	261	mg
Vitamin B6	.104	mg	Zinc	.474	mg
Vitamin B12	0	mcg	Complex Carbs	1.96	g
Folate	35.5	mcg	Sugars	3.96	g
Pantothenic	.175	mg	Water	88.4	g

CALORIE BREAKDOWN		FAT	EXCHANGES
Protein	24%	*Saturated : 1.3%	Bread .456
Carbohydrates	68%	Mono Unsat: 1.2%	Vegetables .4
Fat-Total *	8%	Poly Unsat: 3.8%	

COLE SLAW (makes 4 servings)

250 mL	(1 cup)	Chinese cabbage
1 L	(4 cups)	shredded cabbage
125 mL	(1/2 cup)	thinly sliced celery
60 mL	(1/4 cup)	green onions (use tops too)
3 mL	(1/2 tsp.)	salt
180 mL	(3/4 cup)	GARLIC-DILL DRESSING (page 112)
5 mL	(1 tsp.)	honey (optional)

Method:

COMBINE all ingredients. GARNISH with shredded carrots, pepper rings, parsley or USE your own imagination.

Analysis: COLE SLAW (1/4 RECIPE)   Divided by: 4
        Wgt: 140g (4.92 oz..)   Water: 89%

Calories	52.2	Vitamin C	29.1 mg
Protein	3.82 g	Vitamin D	0 mcg
Carbohydrates	7.66 g	Vit E-Alpha E	2.21 mg
Fat - Total	1.6 g	Vitamin K	mcg
Saturated Fat	.229 g	Biotin	mcg
Mono Fat	.319 g	Calcium	80.9 mg
Poly Fat	.871 g	Copper	.086 mg
Cholesterol	0 mg	Iodine	mcg
Dietary Fibre	2.03 g	Iron	2.2 mg
Soluble Fibre	.62 g	Magnesium	45.2 mg
Total Vit A	16.2 RE	Manganese	.138 mg
Thiamin-B1	.076 mg	Phosphorus	55.6 mg
Riboflavin-B2	.06 mg	Potassium	305 mg
Niacin-B3	.429 mg	Selenium	2.53 mcg
Niacin Equiv.	.294 mg	Sodium	432 mg
Vitamin B6	.105 mg	Zinc	.415 mg
Vitamin B12	0 mcg	Complex Carbs	.364 g
Folate	52.3 mcg	Sugars	4.32 g
Pantothenic	.159 mg	Water	125 g

CALORIE BREAKDOWN		FAT	EXCHANGES
Protein	25%	* Saturated: 3.4%	Fruit .083
Carbohydrates	51%	Mono Unsat: 4.8%	Vegetables .894
Fat-Total *	24%	Poly Unsat: 13%	

CRANBERRY-ORANGE RELISH (makes about 24 servings)

340 gm	(12 ounces)	fresh or frozen cranberries
1	(1)	orange
15 mL	(1 Tbsp.)	orange rind
2	(2)	medium apples, (washed and cored, and diced or grated)
375 mL	(1 1/2 cups)	date pieces, softened in water

Method:

   CHOP all ingredients in food processor or grinder. **REFRIGERATE.**

```
------------------------------------------------------------------------------
| Analysis: CRANBERRY ORANGE RELISH (1 TBSP SERVING) Divided by: 24           |
|           Wgt: 43.3 g (1.53 oz.)                    Water:       69%        |
------------------------------------------------------------------------------
```

Calories	47.5		Vitamin C	5.74 mg
Protein	.344 g		Vitamin D	0 mcg
Carbohydrates	12.5 g		Vit E-Alpha E	.109 mg
Fat - Total	.134 g		Vitamin K	mcg
Saturated Fat	.034 g		Biotin	mcg
Mono Fat	.027 g		Calcium	8.47 mg
Poly Fat	.034 g		Copper	.048 mg
Cholesterol	0 mg		Iodine	mcg
Dietary Fibre	1.94 g		Iron	.185 mg
Soluble Fibre	.605 g		Magnesium	5.86 mg
Total Vit A	3.2 RE		Manganese	.062 mg
Thiamin-B1	.023 mg		Phosphorus	7.34 mg
Riboflavin-B2	.018 mg		Potassium	107 mg
Niacin-B3	.295 mg		Selenium	.314 mcg
Niacin Equiv.	.295 mg		Sodium	.483 mg
Vitamin B6	.04 mg		Zinc	.061 mg
Vitamin B12	0 mcg		Complex Carbs	.055 g
Folate	3.13 mcg		Sugars	10.5 g
Pantothenic	.142 mg		Water	30.1 g

CALORIE BREAKDOWN		FAT		EXCHANGES	
Protein	3%	*Saturated :	.6%	Fruit	.902
Carbohydrates	95%	Mono Unsat:	.5%		
Fat-Total *	2%	Poly Unsat:	.6%		

OSTEOPOROSIS:

   Osteoporosis is caused, **NOT** from a lack of calcium, but from a surplus of protein. The question is not, "Where is the calcium coming from:" The question is, "Where is the calcium going?" (It is going into the toilet in the urine because of calcium leaching habits of protein, especially animal protein.)

   The uncontrollable risk factors are age, family history of osteoporosis, Caucasian race, menopause (due to insufficient estrogon levels.)

   The lifestyle factors include an excess of protein in the diet, excess phosphorus (as in soda pop), lack of sufficient exercise, low body fat (underweight), heavy smoking, lean build and small bone frame, low calcium intake over a long time, moderate use of alcohol, use of aluminum-containing antacids, other dietary factors, including caffeine, and amenorrhea.   Winston Craig PhD., R.D. *Nutrition for the Nineties*, pages 133-134.

CRANBERRY STRAWBERRY MOULD (makes 12 servings)

355 mL	(12 oz)	frozen apple juice concentrate
250 mL	(1 cup)	fresh or frozen cranberries
250 mL	(1 cup)	fresh or frozen whole strawberries
60 mL	(1/4 cup)	agar flakes or Emes Kosher jel

Method:

PLACE one half can of apple juice concentrate, cranberries, and strawberries in blender or food processor. **BLEND** until smooth. **POUR** blended berries and juice into saucepan. **ADD** remaining apple juice concentrate and the agar flakes. **BRING** to boil, **POUR** into mould and **CHILL**. (This is a good sauce to serve at Thanksgiving with BREAD DRESSING (page 6) or a vegetarian loaf (pages 49-55).

```
------------------------------------------------------------------------
| Analysis: CRANBERRY-STRAWBERRY MOULD           Divided by: 12        |
|           Wgt: 55.8 g (1.97 oz.)               Water:      68%       |
------------------------------------------------------------------------
```

Calories	67.5	Vitamin C	6.92 mg
Protein	.284 g	Vitamin D	0 mcg
Carbohydrates	16.8 g	Vit E-Alpha E	.059 mg
Fat - Total	.161 g	Vitamin K	mcg
Saturated Fat	.024 g	Biotin	mcg
Mono Fat	.012 g	Calcium	11.5 mg
Poly Fat	.054 g	Copper	.03 mg
Cholesterol	0 mg	Iodine	mcg
Dietary Fibre	.752 g	Iron	.496 mg
Soluble Fibre	.318 g	Magnesium	10.1 mg
Total Vit A	.998 RE	Manganese	.141 mg
Thiamin-B1	.009 mg	Phosphorus	11.3 mg
Riboflavin-B2	.026 mg	Potassium	185 mg
Niacin-B3	.113 mg	Selenium	.262 mcg
Niacin Equiv.	.113 mg	Sodium	9.45 mg
Vitamin B6	.05 mg	Zinc	.09 mg
Vitamin B12	0 mcg	Complex Carbs	.014 g
Folate	4.37 mcg	Sugars	15.8 g
Pantothenic	.119 mg	Water	38.1 g

CALORIE BREAKDOWN		FAT		EXCHANGES	
Protein	2%	* Saturated :	.3%	Fruit	1.16
Carbohydrates	96%	Mono Unsat:	.1%	Vegetables	.039
Fat-Total *	2%	Poly Unsat:	.7%		

FINNISH BEET SALAD (Rosolli) - (makes 18 half-cup servings)

750 mL	(3 cups) **EACH**	finely chopped cooked beets, carrots, **and** potatoes
250 mL	(1 cup)	finely chopped onion
5 mL	(1 tsp)	salt
125 mL	(1/2 cup)	olives

Method:

MIX all ingredients together and **GARNISH** with parsley. May **SERVE** with GARLIC-DILL DRESSING (page 112). Recipe: (Courtesy of Marjatta Aakko)

| Analysis: FINNISH BEET SALAD   Divided by: 18
| Wgt: 98.4 g (3.47 oz.)   Water: 85%

Calories	55.2	Vitamin C	4.43 mg
Protein	1.98 g	Vitamin D	0 mcg
Carbohydrates	10.6 g	Vit E-Alpha Eq	.58 mg
Fat - Total	.922 g	Vitamin K	mcg
Saturated Fat	.133 g	Biotin	mcg
Mono Fat	.4 g	Calcium	28 mg
Poly Fat	.309 g	Copper	.108 mg
Cholesterol	0 mg	Iodine	mcg
Dietary Fibre	1.97 g	Iron	1.01 mg
Soluble Fibre	.499 g	Magnesium	23.5 mg
Total Vit A	434 RE	Manganese	.236 mg
Thiamin-B1	.048 mg	Phosphorus	37.7 mg
Riboflavin-B2	.031 mg	Potassium	225 mg
Niacin-B3	.531 mg	Selenium	.961 mcg
Niacin Equiv.	.51 mg	Sodium	221 mg
Vitamin B6	.128 mg	Zinc	.315 mg
Vitamin B12	0 mcg	Complex Carbs	4.54 g
Folate	30.4 mcg	Sugars	3.93 g
Pantothenic	.213 mg	Water	83.7 g

CALORIE BREAKDOWN		FAT		EXCHANGES	
Protein	13%	* Saturated:	2%	Bread	.25
Carbohydrates	72%	Mono Unsat:	6.1%	Vegetables	.954
Fats-Total *	14%	Poly Unsat:	4.7%	Fat	.083

FINNISH COOKERY:

In the old days, the Finns lived largely on cereal grains and root vegetables in winter. In some of the rural districts they still do, but the revolution brought by canned and frozen foods, and by the rapid transportation that whisks food from Europe's southern countries to the frozen north, are changing the food habits of the Finns. Today, the gruels, porridges, dumplings, cereal puddings, and pancakes made from wheat, rye, barley, and oats are gradually giving way to a lighter diet; and carrots, turnips, and dried peas are used more imaginatively. Dried fruits are eaten very frequently and potatoes remain king of the table as in all of Scandinavia. The Finns eat them daily. The high vitamin content of potatoes is a safeguard of the nation's health. *Woman's Day Encyclopedia of Cookery - Vol. 8*, page 68.

FIVE BEAN SALAD (makes 10 servings)

500 mL	(2 cups)	**EACH** cooked, cut green beans and cooked garbanzos
500 mL	(2 cups)	cooked red kidney beans
250 mL	(1 cup)	cooked green lima beans
250 mL	(1 cup)	cooked, cut wax beans
125 mL	(1/2 cup)	finely sliced red onion
125 mL	(1/2 cup)	chopped celery
60 mL	(1/4 cup)	finely diced red pepper
45 mL	(3 Tbsp.)	honey
15 mL	(1 Tbsp.)	olive oil
75 mL	(1/3 cup)	fresh lemon juice
10 mL	(2 tsp.)	salt

Method:
COMBINE first 8 ingredients. **MAKE** dressing from the honey, oil, lemon juice and salt. **ADD** to mixture. Flavour improves if allowed to sit in refrigerator overnight. (This salad will keep in the refrigerator for a week.)

```
Analysis:  FIVE BEAN SALAD                    Divided by: 10
           Wgt: 156 g (5.51 oz.)              Water: 73%

        Calories        162        Vitamin C       13.3 mg
        Protein         7.7 g      Vitamin D          0 mcg
        Carbohydrates   29.1 g     Vit E-Alpha E   .489 mg
        Fat - Total     2.53 g     Vitamin K           mcg
        Saturated Fat   .328 g     Biotin              mcg
        Mono Fat        1.21 g     Calcium         50.9 mg
        Poly Fat        .662 g     Copper          .247 mg
        Cholesterol       0 mg     Iodine              mcg
        Dietary Fibre   7.41 g     Iron            2.65 mg
        Soluble Fibre   2.64 g     Magnesium       47.5 mg
        Total Vit A     35.3 RE    Manganese       .712 mg
        Thiamin-B1      .132 mg    Phosphorus       130 mg
        Riboflavin-B2   .087 mg    Potassium        394 mg
        Niacin-B3       .761 mg    Selenium        2.86 mcg
        Niacin Equiv.   .761 mg    Sodium           483 mg
        Vitamin B6      .152 mg    Zinc            1.21 mg
        Vitamin B12       0 mcg    Complex Carbs     13 g
        Folate          116 mcg    Sugars          8.72 g
        Pantothenic     .262 mg    Water            114 g
```

CALORIE BREAKDOWN		FAT		EXCHANGES	
Protein	18%	*Saturated :	1.7%	Bread	1.31
Carbohydrates	68%	Mono Unsat:	6.4%	Lean Meat	.164
Fat-Total *	13%	Poly Unsat:	3.5%	Fruit	.33
				Vegetables	.63
				Fat	.262

GARBANZO SALAD (makes about 5 servings)

500 mL	(2 cups)	cooked garbanzos
250 mL	(1 cup)	thinly sliced celery
45 mL	(3 Tbsp.)	chopped pimento or red pepper
30 mL	(2 Tbsp.)	thinly sliced red onion
30 mL	(2 Tbsp.)	chopped parsley
75 mL	(1/3 cup)	GARLIC-DILL DRESSING (page 112)
15 mL	(1 Tbsp.)	fresh lemon juice
2 mL	(1/4 tsp.)	salt or to taste

Method:

MIX all ingredients. CHILL overnight. SERVE on lettuce leaves or endive. GARNISH with black olives or tomato.

```
Analysis: GARBANZO SALAD                      Divided by: 5
          Wgt: 117 g (4.11 oz.)               Water:     74%
```

Calories	123		Vitamin C	11.2 mg
Protein	6.99 g		Vitamin D	0 mcg
Carbohydrates	20.2 g		Vit E-Alpha E	.738 mg
Fat - Total	2.27 g		Vitamin K	mcg
Saturated Fat	.263 g		Biotin	mcg
Mono Fat	.499 g		Calcium	55.3 mg
Poly Fat	1.07 g		Copper	.266 mg
Cholesterol	0 mg		Iodine	mcg
Dietary Fibre	4.94 g		Iron	2.76 mg
Soluble Fibre	1.3 g		Magnesium	46.4 mg
Total Vit A	34.1 RE		Manganese	.715 mg
Thiamin-B1	.102 mg		Phosphorus	130 mg
Riboflavin-B2	.065 mg		Potassium	305 mg
Niacin-B3	.514 mg		Selenium	3.18 mcg
Niacin Equiv.	.49 mg		Sodium	182 mg
Vitamin B6	.145 mg		Zinc	1.15 mg
Vitamin B12	0 mcg		Complex Carbs	13.5 g
Folate	125 mcg		Sugars	1.5 g
Pantothenic	.254 mg		Water	85.8 g

CALORIE BREAKDOWN		FAT	EXCHANGES	
Protein	22%	*Saturated : 1.8%	Bread	1.15
Carbohydrates	63%	Mono Unsat: 3.5%	Lean Meat	.328
Fat-Total *	16%	Poly Unsat: 7.5%	Fruit	.021
			Vegetables	.25

GOLDEN POTATO SALAD (makes 6 servings)

1500 mL	(6 cups)		potatoes, cut into bite-sized pieces
250 mL	(1 cup)		water
3 mL	(1/2 tsp.)		salt
250 mL	(1 cup)	**EACH**	carrots, (peeled and sliced) **and** water
5 mL	(1 tsp.)		olive or canola oil
15 mL	(1 Tbsp.)		fresh lemon juice
3 mL	(1/2 tsp.)	**EACH**	rosemary **and** salt
1	(1)		clove of garlic, minced
125 mL	(1/2 cup)		GARLIC-DILL DRESSING (page 112)
250 mL	(1 cup)	**EACH**	finely chopped celery **and** minced green onion
			parsley

Method:

COMBINE the potatoes, water, and salt and **COOK** until potatoes are tender. **REMOVE** from heat, **DRAIN**, and **ALLOW** to cool. Meanwhile, in another pot **COOK** the carrots in 1 cup of water. **REMOVE** from heat, but do NOT drain. **ALLOW** to cool. Then **POUR** carrots, oil, lemon juice, rosemary, and GARLIC-DILL DRESSING into blender and **WHIZ** until smooth. Then **COMBINE** potatoes, carrot dressing, celery, and onion in a bowl and **MIX** well. **CHILL** thoroughly and **SERVE** garnished with parsley.

```
-------------------------------------------------------------------
| Analysis: GOLDEN POTATO SALAD              Divided by: 6        |
|            Wgt: 297 g (10.5 oz.)           Water:      86%      |
-------------------------------------------------------------------
```

Calories	155	Vitamin C	16.7 mg
Protein	4.13 g	Vitamin D	0 mcg
Carbohydrates	32.5 g	Vit E-Alpha E	.796 mg
Fat - Total	1.63 g	Vitamin K	mcg
Saturated Fat	.247 g	Biotin	mcg
Mono Fat	.701 g	Calcium	57.7 mg
Poly Fat	.517 g	Copper	.315 mg
Cholesterol	0 mg	Iodine	mcg
Dietary Fibre	3.82 g	Iron	1.65 mg
Soluble Fibre	.942 g	Magnesium	50.9 mg
Total Vit A	648 RE	Manganese	.444 mg
Thiamin-B1	.174 mg	Phosphorus	86.9 mg
Riboflavin-B2	.07 mg	Potassium	628 mg
Niacin-B3	2.09 mg	Selenium	2.55 mcg
Niacin Equiv.	2.06 mg	Sodium	552 mg
Vitamin B6	.471 mg	Zinc	.679 mg
Vitamin B12	0 mcg	Complex Carbs	25.8 g
Folate	34.3 mcg	Sugars	2.6 g
Pantothenic	.833 mg	Water	256 g

CALORIE BREAKDOWN		FAT		EXCHANGES	
Protein	10%	*Saturated :	1.4%	Bread	1.5
Carbohydrates	81%	Mono Unsat:	3.9%	Fruit	.01
Total-Total *	9%	Poly Unsat:	2.9%	Vegetables	.609
				Fat	.145

GREEK SALAD (makes about 8 servings)

60 mL	(1/4 cup)		olive oil
125 mL	(1/2 cup)		lemon juice
3 mL	(1/2 tsp.)		garlic powder
2 mL	(1/4 tsp.)		ground cumin
5 mL	(1 tsp.)		basil
3 mL	(1/2 tsp.)	EACH	oregano and dill weed (preferably fresh)
250 mL	(1 cup)		tofu, blanched and cubed
2	(2)		medium chopped tomatoes
2	(2)		medium thinly sliced cucumber
60 mL	(1/4 cup)		onion slices
15	(15)		pitted black olives
8	(8)		lettuce leaves

Method:

COMBINE the oil, lemon juice, garlic powder, cumin, basil, oregano, and dill weed. POUR over the cubed tofu. MARINATE overnight. STIR in tomatoes, cucumber, and onion slices. ARRANGE on lettuce leaves and GARNISH with the olives.

```
Analysis: GREEK SALAD                          Divided by: 8
          Wgt: 195 g (6.88 oz.)                Water:      89%
```

Calories	102	Vitamin C	20.9 mg
Protein	5.1 g	Vitamin D	0 mcg
Carbohydrates	8.12 g	Vit E-Alpha E	.957 mg
Fat - Total	6.69 g	Vitamin K	mcg
Saturated Fat	.935 g	Biotin	mcg
Mono Fat	3.64 g	Calcium	81.5 mg
Poly Fat	1.67 g	Copper	.188 mg
Cholesterol	0 mg	Iodine	mcg
Dietary Fibre	1.93 g	Iron	3.48 mg
Soluble Fibre	.333 g	Magnesium	40.4 mg
Total Vit A	60.6 RE	Manganese	.438 mg
Thiamin-B1	.099 mg	Phosphorus	79.6 mg
Riboflavin-B2	.072 mg	Potassium	334 mg
Niacin-B3	.625 mg	Selenium	9.54 mcg
Niacin Equiv.	.626 mg	Sodium	66 mg
Vitamin B6	.146 mg	Zinc	.666 mg
Vitamin B12	0 mcg	Complex Carbs	.437 g
Folate	37.4 mcg	Sugars	4.78 g
Pantothenic	.325 mg	Water	174 g

CALORIE BREAKDOWN		FAT		EXCHANGES	
Protein	18%	* Saturated : 7.4%		Bread	.05
Carbohydrates	29%	Mono Unsat: 28.9%		Lean Meat	.562
Fat-Total *	53%	Poly Unsat: 13.3%		Fruit	.062
				Vegetables	.763
				Fat	.842

HOT RICE SALAD (makes about 8 servings)

1 L	(4 cups)	warm, cooked brown rice
250 mL	(1 cup)	chopped tomato
60 mL	(1/4 cup)	chopped green pepper
250 mL	(1 cup)	shredded zucchini
250 mL	(1 cup)	chopped green onion
250 mL	(1 cup)	celery, thinly sliced
125 mL	(1/2 cup)	grated carrots
60 mL	(1/4 cup)	soy sauce
60 mL	(1/4 cup)	toasted sunflower seeds

Method:

COOK rice. ADD remaining ingredients except sunflower seeds. GARNISH with toasted sunflower seeds. SERVE warm.

```
Analysis: HOT RICE SALAD                    Divided by: 10
          Wgt: 149 g (5.27 oz.)             Water:        80%
```

Calories	123		Vitamin C	10.1 mg
Protein	3.66 g		Vitamin D	0 mcg
Carbohydrates	22.4 g		Vit E-Alpha E	2.57 mg
Fat - Total	2.43 g		Vitamin K	mcg
Saturated Fat	.33 g		Biotin	mcg
Mono Fat	.578 g		Calcium	27.8 mg
Poly Fat	1.36 g		Copper	.182 mg
Cholesterol	0 mg		Iodine	mcg
Dietary Fibre	2.6 g		Iron	.965 mg
Soluble Fibre	.382 g		Magnesium	49.4 mg
Total Vit A	177 RE		Manganese	.876 mg
Thiamin-B1	.12 mg		Phosphorus	127 mg
Riboflavin-B2	.067 mg		Potassium	230 mg
Niacin-B3	1.98 mg		Selenium	13.5 mcg
Niacin Equiv.	1.98 mg		Sodium	431 mg
Vitamin B6	.208 mg		Zinc	.799 mg
Vitamin B12	0 mcg		Complex Carbs	17.5 g
Folate	28.5 mcg		Sugars	2.34 g
Pantothenic	.569 mg		Water	119 g

CALORIE BREAKDOWN		FAT	EXCHANGES	
Protein	12%	Saturated : 2.4%	Bread	1.1
Carbohydrates	71%	Mono Unsat: 4.1%	Lean Meat	.037
Fats - Total	17%	Poly Unsat: 9.7%	Vegetables	.5
			Fat	.29

LIMA BEAN AND VEGETABLE SALAD (makes 7 cups)

500 mL	(2 cups)	dry large lima or great northern beans
250 mL	(1 cup)	cooked fresh green peas
250 mL	(1 cup)	sliced celery
125 mL	(1/2 cup)	finely chopped white onion
250 mL	(1 cup)	chopped green and red sweet pepper (mixed)
250 mL	(1 cup)	diced or sliced carrot, lightly boiled and still crisp
5 mL	(1 tsp.)	salt
15 mL	(1 Tbsp.)	fresh lemon juice
250 mL	(1 cup)	GARLIC-DILL DRESSING (page 112)
30 mL	(2 Tbsp.)	snipped fresh chives

Method:
WASH beans well, COVER with 7 cups of water and SOAK overnight or use quick soak method (pages 15 & 21). DRAIN, ADD fresh water to cover and BRING to the boil. BOIL gently, covered, for 1 1/2 hours or until tender but not broken. DRAIN and combine with remaining ingredients except the chives. TURN into a serving bowl and SPRINKLE with chives. CHILL until required. Variation: This salad may also be used to stuff tomatoes.

```
Analysis: LIMA BEAN AND VEGETABLE SALAD (7 cups)   Divided by: 10
          Wgt: 118 g (4.18 oz.)                    Water:      64%
```

Calories	161		Vitamin C	14.1 mg
Protein	10.2 g		Vitamin D	0 mcg
Carbohydrates	28.8 g		Vit E-Alpha E	.881 mg
Fat - Total	1.11 g		Vitamin K	mcg
Saturated Fat	.187 g		Biotin	mcg
Mono Fat	.194 g		Calcium	63 mg
Poly Fat	.582 g		Copper	.355 mg
Cholesterol	0 mg		Iodine	mcg
Dietary Fibre	12.7 g		Iron	3.98 mg
Soluble Fibre	3.24 g		Magnesium	106 mg
Total Vit A	405 RE		Manganese	.815 mg
Thiamin-B1	.261 mg		Phosphorus	179 mg
Riboflavin-B2	.116 mg		Potassium	767 mg
Niacin-B3	1.01 mg		Selenium	3.62 mcg
Niacin Equiv.	.972 mg		Sodium	328 mg
Vitamin B6	.296 mg		Zinc	1.38 mg
Vitamin B12	0 mcg		Complex Carbs	10.2 g
Folate	163 mcg		Sugars	5.56 g
Pantothenic	.607 mg		Water	75.4 g

CALORIE BREAKDOWN		FAT		EXCHANGES	
Protein	25%	*Saturated :	1%	Bread	1.57
Carbohydrates	69%	Mono Unsat:	1.1%	Lean Meat	.089
Fat-Total *	6%	Poly Unsat:	3.2%	Fruit	.006
				Vegetables	.473

MACARONI SALAD (makes 10 servings)

1500 L	(6 cups)		cooked macaroni, rinsed and drained
250 mL	(1 cup)	**EACH**	diced cucumber, sliced celery, **and** sliced green onions
125 mL	(1/2 cup)		chopped green pepper
60 mL	(1/4 cup)		chopped red pepper
5 mL	(1 tsp.)		salt
3 mL	(1/2 tsp.)		celery seed
3 mL	(1/2 tsp.)		garlic powder
3 mL	(1/2 tsp.)		dill
250 mL	(1 cup)		GARLIC-DILL DRESSING (page 112)
250 mL	(1 cup)		cubed CASHEW SLICING "CHEESE" (page 194)

Method:

COMBINE all ingredients in a large bowl stirring in CASHEW-SLICING "CHEESE" last. CHILL until ready to serve. GARNISH with radish roses and parsley.

```
Analysis: MACARONI SALAD (makes 10 servings)     Divided by: 10
          Wgt: 183 g (6.45 oz.)                  Water:      78
```

Calories	161		Vitamin C	17.1 mg
Protein	7.49 g		Vitamin D	0 mcg
Carbohydrates	28.6 g		Vit E-Alpha E	.705 mg
Fat - Total	2.24 g		Vitamin K	mcg
Saturated Fat	.369 g		Biotin	mcg
Mono Fat	.721 g		Calcium	50.6 mg
Poly Fat	.829 g		Copper	.207 mg
Cholesterol	0 mg		Iodine	mcg
Dietary Fibre	2.7 g		Iron	2.77 mg
Soluble Fibre	.357 g		Magnesium	46.8 mg
Total Vit A	41.6 RE		Manganese	.331 mg
Thiamin-B1	.356 mg		Phosphorus	104 mg
Riboflavin-B2	.173 mg		Potassium	213 mg
Niacin-B3	2.14 mg		Selenium	27.9 mcg
Niacin Equiv.	1.66 mg		Sodium	447 mg
Vitamin B6	.17 mg		Zinc	.848 mg
Vitamin B12	0 mcg		Complex Carbs	22.5 g
Folate	56.1 mcg		Sugars	2.65 g
Pantothenic	.355 mg		Water	143 g

CALORIE BREAKDOWN		FAT		EXCHANGES	
Protein	18%	* Saturated :	2 %	Bread	1.51
Carbohydrates	69%	Mono Unsat:	3.9%	Lean Meat	.112
Fat-Total*	12%	Poly Unsat:	4.5%	Fruit	.04
				Vegetables	.4
				Fat	.122

CELERY:

Celery belongs to the parsley family which also includes caraway, carrots, dill, parsley, and parsnips. Celery stalks are an excellent source of potassium. The leaves are much richer than stalks in calcium, iron, potassium, Vitamins A and C.

QUICK VEGETABLE RELISH (Makes 2 1/2 cups)

500 mL	(2 cups)	green cabbage (Pack to measure)
125 mL	(1/2 cup)	grated carrot (Pack to measure)
125 mL	(1/2 cup)	sliced red onion
125 mL	(1/2 cup)	sliced green pepper
10 mL	(2 tsp.)	salt
75 mL	(1/3 cup)	lemon juice
		water to cover

Method:

SHRED the cabbage and carrots. COMBINE all ingredients. PACK into pint jar. ADD enough water to cover. REFRIGERATE overnight. SERVE in sandwiches or as a side dish.

```
------------------------------------------------------------------------
| Analysis: QUICK VEGETABLE SALAD              Divided by: 6           |
|           Wgt: 63.6 g (2.24 oz.)             Water:      88%         |
------------------------------------------------------------------------
```

Calories	18.5		Vitamin C	20.4 mg
Protein	.695 g		Vitamin D	0 mcg
Carbohydrates	4.37 g		Vit E-Alpha E	.514 mg
Fat - Total	.141 g		Vitamin K	mcg
Saturated Fat	.022 g		Biotin	mcg
Mono Fat	.012 g		Calcium	18.9 mg
Poly Fat	.064 g		Copper	.023 mg
Cholesterol	0 mg		Iodine	mcg
Dietary Fibre	1.06 g		Iron	.275 mg
Soluble Fibre	.432 g		Magnesium	8.1 mg
Total Vit A	266 RE		Manganese	.081 mg
Thiamin-B1	.036 mg		Phosphorus	15.3 mg
Riboflavin-B2	.019 mg		Potassium	132 mg
Niacin-B3	.218 mg		Selenium	.811 mcg
Niacin Equiv.	.218 mg		Sodium	718 mg
Vitamin B6	.081 mg		Zinc	.105 mg
Vitamin B12	0 mcg		Complex Carbs	.292 g
Folate	16.8 mcg		Sugars	3.02 g
Pantothenic	.08 mg		Water	56.3 g

CALORIE BREAKDOWN		FAT		EXCHANGES	
Protein	13%	*Saturated :	.9%	Fruit	.031
Carbohydrates	81%	Mono Unsat:	.5%	Vegetables	.644
Fat-Total *	6%	Poly Unsat:	2.7%		

TABBULI (makes 10 servings)

250 mL	(1 cup)	**EACH**	bulgur wheat **and** hot water
5 mL	(1 tsp.)		salt
75 mL	(1/3 cup)		fresh lemon juice
15 mL	(1 Tbsp.)		olive oil
750 mL	(3 cups)		fresh parsley, finely chopped
125 mL	(1/2 cup)		thinly sliced green onions with tops
250 mL	(1 cup)		diced tomatoes
			fresh mint (optional)

Method:

PLACE bulgur in a pot, **ADD** salt and **POUR** hot water over it. **COVER** and **LET** stand for 10 or 15 minutes. **STIR** to fluff. **ADD** lemon juice and olive oil. **MIX** well. **STIR** in remaining ingredients. **CHILL** for at least an hour. (Will keep for several days.)

```
Analysis: TABBULI                                   Divided by: 10
          Wgt: 85.9 g (3.03 oz.)                    Water:      78%

        Calories        72.7          Vitamin C        31.3 mg
        Protein         2.49 g        Vitamin D           0 mcg
        Carbohydrates   13.4 g        Vit E-Alpha E    .605 mg
        Fat - Total     1.75 g        Vitamin K             mcg
        Saturated Fat   .251 g        Biotin                mcg
        Mono Fat        1.08 g        Calcium            34 mg
        Poly Fat        .246 g        Copper           .094 mg
        Dietary Fibre   3.68 g        Iron              1.6 mg
        Soluble Fibre   .695 g        Magnesium        35.4 mg
        Total Vit A      106 RE       Manganese        .481 mg
        Thiamin-B1      .063 mg       Phosphorus       58.3 mg
        Riboflavin-B2   .045 mg       Potassium         214 mg
        Niacin-B3       1.09 mg       Selenium         3.19 mcg
        Niacin Equiv.   1.09 mg       Sodium            228 mg
        Vitamin B6      .084 mg       Zinc             .506 mg
        Vitamin B12        0 mcg      Complex Carbs    8.11 g
        Folate          36.7 mcg      Sugars           1.63 g
        Pantothenic     .272 mg       Water            66.9 g
```

CALORIE BREAKDOWN		FAT		EXCHANGES	
Protein	13%	*Saturated:	2.8%	Bread	.533
Carbohydrates	68%	Mono Unsat:	12.3%	Fruit	.03
Fat-Total *	20%	Poly Unsat:	2.8%	Vegetables	.437
				Fat	.262

BULGUR:

Bulgur is whole wheat that has been cracked into bits and parboiled, i.e., partly cooked. It requires very little cooking. In fact you can just pour boiling water over it, cover and let soak for 15 minutes as is done in the popular Middle Eastern salad tabbuli. Bulgur is almost as nutritious as whole wheat, but of course some nutrients are lost in cracking and cooking. It is often used as a substitute for rice; e.g. in pilaff, and Eastern European dishes consisting of wheat, oil, and herbs cooked together.

TABOULI SALAD (makes 10 servings)

250 mL	(1 cup)	bulgur wheat
5 mL	(1 tsp.)	salt
250 mL	(1 cup)	hot water
75 mL	(1/3 cup)	fresh lemon juice
45 mL	(3 Tbsp.)	olive oil
750 mL	(3 cups)	fresh parsley, chopped fine
250 mL	(1 cup)	diced or thinly sliced cucumber
125 mL	(1/2 cup)	thinly sliced green onions with tops
125 mL	(1/2 cup)	diced tomatoes
125 mL	(1/2 cup)	chopped green pepper
250 mL	(1 cup)	cooked garbanzos

Method:

PLACE bulgur in a pot. ADD salt and POUR hot water over it. COVER and LET stand for 10 or 15 minutes. STIR to fluff. ADD lemon juice and olive oil. MIX well. STIR in remaining ingredients. CHILL for at least an hour. (Will keep for several days.)

```
---------------------------------------------------------------------
| Analysis: TABOULI SALAD                    Divided by: 10          |
|           Wgt: 123 g (4.34 oz.)            Water:      80%         |
---------------------------------------------------------------------
```

Calories	89.3		Vitamin C	28.3 mg
Protein	3.98 g		Vitamin D	0 mcg
Carbohydrates	18.4 g		Vit E-Alpha E	.436 mg
Fat - Total	.803 g		Vitamin K	mcg
Saturated Fat	.113 g		Biotin	mcg
Mono Fat	.164 g		Calcium	39.4 mg
Poly Fat	.324 g		Copper	.15 mg
Cholesterol	0 mg		Iodine	mcg
Dietary Fibre	4.72 g		Iron	1.78 mg
Soluble Fibre	.993 g		Magnesium	43.5 mg
Total Vit A	80.1 RE		Manganese	.663 mg
Thiamin-B1	.083 mg		Phosphorus	88 mg
Riboflavin-B2	.055 mg		Potassium	267 mg
Niacin-B3	1.14 mg		Selenium	7.38 mcg
Niacin Equiv.	1.14 mg		Sodium	226 mg
Vitamin B6	.121 mg		Zinc	.757 mg
Vitamin B12	0 mcg		Complex Carbs	11.5 g
Folate	60.7 mcg		Sugars	2.22 g
Pantothenic	.332 mg		Water	98.4 g

CALORIE BREAKDOWN		FAT	EXCHANGES	
Protein	16%	*Saturated : 1 %	Bread	.82
Carbohydrates	76%	Mono Unsat: 1.5%	Lean Meat	.082
Fat-Total *	7%	Poly Unsat: 3 %	Fruit	.03
			Vegetables	.48

ZUCCHINI SALAD (makes 4 servings)

60 mL	(1/4 cup)	thinly sliced green onion
125 mL	(1/2 cup)	fresh lemon juice
125 mL	(1/2 cup)	white grape juice
3 mL	(1/2 tsp.)	salt
3 mL	(1/2 tsp.)	celery seed
1	(1)	garlic clove, crushed
1500 L	(6 cups)	sliced zucchini

Method:
COMBINE all ingredients in a jar except zucchini and SHAKE well. ADD zucchini. REFRIGERATE. LET stand. It is better the following day.

Analysis: ZUCCHINI SALAD (makes 4 servings)   Divided by: 4
Wgt: 183 g (6.45 oz.)   Water: 91%

Calories	48		Vitamin C	18.6 mg
Protein	2.76 g		Vitamin D	0 mcg
Carbohydrates	10.6 g		Vit E-Alpha E	.307 mg
Fat - Total	.286 g		Vitamin K	mcg
Saturated Fat	.063 g		Biotin	mcg
Mono Fat	.03 g		Calcium	34.7 mg
Poly Fat	.114 g		Copper	.163 mg
Cholesterol	0 mg		Iodine	mcg
Dietary Fibre	3.31 g		Iron	1.07 mg
Soluble Fibre	.626 g		Magnesium	39.4 mg
Total Vit A	817 RE		Manganese	.225 mg
Thiamin-B1	.438 mg		Phosphorus	93.6 mg
Riboflavin-B2	.145 mg		Potassium	480 mg
Niacin-B3	1.56 mg		Selenium	3.44 mcg
Niacin Equiv.	1.56 mg		Sodium	283 mg
Vitamin B6	.277 mg		Zinc	.509 mg
Vitamin B12	.001 mcg		Complex Carbs	.384 g
Folate	114 mcg		Sugars	6.89 g
Pantothenic	.354 mg		Water	167 g

CALORIE BREAKDOWN		FAT	EXCHANGES	
Protein	20%	* Saturated : 1 %	Bread	.062
Carbohydrates	76%	Mono Unsat: .5%	Fruit	.115
Fat-Total *	5%	Poly Unsat: 1.8%	Vegetables	1.55

FRENCH DRESSING (makes 1 1/2 cups)

250 mL	(1 cup)	tomato puree
30 mL	(2 Tbsp.)	honey
125 mL	(1/2 cup)	fresh lemon juice
1	(1)	clove of garlic, minced
10 mL	(2 tsp.)	Italian seasoning
5 mL	(1 tsp.)	dill weed
5 mL	(1 tsp.)	salt

Method:

WHIZ tomato puree, honey, lemon juice, and garlic in a blender until smooth. Then **STIR** in the remaining ingredients. **CHILL** and **SERVE. KEEP REFRIGERATED. USE** this dressing within 7-8 days.

```
Analysis: FRENCH DRESSING                        Divided by: 24
          Wgt: 17.7 g (.625 oz.)                 Water:      79%
```

Calories	11.3		Vitamin C	6.11 mg
Protein	.223 g		Vitamin D	0 mcg
Carbohydrates	3.04 g		Vit E-Alpha Eq	.09 mg
Fat - Total	.026 g		Vitamin K	mcg
Saturated Fat	.005 g		Biotin	mcg
Mono Fat	.003 g		Calcium	4.26 mg
Poly Fat	.011 g		Copper	.02 mg
Cholesterol	0 mg		Iodine	mcg
Dietary Fibre	.293 g		Iron	.156 mg
Soluble Fibre	.067 g		Magnesium	3.36 mg
Total Vit A	14.8 RE		Manganese	.035 mg
Thiamin-B1	.01 mg		Phosphorus	5.17 mg
Riboflavin-B2	.007 mg		Potassium	54.5 mg
Niacin-B3	.193 mg		Selenium	.146 mcg
Niacin Equiv.	.193 mg		Sodium	131 mg
Vitamin B6	.021 mg		Zinc	.036 mg
Vitamin B12	0 mcg		Complex Carbs	.194 g
Folate	1.84 mcg		Sugars	2.56 g
Pantothenic	.053 mg		Water	14.1 g

CALORIE BREAKDOWN		FAT		EXCHANGES	
Protein	7%	*Saturated :	.3%	Fruit	.104
Carbohydrates	92%	Mono Unsat:	92%	Vegetables	.17
Fat-Total *	2%	Poly Unsat:	2%		

LECITHIN-OIL PAN TREATMENT:

Combine one tablespoon of liquid lecithin with one quarter cup of corn oil in a small jar (baby food jar). When you need a greased pan take paper towel and dip it into the mixture. Rub the surface of the pan. Then store the paper towel in another jar to use the next time. Wipe the pan with a clean paper towel just leaving a thin film on on the pan. This will prevent ending up with a sticky surface after the product is baked. This is cheaper than PAM etc., is environmentally friendly, and is just as effective.

GARBANZO DIP (makes about 2 cups)

125 mL	(1/2 cup)	sesame seeds or 1/4 cup Tahini
1	(1)	medium clove of garlic, pressed
625 mL	(2 1/2 cups)	cooked garbanzos
60 mL	(1/4 cup)	garbanzo liquid or hot water
75 mL	(1/3 cup)	fresh lemon juice
5 mL	(1 tsp.)	salt

Method:

WHIZ sesame seeds in food processor until almost a paste. **ADD** remaining ingredients and **WHIZ** until very smooth. **POUR** into a small serving dish. **GARNISH** with parsley. **STORE** in refrigerator.

Serving Suggestion: **SERVE** as a dip with vegetables, on baked potatoes, in a pita bread sandwich with falafels.

```
Analysis: LEBANESE GARBANZO DIP                    Divided by: 16
          Wgt: 31.6 g (1.11 oz.)                   Water:      65%
```

Calories	48.3	Vitamin C	1.43 mg
Protein	2.46 g	Vitamin D	0 mcg
Carbohydrates	6.16 g	Vit E-Alpha E	.147 mg
Fat - Total	1.83 g	Vitamin K	mcg
Saturated Fat	.237 g	Biotin	mcg
Mono Fat	.606 g	Calcium	14 mg
Poly Fat	.804 g	Copper	.109 mg
Cholesterol	0 mg	Iodine	mcg
Dietary Fibre	1.46 g	Iron	.784 mg
Soluble Fibre	.398 g	Magnesium	18.5 mg
Total Vit A	.871 RE	Manganese	.248 mg
Thiamin-B1	.043 mg	Phosphorus	53.2 mg
Riboflavin-B2	.015 mg	Potassium	74.2 mg
Niacin-B3	.227 mg	Selenium	.993 mcg
Niacin Equiv.	.228 mg	Sodium	137 mg
Vitamin B6	.035 mg	Zinc	.562 mg
Vitamin B12	0 mcg	Complex Carbs	4.16 g
Folate	38 mcg	Sugars	.558 g
Pantothenic	.079 mg	Water	20.4 g

CALORIE BREAKDOWN		FATS		EXCHANGES	
Protein	19%	*Saturated :	4.2%	Bread	.359
Carbohydrates	48%	Mono Unsat:	10.7%	Lean Meat	.103
Fat-Total *	32%	Poly Unsat:	14.2%	Fruit	.019
				Fat	.252

GARLIC-DILL DRESSING (makes about 1 1/4 cups)

250 mL	(1 cup)	fresh, drained tofu
45 mL	(3 Tbsp.)	fresh lemon juice (May prefer to use less.)
1	(1)	clove of garlic, minced
3 mL	(1/2 tsp.)	salt
3 mL	(1/2 tsp.)	dill weed (preferably fresh)

Method:

　　　　DROP tofu into boiling water, LEAVE about two minutes, DRAIN well. WHIZ all ingredients in blender. TOSS with salads, USE over cooked vegetables, such as broccoli, or USE as a spread for sandwiches in place of mayonnaise. (May substitute basil for garlic.)

```
------------------------------------------------------------------------
| Analysis:  GARLIC-DILL DRESSING                        Divided by: 20 |
|            Wgt: 15.2 g (.535 oz.)                      Water:     72% |
------------------------------------------------------------------------
```

Calories	18.8	Vitamin C	.643	mg
Protein	2.01 g	Vitamin D	0	mcg
Carbohydrates	.737 g	Vit E-Alpha E	.005	mg
Fat - Total	1.11 g	Vitamin K		mcg
Saturated Fat	.16 g	Biotin		mcg
Mono Fat	.243 g	Calcium	26.4	mg
Poly Fat	.622 g	Copper	.049	mg
Cholesterol	0 mg	Iodine		mcg
Dietary Fibre	.035 g	Iron	1.33	mg
Soluble Fibre	.003 g	Magnesium	12.1	mg
Total Vit A	2.22 RE	Manganese	.152	mg
Thiamin-B1	.021 mg	Phosphorus	24.3	mg
Riboflavin-B2	.013 mg	Potassium	32.9	mg
Niacin-B3	.054 mg	Selenium	.046	mcg
Niacin Equiv.	.054 mg	Sodium	55.6	mg
Vitamin B6	.014 mg	Zinc	.202	mg
Vitamin B12	0 mcg	Complex Carbs	.036	g
Folate	3.93 mcg	Sugars	.146	g
Pantothenic	.02 mg	Water	11	g

CALORIE BREAKDOWN		FAT		EXCHANGES	
Protein	38%	* Saturated :	6.9%	Bread	.025
Carbohydrates	14%	Mono Unsat:	10.5%	Lean Meat	.3
Fat-Total *	48%	Poly Unsat:	26.7%	Fruit	.009

SALAD DRESSING COMPARISON:

SALAD DRESSING	Cal	Pro G	CHO G	Tot Fat G	Sat G	Poly G
1 Tbsp Miracle Whip	69	.1	1.7	6.9	1.1	4.1
1 Tbsp Miracle Whip, Light	44	.1	2.2	3.9	.6	2.2
1 Tbsp Hellmann's Mayonnaise	100	.2	.1	11.2	1.7	6.1
1 Tbsp Garlic-Dill	7.8	.78	.35	.459	.006	.257

SUNNY SOUR CREME (makes about 1 cup)

150 mL	(2/3 cup)		raw, unsalted sunflower seeds
150 mL	(2/3 cup)		water
3 mL	(1/2 tsp.)	**EACH**	salt **and** garlic powder
5 mL	(1 tsp.)		onion powder
45 mL	(3 Tbsp.)		fresh lemon juice (May prefer less.)

Method:

WHIZ sunflower seeds in food processor or blender. (If using blender blend it with the water.) **ADD** remaining ingredients and **WHIZ** until well blended. **ADJUST** water and seasonings to taste and consistency desired. **USE** on baked potatoes or as a sandwich spread.

```
Analysis: SUNNY SOUR CREME                   Divided by: 12
          Wgt: 23.4 g (.825 oz.)             Water:      67%
```

Calories	42.8		Vitamin C	1.07 mg
Protein	1.7 g		Vitamin D	0 mcg
Carbohydrates	1.83 g		Vit E-Alpha E	3.62 mg
Fat - Total	3.57 g		Vitamin K	mcg
Saturated Fat	.376 g		Biotin	mcg
Mono Fat	.683 g		Calcium	9.87 mg
Poly Fat	2.36 g		Copper	.129 mg
Cholesterol	0 mg		Iodine	mcg
Dietary Fibre	.526 g		Iron	.502 mg
Soluble Fibre	.005 g		Magnesium	26.2 mg
Total Vit A	.436 RE		Manganese	.148 mg
Thiamin-B1	.168 mg		Phosphorus	52 mg
Riboflavin-B2	.019 mg		Potassium	56.5 mg
Niacin-B3	.333 mg		Selenium	5.25 mcg
Niacin Equiv.	.333 mg		Sodium	90.3 mg
Vitamin B6	.083 mg		Zinc	.378 mg
Vitamin B12	0 mcg		Complex Carbs	.761 g
Folate	17.1 mcg		Sugars	.544 g
Pantothenic	.504 mg		Water	15.8 g

CALORIE BREAKDOWN		FAT	EXCHANGES	
Protein	15%	*Saturated : 7.3%	Lean Meat	.266
Carbohydrates	16%	Mono Unsat: 13.3%	Fruit	.816
Fat-Total *	70%	Poly Unsat: 46%	Fat	.5

SUNFLOWER SEEDS:

These are generally the least expensive of the popular edible seeds. Like all seeds they are relatively high in fat, mostly unsaturated, moderate in protein, and contain some significant amounts of vitamins and minerals. Sunflower seeds are eaten raw or roasted, hulled or unhulled (they are mechanically hulled). Roy Bruder, Ph.D. *Discovering Natural Foods*, page 187.

TOMATO TOFU DRESSING (makes 32 servings)

250 mL	(1 cup)	tofu
250 mL	(1 cup)	diced tomatoes
45 mL	(3 Tbsp.)	fresh lemon juice
15 mL	(1 Tbsp.)	chicken style seasoning
15 mL	(1 Tbsp.)	chopped parsley
5 mL	(1 tsp.)	onion powder
2 mL	(1/4 tsp.)	garlic powder

Method:

COMBINE all ingredients in blender. BLEND until smooth. This may be used as a vegetable dip as well as a salad dressing.

```
Analysis: TOMATO TOFU DRESSING              Divided by: 16
          Wgt: 34.4 g (1.21 oz.)            Water:        87%
```

Calories	18.2	Vitamin C	3.32 mg
Protein	1.43 g	Vitamin D	0 mcg
Carbohydrates	1.65 g	Vit E-Alpha E	.065 mg
Fat - Total	.811 g	Vitamin K	mcg
Saturated Fat	.114 g	Biotin	mcg
Mono Fat	.171 g	Calcium	21.3 mg
Poly Fat	.437 g	Copper	.048 mg
Cholesterol	0 mg	Iodine	mcg
Dietary Fibre	.416 g	Iron	.944 mg
Soluble Fibre	.096 g	Magnesium	18.1 mg
Total Vit A	11.7 RE	Manganese	.114 mg
Thiamin-B1	.021 mg	Phosphorus	18.7 mg
Riboflavin-B2	.013 mg	Potassium	57.4 mg
Niacin-B3	.15 mg	Selenium	.299 mcg
Niacin Equiv.	.15 mg	Sodium	26.4 mg
Vitamin B6	.024 mg	Zinc	.155 mg
Vitamin B12	0 mcg	Complex Carbs	.12 g
Folate	4.33 mcg	Sugars	.71 g
Pantothenic	.041 mg	Water	30 g

CALORIE BREAKDOWN		FAT		EXCHANGES	
Protein	29%	*Saturated :	5.2%	Lean Meat	.125
Carbohydrates	34%	Mono Unsat:	7.8%	Fruit	.012
Fat-Total *	37%	Poly Unsat:	20. %	Vegetables	.191
				Fat	.062

BARLEY AND PINTO BEAN SOUP (makes 10 servings)

250 mL	(1 cup)	pinto beans (cleaned and soaked by the quick soak method)
1 L	(4 cups)	water
250 mL	(1 cup)	barley
1500 mL	(6 cups)	water
250 mL	(1 cup)	tomato sauce
125 mL	(1/2 cup)	finely chopped onion
1	(1)	garlic clove, minced
375 mL	(1 1/2 cups)	grated carrots
125 mL	(1/2 cup)	parsley flakes
		salt and onion salt to taste

Method:

BRING beans to boil in 4 cups of water. TURN off heat and LET stand one hour. ADD barley and remaining water. COOK until beans are tender. ADD remaining ingredients and SIMMER until all are cooked and flavours well-blended.

```
Analysis: BARLEY AND PINTO BEAN SOUP (10 CUPS)      Divided by: 10
          Wgt: 171 g (6.05 oz.)                     Water:      78%
```

Calories	138		Vitamin C	5.66 mg
Protein	6.39 g		Vitamin D	0 mcg
Carbohydrates	27.8 g		Vit E-Alpha E	.219 mg
Fat - Total	.727 g		Vitamin K	mcg
Saturated Fat	.147 g		Biotin	mcg
Mono Fat	.109 g		Calcium	36.2 mg
Poly Fat	.318 g		Copper	.263 mg
Cholesterol	0 mg		Iodine	mcg
Dietary Fibre	8.94 g		Iron	2.18 mg
Soluble Fibre	2.71 g		Magnesium	56.5 mg
Total Vit A	197 RE		Manganese	.68 mg
Thiamin-B1	.227 mg		Phosphorus	132 mg
Riboflavin-B2	.117 mg		Potassium	424 mg
Niacin-B3	1.39 mg		Selenium	12.6 mcg
Niacin Equiv.	1.4 mg		Sodium	370 mg
Vitamin B6	.189 mg		Zinc	1.11 mg
Vitamin B12	0 mcg		Complex Carbs	15.7 g
Folate	86 mcg		Sugars	3.11 g
Pantothenic	.279 mg		Water	134 g

CALORIE BREAKDOWN		FAT		EXCHANGES	
Protein	18%	*Saturated :	.9%	Bread	1.15
Carbohydrates	78%	Mono Unsat:	.7%	Lean Meat	.25
Fat-Total *	5%	Poly Unsat:	2 %	Vegetables	.475

BEAN SOUP SPECIAL (makes 12 servings)

500 mL	(2 cups)	dry white kidney beans (measured before cooking)
2.5 L	(10 cups)	water to cook the beans
5 mL	(1 tsp.)	olive oil
1	(1)	large garlic clove, minced
500 mL	(2 cups)	chopped onion
500 mL	(2 cups)	sliced or diced carrots
500 mL	(2 cups)	thinly sliced celery
250 mL	(1 cup)	diced raw potatoes
250 mL	(I cup)	shredded cabbage
500 mL	(2 cups)	cooked tomatoes
125 mL	(1/2 cup)	uncooked macaroni
15 mL	(1 Tbsp.)	salt
		parsley to garnish just before serving

METHOD:

COOK the beans. STEAM the garlic, onions, carrots, celery, potatoes, and cabbage in the olive oil and a little water. ADD to cooked beans. STIR in tomatoes, macaroni, and salt. CONTINUE cooking until macaroni is done. At serving time ADD minced parsley.

```
-----------------------------------------------------------------------------
| Analysis: BEAN SOUP SPECIAL (12)              Divided by: 12              |
|           Wgt: 169 g (5.97 oz.)               Water:      73%             |
-----------------------------------------------------------------------------
```

Calories	168	Vitamin C	17.2	mg
Protein	8.97 g	Vitamin D	0	mcg
Carbohydrates	32.2 g	Vit E-Alpha E	.627	mg
Fat - Total	1.03 g	Vitamin K		mcg
Saturated Fat	.154 g	Biotin		mcg
Mono Fat	.347 g	Calcium	66.1	mg
Poly Fat	.349 g	Copper	.353	mg
Cholesterol	0 mg	Iodine		mcg
Dietary Fibre	9.25 g	Iron	2.99	mg
Soluble Fibre	3.75 g	Magnesium	62.4	mg
Total Vit A	678 RE	Manganese	.709	mg
Thiamin-B1	.296 mg	Phosphorus	168	mg
Riboflavin-B2	.134 mg	Potassium	736	mg
Niacin-B3	1.7 mg	Selenium	6.43	mcg
Niacin Equiv.	1.71 mg	Sodium	640	mg
Vitamin B6	.316 mg	Zinc	1.2	mg
Vitamin B12	0 mcg	Complex Carbs	16.8	g
Folate	146 mcg	Sugars	6.18	g
Pantothenic	.547 mg	Water	124	g

CALORIE BREAKDOWN		FAT		EXCHANGES	
Protein	21%	*Saturated :	.8%	Bread	1.46
Carbohydrates	74%	Mono Unsat:	1.8%	Lean Meat	.543
Fat-Total *	5%	Poly Unsat:	1.8%	Vegetables	1.21
				Fat	.073

BLACK BEAN BISQUE (6 servings) (6 cups)

375 mL	(1 1/2 cups)	dry black beans
2 L	(8 cups)	water (preferably distilled)
5 mL	(1 tsp.)	olive oil
375 mL	(1 1/2 cups)	chopped onion
1	(1)	clove of garlic, minced
5 mL	(1 tsp.)	celery seed
2 mL	(1/4 tsp.)	thyme
15 mL	(1 Tbsp.)	lemon juice
125 mL	(1/2 cup)	diced tomato (optional)

Method:

SOAK and DRAIN. SIMMER the black beans in the water. STEAM the onions and garlic in the oil. ADD to the beans. WHIZ most of the beans in the blender, adding about 2 cups more water as needed for operating the blender. ADD seasonings. LEAVE some beans whole; soup will be thick. REHEAT and ADD lemon juice and diced tomato just before serving. TASTE-TEST for salt. SERVE with lemon wedges and croutons, brown rice, or noodles and a crisp salad.

```
Analysis: BLACK BEAN BISQUE (6 SERVINGS)          Divided by: 6
          Wgt: 468 g (16.5 oz.)                   Water:    91%
```

Calories	167	Vitamin C	3.39	mg
Protein	10.1 g	Vitamin D	0	mcg
Carbohydrates	29.5 g	Vit E-Alpha E	.231	mg
Fat - Total	1.5 g	Vitamin K		mcg
Saturated Fat	.274 g	Biotin		mcg
Mono Fat	.666 g	Calcium	52.6	mg
Poly Fat	.354 g	Copper	.276	mg
Cholesterol	0 mg	Iodine		mcg
Dietary Fibre	7.04 g	Iron	2.69	mg
Soluble Fibre	1.92 g	Magnesium	84.2	mg
Total Vit A	1.6 RE	Manganese	.578	mg
Thiamin-B1	.284 mg	Phosphorus	167	mg
Riboflavin-B2	.074 mg	Potassium	455	mg
Niacin-B3	.633 mg	Selenium	9.34	mcg
Niacin Equiv.	.635 mg	Sodium	13	mg
Vitamin B6	.128 mg	Zinc	1.42	mg
Vitamin B12	0 mcg	Complex Carbs	17.4	g
Folate	167 mcg	Sugars	5.06	g
Pantothenic	.308 mg	Water	425	g

CALORIE BREAKDOWN		FAT		EXCHANGES	
Protein	23%	* Saturated :	1.4%	Bread	1.62
Carbohydrates	69%	Mono Unsat:	3.5%	Lean Meat	.269
Fat-Total *	8%	Poly Unsat:	1.9%	Fruit	.01
				Vegetables	.5
				Fat	.145

"CHICKEN" NOODLE SOUP (makes 12 servings)

250 mL	(1 cup)	chopped onions
1	(1)	large garlic clove, minced
2 L	(8 cups)	water
1 L	(4 cups)	diced potato
1 L	(4 cups)	thinly sliced carrots
500 mL	(2 cups)	diced, frozen tofu (See page 224)
45 mL	(3 Tbsp.)	chicken style seasoning
15 mL	(1 Tbsp.)	dried parsley
5 mL	(1 tsp.)	salt
1	(1)	bay leaf
250 mL	(1 cup - about 4 oz)	broken vermicelli or **eggless** noodles

Method:
STEAM onions and garlic in a small amount of water. ADD remaining ingredients except the pasta and cook until the vegetables are almost done. ADD pasta. COOK until done.

```
------------------------------------------------------------------------
| Analysis: "CHICKEN" NOODLE SOUP              Divided by: 12           |
|            Wgt: 323 g (11.4 oz.)             Water:      87%          |
------------------------------------------------------------------------
```

Calories	170	Vitamin C	8.22 mg
Protein	9.4 g	Vitamin D	0 mcg
Carbohydrates	25.8 g	Vit E-Alpha E	.282 mg
Fat - Total	4.06 g	Vitamin K	mcg
Saturated Fat	.585 g	Biotin	mcg
Mono Fat	.836 g	Calcium	114 mg
Poly Fat	2.2 g	Copper	.355 mg
Cholesterol	0 mg	Iodine	mcg
Dietary Fibre	2.9 g	Iron	5.34 mg
Soluble Fibre	.777 g	Magnesium	63.6 mg
Total Vit A	1284 RE	Manganese	1.05 mg
Thiamin-B1	.229 mg	Phosphorus	133 mg
Riboflavin-B2	.124 mg	Potassium	428 mg
Niacin-B3	1.76 mg	Selenium	6.3 mcg
Niacin Equiv.	1.76 mg	Sodium	226 mg
Vitamin B6	.331 mg	Zinc	1.14 mg
Vitamin B12	0 mcg	Complex Carbs	15.8 g
Folate	29.2 mcg	Sugars	3.72 g
Pantothenic	.505 mg	Water	281 g

CALORIE BREAKDOWN		FAT		EXCHANGES	
Protein	21%	*Saturated :	3 %	Bread	1.08
Carbohydrates	58%	Mono Unsat:	4.2%	Lean Meat	1
Fat-Total *	21%	Poly Unsat:	11.2%	Vegetables	.846

CORN-TOMATO CHOWDER (makes 5 cups)

250 mL	(1 cup)	diced potatoes
250 mL	(1 cup)	diced celery
250 mL	(1 cup)	chopped onions
125 mL	(1/2 cup)	chopped green pepper
750 mL	(3 cups)	water
500 mL	(2 cups)	corn
500 mL	(2 cups)	canned tomatoes
2 mL	(1/4 tsp.)	paprika (mild Spanish)
2 mL	(1/4 tsp.)	oregano
5 mL	(1 tsp.)	salt
250 mL	(1 cup)	peas
45 mL	(3 Tbsp.)	flour
375 mL	(1 1/2 cups)	cashew-rice milk or soy milk

Method:

COOK potatoes, celery, onions, and peppers in the water until tender. ADD the corn, tomatoes, paprika, oregano, and salt. BRING to a boil. MIX part of the milk with the flour until smooth. ADD to vegetables slowly, stirring to prevent lumping. CONTINUE cooking for about five minutes, until the flour is cooked. STIR in peas. SERVE piping hot.

```
--------------------------------------------------------------------
| Analysis: CORN-TOMATO CHOWDER              Divided by: 5         |
|           Wgt: 439 g (15.5 oz.)            Water:    87%         |
--------------------------------------------------------------------
```

Calories	216		Vitamin C	37.4 mg
Protein	8.14 g		Vitamin D	0 mcg
Carbohydrates	43.3 g		Vit E-Alpha E	1.02 mg
Fat - Total	3.21 g		Vitamin K	mcg
Saturated Fat	.227 g		Biotin	mcg
Mono Fat	.315 g		Calcium	88.5 mg
Poly Fat	.65 g		Copper	.273 mg
Cholesterol	0 mg		Iodine	mcg
Dietary Fibre	7.68 g		Iron	2.67 mg
Soluble Fibre	1.02 g		Magnesium	55.6 mg
Total Vit A	128 RE		Manganese	.515 mg
Thiamin-B1	.383 mg		Phosphorus	145 mg
Riboflavin-B2	.216 mg		Potassium	716 mg
Niacin-B3	3.3 mg		Selenium	7.22 mcg
Niacin Equiv.	3.18 mg		Sodium	555 mg
Vitamin B6	.337 mg		Zinc	1.25 mg
Vitamin B12	.54 mcg		Complex Carbs	22.8 g
Folate	71.6 mcg		Sugars	8.61 g
Pantothenic	1.21 mg		Water	381 g

CALORIE BREAKDOWN		FAT	EXCHANGES	
Protein	14%	*Saturated : .9%	Bread	1.66
Carbohydrates	74%	Mono Unsat: 1.2%	Vegetables	1.41
Fat-Total *	12%	Poly Unsat: 2.5%	Milk	.225

CREAM OF TOMATO SOUP - (makes 6 cups)

125 mL	(1/2 cup)		raw cashews
1.36 L	(48 oz.)		tomato juice
30 mL	(2 Tbsp.)		unbleached flour
2 mL	(1 1/2 tsp.)		onion powder
3 mL	(1/2 tsp.)	**EACH**	garlic powder, oregano, **and** basil
2 mL	(1/4 tsp.)		salt

Method:

BLEND cashews until smooth and creamy. ADD some of the tomato juice and CONTINUE to blend. ADD flour, onion powder, garlic powder, oregano, basil and salt. BLEND until mixture is smooth. HEAT remaining tomato juice. STIR in contents of blender and CONTINUE to stir and cook until flour is cooked. MAY add cooked pasta alphabets or stars after the soup is cooked. SIMMER together to blend flavours.

```
-----------------------------------------------------------------------
|Analysis:    CREAM OF TOMATO SOUP                    Divided by: 6    |
|             Wgt: 259 g (9.15 oz.)                   Water:     89%   |
-----------------------------------------------------------------------
```

Calories	120		Vitamin C	44.9 mg
Protein	3.99 g		Vitamin D	0 mcg
Carbohydrates	16.8 g		Vit E-Alpha E	.856 mg
Fat - Total	5.5 g		Vitamin K	mcg
Saturated Fat	1.07 g		Biotin	mcg
Mono Fat	3.14 g		Calcium	34.4 mg
Poly Fat	.971 g		Copper	.507 mg
Cholesterol	0 mg		Iodine	mcg
Dietary Fibre	2.91 g		Iron	2.35 mg
Soluble Fibre	.5 g		Magnesium	58.8 mg
Total Vit A	139 RE		Manganese	.313 mg
Thiamin-B1	.162 mg		Phosphorus	109 mg
Riboflavin-B2	.113 mg		Potassium	618 mg
Niacin-B3	1.98 mg		Selenium	4.11 mcg
Niacin Equiv.	1.98 mg		Sodium	972 mg
Vitamin B6	.357 mg		Zinc	1.03 mg
Vitamin B12	0 mcg		Complex Carbs	4.72 g
Folate	58.1 mcg		Sugars	9.15 g
Pantothenic	.793 mg		Water	230 g

CALORIE BREAKDOWN		FAT	EXCHANGES	
Protein	12%	* Saturated: 7.3%	Bread	.118
Carbohydrates	51%	Mono Unsat: 21.3%	Lean Meat	.167
Fat-Total	37%	Poly Unsat: 6.6%	Vegetables	2.01
			Fat	.667

CASHEWS:

Cashews are imported primarily from China, Africa, India, and South America. They are the seed of the cashew apple. They are similar in nutritive value to almonds except they contain more phosphorus and thiamine. When using raw cashews be sure to thoroughly wash them before using. There is some danger of raw, unwashed cashews being contaminated with salmonella.

FRESH GREEN PEA SOUP (makes 4 servings)

250 mL	(1 cup)	boiling water
500 mL	(2 cups)	frozen peas
60 mL	(1/4 cup)	raw cashews or almonds
75 mL	(1/3 cup)	flour
5 mL	(1 tsp.)	salt
15 mL	(1 Tbsp.)	chopped onion
750 mL	(3 cups)	water

Method:

ADD peas to boiling water. **BRING** to a boil and **COOK** one or two minutes. **BLEND** cashews until very fine. **ADD** flour, salt, onion, and part of the 3 cups of water. **ADD** the cooked peas with the cooking water and **BLEND** until the entire mixture is smooth. **POUR** blender mixture into cooking pot. **RINSE** blender with remaining water and **ADD** to pot. **BRING** the entire mixture to a boil. **CONTINUE** stirring until mixture boils and thickens.

```
-------------------------------------------------------------------
| Analysis: FRESH GREEN PEA SOUP              Divided by: 4        |
|           Wgt: 339 g (12 oz.)               Water:      90%      |
-------------------------------------------------------------------
```

Calories	147		Vitamin C	8.08 mg
Protein	6.43 g		Vitamin D	0 mcg
Carbohydrates	21.6 g		Vit E-Alpha E	.407 mg
Fat - Total	4.29 g		Vitamin K	mcg
Saturated Fat	.835 g		Biotin	mcg
Mono Fat	2.37 g		Calcium	30.3 mg
Poly Fat	.812 g		Copper	.33 mg
Cholesterol	0 mg		Iodine	mcg
Dietary Fibre	4.49 g		Iron	2.24 mg
Soluble Fibre	.532 g		Magnesium	50.6 mg
Total Vit A	53.6 RE		Manganese	.473 mg
Thiamin-B1	.318 mg		Phosphorus	125 mg
Riboflavin-B2	.144 mg		Potassium	196 mg
Niacin-B3	1.86 mg		Selenium	8.14 mcg
Niacin Equiv.	1.86 mg		Sodium	611 mg
Vitamin B6	.119 mg		Zinc	1.38 mg
Vitamin B12	0 mcg		Complex Carbs	11.8 g
Folate	55.7 mcg		Sugars	5.32 g
Pantothenic	.262 mg		Water	304 g

CALORIE BREAKDOWN		FAT		EXCHANGES	
Protein	17%	* Saturated :	5%	Bread	1.17
Carbohydrates	57%	Mono Unsat:	14.1%	Lean Meat	.125
Fat-Total *	26%	Poly Unsat:	4.9%	Vegetables	.031
				Fat	.5

GREEK BEAN SOUP (Fassoulatha) (makes 6-8 servings)

500 mL	(2 cups)	dried lima or navy beans
2 L	(8 cups)	water
375 mL	(1 1/2 cups)	finely chopped onion
1	(1)	large clove of garlic, minced
500 mL	(2 cups)	canned or fresh chopped tomatoes
30 mL	(2 Tbsp.)	tomato paste
250 mL	(1 cup)	chopped celery including leaves
250 mL	(1 cup)	diced carrot
60 mL	(1/4 cup)	chopped parsley
30 mL	(2 Tbsp.)	olive oil
15 mL	(1 Tbsp.)	salt

Method:

WASH beans. PLACE in a large pot with 8 cups of water and BRING to the boil. BOIL for 2 minutes, REMOVE from the heat and LEAVE pan covered for 1-2 hours until beans become plump. ADD onions and garlic. COVER and BOIL gently for 1 1/2 hours or until beans are tender. ADD remaining ingredients and COOK a further 30 minutes. GARNISH each serving with fresh parsley. SERVE hot with crusty bread and black olives.

```
-------------------------------------------------------------------
| Analysis: GREEK BEAN SOUP (8 servings)      Divided by: 8       |
|           Wgt: 415 g (14.6 oz.)             Water:     87%      |
-------------------------------------------------------------------
```

Calories	199		Vitamin C	21.4 mg
Protein	11.1 g		Vitamin D	0 mcg
Carbohydrates	37.7 g		Vit E-Alpha E	.778 mg
Fat - Total	1.27 g		Vitamin K	mcg
Saturated Fat	.21 g		Biotin	mcg
Mono Fat	.503 g		Calcium	68 mg
Poly Fat	.352 g		Copper	.478 mg
Cholesterol	0 mg		Iodine	mcg
Dietary Fibre	16.1 g		Iron	4.21 mg
Soluble Fibre	4.27 g		Magnesium	121 mg
Total Vit A	545 RE		Manganese	1.06 mg
Thiamin-B1	.303 mg		Phosphorus	214 mg
Riboflavin-B2	.158 mg		Potassium	1118 mg
Niacin-B3	1.49 mg		Selenium	4.07 mcg
Niacin Equiv.	1.49 mg		Sodium	881 mg
Vitamin B6	.403 mg		Zinc	1.6 mg
Vitamin B12	0 mcg		Complex Carbs	12.9 g
Folate	200 mcg		Sugars	8.69 g
Pantothenic	.937 mg		Water	360 g

CALORIE BREAKDOWN		FAT		EXCHANGES	
Protein	22%	*Saturated :	.9%	Bread	1.78
Carbohydrates	73%	Mono Unsat:	2.2%	Lean Meat	.111
Fat-Total *	6%	Poly Unsat:	1.5%	Fruit	.031
				Vegetables	1.42
				Fat	.109

ITALIAN LENTIL SOUP (makes 10 servings)

375 mL	(1 1/2 cups)	chopped onions (steamed)
3	(3)	large cloves of garlic (minced and steamed)
250 mL	(1 cup)	dry lentils (washed)
2 L	(8 cups)	tomato juice
5 mL	(1 tsp.)	basil
3 mL	(1/2 tsp.)	oregano
		salt to taste or as allowed
125 mL	(1/2 cup)	broken spaghetti or other pasta

Method:

STEAM onions and garlic. ADD remaining ingredients except pasta. SIMMER gently until lentils are tender. (Lentils don't seem to mind the acidic juice as other legumes do.) ADD pasta and COOK until pasta is tender.

```
-------------------------------------------------------------------------
| Analysis: ITALIAN LENTIL SOUP                  Divided by: 10          |
|      Wgt: 245 g (8.65 oz.)                      Water: 85%             |
-------------------------------------------------------------------------
```

Calories	129	Vitamin C	38.9 mg
Protein	7.92 g	Vitamin D	0 mcg
Carbohydrates	25.6 g	Vit E-Alpha E	.719 mg
Fat - Total	.44 g	Vitamin K	mcg
Saturated Fat	.063 g	Biotin	mcg
Mono Fat	.065 g	Calcium	39.4 mg
Poly Fat	.188 g	Copper	.394 mg
Cholesterol	0 mg	Iodine	mcg
Dietary Fibre	4.47 g	Iron	3.23 mg
Soluble Fibre	1.04 g	Magnesium	48.1 mg
Total Vit A	112 RE	Manganese	.519 mg
Thiamin-B1	.25 mg	Phosphorus	142 mg
Riboflavin-B2	.137 mg	Potassium	659 mg
Niacin-B3	2.27 mg	Selenium	6.11 mcg
Niacin Equiv.	2.27 mg	Sodium	921 mg
Vitamin B6	.364 mg	Zinc	1.1 mg
Vitamin B12	0 mcg	Complex Carbs	11.9 g
Folate	127 mcg	Sugars	9.2 g
Pantothenic	.897 mg	Water	208 g

CALORIE BREAKDOWN		FAT		EXCHANGES	
Protein	23%	*Saturated :	.4%	Bread	1.07
Carbohydrates	74%	Mono Unsat:	.4%	Lean Meat	.048
Fat-Total *	3%	Poly Unsat:	1.2%	Vegetables	1.92

LEEK-POTATO SOUP (makes 8 cups)

75 mL	(1/3 cup)	almonds
250 mL	(1 cup)	water
1 L	(4 cups)	leeks, sliced (white part only)
750 mL	(3 cups)	diced potatoes
1500 mL	(6 cups)	water
30 mL	(2 Tbsps.)	chicken style seasoning
3 mL	(1/2 tsp.)	salt
60 mL	(1/4 cup)	chives for garnish (optional)

Method:

WHIZ almonds in blender until a paste. **ADD** 1 cup of water and **CONTINUE** whizzing until well blended. **COOK** leeks and potatoes in 6 cups of water until soft. **ADD** to almond milk in blender and **WHIZ** again. (It won't all fit at once.) **SERVE** with open-faced TOFU-COTTAGE "CHEESE" (page 196) sandwiches. **MAY** be served hot or cold.

```
-----------------------------------------------------------------
| Analysis: LEEK-POTATO SOUP (makes 8 cups)      Divided by: 8   |
|           Wgt: 327 g (11.5 oz.)                Water:     91%  |
-----------------------------------------------------------------
```

Calories	119		Vitamin C	14.8 mg
Protein	2.92 g		Vitamin D	0 mcg
Carbohydrates	21.8 g		Vit E-Alpha E	.765 mg
Fat - Total	2.7 g		Vitamin K	mcg
Saturated Fat	.264 g		Biotin	mcg
Mono Fat	1.55 g		Calcium	51.2 mg
Poly Fat	.617 g		Copper	.237 mg
Cholesterol	0 mg		Iodine	mcg
Dietary Fibre	2.59 g		Iron	1.49 mg
Soluble Fibre	.776 g		Magnesium	43.3 mg
Total Vit A	11.6 RE		Manganese	.411 mg
Thiamin-B1	.102 mg		Phosphorus	69.5 mg
Riboflavin-B2	.06 mg		Potassium	355 mg
Niacin-B3	1.2 mg		Selenium	4.32 mcg
Niacin Equiv.	1.2 mg		Sodium	153 mg
Vitamin B6	.307 mg		Zinc	.457 mg
Vitamin B12	0 mcg		Complex Carbs	14.6 g
Folate	42.5 mcg		Sugars	2.9 g
Pantothenic	.406 mg		Water	297 g

CALORIE BREAKDOWN		FAT		EXCHANGES	
Protein	9%	*Saturated :	1.9%	Bread	.643
Carbohydrates	71%	Mono Unsat:	11.3%	Vegetables	1.52
Fat-Total *	20%	Poly Unsat:	4.5%	Fat	.5

LENTIL-BARLEY STEW (makes about 8 cups)

1500 mL	(10 cups)	boiling water
250 mL	(1 cup)	washed lentils
125 mL	(1/2 cup)	washed pot barley
250 mL	(1 cup)	thinly-sliced celery (include tops)
500 mL	(2 cups)	chopped onion
3	(3)	large garlic cloves, minced
500 mL	(2 cups)	cubed potatoes
250 mL	(1 cup)	thinly-sliced carrots
60 mL	(1/4 cup)	minced fresh parsley
5 mL	(1 tsp.)	onion powder
15 mL	(1 Tbsp.)	Savorex or Marmite

Method:

ADD lentils and barley to boiling water. COOK for about 20 minutes. PREPARE vegetables and ADD to partially-cooked lentils and barley. COOK until lentils and vegetables are tender. ADD seasonings.

```
------------------------------------------------------------------------
| Analysis: LENTIL-BARLEY STEW                    Divided by: 10        |
|           Wgt: 339 g (12 oz.)                   Water:      89%       |
------------------------------------------------------------------------
```

Calories	140		Vitamin C	8.42 mg
Protein	7.46 g		Vitamin D	0 mcg
Carbohydrates	27.8 g		Vit E-Alpha E	.242 mg
Fat - Total	.413 g		Vitamin K	mcg
Saturated Fat	.073 g		Biotin	mcg
Mono Fat	.06 g		Calcium	34.7 mg
Poly Fat	.186 g		Copper	.29 mg
Cholesterol	0 mg		Iodine	mcg
Dietary Fibre	5.27 g		Iron	2.38 mg
Soluble Fibre	1.32 g		Magnesium	43 mg
Total Vit A	415 RE		Manganese	.513 mg
Thiamin-B1	.167 mg		Phosphorus	139 mg
Riboflavin-B2	.085 mg		Potassium	411 mg
Niacin-B3	1.6 mg		Selenium	7.16 mcg
Niacin Equiv.	1.6 mg		Sodium	131 mg
Vitamin B6	.288 mg		Zinc	1.16 mg
Vitamin B12	0 mcg		Complex Carbs	19 g
Folate	99 mcg		Sugars	3.59 g
Pantothenic	.618 mg		Water	302 g

CALORIE BREAKDOWN		FAT		EXCHANGES	
Protein	21%	*Saturated :	.5%	Bread	1.47
Carbohydrates	77%	Mono Unsat:	.4%	Lean Meat	.048
Fat-Total *	3%	Poly Unsat:	1.2%		

LENTIL-RICE POTAGE (8 one-cup servings)

250 mL	(1 cup)	dry green lentils
125 mL	(1/2 cup)	dry brown rice
250 mL	(1 cup)	chopped onion
1500 mL	(6 cups)	boiling water
625 mL	(2 1/2 cups)	canned tomatoes
75 mL	(1/3 cups)	tomato paste
7 mL	(1 1/2 tsp.)	salt
2 mL	(1/4 tsp.)	basil
2 mL	(1/4 tsp.)	thyme

Method:

ADD lentils, rice, and onions to boiling water; SIMMER until done. ADD remaining ingredients and SIMMER a few minutes to blend flavours.

```
-------------------------------------------------------------------------
| Analysis:  LENTIL-RICE POTAGE                        Divided by: 8     |
|            Wgt: 312 g (11 oz.)                       Water:      87%   |
-------------------------------------------------------------------------
```

Calories	153		Vitamin C	17.1 mg
Protein	8.91 g		Vitamin D	0 mcg
Carbohydrates	29 g		Vit E-Alpha E	.518 mg
Fat - Total	.854 g		Vitamin K	mcg
Saturated Fat	.143 g		Biotin	mcg
Mono Fat	.205 g		Calcium	45.7 mg
Poly Fat	.342 g		Copper	.393 mg
Cholesterol	0 mg		Iodine	mcg
Dietary Fibre	4.93 g		Iron	3.17 mg
Soluble Fibre	1.3 g		Magnesium	59.7 mg
Total Vit A	66.2 RE		Manganese	.948 mg
Thiamin-B1	.215 mg		Phosphorus	175 mg
Riboflavin-B2	.113 mg		Potassium	517 mg
Niacin-B3	2.06 mg		Selenium	7.82 mcg
Niacin Equiv.	2.06 mg		Sodium	596 mg
Vitamin B6	.309 mg		Zinc	1.39 mg
Vitamin B12	0 mcg		Complex Carbs	19.3 g
Folate	117 mcg		Sugars	4.75 g
Pantothenic	.824 mg		Water	270 g

CALORIE BREAKDOWN		FAT		EXCHANGES	
Protein	22%	*Saturated :	.8%	Bread	1.49
Carbohydrates	73%	Mono Unsat:	1.2%	Lean Meat	.06
Fat-Total *	5%	Poly Unsat:	1.9%	Fruit	.075
				Vegetables	.967

LENTILS:

There are two noteworthy references to lentils in the Bible. In Genesis 25:29-34 where it tells about Esau selling his birthright for some red lentils and Ezekiel 4:9 where it describes the making of bread from grains, beans, lentils, and vetches during the Babylonian captivity of the Jews. Lentils are readily available, moderately priced, tasty, versatile, and easy to prepare. Because they are so flat and thin they do not need to be soaked before cooking. They are high in protein and iron. One cup of cooked lentils has 6.59 mg of iron.

LIMA BEAN CHOWDER (makes 9 cups - 10 servings)

500 mL	(2 cups)	**EACH**	frozen green lima beans **and** diced raw potatoes
10 mL	(2 tsp.)		olive oil
500 mL	(2 cups)		chopped onions
1	(1)		garlic clove, minced
250 mL	(1 cup)		grated raw carrots
1 L	(4 cups)		liquid from vegetables + water
60 mL	(1/4 cup)		flour
5 mL	(1 tsp.)		salt
30 mL	(2 Tbsp.)		chicken style seasoning
250 mL	(1 cup)	**EACH**	kernel corn **and** frozen (thawed) or fresh peas
250 mL	(1 cup)		GARLIC-DILL DRESSING or TOFU MAYONNAISE
15 mL	(1 Tbsp.)		fresh dill or 1 tsp dried dill (optional)

Method:

COOK the lima beans in 2 cups of water. ADD potatoes after about 5 minutes. SAUTE the onions, carrots, and garlic in the oil. WHIZ the flour, chicken style seasoning, and part of the water in blender. ADD sauteed vegetables, flour mixture, and remaining water to the cooked beans and potatoes. BRING to a boil to COOK the flour. ADD the corn and peas and BRING to a boil again. ADD GARLIC-DILL DRESSING and dill just before serving. ADD more water if desired. SERVE with whole grain bread or crackers and a salad for lunch or supper.

```
Analysis: LIMA BEAN CHOWDER              Divided by: 10
          Wgt: 252 g (8.88 oz.)          Water:      86%
```

Calories	135	Vitamin C	12.8 mg
Protein	6.31 g	Vitamin D	0 mcg
Carbohydrates	25.8 g	Vit E-Alpha Eq	.79 mg
Fat - Total	1.54 g	Vitamin K	mcg
Saturated Fat	.242 g	Biotin	mcg
Mono Fat	.55 g	Calcium	46.5 mg
Poly Fat	.582 g	Copper	.206 mg
Cholesterol	0 mg	Iodine	mcg
Dietary Fibre	5.83 g	Iron	2.21 mg
Soluble Fibre	1.07 g	Magnesium	50.2 mg
Total Vit A	335 RE	Manganese	.333 mg
Thiamin-B1	.434 mg	Phosphorus	123 mg
Riboflavin-B2	.156 mg	Potassium	439 mg
Niacin-B3	2.18 mg	Selenium	3.9 mcg
Niacin Equiv.	1.56 mg	Sodium	378 mg
Vitamin B6	.301 mg	Zinc	.823 mg
Vitamin B12	0 mcg	Complex Carbs	14.4 g
Folate	97.4 mcg	Sugars	5.1 g
Pantothenic	.579 mg	Water	216 g

CALORIE BREAKDOWN		FAT		EXCHANGES	
Protein	18%	*Saturated :	1.5%	Bread	1.19
Carbohydrates	73%	Mono Unsat:	3.5%	Vegetables	.553
Fat-Total *	10%	Poly Unsat:	3.7%	Fat	.087

MINESTRONE (makes 10 servings)

5 mL	(1 tsp.)		olive oil
500 mL	(2 cups)		chopped onion
4	(4)		large garlic cloves, minced
250 mL	(1 cup)	**EACH**	sliced carrots, diced potatoes, **and** sliced celery
2 L	(8 cups)		hot water
30 mL	(2 Tbsp.)		chicken style seasoning
15 mL	(1 Tbsp.)		flake food yeast
5 mL	(1 tsp.)	**EACH**	dried basil **and** salt
250 mL	(1 cup)		canned tomatoes
750 mL	(3 cups)		cooked beans (any mixture of navy, soy, kidney, pinto)
125 mL	(1/2 cup)		uncooked macaroni
500 mL	(2 cups)		chopped raw cabbage
250 mL	(1 cup)		green beans
750 mL	(3 cups)		sliced zucchini (about 2 small)
15 mL	(1 Tbsp.)		snipped parsley

Method:

HEAT the oil. **SAUTE** the onions, garlic, carrots, celery and potatoes. (May **ADD** part of the water to prevent sticking) **ADD** remaining water, chicken style seasoning, food yeast, basil, salt, tomatoes, beans, and macaroni. **SIMMER** for another 20-30 minutes. **ADD** cabbage, beans, and zucchini. **SIMMER** until all ingredients are cooked. **ADD** parsley to garnish. **SERVE** with whole wheat bread.

Analysis: MINESTRONE   Divided by: 10
         Wgt: 417 g (14.7 oz.)   Water: 90%

Calories	159		Vitamin C	21 mg
Protein	7.39 g		Vitamin D	0 mcg
Carbohydrates	31.2 g		Vit E-Alpha Eq	.69 mg
Fat - Total	1.22 g		Vitamin K	mcg
Saturated Fat	.186 g		Biotin	mcg
Mono Fat	.431 g		Calcium	76.9 mg
Poly Fat	.311 g		Copper	.289 mg
Dietary Fibre	9.11 g		Iron	2.61 mg
Soluble Fibre	3.09 g		Magnesium	62 mg
Total Vit A	428 RE		Manganese	.698 mg
Thiamin-B1	.389 mg		Phosphorus	161 mg
Riboflavin-B2	.188 mg		Potassium	663 mg
Niacin-B3	1.86 mg		Selenium	8.83 mcg
Niacin Equiv.	1.42 mg		Sodium	251 mg
Vitamin B6	.335 mg		Zinc	1.1 mg
Vitamin B12	0 mcg		Complex Carbs	14 g
Folate	152 mcg		Sugars	6.47 g
Pantothenic	.598 mg		Water	374 g

CALORIE BREAKDOWN		FAT		EXCHANGES	
Protein	18%	* Saturated :	1%	Bread	1.07
Carbohydrates	76%	Mono Unsat:	2.3%	Lean Meat	.3
Fat-Total *	7%	Poly Unsat:	1.7%	Vegetables	1.59
				Fat	.087

NEWFOUNDLAND PEA SOUP (makes 12 servings)

15 mL	(1 Tbsp.)	olive oil
325 mL	(1 1/2 cups)	chopped onions
2.5 L	(10 cups)	water
10 mL	(2 tsp.)	salt
454 gm	(1 lb. - 2 cups)	dry green split peas (raw)
500 mL	(2 cups)	sliced carrots
250 mL	(1 cup)	shredded cabbage or chopped turnip
30 mL	(2 Tbsp.)	flake food yeast
2	(2)	bay leaves

Method:
SAUTE the onions in the oil in a large pot until transparent. ADD remaining ingredients and SIMMER about 2 hours.

Serving Suggestion: SERVE with whole grain bread or crackers (Wasa, Rice cakes, etc.) and a relish plate of fresh vegetables.

```
Analysis: NEWFOUNDLAND PEA SOUP                    Divided by: 12
          Wgt: 279 g (9.86 oz.)                    Water: 86%
```

Calories	146	Vitamin C	3.15	mg
Protein	9.26 g	Vitamin D	0	mcg
Carbohydrates	24.7 g	Vit E-Alpha E	.747	mg
Fat - Total	1.63 g	Vitamin K		mcg
Saturated Fat	.223 g	Biotin		mcg
Mono Fat	.916 g	Calcium	42.7	mg
Poly Fat	.304 g	Copper	.342	mg
Cholesterol	0 mg	Iodine		mcg
Dietary Fibre	5.81 g	Iron	2.03	mg
Soluble Fibre	2.02 g	Magnesium	48.2	mg
Total Vit A	644 RE	Manganese	.687	mg
Thiamin-B1	.49 mg	Phosphorus	162	mg
Riboflavin-B2	.177 mg	Potassium	443	mg
Niacin-B3	1.86 mg	Selenium	9.62	mcg
Niacin Equiv.	1.12 mg	Sodium	384	mg
Vitamin B6	.195 mg	Zinc	1.2	mg
Vitamin B12	0 mcg	Complex Carbs	13.4	g
Folate	147 mcg	Sugars	4.91	g
Pantothenic	.864 mg	Water	241	g

CALORIE BREAKDOWN		FAT		EXCHANGES	
Protein	25%	* Saturated : 1.3%		Bread	1.15
Carbohydrates	66%	Mono Unsat: 5.5%		Lean Meat	.41
Fat-Total *	10%	Poly Unsat: 1.8%		Vegetables	.641
				Fat	.218

RED CABBAGE AND BEAN SOUP (makes 6 servings)

500 mL	(2 cups)	chopped red cabbage
30 mL	(2 Tbsp.)	lemon juice
5 mL	(1 tsp.)	olive oil
375 mL	(1 1/2 cups)	chopped onion
625 mL	(2 1/2 cups)	water
30 mL	(2 Tbsp.)	chicken style seasoning
250 mL	(1 cup)	canned tomatoes
75 mL	(1/3 cup)	tiny pasta (stars, alphabets, orzo)
540 mL	(19 oz.)	cooked Romano beans (drained and rinsed)
		salt (to taste)
		chopped parsley

Method:

TOSS cabbage with lemon juice and SET aside. In a medium saucepan, HEAT oil over medium heat; ADD onion and SAUTE. ADD cabbage and COOK until tender. STIR in water, chicken style seasoning, and tomatoes; BRING to a boil. ADD pasta and beans; RETURN to simmer and COOK, uncovered for 6 to 8 minutes, stirring occasionally. SEASON to taste. SERVE in heated bowls. SPRINKLE with parsley.

```
-------------------------------------------------------------------------
| Analysis: RED CABBAGE AND BEAN SOUP          Divided by: 6            |
|           Wgt: 278 g (9.8 oz.)               Water:       84%         |
-------------------------------------------------------------------------
```

Calories	169		Vitamin C	26.7 mg
Protein	8.4 g		Vitamin D	0 mcg
Carbohydrates	29.6 g		Vit E-Alpha E	.812 mg
Fat - Total	2.26 g		Vitamin K	mcg
Saturated Fat	.333 g		Biotin	mcg
Mono Fat	1.18 g		Calcium	69.7 mg
Poly Fat	.397 g		Copper	.27 mg
Cholesterol	0 mg		Iodine	mcg
Dietary Fibre	8.86 g		Iron	2.27 mg
Soluble Fibre	2.18 g		Magnesium	51.4 mg
Total Vit A	38 RE		Manganese	.434 mg
Thiamin-B1	.251 mg		Phosphorus	130 mg
Riboflavin-B2	.102 mg		Potassium	477 mg
Niacin-B3	1.24 mg		Selenium	5.73 mcg
Niacin Equiv.	1.24 mg		Sodium	429 mg
Vitamin B6	.183 mg		Zinc	1.09 mg
Vitamin B12	0 mcg		Complex Carbs	4.33 g
Folate	163 mcg		Sugars	4.26 g
Pantothenic	.378 mg		Water	234 g

CALORIE BREAKDOWN		FAT		EXCHANGES	
Protein	19%	* Saturated :	1.7%	Bread	1.38
Carbohydrates	69%	Mono Unsat:	6.1%	Lean Meat	.209
Fat-Total *	12%	Poly Unsat:	2.1%	Fruit	.021
				Vegetables	.953
				Fat	.291

SUPER SEASHELL STEW (makes 9 cups)

125 mL	(1/2 cup)		sliced celery
1	(1)		large garlic clove, minced
75 mL	(1/3 cup)		chopped green sweet pepper
75 mL	(1/3 cup)		chopped red sweet pepper
250 mL	(1 cup)		chopped onion
250 mL	(1 cup)		sliced carrots
500 mL	(2 cups)		canned tomatoes
750 mL	(3 cups)		water
10 mL	(2 tsp.)		salt
3 mL	(1/2 tsp.)	**EACH**	oregano **and** basil
375 mL	(1 1/2 cups)		small shell macaroni
500 mL	(2 cups)		cooked garbanzos
250 mL	(1 cup)		sliced zucchini
60 mL	(1/4 cup)		chopped parsley

Method:

STEAM celery, garlic, peppers, onion, and carrots in a small amount of water until tender. **ADD** tomatoes, water, salt, oregano, basil, macaroni, and garbanzos. **SIMMER** until vegetables are tender. **ADD** zucchini and parsley and **COOK** until tender-crisp.

```
Analysis: SUPER SEASHELL STEW                    Divided by: 9
          Wgt: 247 g (8.73 oz.)                  Water:  84%
```

Calories	153	Vitamin C	24.3 mg
Protein	6.65 g	Vitamin D	0 mcg
Carbohydrates	29.5 g	Vit E-Alpha E	.566 mg
Fat - Total	1.47 g	Vitamin K	mcg
Saturated Fat	.178 g	Biotin	mcg
Mono Fat	.28 g	Calcium	55.3 mg
Poly Fat	.636 g	Copper	.273 mg
Cholesterol	0 mg	Iodine	mcg
Dietary Fibre	4.59 g	Iron	2.46 mg
Soluble Fibre	1.41 g	Magnesium	43.2 mg
Total Vit A	414 RE	Manganese	.656 mg
Thiamin-B1	.286 mg	Phosphorus	119 mg
Riboflavin-B2	.139 mg	Potassium	401 mg
Niacin-B3	2.18 mg	Selenium	12.6 mcg
Niacin Equiv.	2.18 mg	Sodium	579 mg
Vitamin B6	.197 mg	Zinc	1.02 mg
Vitamin B12	0 mcg	Complex Carbs	19.9 g
Folate	84.1 mcg	Sugars	5.05 g
Pantothenic	.35 mg	Water	207 g

CALORIE BREAKDOWN		FAT		EXCHANGES	
Protein	17%	*Saturated:	1%	Bread	1.64
Carbohydrates	75%	Mono Unsat:	1.6%	Lean Meat	.182
Fat-Total *	8%	Poly Unsat:	3.6%	Vegetables	1.08

UKRAINIAN BORSCHT (makes 10 cups - 10 servings)

30 mL	(2 Tbsp.)	water to steam onions, carrots, and celery
125 mL	(1/2 cup)	chopped onion
250 mL	(1 cup)	thinly sliced carrot
125 mL	(1/2 cup)	thinly sliced celery
750 mL	(3 cups)	grated raw beets
500 mL	(2 cups)	shredded cabbage
500 mL	(2 cups)	cubed potatoes
250 mL	(1 cup)	cooked tomatoes, cut up
8 mL	(1 1/2 tsp.)	lemon juice
1.5 L	(6 cups)	water
30 mL	(2 Tbsp.)	chopped dill or 2 tsp. ground dill seed
3 mL	(1/2 tsp.)	salt
125 mL	(1/2 cup)	GARLIC-DILL DRESSING (optional)

Method:

STEAM onions, carrots, and celery for about 5 minutes. ADD beets, cabbage, potatoes, tomatoes, and lemon juice. SIMMER about 15 minutes. ADD water and seasoning. SIMMER for half an hour. ADD dill and salt to taste. At serving time ADD a tablespoon of GARLIC-DILL DRESSING to each individual bowl.

```
-----------------------------------------------------------------
| Analysis: UKRAINIAN BORSCHT (10)         Divided by: 10        |
|           Wgt: 289 g (10.2 oz.)          Water:      93%       |
-----------------------------------------------------------------
```

Calories	69.2		Vitamin C	16 mg
Protein	2.72 g		Vitamin D	0 mcg
Carbohydrates	14.4 g		Vit E-Alpha E	.848 mg
Fat - Total	.653 g		Vitamin K	mcg
Saturated Fat	.099 g		Biotin	mcg
Mono Fat	.117 g		Calcium	40.1 mg
Poly Fat	.323 g		Copper	.153 mg
Cholesterol	0 mg		Iodine	mcg
Dietary Fibre	3.14 g		Iron	1.35 mg
Soluble Fibre	.918 g		Magnesium	33.3 mg
Total Vit A	406 RE		Manganese	.364 mg
Thiamin-B1	.088 mg		Phosphorus	54.5 mg
Riboflavin-B2	.087 mg		Potassium	401 mg
Niacin-B3	1.04 mg		Selenium	1.28 mcg
Niacin Equiv.	.826 mg		Sodium	202 mg
Vitamin B6	.209 mg		Zinc	.449 mg
Vitamin B12	0 mcg		Complex Carbs	5.96 g
Folate	62.9 mcg		Sugars	5.07 g
Pantothenic	.393 mg		Water	269 g

CALORIE BREAKDOWN		FAT	EXCHANGES	
Protein	15%	*Saturated : 1.2%	Bread	.3
Carbohydrates	77%	Mono Unsat: 1.4%	Fruit	.003
Fat-Total *	8%	Poly Unsat: 3.9%	Vegetables	.45

ZUCCHINI VELVET SOUP (makes 6 servings)

375 mL	(1 1/2 cups)	chopped onion
1 L	(4 cups)	water
2.5 L	(10 cups)	zucchini, cut in chunks
125 mL	(1/2 cup)	rolled oats
75 mL	(1/3 cup)	fresh dill, finely chopped
30 mL	(2 Tbsp.)	soy sauce

Method:

COOK the onion in 1/2 cup of the water in a medium saucepan for 5 minutes. **ADD** the remaining ingredients. **BRING** to a boil, **COVER, SIMMER** about 20 minutes. **PROCESS** in blender or food processor, small amounts at a time, until velvety smooth. **SERVE** warm.

```
Analysis: ZUCCHINI VELVET SOUP (8 cups)        Divided by: 8
          Wgt: 321 g (11.3 oz.)                Water:    95%
```

Calories	56.1		Vitamin C	16.8 mg
Protein	3.29 g		Vitamin D	0 mcg
Carbohydrates	11.1 g		Vit E-Alpha E	.269 mg
Fat - Total	.602 g		Vitamin K	mcg
Saturated Fat	.112 g		Biotin	mcg
Mono Fat	.128 g		Calcium	36.8 mg
Poly Fat	.234 g		Copper	.141 mg
Cholesterol	0 mg		Iodine	mcg
Dietary Fibre	2.96 g		Iron	1.09 mg
Soluble Fibre	.599 g		Magnesium	49.1 mg
Total Vit A	58.3 RE		Manganese	.455 mg
Thiamin-B1	.166 mg		Phosphorus	91 mg
Riboflavin-B2	.069 mg		Potassium	478 mg
Niacin-B3	.89 mg		Selenium	4.32 mcg
Niacin Equiv.	.891 mg		Sodium	266 mg
Vitamin B6	.194 mg		Zinc	.593 mg
Vitamin B12	0 mcg		Complex Carbs	3.33 g
Folate	44.4 mcg		Sugars	4.81 g
Pantothenic	.246 mg		Water	304 g

CALORIE BREAKDOWN		FAT		EXCHANGES	
Protein	21%	* Saturated:	1.6%	Bread	.179
Carbohydrates	70%	Mono Unsat:	1.8%	Vegetables	1.62
Fat-Total *	9%	Poly Unsat:	3.3%		

APPLE MARMALADE (makes about 2 cups)

355 mL	(12 1/2 oz.)	water
355 mL	(12 1/2 oz.)	frozen apple juice concentrate
60 mL	(1/4 cup)	cornstarch
1 mL	(1/4 tsp.)	coriander
1 mL	(1/4 tsp.)	cardamon
2	(2)	large unpeeled apples

Method:

RESERVE 125 mL (1/2 cup) of the water. BRING remaining water and juice to a boil. COMBINE cornstarch and reserved water. STIR in some of the hot liquid. POUR into remaining hot liquid, and BOIL until clear, stirring constantly. ADD coriander and cardamon. SHRED the apple and STIR it into the thickened juice.

Serving Suggestions: Chill and use as jam or use hot on toast, waffles, granola or muffins.

```
-------------------------------------------------------------------
| Analysis: APPLE MARMALADE                      Divided by: 16   |
|           Wgt: 74.6 g (2.63 oz.)               Water:      86%  |
-------------------------------------------------------------------
```

Calories	41.7	Vitamin C	1.11 mg
Protein	.119 g	Vitamin D	0 mcg
Carbohydrates	10.3 g	Vit E-Alpha E	.084 mg
Fat - Total	.115 g	Vitamin K	mcg
Saturated Fat	.019 g	Biotin	mcg
Mono Fat	.007 g	Calcium	4.83 mg
Poly Fat	.033 g	Copper	.015 mg
Cholesterol	0 mg	Iodine	mcg
Dietary Fibre	.368 g	Iron	.195 mg
Soluble Fibre	.166 g	Magnesium	3.86 mg
Total Vit A	.713 RE	Manganese	.053 mg
Thiamin-B1	.004 mg	Phosphorus	5.45 mg
Riboflavin-B2	.011 mg	Potassium	91.1 mg
Niacin-B3	.034 mg	Selenium	.134 mcg
Niacin Equiv.	.034 mg	Sodium	4.32 mg
Vitamin B6	.026 mg	Zinc	.034 mg
Vitamin B12	0 mcg	Complex Carbs	1.37 g
Folate	.551 mcg	Sugars	8.55 g
Pantothenic	.046 mg	Water	63.8 g

CALORIE BREAKDOWN		FAT		EXCHANGES	
Protein	1%	* Saturated :	.4%	Bread	.096
Carbohydrates	96%	Mono Unsat:	.2%	Fruit	.644
Fat-Total *	2%	Poly Unsat:	.7%		

APPLE MILLET (makes 4 cups - 8 half-cup servings)

45 mL	(3 Tbsp.)	blanched almonds
60 mL	(1/4 cup)	water
125 mL	(1/2 cup)	dry hulled millet seed
125 mL	(1/2 cup)	washed raisins
2	(2)	large apples, washed and grated
1 mL	(1/4 tsp.)	salt
500 mL	(2 cups)	boiling water (or less if a firmer pudding is desired)

Method:
BLEND almonds to a paste. ADD water and CONTINUE to blend. MIX all ingredients together. POUR into a casserole. BAKE at 350° F. for one hour.

```
----------------------------------------------------------------
| Analysis: APPLE MILLET                      Divided by: 8     |
|           Wgt: 145 g (5.13 oz.)             Water:      77%   |
----------------------------------------------------------------
```

Calories	133		Vitamin C	3.89 mg
Protein	2.26 g		Vitamin D	0 mcg
Carbohydrates	27.9 g		Vit E-Alpha E	.579 mg
Fat - Total	2.47 g		Vitamin K	mcg
Saturated Fat	.221 g		Biotin	mcg
Mono Fat	1.17 g		Calcium	22.5 mg
Poly Fat	.454 g		Copper	.098 mg
Cholesterol	0 mg		Iodine	mcg
Dietary Fibre	2.19 g		Iron	.519 mg
Soluble Fibre	.742 g		Magnesium	17.9 mg
Total Vit A	2.78 RE		Manganese	.126 mg
Thiamin-B1	.061 mg		Phosphorus	64 mg
Riboflavin-B2	.067 mg		Potassium	203 mg
Niacin-B3	.425 mg		Selenium	1.08 mcg
Niacin Equiv.	.245 mg		Sodium	72.2 mg
Vitamin B6	.065 mg		Zinc	.186 mg
Vitamin B12	0 mcg		Complex Carbs	.131 g
Folate	3.22 mcg		Sugars	18.3 g
Pantothenic	.072 mg		Water	112 g

CALORIE BREAKDOWN		FAT	EXCHANGES	
Protein	6%	Saturated : 1.4%	Fruit	1.33
Carbohydrates	78%	Mono Unsat: 7.4%	Fat	.38
Fat - Total *	16%	Poly Unsat: 2.9%		

MILLET:
Millet is used extensively throughout much of the world. It is a very nutritious grain, containing ample protein and an abundance of minerals, especially iron. Millet is high in starch, hence it is an energy food. It is generally superior to wheat, rice, and corn in protein quality, but it is low in the essential amino acid lysine. Millet comes both hulled and unhulled, but recipes referring to "whole millet" mean the hulled variety, since it is the most common. Although the unhulled seed has higher fibre content, ample fibre remains in the hulled variety. Hulled millet cooks up quickly and makes a delicious, highly digestible cereal. It does not contain any gluten, so it is unsuitable for making leavened breads.

APPLE RICE PUDDING (makes 6 servings)

125 mL	(1/2 cup)		dry brown rice (Uncle Ben's Works well.)
500 mL	(2 cups)		apple juice
30 mL	(2 Tbsp.)	**EACH**	raisins **and** honey
375 mL	(1 1/2 cups)		diced or grated apples

Method:

COMBINE rice, apple juice, and raisins. COVER and COOK on low heat for 40 minutes or until rice is done. ADD apples and honey. COOK 10 minutes longer. TOP with nuts and SERVE plain or with whipped topping.

```
Analysis: APPLE RICE PUDDING              Divided by: 8
          Wgt: 99.6 g (3.51 oz.)          Water:      73%
```

Calories	106		Vitamin C	1.66 mg
Protein	1.13 g		Vitamin D	0 mcg
Carbohydrates	25 g		Vit E-Alpha E	.144 mg
Fat - Total	.482 g		Vitamin K	mcg
Saturated Fat	.094 g		Biotin	mcg
Mono Fat	.127 g		Calcium	9.15 mg
Poly Fat	.163 g		Copper	.058 mg
Cholesterol	0 mg		Iodine	mcg
Dietary Fibre	1.02 g		Iron	.432 mg
Soluble Fibre	.294 g		Magnesium	21.5 mg
Total Vit A	1.1 RE		Manganese	.491 mg
Thiamin-B1	.055 mg		Phosphorus	46.5 mg
Riboflavin-B2	.027 mg		Potassium	144 mg
Niacin-B3	.652 mg		Selenium	4.84 mcg
Niacin Equiv.	.652 mg		Sodium	38.8 mg
Vitamin B6	.095 mg		Zinc	.284 mg
Vitamin B12	0 mcg		Complex Carbs	8.38 g
Folate	3.25 mcg		Sugars	15.6 g
Pantothenic	.227 mg		Water	72.3 g

CALORIE BREAKDOWN		FAT		EXCHANGES	
Protein	4%	*Saturated	.8%	Bread	.532
Carbohydrates	92%	Mono Unsat:	1.1%	Fruit	1.08
Fat-Total *	4%	Poly Unsat:	1.3%		

VITAMIN B$_{12}$

Since there isn't a reliable and adequate known source of Vitamin B$_{12}$ in plant food, vegans should obtain their dietary needs either from foods fortified with Vitamin B$_{12}$, such as some ready-to-eat cereals, fortified soy beverages, fortified meat analogues, or from the regular use of a Vitamin B$_{12}$ supplement. A B$_{12}$ supplement of 10-15 micrograms taken once a week is probably adequate. Results of studies done with vegans at Weimar Institute in California show that for an oral supplement to have any beneficial effect, the tablet should be thoroughly chewed and not swallowed whole. Winston J. Craig, PhD., R.D. *Nutrition for the Nineties*, pages 187-188.

BERRIED PLEASURE (makes 6 servings)

156 mL	(5 1/2 oz.)	frozen grape juice concentrate, undiluted
375 mL	(1 1/2 cups)	water
60 mL	(1/4 cup)	quick cooking tapioca
5 mL	(1 tsp.)	fresh lemon juice
250 mL	(1 cup)	blueberries or other berries

Method:
LET grape juice concentrate, water, and tapioca stand in saucepan 5 minutes. BRING to a boil over medium heat. SIMMER slowly, stirring often, until tapioca is clear and juice is thickened. ADD lemon juice and STIR in berries. COOL. STIR. SERVE as a simple chilled dessert in little glass dishes with a spoonful of whipped topping, or with fruit, such as bananas and berries, stirred or layered in, or SERVE hot on whole wheat toast, waffles or pancakes.

```
Analysis: BERRIED PLEASURE                    Divided by: 6
          Wgt: 128 g (4.51 oz.)               Water:     80%
```

Calories	99.2		Vitamin C	30.9 mg
Protein	.412 g		Vitamin D	0 mcg
Carbohydrates	24.4 g		Vit E-Alpha E	.322 mg
Fat - Total	.278 g		Vitamin K	mcg
Saturated Fat	.067 g		Biotin	mcg
Mono Fat	.048 g		Calcium	8.66 mg
Poly Fat	.121 g		Copper	.032 mg
Cholesterol	0 mg		Iodine	mcg
Dietary Fibre	1.49 g		Iron	.209 mg
Soluble Fibre	.428 g		Magnesium	7.33 mg
Total Vit A	3.16 RE		Manganese	.26 mg
Thiamin-B1	.027 mg		Phosphorus	8.97 mg
Riboflavin-B2	.042 mg		Potassium	42.8 mg
Niacin-B3	.29 mg		Selenium	1.25 mcg
Niacin Equiv.	.29 mg		Sodium	4.56 mg
Vitamin B6	.069 mg		Zinc	.083 mg
Vitamin B12	0 mcg		Complex Carbs	0 g
Folate	3.43 mcg		Sugars	17.7 g
Pantothenic	.063 mg		Water	102 g

CALORIE BREAKDOWN		FAT		EXCHANGES	
Protein	2%	Saturated :	.6%	Fruit	.97
Carbohydrate	96%	Mono Unsat:	.4%		
Fat	2%	Poly Unsat:	1.1%		

DATE BUTTER:
SIMMER equal amounts of dates and water until the dates are soft and can be stirred to a smooth paste or WHIZ in the food processor after the dates are cooked. USE as a sweetener in muffins, bread, cookies, pudding, granola or as jam on toast.

CURRANT DELIGHT (makes 16 - 1/8 cup servings)

375 mL	(1 1/2 cups)	unsweetened grape juice (purple)
250 mL	(1 cup)	dried currants
15 mL	(1 Tbsp.)	minute tapioca

Method:

PLACE all ingredients in saucepan. BRING to a simmer, then TURN off heat. COVER and LET stand for 30 minutes. Then TURN on heat and SIMMER very slowly about 5-7 minutes until tapioca turns translucent. USE as a topping for waffles or REFRIGERATE and USE as a spread for bread. (This is best if made the evening before you need it so the currants hydrate more and appear like little berries.)

```
Analysis:  CURRANT DELIGHT (2 Tbsp servings)       Divided by: 16
           Wgt: 33.3 g (1.17 oz.)                  Water:      65%
```

Calories	41.9		Vitamin C	.447 mg
Protein	.507 g		Vitamin D	0 mcg
Carbohydrates	10.6 g		Vit E-Alpha E	.011 mg
Fat - Total	.043 g		Vitamin K	mcg
Saturated Fat	.008 g		Biotin	mcg
Mono Fat	.005 g		Calcium	9.89 mg
Poly Fat	.021 g		Copper	.049 mg
Cholesterol	0 mg		Iodine	mcg
Dietary Fibre	.778 g		Iron	.353 mg
Soluble Fibre	.146 g		Magnesium	6.06 mg
Total Vit A	.893 RE		Manganese	.128 mg
Thiamin-B1	.021 mg		Phosphorus	13.9 mg
Riboflavin-B2	.022 mg		Potassium	112 mg
Niacin-B3	.208 mg		Selenium	.345 mcg
Niacin Equiv.	.208 mg		Sodium	1.43 mg
Vitamin B6	.042 mg		Zinc	.071 mg
Vitamin B12	0 mcg		Complex Carbs	0 g
Folate	1.54 mcg		Sugars	9.38 g
Pantothenic	.014 mg		Water	21.7 g

CALORIE BREAKDOWN		FAT		EXCHANGES	
Protein	5%	*Saturated :	.2%	Fruit	.657
Carbohydrates	95%	Mono Unsat:	.1%		
Fat-Total *	1%	Poly Unsat:	.4%		

FRUIT AND MILLET PUDDING (makes eight 130 gram servings)

500 mL	(2 cups)	cooked millet (May substitute rice.)
60 mL	(1/4 cup)	raisins
250 mL	(1 cup)	crushed unsweetened pineapple
60 mL	(1/4 cup)	raw cashews
5 mL	(1 tsp.)	vanilla
3 mL	(1/2 tsp.)	almond extract
180 mL	(3/4 cup)	hot water
1	(1)	medium banana
45 mL	(3 Tbsp.)	orange juice concentrate

Method:

MIX millet, raisins, and pineapple together and PLACE in a casserole. BLEND the cashews until a smooth paste in blender or food processor. ADD remaining ingredients and WHIZ until smooth. POUR over ingredients in casserole. BAKE at 350° F. for 45 minutes and SERVE hot.

```
Analysis: FRUIT AND MILLET              Divided by: 8
          Wgt: 140 g (4.95 oz.)         Water:     75%
```

Calories	148		Vitamin C	8.83 mg
Protein	3.26 g		Vitamin D	0 mcg
Carbohydrates	28.8 g		Vit E-Alpha E	.352 mg
Fat - Total	2.71 g		Vitamin K	mcg
Saturated Fat	.529 g		Biotin	mcg
Mono Fat	1.29 g		Calcium	12.6 mg
Poly Fat	.669 g		Copper	.254 mg
Cholesterol	0 mg		Iodine	mcg
Dietary Fibre	1.7 g		Iron	.874 mg
Soluble Fibre	.55 g		Magnesium	48.8 mg
Total Vit A	3.33 RE		Manganese	.586 mg
Thiamin-B1	.124 mg		Phosphorus	91.9 mg
Riboflavin-B2	.084 mg		Potassium	211 mg
Niacin-B3	1.09 mg		Selenium	1.67 mcg
Niacin Equiv.	1.09 mg		Sodium	3.65 mg
Vitamin B6	.198 mg		Zinc	.863 mg
Vitamin B12	0 mcg		Complex Carbs	14.7 g
Folate	23.7 mcg		Sugars	12.3 g
Pantothenic	.243 mg		Water	105 g

CALORIE BREAKDOWN	FAT	EXCHANGES
Protein 9%	*Saturated : 3.1%	Bread .875
Carbohydrates 75%	Mono Unsat: 7.6%	Lean Meat .062
Fat-Total * 16%	Poly Unsat: 3.9%	Fruit .854

FRUIT SOUP (makes 12 servings)

375 gm	(2 cups)	dried prunes
10	(10)	dried apricots
10	(10)	dried figs
1 L	(4 cups)	water
540 mL	(19 oz.)	unsweetened pineapple tidbits (Do not drain)
175 mL	(6 1/4 oz.)	orange juice concentrate
60 mL	(1/4 cup)	minute tapioca
250 mL	(1 cup)	frozen strawberries

Method:

SOAK the prunes, apricots, and figs in the water overnight. **COOK** until soft. **ADD** pineapple, orange juice, and minute tapioca. **COOK** until tapioca is clear. **ADD** strawberries just before serving. **EXPERIMENT** with other combinations of fruits such as apples, raisins, peaches, or rhubarb in place of or in addition to some other ingredient.

```
-----------------------------------------------------------------------
| Analysis: FRUIT SOUP                      Divided by: 16            |
|           Wgt: 146 g (5.15 oz.)           Water:        75%         |
-----------------------------------------------------------------------
```

Calories	131		Vitamin C	16.9 mg
Protein	1.4 g		Vitamin D	0 mcg
Carbohydrates	33.9 g		Vit E-Alpha E	.078 mg
Fat - Total	.318 g		Vitamin K	mcg
Saturated Fat	.042 g		Biotin	mcg
Mono Fat	.121 g		Calcium	39.2 mg
Poly Fat	.111 g		Copper	.193 mg
Cholesterol	0 mg		Iodine	mcg
Dietary Fibre	3.42 g		Iron	1.14 mg
Soluble Fibre	1.36 g		Magnesium	26.7 mg
Total Vit A	67.4 RE		Manganese	.484 mg
Thiamin-B1	.078 mg		Phosphorus	36.1 mg
Riboflavin-B2	.065 mg		Potassium	385 mg
Niacin-B3	.787 mg		Selenium	1.71 mcg
Niacin Equiv.	.787 mg		Sodium	4.92 mg
Vitamin B6	.128 mg		Zinc	.273 mg
Vitamin B12	0 mcg		Complex Carbs	0 g
Folate	15.3 mcg		Sugars	28.6 g
Pantothenic	.254 mg		Water	109 g

CALORIE BREAKDOWN		FAT		EXCHANGES	
Protein	4%	*Saturated:	.3%	Fruit	2.08
Carbohydrates	94%	Mono Unsat:	.8%		
Fat	2%	Poly Unsat:	.7%		

INDIAN CORNMEAL DELIGHT (makes 5 1/4 cups, - 4 2/3-cup servings)

250 mL	(1 cup)	cornmeal
250 mL	(1 cup)	cold water
750 mL	(3 cups)	hot water
5 mL	(1 tsp.)	salt
500 mL	(2 cups)	grated raw apple
60 mL	(1/4 cup)	raisins

Method:

STIR cornmeal into cold water and the cornmeal mixture into the hot water. COOK until thick. STIR in remaining ingredients and PUT into a baking dish. BAKE 45 minutes at 350° F.

```
-------------------------------------------------------------------------
| Analysis: INDIAN CORNMEAL DELIGHT            Divided by: 4             |
|           Wgt: 354 g (12.5 oz.)              Water:      85%           |
-------------------------------------------------------------------------
```

Calories	199		Vitamin C	4.38 mg
Protein	3.39 g		Vitamin D	0 mcg
Carbohydrates	45.7 g		Vit E-Alpha E	.542 mg
Fat - Total	.873 g		Vitamin K	mcg
Saturated Fat	.134 g		Biotin	mcg
Mono Fat	.155 g		Calcium	17.1 mg
Poly Fat	.333 g		Copper	.102 mg
Cholesterol	0 mg		Iodine	mcg
Dietary Fibre	3.83 g		Iron	1.79 mg
Soluble Fibre	1.23 g		Magnesium	23.6 mg
Total Vit A	17.8 RE		Manganese	.104 mg
Thiamin-B1	.275 mg		Phosphorus	43.7 mg
Riboflavin-B2	.159 mg		Potassium	214 mg
Niacin-B3	1.88 mg		Selenium	3.37 mcg
Niacin Equiv.	1.88 mg		Sodium	542 mg
Vitamin B6	.148 mg		Zinc	.381 mg
Vitamin B12	0 mcg		Complex Carbs	24.9 g
Folate	18.9 mcg		Sugars	16.9 g
Pantothenic	.156 mg		Water	302 g

CALORIE BREAKDOWN		FAT		EXCHANGES	
Protein	7%	*Saturated :	.6%	Bread	1.5
Carbohydrates	90%	Mono Unsat:	.7%	Fruit	1.27
Fat-Total *	4%	Poly Unsat:	1.5%		

IODINE:

One important physiological function of salt is that it provides a vehicle for meeting the body's iodine requirement. Until iodized salt was introduced, iodine-deficiency goiter was common in certain areas of North America. Iodized salt contains 0.01% potassium iodide or 76 mcg of iodine per gram. Thus, the average use of 3.4 g. of iodized salt per person per day adds approximately 260 mcg to the daily intake, more than meeting the normal requirement of about 150 mcg. *Foods and Nutrition Encyclopedia* - Volume 2, page 1959.

JOHNNY APPLESEED RICE PUDDING (makes 6 servings)

125 mL	(1/2 cup)	dry brown rice
500 mL	(2 cups)	apple juice
30 mL	(2 Tbsp)	raisins
375 mL	(1 1/2 cups)	diced or grated apples
30 mL	(2 Tbsp)	honey

Method:

COMBINE rice, apple juice, and raisins. COVER and COOK on low heat for 40 minutes. ADD apples and honey. COOK 10 minutes longer. TOP with nuts and SERVE plain or with whipped topping. (See SOYAGEN DESSERT TOPPING or ORANGE TOFU TOPPING.)

```
Analysis: JOHNNY APPLESEED RICE            Divided by: 8
          Wgt: 99.6 g (3.51 oz.)           Water:     73%
```

Calories	106		Vitamin C	1.66 mg
Protein	1.13 g		Vitamin D	0 mcg
Carbohydrates	25 g		Vit E-Alpha E	.144 mg
Fat - Total	.482 g		Vitamin K	mcg
Saturated Fat	.094 g		Biotin	mcg
Mono Fat	.127 g		Calcium	9.15 mg
Poly Fat	.163 g		Copper	.058 mg
Cholesterol	0 mg		Iodine	mcg
Dietary Fibre	1.02 g		Iron	.432 mg
Soluble Fibre	.294 g		Magnesium	21.5 mg
Total Vit A	1.1 RE		Manganese	.491 mg
Thiamin-B1	.055 mg		Phosphorus	46.5 mg
Riboflavin-B2	.027 mg		Potassium	144 mg
Niacin-B3	.652 mg		Selenium	4.84 mcg
Niacin Equiv.	.652 mg		Sodium	38.8 mg
Vitamin B6	.095 mg		Zinc	.284 mg
Vitamin B12	0 mcg		Complex Carbs	8.38 g
Folate	3.25 mcg		Sugars	15.6 g
Pantothenic	.227 mg		Water	72.3 g

CALORIE BREAKDOWN		FAT		EXCHANGES	
Protein	4%	*Saturated	.8%	Bread	.532
Carbohydrates	92%	Mono Unsat:	1.1%	Fruit	1.08
Fat-Total *	4%	Poly Unsat:	1.3%		

FLAKE FOOD YEAST:

This product is a pale yellow colour flake, and has a distinct but pleasant aroma. It is grown by aerobic fermentation on molasses. After the conversion of all the molasses sugar, the yeasts are partially autolysed, and completely inactivated in order to make the nutrients available as food. It contains a full complement of amino acids, iron, and B vitamins, as well as a few hard-to-get trace elements like selenium and chromium. It is, however, a high phosphorus food so this should be remembered when using it. Excessive use could cause a calcium-phosphorus imbalance. Often it is used for the cheesy flavour it provides, and it would not be harmful in modest amounts.

MARMALADE DELUXE (16 servings)

250 mL	(1 cup)	**EACH**	dried apricots and pitted dates
15 mL	(1 Tbsp.)		fresh lemon juice
430 mL	(1 3/4 cups)		pineapple juice

Method:

WASH and SOAK fruit in the juice overnight. BLEND after soaking. USE in place of jams or jellies.

```
-------------------------------------------------------------------------
| Analysis: MARMALADE DELUXE (16 servings)          Divided by: 16      |
|           Wgt: 47.5 g (1.68 oz.)                  Water:      62%     |
-------------------------------------------------------------------------
```

Calories	65.5		Vitamin C	3.56 mg
Protein	.608 g		Vitamin D	0 mcg
Carbohydrates	17 g		Vit E-Alpha E	.015 mg
Fat - Total	.111 g		Vitamin K	mcg
Saturated Fat	.026 g		Biotin	mcg
Mono Fat	.034 g		Calcium	11.9 mg
Poly Fat	.019 g		Copper	.092 mg
Cholesterol	0 mg		Iodine	mcg
Dietary Fibre	1.61 g		Iron	.582 mg
Soluble Fibre	.648 g		Magnesium	11.3 mg
Total Vit A	59.5 RE		Manganese	.327 mg
Thiamin-B1	.026 mg		Phosphorus	16.2 mg
Riboflavin-B2	.029 mg		Potassium	222 mg
Niacin-B3	.56 mg		Selenium	.563 mcg
Niacin Equiv.	.56 mg		Sodium	1.43 mg
Vitamin B6	.061 mg		Zinc	.123 mg
Vitamin B12	0 mcg		Complex Carbs	0 g
Folate	8.68 mcg		Sugars	15.4 g
Pantothenic	.176 mg		Water	29.3 g

CALORIE BREAKDOWN		FATS		EXCHANGES
Protein	3%	*Saturated:	.3%	Fruit 1.05
Carbohydrates	95%	Mono Unsat:	.4%	
Fat-Total *	1%	Poly Unsat:	.2%	

HOW TO EAT MORE AND WEIGH LESS!

1. Let diets die! Eat for health, and let the pounds take care of themselves.
2. Eat more natural foods, simply prepared!
3. Avoid refined, processed foods and snacks high in fat and sugar.
    - Freely use whole grain products, even pasta
    - Freely use tubers and legumes, like potatoes, yams, squash, beans
    - Freely use fresh fruits and vegetables (with low-calorie dressings)
    - Eat a substantial breakfast daily
4. If you use any animal products use them sparingly, more like a condiment.
5. Drink 6-8 glasses of plain water daily.
6. Walk briskly every day.
7. Picture yourself successful; tie into supportive and spiritual resources.
8. Beware of weak moments. (Don't buy problem foods. If they are not around you won't eat them.) Hans Diehl, DrHSc, MPH, *To Your Health*, 52-53.

MILLET BREAKFAST PUDDING (makes 6 servings)

250 mL	(1 cup)	uncooked millet (Wash)
125 mL	(1/2 cup)	chopped dates
125 mL	(1/2 cup)	chopped prunes
3	(3)	dried figs
3 mL	(1/2 tsp.)	salt
1 L	(4 cups)	boiling water
5 mL	(1 tsp.)	vanilla

Method:

MIX millet, dates, prunes, figs, and salt in a casserole. **ADD** boiling water and vanilla. **BAKE** in a 350° F. oven for one hour. This can be made ahead and reheated.

```
Analysis: MILLET BREAKFAST PUDDING (6 SERVINGS)     Divided by: 6
          Wgt: 231 g (8.16 oz.)                     Water:     71%
```

Protein	4.55 g		Vitamin D	0 mcg
Carbohydrates	55.7 g		Vit E-Alpha E	.135 mg
Fat - Total	3.51 g		Vitamin K	mcg
Saturated Fat	1.91 g		Biotin	mcg
Mono Fat	.142 g		Calcium	41.3 mg
Poly Fat	.089 g		Copper	.197 mg
Cholesterol	0 mg		Iodine	mcg
Dietary Fibre	3.22 g		Iron	1.1 mg
Soluble Fibre	.562 g		Magnesium	22.9 mg
Total Vit A	8.59 RE		Manganese	.183 mg
Thiamin-B1	.179 mg		Phosphorus	123 mg
Riboflavin-B2	.124 mg		Potassium	431 mg
Niacin-B3	1.28 mg		Selenium	2.21 mcg
Niacin Equiv.	.579 mg		Sodium	185 mg
Vitamin B6	.128 mg		Zinc	.294 mg
Vitamin B12	0 mcg		Complex Carbs	0 g
Folate	39.7 mcg		Sugars	24 g
Pantothenic	.375 mg		Water	165 g

CALORIE BREAKDOWN		FAT		EXCHANGES	
Protein	7%	* Saturated :	6.3%	Fruit	1.73
Carbohydrates	82%	Mono Unsat:	.5%	Fat	.335
Fat-Total *	12%	Poly Unsat:	.3%		

WARNING ABOUT SALT SUBSTITUTES:

Avoid salt substitutes. Sea salt is sodium Chloride. Formulations under labels such as "Lite Salt" replace much of the sodium chloride with potassium chloride. Consumptions of high levels of potassium can cause irregular heartbeats and **even death**. Marc Sorenson, Ed. D, *Mega Health*, page 389.

MILLET PUDDING (makes 6 cups, 12-half-cup servings)

1 L	(4 cups)	cooked millet (1/2 cup before cooking)
125 mL	(1/2 cup)	raisins
15 mL	(1 Tbsp.)	freshly grated orange rind
60 mL	(1/4 cup)	raw cashews
75 mL	(1/3 cup)	dates (softened in part of water)
1 L	(4 cups)	water
1 mL	(1/4 tsp.)	salt
5 mL	(1 tsp.)	vanilla
10 mL	(2 tsp.)	maple flavouring

Method:

PLACE millet, raisins, and orange rind in bowl. WHIZ cashews in blender or food processor until a smooth paste. ADD remaining ingredients. POUR over ingredients in bowl. MIX well. PLACE in baking dish. BAKE at 350° F. until set.

```
Analysis: MILLET PUDDING (2) 12 half-cup servings  Divided by: 12
          Wgt: 173 g (6.1 oz.)                      Water:     80%
```

Calories	140		Vitamin C	.891 mg
Protein	3.5 g		Vitamin D	0 mcg
Carbohydrates	27.9 g		Vit E-Alpha E	.445 mg
Fat - Total	1.87 g		Vitamin K	mcg
Saturated Fat	.253 g		Biotin	mcg
Mono Fat	.82 g		Calcium	14.6 mg
Poly Fat	.631 g		Copper	.185 mg
Cholesterol	0 mg		Iodine	mcg
Dietary Fibre	1.84 g		Iron	.771 mg
Soluble Fibre	.682 g		Magnesium	45.7 mg
Total Vit A	.518 RE		Manganese	.296 mg
Thiamin-B1	.103 mg		Phosphorus	98.1 mg
Riboflavin-B2	.091 mg		Potassium	143 mg
Niacin-B3	1.3 mg		Selenium	.593 mcg
Niacin Equiv.	1.3 mg		Sodium	49.5 mg
Vitamin B6	.114 mg		Zinc	.84 mg
Vitamin B12	0 mcg		Complex Carbs	18.2 g
Folate	17.3 mcg		Sugars	7.86 g
Pantothenic	.19 mg		Water	139 g

CALORIE BREAKDOWN		FAT		EXCHANGES	
Protein	10%	* Saturated :	1.6%	Bread	1.17
Carbohydrates	78%	Mono Unsat:	5.2%	Lean Meat	.055
Fat-Total *	12%	Poly Unsat:	4 %	Fruit	.559
				Fat	.168

ISAIAH 55:2

"Wherefore do you spend money for that which is not bread? and your labour for that which satisfieth not? hearken diligently unto me, and eat that which is good."

NATURAL FRUIT JELLY (makes 8 two-tablespoon servings)

| 250 mL | (1 cup) | grape juice or other fruit juice |
| 30 mL | (2 Tbsp.) | cornstarch or tapioca |

Method:

MIX with a wire whip. **COOK** until thickened, stirring almost constantly. **USE hot** on waffles or cereal or **REFRIGERATE** and **USE** on toast.

```
Analysis: NATURAL FRUIT JELLY              Divided by: 8
          Wgt: 33.3 g (1.17 oz.)           Water:      82%
```

Calories	23.5		Vitamin C	7.48 mg
Protein	.065 g		Vitamin D	0 mcg
Carbohydrates	5.83 g		Vit E-Alpha E	.016 mg
Fat - Total	.029 g		Vitamin K	mcg
Saturated Fat	.009 g		Biotin	mcg
Mono Fat	.001 g		Calcium	1.29 mg
Poly Fat	.009 g		Copper	.005 mg
Cholesterol	0 mg		Iodine	mcg
Dietary Fibre	.239 g		Iron	.041 mg
Soluble Fibre	.062 g		Magnesium	1.31 mg
Total Vit A	.312 RE		Manganese	.056 mg
Thiamin-B1	.005 mg		Phosphorus	1.51 mg
Riboflavin-B2	.008 mg		Potassium	6.62 mg
Niacin-B3	.039 mg		Selenium	.32 mcg
Niacin Equiv.	.039 mg		Sodium	.805 mg
Vitamin B6	.013 mg		Zinc	.014 mg
Vitamin B12	0 mcg		Complex Carbs	1.8 g
Folate	.406 mcg		Sugars	3.79 g
Pantothenic	.007 mg		Water	27.3 g

CALORIE BREAKDOWN		FAT		EXCHANGES	
Protein	1%	*Saturated:	.4%	Bread	.125
Carbohydrates	98%	Mono Unsat:	.1%	Fruit	.25
Fat-Total *	1%	Poly Unsat:	.3%		

HOW TO LOWER YOUR CHOLESTEROL:

1. Avoid all animal products, such as meats, eggs, and dairy products.
2. Severely reduce saturated fats--especially by avoiding animal products.
3. Get down to your ideal weight--avoid highly refined, empty calorie foods, low in fibre. This includes the visible fats and oils, sugar and alcohol. Use nuts sparingly.
4. Eat plenty of natural plant foods--eat all you want of the unrefined whole grain products, of legumes, and of fresh fruits and vegetables. Enjoy those potatoes, yams and sweet potatoes! These foods not only satisfy, but are also rich in fibre.
5. Walk daily--a regular exercise programme can further help in lowering your blood cholesterol. At the same time, it may improve your HDL portion of your cholesterol, which appears protective.
6. See your physician--if possible, replace diuretic drugs.
   (Hans Diehl, *To Your Health*, page 111.)

PINEAPPLE MARMALADE (makes about 6 cups)

341 mL	(12 oz.)	frozen apple juice concentrate
500 mL	(2 cups)	orange juice
30 mL	(2 Tbsp.)	cornstarch
60 mL	(1/4 cup)	quick tapioca (Use more if a thicker product is needed.)
540 mL	(19 oz.)	unsweetened crushed pineapple (Do not drain.)
60 mL	(1/4 cup)	shredded unsweetened coconut (optional)

Method:

PLACE apple juice concentrate and most of the orange juice in a pot and BRING to boil. MIX remaining orange juice with the cornstarch. ADD a small amount of the hot juice to the cornstarch mixture. Then STIR into the hot juice. CONTINUE stirring until mixture boils again. SPRINKLE tapioca on top and stir while mixture simmers long enough to cook the tapioca (about 5 minutes). ADD crushed pineapple and coconut. CHILL and SERVE on toast as jam. May also be served hot on waffles or pancakes.

```
Analysis: PINEAPPLE MARMALADE (6 cups)          Divided by: 24
          Wgt: 66.1 g (2.33 oz.)                Water:      74%
```

Calories	66.6		Vitamin C	10.8 mg
Protein	.409 g		Vitamin D	0 mcg
Carbohydrates	15.4 g		Vit E-Alpha E	.062 mg
Fat - Total	.622 g		Vitamin K	mcg
Saturated Fat	.478 g		Biotin	mcg
Mono Fat	.03 g		Calcium	9.24 mg
Poly Fat	.035 g		Copper	.047 mg
Cholesterol	0 mg		Iodine	mcg
Dietary Fibre	.392 g		Iron	.287 mg
Soluble Fibre	.126 g		Magnesium	9.28 mg
Total Vit A	2.7 RE		Manganese	.342 mg
Thiamin-B1	.042 mg		Phosphorus	11.1 mg
Riboflavin-B2	.019 mg		Potassium	153 mg
Niacin-B3	.141 mg		Selenium	.574 mcg
Niacin Equiv.	.141 mg		Sodium	5.22 mg
Vitamin B6	.05 mg		Zinc	.075 mg
Vitamin B12	0 mcg		Complex Carbs	.609 g
Folate	10.5 mcg		Sugars	13.1 g
Pantothenic	.103 mg		Water	49.1 g

CALORIE BREAKDOWN		FAT	EXCHANGES	
Protein	2%	Saturated: 6.2%	Bread	.04
Carbohydrates	90%	Mono Unsat: .4%	Fruit	.9
Fat - Total *	8%	Poly Unsat: .5%	Fat	.08

STRAWBERRY-PINEAPPLE JAM (makes about 10 cups - 40 quarter-cup servings)

1 L	(4 cups)	frozen strawberries
540 mL	(19 oz.)	unsweetened crushed pineapple (Use juice, too.)
60 mL	(1/4 cup)	minute tapioca

Method:

PLACE the berries in a saucepan and HEAT to boiling. SPRINKLE tapioca on top and STIR constantly. COOK until tapioca is clear. STIR in pineapple. SERVE on pancakes, waffles, toast or on cereal.

```
| Analysis: STRAWBERRY-PINEAPPLE JAM              Divided by: 40    |
|           Wgt: 30.6 g (1.08 oz.)                Water:      84%   |
```

Calories	17.3		Vitamin C	7.55 mg
Protein	.136 g		Vitamin D	0 mcg
Carbohydrates	4.47 g		Vit E-Alpha E	.055 mg
Fat - Total	.028 g		Vitamin K	mcg
Saturated Fat	.002 g		Biotin	mcg
Mono Fat	.004 g		Calcium	4.56 mg
Poly Fat	.012 g		Copper	.021 mg
Cholesterol	0 mg		Iodine	mcg
Dietary Fibre	.436 g		Iron	.158 mg
Soluble Fibre	.109 g		Magnesium	3.72 mg
Total Vit A	1.19 RE		Manganese	.209 mg
Thiamin-B1	.017 mg		Phosphorus	2.93 mg
Riboflavin-B2	.008 mg		Potassium	40.4 mg
Niacin-B3	.111 mg		Selenium	.229 mcg
Niacin Equiv.	.111 mg		Sodium	.446 mg
Vitamin B6	.015 mg		Zinc	.034 mg
Vitamin B12	0 mcg		Complex Carbs	0 g
Folate	3.21 mcg		Sugars	3.26 g
Pantothenic	.031 mg		Water	25.8 g

CALORIE BREAKDOWN		FAT		EXCHANGES	
Protein	3%	*Saturated : .1%		Fruit	.248
Carbohydrates	96%	Mono Unsat: .2%			
Fats-Total*	1%	Poly Unsat: .6%			

SALT:

Salt affects your health only to the degree that it causes your blood pressure to increase. **Less than one fourth of people who have high blood pressure are "salt sensitive."** If you don't have high blood pressure, then you don't have to limit your salt intake drastically. Your body maintains a precise concentration of salt, so when you eat salt, your body tends to retain water in order to dilute the salt to keep it in a constant concentration. All other things being equal, when you increase the amount of volume (water) in a closed system (your body), the pressure increases. Because salt causes water retention, it was once thought that eating salt would cause everyone's blood pressure to increase. Most people, though, are able to excrete the extra salt and water in their urine, unless they have congestive heart failure or kidney disease. If you do, then you will benefit from restricting your salt intake. *Dean Ornish's Program for Reversing Heart Disease*, page 271.

APPLE-OAT SQUARES (makes 12 servings)

500 mL	(2 cups)	old-fashioned rolled oats
30 mL	(2 Tbsp.)	oil
3 mL	(1/2 tsp.)	salt
375 mL	(1 1/2 cups)	apple juice
8 mL	(1 1/2 tsp.)	vanilla
750 mL	(3 cups)	shredded apples, packed
60 mL	(1/4 cup)	raw sunflower seeds

Method:

MIX well oats, oil, and salt; STIR in apple juice and vanilla (let stand while shredding apples.) STIR in shredded apples. POUR into a 9" x 9" baking pan. SPRINKLE the sunflower seeds over top; PRESS down lightly. BAKE at 350° F about 45 minutes. CUT in squares and SERVE hot with a dollop of SOYAGEN DESSERT TOPPING (page 176).

```
------------------------------------------------------------------
| Analysis: APPLE-OAT SQUARES (12 servings)      Divided by: 12   |
|           Wgt: 82.7 g (2.92 oz.)               Water:     70%   |
------------------------------------------------------------------
```

Calories	112		Vitamin C	2.26 mg
Protein	2.39 g		Vitamin D	0 mcg
Carbohydrates	18.1 g		Vit E-Alpha E	.947 mg
Fat - Total	3.62 g		Vitamin K	mcg
Saturated Fat	.517 g		Biotin	mcg
Mono Fat	2 g		Calcium	12.5 mg
Poly Fat	.791 g		Copper	.082 mg
Cholesterol	0 mg		Iodine	mcg
Dietary Fibre	2.18 g		Iron	.796 mg
Soluble Fibre	.933 g		Magnesium	25 mg
Total Vit A	2.99 RE		Manganese	.549 mg
Thiamin-B1	.107 mg		Phosphorus	73.1 mg
Riboflavin-B2	.029 mg		Potassium	128 mg
Niacin-B3	.185 mg		Selenium	4.39 mcg
Niacin Equiv.	.185 mg		Sodium	90.3 mg
Vitamin B6	.046 mg		Zinc	.473 mg
Vitamin B12	0 mcg		Complex Carbs	7.39 g
Folate	5.69 mcg		Sugars	8.38 g
Pantothenic	.217 mg		Water	57.7 g

CALORIE BREAKDOWN		FAT		EXCHANGES	
Protein	8%	*Saturated :	4.1%	Bread	.633
Carbohydrates	63%	Mono Unsat:	15.7%	Lean Meat	.028
Fat-Total *	28%	Poly Unsat:	6.2%	Fruit	.72
				Fat	.513

APPLE PRUNE COOKIES (makes about 45 one-tablespoon cookies)

250 mL	(1 cup)	chopped dates
125 mL	(1/2 cup)	chopped prunes
125 mL	(1/2 cup)	frozen orange juice concentrate
310 mL	(1 1/4 cups)	shredded, unpeeled apple
125 mL	(1/2 cup)	chopped nuts
125 mL	(1/2 cup)	unsweetened coconut
3 mL	(1/2 tsp.)	salt
5 mL	(1 tsp.)	vanilla
750 mL	(3 cups)	quick-cooking rolled oats

Method:

HEAT dates, prunes, and orange juice concentrate in microwave or in a pot until dates can be mashed. (**MASH** with a fork or in food processor.) **ADD** remaining ingredients and **MIX** well. **DROP** by tablespoonsful on lecithin treated pan. **BAKE** at 350° F. for 15-20 minutes.

```
Analysis: APPLE-PRUNE COOKIES (45 1 tbsp. cookies)    Divided by: 45
          Wgt: 19.7 g (.693 oz.)                      Water:       35%
```

Calories	55.7		Vitamin C	2.48 mg
Protein	1.27 g		Vitamin D	0 mcg
Carbohydrates	9.44 g		Vit E-Alpha E	.121 mg
Fat - Total	1.77 g		Vitamin K	mcg
Saturated Fat	.64 g		Biotin	mcg
Mono Fat	.325 g		Calcium	7.27 mg
Poly Fat	.658 g		Copper	.067 mg
Cholesterol	0 mg		Iodine	mcg
Dietary Fibre	1.17 g		Iron	.414 mg
Soluble Fibre	.384 g		Magnesium	13.1 mg
Total Vit A	1.5 RE		Manganese	.271 mg
Thiamin-B1	.047 mg		Phosphorus	35.4 mg
Riboflavin-B2	.018 mg		Potassium	83.8 mg
Niacin-B3	.187 mg		Selenium	1.95 mcg
Niacin Equiv.	.158 mg		Sodium	24.7 mg
Vitamin B6	.032 mg		Zinc	.244 mg
Vitamin B12	0 mcg		Complex Carbs	3.08 g
Folate	5.19 mcg		Sugars	3.96 g
Pantothenic	.116 mg		Water	6.81 g

CALORIE BREAKDOWN		FAT		EXCHANGES	
Protein	9%	*Saturated :	9.8%	Bread	.267
Carbohydrates	64%	Mono Unsat:	5 %	Fruit	.274
Fat-Total *	27%	Poly Unsat:	10.1%	Fat	.093

CAROB CHUNKIES (makes 36 pieces)

125 mL	(1/2 cup)	**EACH**	carob powder **and** water
250 mL	(1 cup)		peanut butter
250 mL	(1 cup)		DATE BUTTER (1 cup dates, 1/2 cup water)
150 mL	(2/3 cup)		coarsely chopped walnuts or pecans
60 mL	(1/4 cup)		unsweetened coconut
5 mL	(1 tsp.)		vanilla

Method:

COMBINE carob powder and water in a small saucepan and COOK until thick, stirring constantly. REMOVE from heat and ADD remaining ingredients. STIR together well. PRESS evenly into 8"x 8" pyrex dish. REFRIGERATE. CUT into 36 squares. FREEZE for a chewier fudge.

```
----------------------------------------------------------------------
| Analysis: CAROB CHUNKIES (1/36 OF RECIPE)      Divided by: 36       |
|           Wgt: 22.6 g (.796 oz.)               Water:      39%      |
----------------------------------------------------------------------
```

Calories	75		Vitamin C	.082 mg
Protein	2.2 g		Vitamin D	0 mcg
Carbohydrates	5.84 g		Vit E-Alpha E	.651 mg
Fat - Total	5.29 g		Vitamin K	mcg
Saturated Fat	1.12 g		Biotin	mcg
Mono Fat	2.02 g		Calcium	11.3 mg
Poly Fat	1.91 g		Copper	.09 mg
Cholesterol	0 mg		Iodine	mcg
Dietary Fibre	1.1 g		Iron	.288 mg
Soluble Fibre	.015 g		Magnesium	17.6 mg
Total Vit A	.457 RE		Manganese	.219 mg
Thiamin-B1	.022 mg		Phosphorus	33.1 mg
Riboflavin-B2	.022 mg		Potassium	101 mg
Niacin-B3	1.1 mg		Selenium	1.08 mcg
Niacin Equiv.	1.03 mg		Sodium	2.46 mg
Vitamin B6	.058 mg		Zinc	.295 mg
Vitamin B12	0 mcg		Complex Carbs	.746 g
Folate	8.89 mcg		Sugars	.683 g
Pantothenic	.114 mg		Water	8.75 g

CALORIE BREAKDOWN		FAT	EXCHANGE	
Protein	11%	* Saturated : 12.7%	Bread	.044
Carbohydrates	29%	Mono Unsat: 22.8%	Lean Meat	.22
Fat-Total *	60%	Poly Unsat: 21.5%	Fruit	.15
			Fat	.618

SUBSTITUTING CAROB FOR CHOCOLATE:

When substituting carob powder for cocoa, use an equal amount called for in the recipe. When substituting for chocolate, use three tablespoons of carob powder plus one tablespoon of water for each square of chocolate. Since carob powder is 46% natural sugar, less sweetener should be used than when using cocoa or chocolate. Carob is also known as St. John's Bread (See page 152).

CAROB FRUIT BARS (makes 24 bars)

5 mL	(1 tsp.)		yeast
60 mL	(1/4 cup)		warm water
375 mL	(1 1/2 cups)		cooked, pitted prunes
250 mL	(1 cup)	**EACH**	raisins, chopped dates, **and** whole wheat flour
45 mL	(3 Tbsp.)		carob powder
125 mL	(1/2 cup)		chopped nuts

Method:

DISSOLVE yeast in water and **ADD** to fruit. **LET** rise until bubbly. **ADD** rest of ingredients. **MIX** well. **PUT** in oiled pan and **SPREAD** out evenly 1 inch thick. **LET** rise 30 minutes. **BAKE** at 350°F. for 35-40 minutes. **COOL** and **CUT** into bars.

```
Analysis: CAROB FRUIT BARS (25 bars)        Divided by: 25
          Wgt: 33 g (1.16 oz.)              Water:      25%
```

Calories	96.4		Vitamin C	.612 mg
Protein	1.61 g		Vitamin D	0 mcg
Carbohydrates	20.9 g		Vit E-Alpha E	.175 mg
Fat - Total	1.7 g		Vitamin K	mcg
Saturated Fat	.174 g		Biotin	mcg
Mono Fat	.366 g		Calcium	16.7 mg
Poly Fat	.989 g		Copper	.136 mg
Cholesterol	0 mg		Iodine	mcg
Dietary Fibre	1.76 g		Iron	.859 mg
Soluble Fibre	.326 g		Magnesium	15.7 mg
Total Vit A	.72 RE		Manganese	.296 mg
Thiamin-B1	.057 mg		Phosphorus	42.1 mg
Riboflavin-B2	.051 mg		Potassium	196 mg
Niacin-B3	.745 mg		Selenium	4.55 mcg
Niacin Equiv.	.589 mg		Sodium	2.56 mg
Vitamin B6	.085 mg		Zinc	.308 mg
Vitamin B12	0 mcg		Complex Carbs	3.06 g
Folate	7.69 mcg		Sugars	9.03 g
Pantothenic	.178 mg		Water	8.17 g

CALORIE BREAKDOWN		FAT	EXCHANGES	
Protein	6%	* Saturated : 1.5%	Bread	.236
Carbohydrates	79%	Mono Unsat: 3.1%	Fruit	.634
Fat-Total *	15%	Poly Unsat: 8.5%	Vegetables	.011

CAROB:

Carob powder (flour) is a popular substitute for cocoa and chocolate. It is made by pulverizing the dried pod after the seeds have been removed. It is far lower in fat and calories than chocolate, and does not contain any of the harmful compounds like methylxanthine or caffeine common to chocolate. In addition, it contains more natural sugars, (so additional sweetener is not always needed) It also has more fibre, and minerals (calcium, iron, magnesium) than either cocoa or chocolate. It has its own B vitamins needed to digest sugar. Fermentation is essential to develop the chocolate flavour, but insects, rodents and small animals make nests in the piles of bean pods and many kinds of contamination can occur.

DATE APPLE COOKIES (makes 36 one Tbsp cookies)

250 mL	(1 cup)	dates
125 mL	(1/2 cup)	chopped prunes
125 mL	(1/2 cup)	unsweetened apple juice concentrate
250 mL	(1 cup)	shredded, unpeeled apple
125 mL	(1/2 cup)	chopped nuts
125 mL	(1/2 cup)	unsweetened coconut
5 mL	(1 tsp)	vanilla
750 mL	(3 cups)	rolled oats

Method:

    HEAT dates, prunes, and apple juice concentrate sufficiently to soften fruit. **MASH** with a fork or **WHIZ** in blender. **TRANSFER** to a bowl. **ADD** remaining ingredients and **MIX** well. **DROP** by tablespoons on a non-stick or lightly sprayed pan. **BAKE** at 350° F. for 10 minutes and then at 300° F. for 10 more minutes.

```
Analysis: DATE APPLE COOKIES                    Divided by: 36
          Wgt: 24.5 g (.865 oz.)                Water      34%
```

Calories	69.5	Vitamin C	3.1 mg
Protein	1.6 g	Vitamin D	0 mcg
Carbohydrates	11.8 g	Vit E-Alpha E	.152 mg
Fat - Total	2.22 g	Vitamin K	mcg
Saturated Fat	.801 g	Biotin	mcg
Mono Fat	.407 g	Calcium	9.13 mg
Poly Fat	.824 g	Copper	.084 mg
Cholesterol	0 mg	Iodine	mcg
Dietary Fibre	1.47 g	Iron	.52 mg
Soluble Fibre	.484 g	Magnesium	16.4 mg
Total Vit A	1.95 RE	Manganese	.342 mg
Thiamin-B1	.069 mg	Phosphorus	44.6 mg
Riboflavin-B2	.024 mg	Potassium	105 mg
Niacin-B3	.24 mg	Selenium	2.44 mcg
Niacin Equiv.	.204 mg	Sodium	30.8 mg
Vitamin B6	.041 mg	Zinc	.307 mg
Vitamin B12	0 mcg	Complex Carbs	3.9 g
Folate	7.16 mcg	Sugars	4.95 g
Pantothenic	.166 mg	Water	8.46 g

CALORIE BREAKDOWN		FAT		EXCHANGES	
Protein	9%	* Saturated :	9.8%	Bread	.255
Carbohydrates	64%	Mono Unsat:	5 %	Fruit	.34
Fat-Total *	27%	Poly Unsat:	10.1%	Fat	.112

DID YOU KNOW?

    Pink grapefruit has 100 times as much beta carotene as white grapefruit.

GORILLA MUNCHIES (makes one 9"x 13" pan or about 40 balls)

125 mL	(1/2 cup)	chopped sunflower seeds
250 mL	(1 cup)	chopped walnuts
250 mL	(1 cup)	unsweetened coconut
750 mL	(2 1/2 cups)	MALT GRANOLA (page 56) or other homemade granola
25 mL	(1/2 cup)	honey
250 mL	(1 cup)	peanut butter
250 mL	(1 cup)	carob chips **or** 1/3 cup of carob powder + 1/4 cup water

Method:

  MIX sunflower seeds, walnuts, coconut, and granola in a bowl. **HEAT** honey; **ADD** peanut butter; **CONTINUE** to heat and **STIR** until peanut butter and honey are well blended. **REMOVE** from heat. **ADD** carob chips (the unsweetened ones do not melt very readily). **STIR** until chips are melted. **ADD** to dry ingredients in bowl and **MIX** well. **FORM** into balls and **REFRIGERATE** or **PACK** into a 9"x 13" pan, **CUT** into squares before it sets. You may have to add a little water to make it easier to handle.

```
------------------------------------------------------------------------
| Analysis: GORILLA MUNCHIES                    Divided by: 40          |
|           Wgt: 27.2 g (.96 oz.)               Water:      13%         |
------------------------------------------------------------------------
```

Calories	126		Vitamin C	.21 mg
Protein	3.68 g		Vitamin D	.004 mcg
Carbohydrates	11.1 g		Vit E-Alpha E	1.81 mg
Fat - Total	8.32 g		Vitamin K	mcg
Saturated Fat	2.22 g		Biotin	mcg
Mono Fat	2.59 g		Calcium	17.3 mg
Poly Fat	3.09 g		Copper	.161 mg
Cholesterol	0 mg		Iodine	mcg
Dietary Fibre	1.66 g		Iron	.722 mg
Soluble Fibre	.187 g		Magnesium	33.8 mg
Total Vit A	.822 RE		Manganese	.516 mg
Thiamin-B1	.1 mg		Phosphorus	76.5 mg
Riboflavin-B2	.038 mg		Potassium	125 mg
Niacin-B3	1.28 mg		Selenium	4.55 mcg
Niacin Equiv.	1.27 mg		Sodium	37.5 mg
Vitamin B6	.085 mg		Zinc	.65 mg
Vitamin B12	0 mcg		Complex Carbs	3.63 g
Folate	15.9 mcg		Sugars	4.93 g
Pantothenic	.287 mg		Water	3.45 g

CALORIE BREAKDOWN		FAT	EXCHANGES	
Protein	11%	Saturated : 14.9%	Bread	.27
Carbohydrates	33%	Mono Unsat: 17.4%	Lean Meat	.3
Fat - Total *	56%	Poly Unsat: 20.8%	Fruit	.55
			Fat	.97

ORANGE-OAT BALLS (makes 38 balls)

60 mL	(1/4 cup)	chopped dates
60 mL	(1/4 cup)	water
125 mL	(1/2 cup)	orange juice concentrate
125 mL	(1/2 cup)	crunchy peanut butter (Just Peanuts)
125 mL	(1/2 cup)	raisins
125 mL	(1/2 cup)	unsweetened carob chips
125 mL	(1/2 cup)	sunflower seeds (optional)
375 mL	(1 1/2 cups)	rolled oats
		unsweetened fine coconut (optional)

Method:

PLACE dates, water, and orange juice concentrate in a pot and LET soak until dates are soft. BRING to a boil and MASH until dates are well blended. ADD peanut butter and MIX well. ADD remaining ingredients except coconut. MIX well with hands. MAKE balls (1 Tbsp each) and ROLL in coconut. PLACE on waxed paper. CHILL.

```
-------------------------------------------------------------------------------
| Analysis: ORANGE-OAT BALLS                     Divided by: 38               |
|           Wgt: 15.2 g (.536 oz.)               Water:      23%              |
-------------------------------------------------------------------------------
```

Calories	57		Vitamin C	2.57 mg
Protein	1.81 g		Vitamin D	0 mcg
Carbohydrates	6.44 g		Vit E-Alpha E	1.17 mg
Fat - Total	3.06 g		Vitamin K	mcg
Saturated Fat	.745 g		Biotin	mcg
Mono Fat	1.04 g		Calcium	6.26 mg
Poly Fat	1.12 g		Copper	.075 mg
Cholesterol	0 mg		Iodine	mcg
Dietary Fibre	.953 g		Iron	.339 mg
Soluble Fibre	.21 g		Magnesium	14.4 mg
Total Vit A	.983 RE		Manganese	.239 mg
Thiamin-B1	.039 mg		Phosphorus	49.6 mg
Riboflavin-B2	.017 mg		Potassium	87.5 mg
Niacin-B3	.662 mg		Selenium	2.71 mcg
Niacin Equiv.	.662 mg		Sodium	1.31 mg
Vitamin B6	.044 mg		Zinc	.304 mg
Vitamin B12	0 mcg		Complex Carbs	2.21 g
Folate	11.1 mcg		Sugars	3.29 g
Pantothenic	.215 mg		Water	3.51 g

CALORIE BREAKDOWN		FAT		EXCHANGES	
Protein	12%	* Saturated: 11.1%		Bread	.136
Carbohydrates	43%	Mono Unsat: 15.4%		Lean Meat	.124
Fat-Total *	46%	Poly Unsat: 16.6%		Fruit	.235
				Fat	.465

POLYNESIAN BARS (makes 24 bars)

Crumble Crust (makes 4 cups)

250 mL	(1 cup)	whole-wheat pastry flour or millet flour
3 mL	(1/2 tsp.)	salt
125 mL	(1/2 cup)	moist flaked coconut
250 mL	(1 cup)	walnuts
5 mL	(1 tsp.)	grated orange rind
450 mL	(1 3/4 cups)	quick-cooking rolled oats
180 mL	(3/4 cup)	orange juice

Method:

MIX flour and salt in bowl. WHIZ the coconut and 2/3 cup of the walnuts in blender until fine. ADD to flour; CRUMBLE together like fine bread crumbs. CHOP remaining 1/3 cup of nuts; COMBINE with orange rind and rolled oats; TOSS with the above mixture. ADD the orange juice; MIX until moistened. PRESS about 2/3 of the crumble crust into the bottom of a 12" x 8" baking dish that has been coated with Pam. MAKE filling, SPREAD over crumbs. COVER with remaining crust, PRESS down. BAKE at 350°F. (about 25 minutes) Cool and CUT into bars. <u>Serving Suggestion:</u> SERVE with fruit salad or USE in a packed lunch.

Pineapple-date Filling

500 mL	(2 cups)	chopped dates
375 mL	(1 1/2 cups)	unsweetened, crushed pineapple, undrained
125 mL	(1/2 cup)	orange juice
5 mL	(1 tsp.)	vanilla

Method:

SIMMER all filling ingredients, stirring frequently until thickened--consistency of jam.

```
Analysis: POLYNESIAN BARS (Pineapple-date)          Divided by: 24
          Wgt: 61.4 g (2.17 oz.)                     Water:      48%
```

Calories	139		Pantothenic	.308 mg
Protein	2.91 g		Vitamin C	6.83 mg
Carbohydrates	23.7 g		Vit E-Alpha E	.299 mg
Fat - Total	4.7 g		Calcium	18.2 mg
Saturated Fat	1.32 g		Copper	.184 mg
Mono Fat	.904 g		Iron	.847 mg
Poly Fat	2.15 g		Magnesium	34.3 mg
Dietary Fibre	3.09 g		Manganese	.816 mg
Soluble Fibre	.75 g		Phosphorus	73.3 mg
Total Vit A	3.65 RE		Potassium	215 mg
Thiamin-B1	.12 mg		Selenium	6.85 mcg
Riboflavin-B2	.047 mg		Sodium	64.5 mcg
Niacin-B3	.793 mg		Zinc	.564 mg
Niacin Equiv.	.793 mg		Complex Carbs	6.73 mg
Vitamin B6	.101 mg		Sugars	13.8 g
Folate	15.2 mcg			

CALORIE BREAKDOWN		FAT		EXCHANGES	
Protein	8%	* Saturated :	8 %	Bread	.467
Carbohydrates	64%	Mono Unsat:	5.5%	Fruit	.932
Fat-Total *	28%	Poly Unsat:	13.1%	Fat	.175

SESAME SNAPS (makes 25)

500 mL	(2 cups)	white sesame seeds
30 mL	(2 Tbsp.)	honey
30 mL	(2 Tbsp.)	brown sugar

Method:

TOAST sesame seeds in a dry pot, stirring so they won't burn. (They will pop and be shiny. Be careful not to toast them too long because they will turn bitter.) **ADD** brown sugar and honey. **CONTINUE** to cook and **STIR** until all the seeds are sticky). **SPREAD** quickly in a 9" x 9" greased pan. **CUT** into squares and **LET** cool. **BREAK** apart.

```
-----------------------------------------------------------------------
| Analysis: SESAME SNAPS                        Divided by: 25         |
|           Wgt: 13.9 g (.492 oz.)              Water:        6%       |
-----------------------------------------------------------------------
```

Calories	73.9	Vitamin C	.017	mg
Protein	2.05 g	Vitamin D	0	mcg
Carbohydrates	4.8 g	Vit E-Alpha E	.262	mg
Fat - Total	5.73 g	Vitamin K		mcg
Saturated Fat	.8 g	Biotin		mcg
Mono Fat	2.17 g	Calcium	113	mg
Poly Fat	2.51 g	Copper	.473	mg
Cholesterol	0 mg	Iodine		mcg
Dietary Fibre	1.16 g	Iron	1.7	mg
Soluble Fibre	0 g	Magnesium	40.6	mg
Total Vit A	.115 RE	Manganese	.287	mg
Thiamin-B1	.091 mg	Phosphorus	72.7	mg
Riboflavin-B2	.029 mg	Potassium	57.3	mg
Niacin-B3	.523 mg	Selenium	.635	mcg
Niacin Equiv.	.524 mg	Sodium	1.62	mg
Vitamin B6	.092 mg	Zinc	.901	mg
Vitamin B12	0 mcg	Complex Carbs	1.42	g
Folate	11.2 mcg	Sugars	2.23	g
Pantothenic	.008 mg	Water	.842	g

CALORIE BREAKDOWN		FAT		EXCHANGE	
Protein	10%	Saturated :	6.1%	Fruit	.125
Carbohydrates	24%	Mono Unsat:	24.7%	Fat	1.28
Fat	65%	Poly Unsat:	28.6%		

SESAME SEEDS:

The unique quality of sesame protein is the presence of a high level of the sulphur-containing amino acids, methionine and cystine. The limiting amino acid of sesame protein is lysine. Sesame does not contain some of the objectionable characteristics found in soy protein, particularly with regard to the trypsin inhibiting factor. Sesame averages about 50% oil, which is highly resistant to oxidation, and 25% protein which has a unique balance of amino acids. There is an appreciable amount of calcium, magnesium, and phosphorous in sesame seeds. Since they are high in fat this should be taken into consideration when using them.

TAHITIAN TREATS (Makes about 60)

250 mL	(1 cup)	walnuts, ground (May use meal)
250 mL	(1 cup)	almonds, ground (May use meal)
250 mL	(1 cup)	fine unsweetened coconut
250 mL	(1 cup)	ground dates
45 mL	(3 Tbsp.)	carob powder
125 mL	(1/2 cup)	orange juice
45 mL	(3 Tbsp.)	minute tapioca
5 mL	(1 tsp.)	vanilla

Method:

PLACE nuts, coconut, dates and carob powder in mixing bowl. **PLACE** orange juice and tapioca in a small saucepan. **COOK** and **STIR** over medium heat until tapioca is clear, about 6 to 8 minutes. **ADD** vanilla. **COMBINE** all ingredients and **MIX** thoroughly. Fingers work best!) **SHAPE** portions about the size of a date between palms of hands. **ROLL** in ground nuts or coconut. **CHILL** until firm. **STORE** in refrigerator.

```
------------------------------------------------------------------
| Analysis: TAHITIAN TREATS (makes 60)       Divided by: 60       |
|           Wgt: 10.7 g (.377 oz.)           Water:     25%       |
------------------------------------------------------------------
```

Calories	42.6		Vitamin C	.901 mg
Protein	.782 g		Vitamin D	0 mcg
Carbohydrates	4.07 g		Vit E-Alpha E	.164 mg
Fat - Total	2.91 g		Vitamin K	mcg
Saturated Fat	.939 g		Biotin	mcg
Mono Fat	.855 g		Calcium	8.69 mg
Poly Fat	.966 g		Copper	.064 mg
Cholesterol	0 mg		Iodine	mcg
Dietary Fibre	.74 g		Iron	.197 mg
Soluble Fibre	.092 g		Magnesium	10.6 mg
Total Vit A	.566 RE		Manganese	.14 mg
Thiamin-B1	.016 mg		Phosphorus	19 mg
Riboflavin-B2	.021 mg		Potassium	54.6 mg
Niacin-B3	.157 mg		Selenium	.732 mcg
Niacin Equiv.	.157 mg		Sodium	1.08 mg
Vitamin B6	.025 mg		Zinc	.139 mg
Vitamin B12	0 mcg		Complex Carbs	.285 g
Folate	3.73 mcg		Sugars	2.41 g
Pantothenic	.057 mg		Water	2.69 g

CALORIE BREAKDOWN		FAT		EXCHANGES	
Protein	7%	*Saturated :	18.5%	Bread	.025
Carbohydrates	36%	Mono Unsat:	16.9%	Lean Meat	.044
Fat-Total *	57%	Poly Unsat:	19.1%	Fruit	.186
				Fat	.255

YUMMY COOKIE BARS (makes 45)

500 mL	(2 cups)	chopped dates
500 mL	(2 cups)	warm apple juice concentrate
10 mL	(2 tsp.)	vanilla
250 mL	(1 cup)	peanut butter
250 mL	(1 cup)	chopped walnuts
250 mL	(1 cup)	raisins
250 mL	(1 cup)	coconut
500 mL	(2 cups)	rolled oats
500 mL	(2 cups)	whole wheat flour
180 mL	(3/4 cup)	soy flour

Method:

BLEND dates and warm apple juice concentrate. PLACE in mixing bowl. ADD vanilla and peanut butter and MIX well. STIR in remaining ingredients and MIX well. SPREAD about one inch deep in a pyrex cake pan. BAKE at 300° F. for 30 to 45 minutes. CUT in bars while still warm.

```
-----------------------------------------------------------------------
| Analysis: YUMMY COOKIE BARS                      Divided by: 45      |
|           Wgt: 44.2 g (1.56 oz.)                 Water:     24%      |
-----------------------------------------------------------------------
```

Calories	152	Vitamin C	.48	mg
Protein	4.24 g	Vitamin D	0	mcg
Carbohydrates	22.4 g	Vit E-Alpha E	.681	mg
Fat - Total	6.12 g	Vitamin K		mcg
Saturated Fat	1.78 g	Biotin		mcg
Mono Fat	1.89 g	Calcium	18.3	mg
Poly Fat	2.08 g	Copper	.226	mg
Cholesterol	0 mg	Iodine		mcg
Dietary Fibre	2.68 g	Iron	.949	mg
Soluble Fibre	.557 g	Magnesium	37.1	mg
Total Vit A	1.21 RE	Manganese	.671	mg
Thiamin-B1	.087 mg	Phosphorus	83.5	mg
Riboflavin-B2	.05 mg	Potassium	269	mg
Niacin-B3	1.43 mg	Selenium	7.04	mcg
Niacin Equiv.	1.43 mg	Sodium	6.3	mg
Vitamin B6	.114 mg	Zinc	.598	mg
Vitamin B12	0 mcg	Complex Carbs	5.93	g
Folate	17.9 mcg	Sugars	13.8	g
Pantothenic	.302 mg	Water	10.6	g

CALORIE BREAKDOWN		FAT		EXCHANGES	
Protein	11%	* Saturated :	9.9%	Bread	.409
Carbohydrates	55%	Mono Unsat:	10.5%	Lean Meat	.243
Fat-Total *	43%	Poly Unsat:	11.6%	Fruit	.934
				Fat	.624

AMBROSIA (makes 10 servings)

500 mL	(2 cups)	orange juice
75 mL	(1/3 cup)	minute tapioca
125 mL	(1/2 cup)	unsweetened coconut
500 mL	(2 cups)	orange pieces
500 mL	(2 cups)	sliced bananas
540 mL	(19 oz.)	pineapple tidbits
500 mL	(2 cups)	green seedless grapes

Method:

COOK tapioca in juice until tapioca is clear. **REMOVE** from heat. **STIR** in fruit. **CHILL** and **SERVE**. **GARNISH** with kiwi, strawberries, or blueberries.

```
-----------------------------------------------------------------------
| Analysis: AMBROSIA                          Divided by: 10          |
|           Wgt: 209 g (7.36 oz.)             Water:        81%       |
-----------------------------------------------------------------------
```

Calories	153		Vitamin C	49.9 mg
Protein	1.59 g		Vitamin D	0 mcg
Carbohydrates	35.4 g		Vit E-Alpha E	.523 mg
Fat - Total	1.96 g		Vitamin K	mcg
Saturated Fat	1.47 g		Biotin	mcg
Mono Fat	.103 g		Calcium	33.3 mg
Poly Fat	.128 g		Copper	.164 mg
Cholesterol	0 mg		Iodine	mcg
Dietary Fibre	2.78 g		Iron	.563 mg
Soluble Fibre	.713 g		Magnesium	28.9 mg
Total Vit A	18.3 RE		Manganese	.753 mg
Thiamin-B1	.167 mg		Phosphorus	31.5 mg
Riboflavin-B2	.084 mg		Potassium	417 mg
Niacin-B3	.627 mg		Selenium	5.05 mcg
Niacin Equiv.	.627 mg		Sodium	2.89 mg
Vitamin B6	.299 mg		Zinc	.221 mg
Vitamin B12	0 mcg		Complex Carbs	4.8 g
Folate	42.7 mcg		Sugars	27.8 g
Pantothenic	.333 mg		Water	169 g

CALORIE BREAKDOWN		FAT		EXCHANGES	
Protein	4%	*Saturated:	8%	Bread	.18
Carbohydrates	86%	Mono Unsat:	.6%	Fruit	2.07
Fat-Total *	11%	Poly Unsat:	.7%	Fat	.241

COCONUT:

Coconut, of all natural foods has the highest level of fat, a large proportion of which is saturated. It is 92% fat, higher even than meat, eggs, or cheese. However if NO animal fat is in the diet, some authorities believe the saturated fat is not any more of a problem than other fats, but if there is any cholesterol in the diet the saturated fat can be a problem. For children who need extra calories it may be a satisfactory source of calories, especially if it is used in an otherwise nutritious food.

APPLE CRISP (makes 12 servings)

1500 mL	(6 cups)	washed, cored, shredded, raw apples
75 mL	(1/3 cup)	washed raisins
3 mL	(1/2 tsp.)	coriander
125 mL	(1/2 cup)	frozen apple juice concentrate
125 mL	(1/2 cup)	water

Topping:

30 mL	(2 Tbsp.)	olive oil
45 mL	(3 Tbsp.)	honey
75 mL	(1/3 cup)	oat bran
250 mL	(1 cup)	quick cooking rolled oats
5 mL	(1 tsp.)	vanilla

Method:

PRESS shredded apples and raisins into baking dish. **SPRINKLE** coriander over apples. **MIX** apple juice concentrate and water and **POUR** over apples. **LET** stand for 2 hours or more. **MIX** remaining ingredients to form a crumbly mixture. **SPRINKLE** over apple mixture. **BAKE** at 350° F. until apples are done and the topping is a delicate brown. **SERVE** warm or cold.

```
Analysis: APPLE CRISP                    Divided by: 12
          Wgt: 119 g (4.2 oz.)           Water:      70%
```

Calories	144	Vitamin C	3.65 mg
Protein	2.34 g	Vitamin D	0 mcg
Carbohydrates	28.9 g	Vit E-Alpha E	.736 mg
Fat - Total	3.31 g	Vitamin K	mcg
Saturated Fat	.493 g	Biotin	mcg
Mono Fat	1.92 g	Calcium	15.4 mg
Poly Fat	.565 g	Copper	.089 mg
Cholesterol	0 mg	Iodine	mcg
Dietary Fibre	2.87 g	Iron	.878 mg
Soluble Fibre	1.18 g	Magnesium	26.7 mg
Total Vit A	4.14 RE	Manganese	.568 mg
Thiamin-B1	.119 mg	Phosphorus	76 mg
Riboflavin-B2	.039 mg	Potassium	196 mg
Niacin-B3	.2 mg	Selenium	3.35 mcg
Niacin Equiv.	.201 mg	Sodium	4.02 mg
Vitamin B6	.067 mg	Zinc	.446 mg
Vitamin B12	0 mcg	Complex Carbs	6.66 g
Folate	6.36 mcg	Sugars	19.4 g
Pantothenic	.225 mg	Water	83.7 g

CALORIE BREAKDOWN		FAT		EXCHANGES	
Protein	6%	* Saturated:	2.9%	Bread	.432
Carbohydrates	75%	Mono Unsat:	11.2%	Fruit	1.38
Fat-Total *	19%	Poly Unsat:	3.3%	Fat	.436

APPLE-STRAWBERRY CRISP (makes 12 servings)

1500 mL	(6 cups)		washed, cored, shredded, raw apples
500 mL	(2 cups)		fresh or frozen strawberries (Use juice, too.)
540 mL	(19 oz.)		unsweetened crushed pineapple (Use juice, too.)
75 mL	(1/3 cup)	EACH	washed raisins and frozen apple juice concentrate
30 mL	(2 Tbsp.)		cornstarch or arrowroot flour
3 mL	(1/2 tsp.)		coriander seed

Topping:

30 mL	(2 Tbsp.)	olive oil
45 mL	(3 Tbsp.)	honey
75 mL	(1/3 cup)	oat bran
375 mL	(1 1/2 cups)	quick cooking rolled oats
5 mL	(1 tsp.)	vanilla

Method:

COMBINE shredded apples, strawberries, pineapple, raisins, apple juice concentrate, cornstarch, and coriander seed. PLACE in baking dish. LET stand while preparing topping. MIX remaining ingredients to form a crumbly mixture. SPRINKLE over apple mixture. BAKE at 350° F. until apples are done and the topping is a delicate brown. SERVE warm or cold with SOYAGEN DESSERT TOPPING.

```
Analysis: APPLE STRAWBERRY CRISP (12 servings)      Divided by: 12
          Wgt: 214 g (7.56 oz.)                     Water:      75%
```

Calories	214	Vitamin C	21.3 mg
Protein	2.79 g	Vitamin D	0 mcg
Carbohydrates	46.8 g	Vit E-Alpha E	1.16 mg
Fat - Total	3.58 g	Vitamin K	mcg
Saturated Fat	.529 g	Biotin	mcg
Mono Fat	1.95 g	Calcium	29.4 mg
Poly Fat	.651 g	Copper	.165 mg
Cholesterol	0 mg	Iodine	mcg
Dietary Fibre	4.9 g	Iron	1.29 mg
Soluble Fibre	1.82 g	Magnesium	39 mg
Total Vit A	9.35 RE	Manganese	1.22 mg
Thiamin-B1	.182 mg	Phosphorus	87.2 mg
Riboflavin-B2	.064 mg	Potassium	337 mg
Niacin-B3	.492 mg	Selenium	4.08 mcg
Niacin Equiv.	.492 mg	Sodium	4.3 mg
Vitamin B6	.131 mg	Zinc	.555 mg
Vitamin B12	0 mcg	Complex Carbs	7.99 g
Folate	14.4 mcg	Sugars	33.8 g
Pantothenic	.329 mg	Water	160 g

CALORIE BREAKDOWN		FAT		EXCHANGES	
Protein	5%	*Saturated :	2.1%	Bread	.527
Carbohydrates	81%	Mono Unsat:	7.6%	Fruit	2.49
Fat-Total *	14%	Poly Unsat:	2.5%	Fat	.452

BANANA DATE NUT BARS (makes 24 servings)

125 mL	(1/2 cup)	warm water
15 mL	(1 Tbsp.)	honey
30 mL	(2 Tbsp.)	active dry yeast
375 mL	(1 1/2 cups)	oat flour
125 mL	(1/2 cup)	honey
15 mL	(1 Tbsp.)	vanilla
75 mL	(1/3 cup)	oil
500 mL	(2 cups)	mashed ripe bananas
375 mL	(1 1/2 cups) **EACH**	chopped dates **and** whole wheat flour
10 mL	(2 tsp.)	salt
250 mL	(1 cup)	chopped nuts

Method:

In small bowl, **STIR** together first 3 ingredients. **SET** aside in warm place until it bubbles. **MAKE** oat flour by processing rolled oats in blender. **EMPTY** oat flour into large bowl. **ADD** whole wheat flour, salt, and nuts. **PLACE** honey, vanilla, oil, bananas and dates in blender. **WHIZ** until smooth. **ADD** blender mixture, and yeast mixture to dry ingredients. **MIX** well. **SPREAD** evenly into PAM or lecithin-treated (6 parts corn oil and 1 part lecithin and **SHAKE** well) 9" x 13" baking dish. **COVER** and **LET** rise in warm place 10-15 minutes. **BAKE** at 375° F. for 10 minutes. **REDUCE** heat to 350° F and **BAKE** for 30-40 minutes more.

```
Analysis: BANANA-DATE-NUT BARS (24 PIECES)      Divided by: 24
          Wgt: 64.7 g (2.28 oz.)                Water:      38%
```

Calories	176	Vitamin C	1.95 mg
Protein	3.23 g	Vitamin D	0 mcg
Carbohydrates	29.2 g	Vit E-Alpha E	.644 mg
Fat - Total	6.42 g	Vitamin K	mcg
Saturated Fat	.785 g	Biotin	mcg
Mono Fat	2.85 g	Calcium	15.8 mg
Poly Fat	2.38 g	Copper	.175 mg
Cholesterol	0 mg	Iodine	mcg
Dietary Fibre	3.2 g	Iron	.96 mg
Soluble Fibre	.729 g	Magnesium	36.6 mg
Total Vit A	3.18 RE	Manganese	.686 mg
Thiamin-B1	.116 mg	Phosphorus	82.3 mg
Riboflavin-B2	.096 mg	Potassium	237 mg
Niacin-B3	1.13 mg	Selenium	8.15 mcg
Niacin Equiv.	1.13 mg	Sodium	180 mg
Vitamin B6	.198 mg	Zinc	.637 mg
Vitamin B12	0 mcg	Complex Carbs	8.27 g
Folate	27 mcg	Sugars	17.6 g
Pantothenic	.363 mg	Water	24.4 g

CALORIE BREAKDOWN		FAT		EXCHANGES	
Protein	7%	*Saturated : 3.8%		Bread	.541
Carbohydrates	62%	Mono Unsat: 13.7%		Fruit	1.18
Fat-Total *	31%	Poly Unsat: 11.4%		Vegetables	.071
				Fat	.548

BANANA POPSICLES (makes about 10 popsicles)

60 mL	(1/4 cup)		carob powder
180 mL	(3/4 cup)		boiling water
125 mL	(1/2 cup)	**EACH**	dates **and** peanut butter
7 mL	(1 1/2 tsp.)		vanilla
1/2 mL	(1/8 tsp.)		salt (optional)
5	(5)		ripe bananas
250 mL	(1 cup)		finely chopped unsalted roasted peanuts

Method:

   PEEL and **CUT** ripe bananas in half crosswise. **DIP** in diluted orange or lemon juice to prevent darkening. **INSERT** popsicle stick in the cut end of each banana half. **ARRANGE** in a container so they don't touch. **FREEZE. WHIZ** carob, dates and boiling water in a blender. **PUT** into a bowl. **ADD** vanilla and salt. **STIR. COAT** banana with carob mixture and **COVER** with chopped peanuts. **FREEZE.**

```
Analysis: BANANA POPSICLES                    Divided by: 10
          Wgt: 113 g (4 oz.)                  Water:      55%
```

Calories	245		Vitamin C	5.2 mg
Protein	7.32 g		Vitamin D	0 mcg
Carbohydrates	27.5 g		Vit E-Alpha E	2.28 mg
Fat - Total	13.9 g		Vitamin K	mcg
Saturated Fat	2.36 g		Biotin	mcg
Mono Fat	6.67 g		Calcium	20.2 mg
Poly Fat	4.19 g		Copper	.251 mg
Cholesterol	0 mg		Iodine	mcg
Dietary Fibre	4.08 g		Iron	.928 mg
Soluble Fibre	.521 g		Magnesium	65.9 mg
Total Vit A	5 RE		Manganese	.656 mg
Thiamin-B1	.114 mg		Phosphorus	108 mg
Riboflavin-B2	.095 mg		Potassium	477 mg
Niacin-B3	4.24 mg		Selenium	2.91 mcg
Niacin Equiv.	4.24 mg		Sodium	32.7 mg
Vitamin B6	.444 mg		Zinc	.963 mg
Vitamin B12	0 mcg		Complex Carbs	3.78 g
Folate	45 mcg		Sugars	18.1 g
Pantothenic	.545 mg		Water	62.8 g

CALORIE BREAKDOWN		FAT		EXCHANGES	
Protein	11%	*Saturated :	8 %	Bread	.067
Carbohydrates	42%	Mono Unsat:	22.7%	Lean Meat	.896
Fat-Total *	47%	Poly Unsat:	14.2%	Fruit	1.64
				Fat	2.05

BAVARIAN DELIGHT (makes 6 servings)

8	(8)	dates
180 mL	(3/4 cup)	water
75 mL	(1/3 cup)	cashews (roasted, no salt)
45 mL	(3 Tbsp.)	carob powder
8 mL	(1 1/2 tsp.)	vanilla
5	(5)	large frozen ripe bananas

Method:
WHIZ dates, water, cashews, carob, and vanilla in blender until very smooth. **ADD** frozen bananas, a few slices at a time, while blender continues to run. **POUR** into container and **FREEZE** or **EAT** immediately as soft ice cream.

```
Analysis: BAVARIAN DELIGHT                    Divided by: 6
          Wgt: 152 g (5.34 oz.)              Water:     68%
```

Calories	198	Vitamin C	8.67	mg
Protein	3.09 g	Vitamin D	0	mcg
Carbohydrates	37.3 g	Vit E-Alpha E	.353	mg
Fat - Total	5.83 g	Vitamin K		mcg
Saturated Fat	1.24 g	Biotin		mcg
Mono Fat	3.18 g	Calcium	26.2	mg
Poly Fat	.986 g	Copper	.404	mg
Cholesterol	0 mg	Iodine		mcg
Dietary Fibre	3.95 g	Iron	1.2	mg
Soluble Fibre	.707 g	Magnesium	63.2	mg
Total Vit A	8.19 RE	Manganese	.288	mg
Thiamin-B1	.077 mg	Phosphorus	81.9	mg
Riboflavin-B2	.144 mg	Potassium	539	mg
Niacin-B3	.979 mg	Selenium	4.07	mcg
Niacin Equiv.	.979 mg	Sodium	5.12	mg
Vitamin B6	.611 mg	Zinc	.861	mg
Vitamin B12	0 mcg	Complex Carbs	4.79	g
Folate	28.4 mcg	Sugars	25.7	g
Pantothenic	.474 mg	Water	103	g

CALORIE BREAKDOWN		FAT		EXCHANGES	
Protein	6%	* Saturated:	5.2%	Bread	.048
Carbohydrates	70%	Mono Unsat:	13.4%	Lean Meat	.167
Fat-Total *	25%	Poly Unsat:	4.1%	Fruit	2.13
				Fat	.715

BLIND DATE PUDDING (makes 6 servings)

125 mL	(1/2 cup)	chopped dates
625 mL	(2 1/2 cups)	cooked brown rice
3 mL	(1/2 tsp.)	grated lemon or orange rind
375 mL	(1 1/2 cups)	orange juice
75 mL	(1/3 cup)	raw, washed cashews
8 mL	(1 1/2 tsp.)	vanilla
1 mL	(1/4 tsp.)	salt
4 mL	(3/4 tsp.)	ground coriander

Method:

LAY dates in bottom of baking dish. COVER with rice. WHIZ remaining ingredients in blender; POUR over the rice. BAKE at 350° F. about 45 minutes. SERVE hot or chilled in sherbet glasses topped with a spoonful of DATE-ORANGE SYRUP.

DATE-ORANGE SYRUP (makes 1 3/4 cups)

250 mL	(1 cup)	pitted dates
90 mL	(6 Tbsp.)	frozen orange juice concentrate (undiluted)
250 mL	(1 cup)	hot water

Method:

WHIZ in blender until smooth. SERVE on BLIND-DATE PUDDING, pancakes, or as a spread.

```
-------------------------------------------------------------------------
| Analysis: BLIND DATE PUDDING (6 servings)      Divided by: 6          |
|           Wgt: 168 g (5.92 oz.)                Water:      71%        |
-------------------------------------------------------------------------
```

Calories	207		Vitamin C	24.4 mg
Protein	4.01 g		Vitamin D	0 mcg
Carbohydrates	39.3 g		Vit E-Alpha E	.927 mg
Fat - Total	4.41 g		Vitamin K	mcg
Saturated Fat	.876 g		Biotin	mcg
Mono Fat	2.4 g		Calcium	23.7 mg
Poly Fat	.872 g		Copper	.323 mg
Cholesterol	0 mg		Iodine	mcg
Dietary Fibre	3.37 g		Iron	1.07 mg
Soluble Fibre	.491 g		Magnesium	66.9 mg
Total Vit A	5.73 RE		Manganese	.853 mg
Thiamin-B1	.156 mg		Phosphorus	121 mg
Riboflavin-B2	.062 mg		Potassium	296 mg
Niacin-B3	1.81 mg		Selenium	12.8 mcg
Niacin Equiv.	1.81 mg		Sodium	143 mg
Vitamin B6	.194 mg		Zinc	1.02 mg
Vitamin B12	0 mcg		Complex Carbs	18.5 g
Folate	37.7 mcg		Sugars	17.1 g
Pantothenic	.539 mg		Water	118 g

CALORIE BREAKDOWN		FAT		EXCHANGES	
Protein	8%	* Saturated : 3.7%		Bread	1.13
Carbohydrates	74%	Mono Unsat: 10.1%		Lean Meat	.167
Fat-Total *	19%	Poly Unsat: 3.7%		Fruit	1.36
				Fat	.59

CAROB BANANA TAPIOCA (makes 8 half-cup servings)

60 mL	(1/4 cup)	pitted dates
125 mL	(1/2 cup)	water to soften
2	(2)	large bananas
125 mL	(1/2 cup)	well-cooked brown rice
45 mL	(3 Tbsp.)	carob powder
		water
90 mL	(6 Tbsp.)	minute tapioca

Method:

SIMMER dates in the 1/2 cup of water to soften. **BREAK** the bananas into quarters. **PUT** softened dates, bananas, rice, and carob powder into blender. **ADD** enough water to make total contents of blender 2 1/2 cups. **BLEND** until very smooth. **POUR** into sauce pan. **ADD** 1 additional cup of water (use water to rinse blender). **SPRINKLE** in the tapioca gradually while stirring. **LET** set 5 minutes, to soften tapioca, then **BRING** to a boil, stirring constantly. **SIMMER** gently about 2 minutes (until tapioca is clear). **REMOVE** from heat and **COOL**. **SERVE** plain or **GARNISH** with flaked coconut, kiwi, or other topping.

```
---------------------------------------------------------------------
| Analysis: CAROB BANANA TAPIOCA (1/2 cup servings)  Divided by: 8  |
|           Wgt: 130 g (4.6 oz.)                      Water:    75% |
---------------------------------------------------------------------
```

Calories	120		Vitamin C	3.43 mg
Protein	1.07 g		Vitamin D	0 mcg
Carbohydrates	29.5 g		Vit E-Alpha E	.244 mg
Fat - Total	.331 g		Vitamin K	mcg
Saturated Fat	.105 g		Biotin	mcg
Mono Fat	.068 g		Calcium	16.3 mg
Poly Fat	.08 g		Copper	.092 mg
Cholesterol	0 mg		Iodine	mcg
Dietary Fibre	1.7 g		Iron	.369 mg
Soluble Fibre	.325 g		Magnesium	20 mg
Total Vit A	3.3 RE		Manganese	.196 mg
Thiamin-B1	.035 mg		Phosphorus	23.2 mg
Riboflavin-B2	.057 mg		Potassium	213 mg
Niacin-B3	.557 mg		Selenium	2.27 mcg
Niacin Equiv.	.557 mg		Sodium	3.77 mg
Vitamin B6	.254 mg		Zinc	.193 mg
Vitamin B12	0 mcg		Complex Carbs	3.6 g
Folate	9.06 mcg		Sugars	10.7 g
Pantothenic	.177 mg		Water	97.5 g

CALORIE BREAKDOWN		FAT		EXCHANGES	
Protein	3%	*Saturated	.8%	Bread	.204
Carbohydrates	94%	Mono Unsat:	.5%	Fruit	.932
Fat-Total *	2%	Poly Unsat:	.6%		

FRUIT MINCEMEAT (makes 16 servings)

750 mL	(3 cups)	softened cut up prunes
375 mL	(1 1/2 cups)	raisins
125 mL	(1/2 cup)	currants (May use 1/2 cup more raisins instead.)
1 L	(4 cups)	chopped raw apples
30 mL	(2 Tbsp.)	coarsely grated orange rind
30 mL	(2 Tbsp.)	grated lemon rind
1 mL	(1/4 tsp.)	salt
3 mL	(1/2 tsp.)	cardamon
3 mL	(1/2 tsp.)	coriander
500 mL	(2 cups)	boiling water
250 mL	(1 cup)	finely chopped walnuts

Method:

MIX prunes, raisins, currants, orange and lemon rind, salt, cardamon, and coriander. ADD boiling water. LET stand overnight. Next morning ADD nuts. REFRIGERATE or USE at once. ADD apples just before baking. BAKE 1 1/2 hours at 350º degrees F. May use as pie or tart filling, as jam on toast, or on cooked cereal to sweeten.

```
--------------------------------------------------------------------------
| Analysis: FRUIT MINCEMEAT                    Divided by: 16            |
|           Wgt: 114 g (4.03 oz.)              Water:       57%          |
--------------------------------------------------------------------------
```

Calories	195		Vitamin C	5.52 mg
Protein	2.42 g		Vitamin D	0 mcg
Carbohydrates	40.1 g		Vit E-Alpha E	.462 mg
Fat - Total	5.02 g		Vitamin K	mcg
Saturated Fat	.458 g		Biotin	mcg
Mono Fat	1.08 g		Calcium	38.1 mg
Poly Fat	2.99 g		Copper	.311 mg
Cholesterol	0 mg		Iodine	mcg
Dietary Fibre	2.04 g		Iron	1.85 mg
Soluble Fibre	.461 g		Magnesium	21.2 mg
Total Vit A	3.12 RE		Manganese	.295 mg
Thiamin-B1	.09 mg		Phosphorus	68.6 mg
Riboflavin-B2	.085 mg		Potassium	423 mg
Niacin-B3	.782 mg		Selenium	1.5 mcg
Niacin Equiv.	.295 mg		Sodium	39.5 mg
Vitamin B6	.177 mg		Zinc	.457 mg
Vitamin B12	0 mcg		Complex Carbs	1.11 g
Folate	8.15 mcg		Sugars	16.8 g
Pantothenic	.216 mg		Water	65.5 g

CALORIE BREAKDOWN		FAT		EXCHANGES	
Protein	4%	*Saturated :	1.9%	Bread	.077
Carbohydrates	75%	Mono Unsat:	4.5%	Fruit	1.16
Fat-Total *	21%	Poly Unsat:	12.5%		

HOT FUDGE SUNDAE (makes 18 servings)

500 mL	(2 cups)	chopped dates (Chop to be sure there are no pits.)
500 mL	(2 cups)	water
125 mL	(1/2 cup)	carob powder
10 mL	(2 tsp.)	vanilla
10	(10)	large, sliced frozen bananas
60 mL	(1/4 cup)	chopped, unsalted, roasted peanuts

Method:

HEAT the dates in the water until soft. Then **WHIZ** in food processor or blender. **ADD** carob and vanilla. **POUR** over frozen bananas or **WHIZ** bananas in food processor and **SCOOP** into serving dishes. Then **POUR** carob mixture over them. **SPRINKLE** peanuts on top.

```
Analysis: HOT FUDGE SUNDAE              Divided by: 18
          Wgt: 115 g (4.05 oz.)         Water:      68%
```

Calories	137	Vitamin C	5.78 mg
Protein	1.65 g	Vitamin D	0 mcg
Carbohydrates	32.4 g	Vit E-Alpha E	.359 mg
Fat - Total	1.42 g	Vitamin K	mcg
Saturated Fat	.299 g	Biotin	mcg
Mono Fat	.56 g	Calcium	21.7 mg
Poly Fat	.386 g	Copper	.155 mg
Cholesterol	0 mg	Iodine	mcg
Dietary Fibre	3.41 g	Iron	.557 mg
Soluble Fibre	.737 g	Magnesium	30.7 mg
Total Vit A	6.08 RE	Manganese	.212 mg
Thiamin-B1	.057 mg	Phosphorus	30.1 mg
Riboflavin-B2	.098 mg	Potassium	416 mg
Niacin-B3	1.11 mg	Selenium	1.36 mcg
Niacin Equiv.	1.11 mg	Sodium	3.14 mg
Vitamin B6	.42 mg	Zinc	.26 mg
Vitamin B12	0 mcg	Complex Carbs	1.95 g
Folate	18.4 mcg	Sugars	24.7 g
Pantothenic	.349 mg	Water	78.2 g

CALORIE BREAKDOWN		FAT		EXCHANGES	
Protein	4%	Saturated:	1.8%	Bread	.04
Carbohydrates	87%	Mon Unsat:	3.4%	Lean Meat	.07
Fat - Total *	9%	Poly Unsat:	2.3%	Fruit	2.00
				Fat	.16

MILLET-GRANOLA SURPRISE (makes 15 servings)

1 L	(4 cups)		YUMMY GRANOLA or other low-fat granola
750 mL	(3 cups)		cooked millet (measured after cooking)
5 mL	(1 tsp.)		vanilla
500 mL	(2 cups)	**EACH**	pineapple juice **and** sliced bananas
250 mL	(1 cup)		frozen strawberries (thickened)
15 mL	(1 Tbsp.)		cornstarch
30 mL	(2 Tbsp.)		honey

Method:

PUT a layer of granola on the bottom of a rectangular dish or a spring-form pan. ADD a layer of sliced bananas, a layer of the hot millet blended with 1 1/2 cups of the pineapple juice and vanilla. CONTINUE layering ending with the millet mixture. To thicken strawberries MIX remaining juice with cornstarch and honey and BOIL until thickened. SPREAD the thickened strawberries on top. LET set overnight. CUT into squares or slices. (May add strawberries just before serving instead.)

```
---------------------------------------------------------------------------
| Analysis: MILLET-GRANOLA SURPRISE          Divided by: 18                |
|           Wgt: 140 g (4.95 oz.)            Water:       66%              |
---------------------------------------------------------------------------
```

Calories	203	Vitamin C	15.9 mg
Protein	5.77 g	Vitamin D	.013 mcg
Carbohydrates	36.4 g	Vit E-Alpha E	1.26 mg
Fat - Total	4.56 g	Vitamin K	mcg
Saturated Fat	.934 g	Biotin	mcg
Mono Fat	1.63 g	Calcium	30.6 mg
Poly Fat	1.62 g	Copper	.235 mg
Cholesterol	0 mg	Iodine	mcg
Dietary Fibre	3.45 g	Iron	1.6 mg
Soluble Fibre	1.04 g	Magnesium	63.3 mg
Total Vit A	4.28 RE	Manganese	1.22 mg
Thiamin-B1	.209 mg	Phosphorus	154 mg
Riboflavin-B2	.115 mg	Potassium	276 mg
Niacin-B3	1.69 mg	Selenium	6.69 mcg
Niacin Equiv.	1.67 mg	Sodium	126 mg
Vitamin B6	.222 mg	Zinc	1.32 mg
Vitamin B12	.001 mcg	Complex Carbs	19.9 g
Folate	29.6 mcg	Sugars	12.3 g
Pantothenic	.411 mg	Water	92.2 g

CALORIE BREAKDOWN		FAT	EXCHANGES	
Protein	11%	Saturated : 4%	Bread	1.44
Carbohydrates	69%	Mono Unsat: 7%	Lean Meat	.114
Fat -Total	20%	Poly Unsat: 7%	Fruit	.9

PRINCESS PUDDING (makes 6 half-cup servings)

625 mL	(2 1/2 cups)	unsweetened pineapple juice
125 mL	(1/2 cup)	cornmeal
1	(1)	banana
8 mL	(1 1/2 tsp.)	vanilla
60 mL	(1/4 cup)	coconut
250 mL	(1 cup)	granola

Method:

COOK cornmeal in 2 cups of the pineapple juice. **BLEND** 1/2 cup pineapple juice, banana, vanilla, and coconut until smooth. **POUR** freshly cooked cornmeal into blender with other ingredients and **BLEND** until smooth. **PUT** a layer of granola on bottom of dish. **SPOON** ingredients from blender over granola and **CHILL. GARNISH** with sliced fresh strawberries and/or kiwi.

```
-------------------------------------------------------------------
| Analysis: PRINCESS PUDDING (6 half-cup servings)  Divided by: 6  |
|          Wgt: 163 g (5.75 oz.)              Water:      68%       |
-------------------------------------------------------------------
```

Calories	223	Vitamin C	13 mg
Protein	4.7 g	Vitamin D	.01 mcg
Carbohydrates	39.8 g	Vit E-Alpha E	.857 mg
Fat - Total	5.48 g	Vitamin K	mcg
Saturated Fat	2.55 g	Biotin	mcg
Mono Fat	1.31 g	Calcium	36.3 mg
Poly Fat	1.19 g	Copper	.236 mg
Cholesterol	0 mg	Iodine	mcg
Dietary Fibre	3.1 g	Iron	1.71 mg
Soluble Fibre	.76 g	Magnesium	53 mg
Total Vit A	7.67 RE	Manganese	1.73 mg
Thiamin-B1	.252 mg	Phosphorus	107 mg
Riboflavin-B2	.13 mg	Potassium	332 mg
Niacin-B3	1.65 mg	Selenium	7.23 mcg
Niacin Equiv.	1.64 mg	Sodium	95.8 mg
Vitamin B6	.29 mg	Zinc	.941 mg
Vitamin B12	.001 mcg	Complex Carbs	16 g
Folate	42.6 mcg	Sugars	19.8 g
Pantothenic	.39 mg	Water	111 g

CALORIE BREAKDOWN		FAT		EXCHANGES	
Protein	8%	* Saturated :	10.1%	Bread	1.1
Carbohydrates	70%	Mono Unsat:	5.2%	Lean Meat	.086
Fat-Total *	22%	Poly Unsat:	4.7%	Fruit	1.26
				Fat	.766

PUDDING CAKE AND LEMON SAUCE (makes 16 servings)

60 mL	(1/4 cup)	raw, washed cashews
375 mL	(1 1/2 cups) **EACH**	water **and** dates
5 mL	(1 tsp.)	vanilla
2 L	(8 cups)	soft whole wheat bread crumbs
250 mL	(1 cup) **EACH**	crushed pineapple **and** raisins
500 mL	(2 cups)	grated carrots
125 mL	(1/2 cup)	chopped walnuts

SAUCE:

500 mL	(2 cups)	crushed pineapple
30 mL	(2 Tbsp.)	cornstarch
125 mL	(1/2 cup)	fresh lemon juice

Method:

WHIZ cashews until almost nut butter. SIMMER water and dates until dates are soft. ADD softened dates to cashews in food processor and WHIZ. COMBINE remaining ingredients in mixing bowl. ADD date mixture. PACK mixture into a bundt or other suitable pan. BAKE at 300° F. for 1 hour. While pudding is baking HEAT pineapple. MIX cornstarch with the lemon juice and STIR into hot pineapple mixture. COOK until thick. WHIZ in food processor until smooth. SERVE over the warm "cake".

```
------------------------------------------------------------------------
| Analysis: PUDDING CAKE WITH SAUCE          Divided by: 16            |
|           Wgt: 143 g (5.06 oz.)            Water:       65%          |
------------------------------------------------------------------------
```

Calories	195		Vitamin C	9.59 mg
Protein	3.49 g		Vitamin D	.047 mcg
Carbohydrates	42 g		Vit E-Alpha E	.289 mg
Fat - Total	2.83 g		Vitamin K	mcg
Saturated Fat	.5 g		Biotin	mcg
Mono Fat	1.15 g		Calcium	42.3 mg
Poly Fat	1.01 g		Copper	.226 mg
Cholesterol	.675 mg		Iodine	mcg
Dietary Fibre	3.34 g		Iron	1.39 mg
Soluble Fibre	.748 g		Magnesium	30.9 mg
Total Vit A	390 RE		Manganese	.771 mg
Thiamin-B1	.189 mg		Phosphorus	62 mg
Riboflavin-B2	.103 mg		Potassium	331 mg
Niacin-B3	1.5 mg		Selenium	8.21 mcg
Niacin Equiv.	1.5 mg		Sodium	122 mg
Vitamin B6	.134 mg		Zinc	.456 mg
Vitamin B12	0 mcg		Complex Carbs	11.6 g
Folate	17.8 mcg		Sugars	27.1 g
Pantothenic	.349 mg		Water	93.7 g

CALORIE BREAKDOWN		FAT		EXCHANGES	
Protein	7%	* Saturated :	2.2%	Bread	.832
Carbohydrates	81%	Mono Unsat:	5%	Lean Meat	.031
Fat-Total *	12%	Poly Unsat:	4.4%	Fruit	1.69
		Fat .125---->		Vegetables	.191

QUINOA PUDDING (makes 8 half-cup servings)

500 mL	(2 cups)	cooked quinoa (1 cup + 2 cups water before cooking)
250 mL	(1 cup)	apple juice
125 mL	(1/2 cup)	raisins
45 mL	(3 Tbsp.)	sliced almonds
1/2 mL	(1/8 tsp.)	coriander
8 mL	(1 1/2 tsp.)	vanilla
		grated rind of one lemon
500 mL	(2 cups)	hot unsweetened apple sauce

Method:

COMBINE all the ingredients except apple sauce in a saucepan, **COVER** and **BRING** to a boil. **REDUCE** heat. **SIMMER** for 15 minutes. **STIR** in apple sauce. **POUR** pudding into individual dishes. **TOP** with a strawberry or hot fruit.

```
-------------------------------------------------------------------
| Analysis: QUINOA PUDDING (8)                Divided by: 8        |
|           Wgt: 127 g (4.47 oz.)             Water:      67%      |
-------------------------------------------------------------------
```

Calories	172		Vitamin C	1.59 mg
Protein	3.9 g		Vitamin D	0 mcg
Carbohydrates	34.1 g		Vit E-Alpha E	.282 mg
Fat - Total	3 g		Vitamin K	mcg
Saturated Fat	.308 g		Biotin	mcg
Mono Fat	1.41 g		Calcium	30.4 mg
Poly Fat	.882 g		Copper	.256 mg
Dietary Fibre	1.87 g		Iron	2.45 mg
Soluble Fibre	.376 g		Magnesium	60.9 mg
Total Vit A	1.97 RE		Manganese	.649 mg
Thiamin-B1	.074 mg		Phosphorus	120 mg
Riboflavin-B2	.138 mg		Potassium	342 mg
Niacin-B3	.941 mg		Selenium	1.22 mcg
Niacin Equiv.	.941 mg		Sodium	9.38 mg
Vitamin B6	.103 mg		Zinc	.854 mg
Vitamin B12	0 mcg		Complex Carbs	.153 g
Folate	13.1 mcg		Sugars	17.1 g
Pantothenic	.321 mg		Water	84.5 g

CALORIE BREAKDOWN		FAT		EXCHANGES	
Protein	9%	*Saturated :	1.5%	Bread	.957
Carbohydrates	76%	Mono Unsat:	7.1%	Lean Meat	.089
Fat-Total *	15%	Poly Unsat:	4.4%	Fruit	1.31
				Fat	.282

RICE AMBROSIA (makes 8 servings)

250 mL	(1 cup)	cold, cooked brown rice
125 mL	(1/2 cup)	chopped orange sections
1	(1)	large banana, chopped
125 mL	(1/2 cup)	unsweetened pineapple tidbits (Do not drain.)
125 mL	(1/2 cup)	Thompson seedless grapes
60 mL	(1/4 cup)	chopped dates (softened)
2	(2)	figs (softened)
15 mL	(1 Tbsp.)	orange juice concentrate
30 mL	(2 Tbsp.)	moist unsweetened flaked coconut

Method:

MIX all ingredients except coconut. **CHILL. SERVE** in sherbet glasses or serving bowl. **SPRINKLE** coconut on top.

```
Analysis: RICE AMBROSIA (1/8 recipe)              Divided by: 8
          Wgt: 99.3 g (3.5 oz.)                   Water:     73%
```

Calories	104		Vitamin C	17.4 mg
Protein	1.48 g		Vitamin D	0 mcg
Carbohydrates	23.7 g		Vit E-Alpha E	.448 mg
Fat - Total	1.25 g		Vitamin K	mcg
Saturated Fat	.812 g		Biotin	mcg
Mono Fat	.148 g		Calcium	24.7 mg
Poly Fat	.155 g		Copper	.114 mg
Cholesterol	0 mg		Iodine	mcg
Dietary Fibre	2.57 g		Iron	.451 mg
Soluble Fibre	.593 g		Magnesium	25.8 mg
Total Vit A	8.37 RE		Manganese	.497 mg
Thiamin-B1	.085 mg		Phosphorus	36.9 mg
Riboflavin-B2	.05 mg		Potassium	228 mg
Niacin-B3	.757 mg		Selenium	5.49 mcg
Niacin Equiv.	.757 mg		Sodium	2.88 mg
Vitamin B6	.18 mg		Zinc	.279 mg
Vitamin B12	0 mcg		Complex Carbs	5.5 g
Folate	14.5 mcg		Sugars	15.6 g
Pantothenic	.26 mg		Water	72.3 g

CALORIE BREAKDOWN		FAT		EXCHANGES	
Protein	5%	*Saturated :	6.5%	Bread	.336
Carbohydrates	85%	Mono Unsat:	1.2%	Fruit	1.15
Fat-Total *	10%	Poly Unsat:	1.2%	Fat	.125

LIFESTYLE AND CANCER:

Lifestyle has a major influence upon one's risk of cancer. Environmental factors such as cigarette smoking, occupational hazards, diet, environmental pollution and other lifestyle factors are major causes of cancer. About 50-60% of all cancers are believed to be diet-related, while about 35% of all deaths due to cancer are believed to be associated with improper diet.

SMOOTHIES (makes 4 servings)

250 mL	(1 cup)	frozen strawberries
2	(2)	large frozen ripe bananas
125 mL	(1/2 cup)	apple juice concentrate

Method:
    BLEND ingredients until smooth. **SERVE** immediately or **RETURN** to freezer. (If left very long it may be necessary to process it again because it freezes solid.) **SERVE** with chopped nuts, toasted coconut, kiwi slices, CAROB SAUCE, etc.

CAROB SAUCE: (analysis not included)

5 mL	(1 tsp.)	vanilla
3	(3)	chopped, pitted dates
25 mL	(5 tsp.)	cornstarch or arrowroot powder
30 mL	(2 Tbsp.)	carob powder
250 mL	(1 cup)	water

Method:
    BLEND vanilla, dates, cornstarch, and carob powder with a small amount of the water. **ADD** the rest of the water after dates are blended. **COOK** until thick, stirring constantly. May be used cold or hot.

```
Analysis: SMOOTHIES                        Divided by: 3
          Wgt: 167 g (5.89 oz.)            Water:     82%
```

Calories	106	Vitamin C	27.8 mg
Protein	1.02 g	Vitamin D	0 mcg
Carbohydrates	27.2 g	Vit E-Alpha E	.344 mg
Fat - Total	.465 g	Vitamin K	mcg
Saturated Fat	.152 g	Biotin	mcg
Mono Fat	.041 g	Calcium	15.4 mg
Poly Fat	.108 g	Copper	.113 mg
Cholesterol	0 mg	Iodine	mcg
Dietary Fibre	2.59 g	Iron	.762 mg
Soluble Fibre	.699 g	Magnesium	28.8 mg
Total Vit A	8.1 RE	Manganese	.306 mg
Thiamin-B1	.054 mg	Phosphorus	24.6 mg
Riboflavin-B2	.101 mg	Potassium	424 mg
Niacin-B3	.681 mg	Selenium	1.27 mcg
Niacin Equiv.	.681 mg	Sodium	2.99 mg
Vitamin B6	.466 mg	Zinc	.198 mg
Vitamin B12	0 mcg	Complex Carbs	2.13 g
Folate	22.9 mcg	Sugars	22.4 g
Pantothenic	.277 mg	Water	138 g

CALORIE BREAKDOWN		FAT	EXCHANGES	
Protein	3%	*Saturated : 1.2%	Fruit	1.84
Carbohydrates	93%	Mono Unsat: .3%		
Fat-Total *	4%	Poly Unsat: .8%		

SOYAGEN DESSERT TOPPING (makes 1 1/2 cups)

250 mL	(1 cup)	very cold water
125 mL	(1/2 cup)	soyagen milk powder (Other brands don't work.)
15 mL	(1 Tbsp.)	honey
2 mL	(1/4 tsp.)	vanilla
125 mL	(1/2 cup)	corn or safflower oil
15 mL	(1 Tbsp.)	fresh lemon juice

Method:

WHIZ water, soy milk powder, honey, and vanilla in blender or food processor for 1 minute. **ADD** oil slowly while continuing to whiz. **ADD** lemon juice and **MIX** well. **SERVE** as a nondairy topping for desserts or as a dressing for fruit salad. **COVER** and **REFRIGERATE** until used. It may be necessary to beat topping with a spoon before using.

```
Analysis: SOYAGEN DESSERT TOPPING          Divided by: 24
          Wgt: 18.3 g (.646 oz.)           Water:      5%
```

Calories	54		Vitamin C	.6 mg
Protein	.505 g		Vitamin D	.136 mcg
Carbohydrates	1.96 g		Vit E-Alpha E	1.02 mg
Fat - Total	5.04 g		Vitamin K	mcg
Saturated Fat	.577 g		Biotin	mcg
Mono Fat	1.1 g		Calcium	11.5 mg
Poly Fat	2.65 g		Copper	.002 mg
Cholesterol	0 mg		Iodine	mcg
Dietary Fibre	.002 g		Iron	.105 mg
Soluble Fibre	.001 g		Magnesium	.154 mg
Total Vit A	2.93 RE		Manganese	.001 mg
Thiamin-B1	.004 mg		Phosphorus	.115 mg
Riboflavin-B2	.011 mg		Potassium	18.8 mg
Niacin-B3	.028 mg		Selenium	.008 mcg
Niacin Equiv.	.002 mg		Sodium	17.8 mg
Vitamin B6	.001 mg		Zinc	.049 mg
Vitamin B12	.042 mcg		Complex Carbs	0 g
Folate	.1 mcg		Sugars	.78 g
Pantothenic	.02 mg		Water	10.6 g

CALORIE BREAKDOWN		FAT		EXCHANGES	
Protein	4%	* Saturated :	9.4%	Fruit	.045
Carbohydrates	14%	Mono Unsat:	17.9%	Milk	.062
Fat-Total *	82%	Poly Unsat:	43.1%	Fat	.892

STEAMED FRUIT PUDDING (makes 16 servings)

250 mL	(1 cup)	apple juice
250 mL	(1 cup)	washed raisins
250 mL	(1 cup)	chopped dried apricots
250 mL	(1 cup)	chopped prunes
250 mL	(1 cup)	grated fresh apple
250 mL	(1 cup)	hot water
125 mL	(1/2 cup)	raw cashews
10	(10)	dates
500 mL	(2 cups)	whole wheat flour
500 mL	(2 cups)	fresh whole wheat bread crumbs
3 mL	(1/2 tsp.)	salt
30 mL	(2 Tbsp.)	grated lemon rind

METHOD:

SOAK raisins, apricots, and prunes in juice overnight in a large bowl. **STIR** in apples. **BLEND** water, dates, and cashews until smooth. **ADD** to soaked fruit and juice. **STIR** in remaining ingredients. **PUT** into a lecithin treated tube pan or 19 oz. cans. **STEAM** for 2 hours in a covered steamer. **COOL, UNMOULD, SLICE** and **SERVE** with warm apple sauce.

```
Analysis: STEAMED FRUIT PUDDING              Divided by: 16
          Wgt: 81.1 g (2.86 oz.)             Water:      41%
```

Calories	185		Vitamin C	2.13 mg
Protein	4.16 g		Vitamin D	.012 mcg
Carbohydrates	39.9 g		Vit E-Alpha Eq	.34 mg
Fat - Total	2.64 g		Vitamin K	mcg
Saturated Fat	.512 g		Biotin	mcg
Mono Fat	1.31 g		Calcium	28.9 mg
Poly Fat	.532 g		Copper	.288 mg
Dietary Fibre	4.08 g		Iron	2.05 mg
Soluble Fibre	.991 g		Magnesium	42.6 mg
Total Vit A	59.5 RE		Manganese	.698 mg
Thiamin-B1	.13 mg		Phosphorus	108 mg
Riboflavin-B2	.099 mg		Potassium	392 mg
Niacin-B3	1.82 mg		Selenium	15.5 mcg
Niacin Equiv.	1.65 mg		Sodium	127 mg
Vitamin B6	.141 mg		Zinc	.88 mg
Vitamin B12	0 mcg		Complex Carbs	12.1 g
Folate	13.9 mcg		Sugars	17 g
Pantothenic	.386 mg		Water	32.9 g

CALORIE BREAKDOWN		FAT	EXCHANGES	
Protein	8%	*Saturated : 2.3%	Bread	.814
Carbohydrates	80%	Mono Unsat: 5.9%	Lean Meat	.094
Fat-Total *	12%	Poly Unsat: 2.4%	Fruit	1.22
			Fat	.305

STRAWBERRY CLOUD (makes 6 servings)

750 mL	(3 cups)	frozen or fresh strawberries
1	(1)	medium ripe banana
375 mL	(1 1/2 cups)	tofu
30 mL	(2 Tbsp.)	fresh lemon juice
2 mL	(1/4 tsp.)	vanilla

Method:

DRAIN the tofu and PUT into a food processor together with the strawberries, lemon juice, banana, and vanilla. PROCESS until smooth. DIVIDE the mixture between 6 individual serving dishes and DECORATE with kiwi. CHILL until required. NOTE: If using frozen berries the dessert will be like soft ice-cream. If using fresh berries it will be a pudding texture.

```
Analysis: STRAWBERRY CLOUD (6 SERVINGS)          Divided by: 6
          Wgt: 162 g (5.71 oz.)                  Water:      80%
```

Calories	136		Vitamin C	34.9 mg
Protein	10.5 g		Vitamin D	0 mcg
Carbohydrates	14.4 g		Vit E-Alpha E	.269 mg
Fat - Total	5.68 g		Vitamin K	mcg
Saturated Fat	.837 g		Biotin	mcg
Mono Fat	1.23 g		Calcium	142 mg
Poly Fat	3.16 g		Copper	.296 mg
Cholesterol	0 mg		Iodine	mcg
Dietary Fibre	2.13 g		Iron	7.22 mg
Soluble Fibre	.519 g		Magnesium	73 mg
Total Vit A	15.3 RE		Manganese	.99 mg
Thiamin-B1	.126 mg		Phosphorus	133 mg
Riboflavin-B2	.112 mg		Potassium	341 mg
Niacin-B3	.692 mg		Selenium	.87 mcg
Niacin Equiv.	.694 mg		Sodium	10.5 mg
Vitamin B6	.191 mg		Zinc	1.12 mg
Vitamin B12	0 mcg		Complex Carbs	.532 g
Folate	35.2 mcg		Sugars	9.13 g
Pantothenic	.219 mg		Water	130 g

CALORIE BREAKDOWN		FAT		EXCHANGES	
Protein	28%	* Saturated:	5%	Bread	.124
Carbohydrates	38%	Mono Unsat:	7.4%	Lean Meat	1.5
Fat-Total *	18.9%	Poly Unsat:	18.9%	Fruit	.818
				Fat	.008

TOFU "CHEESE" CAKE (makes 16 servings)

Crust:
375 mL	(1 1/2 cups)	toasted rolled oats
125 mL	(1/2 cup)	toasted coconut
60 mL	(1/4 cup)	slivered almonds
30 mL	(2 Tbsp.)	corn oil

Filling:
75 mL	(1/3 cup)		raw cashews
30 mL	(2 Tbsp.)	**EACH**	honey **and** lemon juice
2 mL	(1/2 tsp.)		salt
540 mL	(19 oz.)		unsweetened crushed pineapple (Do not drain.)
500 gm	(1 lb - 2 cups)		tofu
341 mL	(12 oz.)		pineapple juice concentrate
75 mL	(1/3 cup)		agar flakes or Emes Kosher jel (plain)

Method:
WHIZ ingredients for crust in food processor. **PRESS** mixture into a 9 inch spring form pan and flatten with the bottom of a glass. **BAKE** at 350°F. for about 12 minutes. **Filling:** **BLEND** cashews until smooth. **ADD** honey, lemon juice, salt, pineapple and tofu. **BLEND.** **SOAK** agar in the pineapple juice concentrate for five minutes. **BRING** to a boil and **SIMMER** until agar is dissolved. **ADD** to mixture in food processor. **BLEND** well. **POUR** onto crust. **CHILL. TOP** with fruit of your choice.

```
Analysis: TOFU "CHEESE" CAKE (16)              Divided by: 16
          Wgt: 116 g (4.08 oz.)               Water:    60%
```

Calories	217	Vitamin C	15.6 mg
Protein	7.68 g	Vitamin D	0 mcg
Carbohydrates	28 g	Vit E-Alpha E	.807 mg
Fat - Total	9.67 g	Vitamin K	mcg
Saturated Fat	2.54 g	Biotin	mcg
Mono Fat	2.84 g	Calcium	92.2 mg
Poly Fat	3.68 g	Copper	.357 mg
Cholesterol	0 mg	Iodine	mcg
Dietary Fibre	1.9 g	Iron	4.31 mg
Soluble Fibre	.487 g	Magnesium	71 mg
Total Vit A	8.84 RE	Manganese	2.1 mg
Thiamin-B1	.211 mg	Phosphorus	134 mg
Riboflavin-B2	.09 mg	Potassium	320 mg
Niacin-B3	.642 mg	Selenium	4.12 mcg
Niacin Equiv.	.644 mg	Sodium	90.3 mg
Vitamin B6	.15 mg	Zinc	1.14 mg
Vitamin B12	0 mcg	Complex Carbs	4.73 g
Folate	28.1 mcg	Sugars	20 g
Pantothenic	.356 mg	Water	69 g

CALORIE BREAKDOWN		FAT		EXCHANGES	
Protein	13%	*Saturated :	10 %	Bread	.33
Carbohydrates	49%	Mono Unsat:	11.1%	Lean Meat	.864
Fat-Total *	38%	Poly Unsat:	14.4%	Fruit	1.36
		Fat 1.09--->		Vegetables	.018

TOFU-FRUIT "YOGHURT" (makes 8 one-half-cup servings)

750 mL	(3 cups)	tofu
500 mL	(2 cups)	frozen strawberries or raspberries
250 mL	(1 cup)	mashed bananas
30 mL	(2 Tbsp.)	honey
30 mL	(2 Tbsp.)	lemon juice (preferably fresh)
8 mL	(1 1/2 tsp.)	vanilla

Method:

PLACE all ingredients in a food processor and WHIZ until smooth. CHILL for at least 2 hours. SERVE very cold.

```
--------------------------------------------------------------------------
| Analysis: TOFU- FRUIT YOGHURT (1/2 CUP SERVINGS)   Divided by: 8       |
|           170 g (5.99 oz.)                         Water:      74%     |
--------------------------------------------------------------------------
```

Calories	194		Vitamin C	19.9 mg
Protein	15.4 g		Vitamin D	0 mcg
Carbohydrates	19 g		Vit E-Alpha E	.199 mg
Fat - Total	8.43 g		Vitamin K	mcg
Saturated Fat	1.25 g		Biotin	mcg
Mono Fat	1.84 g		Calcium	202 mg
Poly Fat	4.7 g		Copper	.408 mg
Dietary Fibre	1.51 g		Iron	10.3 mg
Soluble Fibre	.355 g		Magnesium	101 mg
Total Vit A	19.9 RE		Manganese	1.27 mg
Thiamin-B1	.171 mg		Phosphorus	190 mg
Riboflavin-B2	.141 mg		Potassium	398 mg
Niacin-B3	.695 mg		Selenium	.666 mcg
Niacin Equiv.	.698 mg		Sodium	14.5 mg
Vitamin B6	.263 mg		Zinc	1.59 mg
Vitamin B12	0 mcg		Complex Carbs	.787 g
Folate	39.9 mcg		Sugars	12.5 g
Pantothenic	.247 mg		Water	125 g

CALORIE BREAKDOWN		FAT		EXCHANGES	
Protein	29%	*Saturated :	5.3%	Bread	.187
Carbohydrates	36%	Mono Unsat:	7.8%	Lean Meat	2.25
Fat-Total *	36%	Poly Unsat:	19.8%	Fruit	.969
				Fat	.039

HAZARDS OF REFINED SUGAR:

Depletion of body stores of Vitamin B_1, promotion of dental caries, depression of immune system (interfering with germ-killing capacity of white cells), elevated blood fat (from conversion of glucose to triglycerides), promotion of hypoglycemia, gastric irritation when stomach contents have more than 10% sugar, and constipation (Usually diets rich in sugar are low in fibre.)

TOFU ORANGE TOPPING (makes about 2 cups - 22 servings)

500 mL	(2 cups)	tofu (blanched in boiling water for 2 minutes)
20 mL	(4 tsp.)	vanilla
60 mL	(1/4 cup)	honey
1 mL	(1/4 tsp.)	salt
60 mL	(1/4 cup)	frozen orange juice concentrate
125 mL	(1/2 cup)	corn oil

Method:

DRAIN and **COOL** tofu. **PLACE** all ingredients in blender and blend until smooth, stopping blender 2 or 3 times to stir contents. **KEEP** refrigerated. (Keeps several days.)

```
Analysis: TOFU ORANGE TOPPING (22 X 2 TBSP.)          Divided by: 22
          Wgt: 33.9 g (1.2 oz.)                       Water: 62%
```

Calories	77.7		Vitamin C	2.2 mg
Protein	1.86 g		Vitamin D	0 mcg
Carbohydrates	4.45 g		Vit E-Alpha E	1.05 mg
Fat - Total	6.04 g		Vitamin K	mcg
Saturated Fat	.786 g		Biotin	mcg
Mono Fat	1.44 g		Calcium	24.4 mg
Poly Fat	3.5 g		Copper	.048 mg
Cholesterol	0 mg		Iodine	mcg
Dietary Fibre	.282 g		Iron	1.23 mg
Soluble Fibre	.003 g		Magnesium	23.6 mg
Total Vit A	2.47 RE		Manganese	.141 mg
Thiamin-B1	.023 mg		Phosphorus	22.9 mg
Riboflavin-B2	.014 mg		Potassium	39.8 mg
Niacin-B3	.06 mg		Selenium	.371 mcg
Niacin Equiv.	.06 mg		Sodium	50.2 mg
Vitamin B6	.014 mg		Zinc	.193 mg
Vitamin B12	0 mcg		Complex Carbs	.062 g
Folate	5.86 mcg		Sugars	3.84 g
Pantothenic	.027 mg		Water	21 g

CALORIE BREAKDOWN		FAT		EXCHANGES	
Protein	9%	*Saturated :	8.9%	Lean Meat	.182
Carbohydrates	22%	Mono Unsat:	16.3%	Fruit	.243
Fat-Total *	68%	Poly Unsat:	39.5%	Vegetables	.091
				Fat	1.1

PLANT SOURCES OF CALCIUM:

1 cup of:				
	collards	357 mg	3 large figs	78 mg
	kale	179 mg	1 oz. almonds	75 mg
	broccoli pieces	177 mg	1/2 cup pitted dates	58 mg
	cooked soy beans	131 mg	1 medium orange	55 mg
	garbanzos	80 mg	4 oz. tofu (precipitated with calcium	
	pinto beans	86 mg	salts)	300 mg
	1/2 cup prunes	30 mg	1 Tbsp. blackstrap molasses	137 mg

TOFU TROPICAL DESSERT (makes 6 servings)

125 mL	(1/2 cup)	**EACH**	chopped dates, water, **and** pineapple juice
250 mL	(1 cup)		tofu
375 mL	(1 1/2 cups)		sliced ripe banana
45 mL	(3 Tbsp.)		lemon juice
10 mL	(2 tsp.)		vanilla
60 mL	(1/4 cup)		cornstarch or arrowroot
1 mL	(1/4 tsp.)		salt
250 mL	(1 cup)		crushed pineapple
30 mL	(2 Tbsp.)		grated lemon rind

Method:

SOFTEN dates in the water by cooking until soft. **DRAIN** crushed pineapple, reserving the juice. **MIX** the cornstarch with part of the pineapple juice. **COMBINE** softened dates, tofu, bananas, and vanilla in blender and **BLEND** until smooth. **POUR** into a saucepan and **BRING** to a boil, stirring constantly. **ADD** cornstarch pineapple juice mixture, and **COOK** until thick, stirring constantly. **REMOVE** from heat and **ADD** lemon juice, lemon rind, remaining pineapple juice, salt, and pineapple. **POUR** into parfait glasses that have granola at the bottom. **REFRIGERATE** at least 2 hours. May top with crushed pineapple, or blueberry topping, or slivered almonds.

```
-------------------------------------------------------------------------
| Analysis: TOFU TROPICAL DESSERT (6 servings)      Divided by: 6        |
|      Wgt: 193 g (6.82 oz.)                        Water: 73%           |
-------------------------------------------------------------------------
```

Calories	201		Vitamin C	15.5 mg
Protein	7.65 g		Vitamin D	0 mcg
Carbohydrates	37.6 g		Vit E-Alpha E	.198 mg
Fat - Total	3.98 g		Vitamin K	mcg
Saturated Fat	.637 g		Biotin	mcg
Mono Fat	.854 g		Calcium	106 mg
Poly Fat	2.13 g		Copper	.302 mg
Cholesterol	0 mg		Iodine	mcg
Dietary Fibre	2.64 g		Iron	4.91 mg
Soluble Fibre	.639 g		Magnesium	65.3 mg
Total Vit A	13.6 RE		Manganese	1.3 mg
Thiamin-B1	.16 mg		Phosphorus	98.2 mg
Riboflavin-B2	.11 mg		Potassium	434 mg
Niacin-B3	.882 mg		Selenium	1.24 mcg
Niacin Equiv.	.884 mg		Sodium	97.4 mg
Vitamin B6	.337 mg		Zinc	.844 mg
Vitamin B12	0 mcg		Complex Carbs	6.08 g
Folate	25.9 mcg		Sugars	26.6 g
Pantothenic	.346 mg		Water	142 g

CALORIE BREAKDOWN		FAT		EXCHANGES	
Protein	14%	* Saturated :	2.6%	Bread	.416
Carbohydrates	69%	Mono Unsat:	3.5%	Lean Meat	1
Fat-Total *	17%	Poly Unsat:	8.9%	Fruit	1.94
				Fat	.064

BEETS HAWAIIAN STYLE (makes 6 servings)

500 mL	(2 cups)	cooked beets (sliced or diced)
150 mL	(2/3 cup)	water
5 mL	(1 tsp.)	honey
1 mL	(1/4 tsp.)	salt
15 mL	(1 Tbsp.)	cornstarch
30 mL	(2 Tbsp.)	water
30 mL	(2 Tbsp.)	lemon juice
398 mL	(14 oz. can)	unsweetened pineapple chunks

Method:

   COMBINE beets, water, honey and salt and **BRING** to boil. **ADD** cornstarch dissolved in water. **BRING** to boil, **REMOVE** from heat and **ADD** lemon juice and pineapple. **SERVE** hot or cold.

```
Analysis: BEETS, HAWAIIAN STYLE (6 SERVINGS)      Divided by: 6
          Wgt: 169 g (5.95 oz.)                   Water:     87%
```

Calories	78.6	Vitamin C	11.3 mg
Protein	1.29 g	Vitamin D	0 mcg
Carbohydrates	19.7 g	Vit E-Alpha E	.247 mg
Fat - Total	.168 g	Vitamin K	mcg
Saturated Fat	.022 g	Biotin	mcg
Mono Fat	.028 g	Calcium	20.5 mg
Poly Fat	.062 g	Copper	.109 mg
Cholesterol	0 mg	Iodine	mcg
Dietary Fibre	1.9 g	Iron	.668 mg
Soluble Fibre	.588 g	Magnesium	24 mg
Total Vit A	5.29 RE	Manganese	1 mg
Thiamin-B1	.086 mg	Phosphorus	26.4 mg
Riboflavin-B2	.038 mg	Potassium	269 mg
Niacin-B3	.401 mg	Selenium	.725 mcg
Niacin Equiv.	.401 mg	Sodium	134 mg
Vitamin B6	.095 mg	Zinc	.288 mg
Vitamin B12	0 mcg	Complex Carbs	1.37 g
Folate	49.5 mcg	Sugars	16.5 g
Pantothenic	.161 mg	Water	146 g

CALORIE BREAKDOWN		FAT		EXCHANGES	
Protein	6%	*Saturated :	.2%	Bread	.083
Carbohydrates	92%	Mono Unsat:	.3%	Fruit	.806
Fat-Total *	2%	Poly Unsat:	.7%	Vegetables	1.02

BEETS PIQUANT (makes 6 servings)

1 L	(4 cups)	grated, peeled, raw beets
310 mL	(1 1/4 cups)	orange juice
30 mL	(2 Tbsp.)	lemon juice
30 mL	(2 Tbsp.)	corn starch
3 mL	(1/2 tsp.)	salt
2 mL	(1/4 tsp.)	ground cardamon

Method:

COOK the beets in the orange juice. COMBINE lemon juice, corn starch, salt, and cardamon. STIR into cooked beets. LET continue to cook until whole mixture boils and the liquid has thickened.

```
-----------------------------------------------------------------------------
| Analysis: BEETS PIQUANT                        Divided by: 6              |
|           Wgt: 173 g (6.1 oz.)                 Water:       86%           |
-----------------------------------------------------------------------------
```

Calories	84.7		Vitamin C	25.5 mg
Protein	2.31 g		Vitamin D	0 mcg
Carbohydrates	19.7 g		Vit E-Alpha E	.391 mg
Fat - Total	.257 g		Vitamin K	mcg
Saturated Fat	.038 g		Biotin	mcg
Mono Fat	.047 g		Calcium	23.7 mg
Poly Fat	.084 g		Copper	.11 mg
Cholesterol	0 mg		Iodine	mcg
Dietary Fibre	2.88 g		Iron	.978 mg
Soluble Fibre	.946 g		Magnesium	32 mg
Total Vit A	8.78 RE		Manganese	.401 mg
Thiamin-B1	.074 mg		Phosphorus	52.3 mg
Riboflavin-B2	.055 mg		Potassium	450 mg
Niacin-B3	.49 mg		Selenium	.577 mcg
Niacin Equiv.	.49 mg		Sodium	89.2 mg
Vitamin B6	.101 mg		Zinc	.434 mg
Vitamin B12	0 mcg		Complex Carbs	2.77 g
Folate	114 mcg		Sugars	14.1 g
Pantothenic	.25 mg		Water	149 g

CALORIE BREAKDOWN		FAT		EXCHANGES	
Protein	10%	*Saturated : .4%		Bread	.17
Carbohydrates	87%	Mono Unsat: .5%		Fruit	.437
Fat-Total *	3%	Poly Unsat: .8%		Vegetables	2.04

CREAMED POTATOES (makes 8 servings)

2 L	(8 cups)	diced, cooked potatoes (peel after cooking)
500 mL	(2 cups)	chopped onions (steamed until transparent)
2	(2)	large cloves of garlic, minced and steamed
75 mL	(1/3 cup)	raw cashews (whizzed to a paste)
5 mL	(1 tsp.)	salt
30 mL	(2 Tbsp.)	chicken style seasoning
125 mL	(1/2 cup)	all-purpose unbleached flour
750 mL	(3 cups)	water

Method:

ADD salt, chicken style seasoning, flour, and part of the water to the cashew paste in blender. WHIZ until very smooth. EMPTY contents of blender into a large pot. RINSE blender with remaining water. ADD to pot. BRING to a boil, stirring constantly until thickened. STIR potatoes, onions, and garlic into the sauce. HEAT entire mixture to blend flavours either on top of stove or in the oven. GARNISH with chopped parsley, red pepper rings, or CASHEW SLICING "CHEESE" slices.

```
Analysis: CREAMED POTATOES                    Divided by: 8
          Wgt: 283 g (9.97 oz.)               Water:     82%
```

Calories	205	Vitamin C	20.5 mg
Protein	4.78 g	Vitamin D	0 mcg
Carbohydrates	40.4 g	Vit E-Alpha E	.182 mg
Fat - Total	3.02 g	Vitamin K	mcg
Saturated Fat	.579 g	Biotin	mcg
Mono Fat	1.58 g	Calcium	22 mg
Poly Fat	.563 g	Copper	.426 mg
Cholesterol	0 mg	Iodine	mcg
Dietary Fibre	3.33 g	Iron	1.24 mg
Soluble Fibre	.273 g	Magnesium	51.8 mg
Total Vit A	0 RE	Manganese	.357 mg
Thiamin-B1	.235 mg	Phosphorus	111 mg
Riboflavin-B2	.086 mg	Potassium	621 mg
Niacin-B3	2.57 mg	Selenium	5.79 mcg
Niacin Equiv.	2.57 mg	Sodium	277 mg
Vitamin B6	.481 mg	Zinc	.896 mg
Vitamin B12	0 mcg	Complex Carbs	31.1 g
Folate	27.2 mcg	Sugars	4.4 g
Pantothenic	.858 mg	Water	231 g

CALORIE BREAKDOWN		FAT		EXCHANGES	
Protein	9%	*Saturated : 2.5%		Bread	1.85
Carbohydrates	78%	Mono Unsat: 6.8%		Lean Meat	.083
Fat-Total *	13%	Poly Unsat: 2.4%		Vegetables	.5
				Fat	.333

CREOLE CORN (makes 6 half-cup servings)

500 mL	(2 cups)	fresh or frozen corn
60 mL	(1/4 cup)	chopped onion
60 mL	(1/4 cup)	thinly sliced green pepper
250 mL	(1 cup)	canned or stewed tomatoes
1 mL	(1/8 tsp.)	dill weed
1 mL	(1/8 tsp.)	ground cumin
3 mL	(1/2 tsp.)	salt (or to taste)

Method:

COOK corn, onion, green pepper over low heat until tender. ADD a small amount of water if necessary to prevent sticking. ADD remaining ingredients and heat thoroughly.

```
------------------------------------------------------------------
| Analysis: CREOLE CORN                          Divided by: 6    |
|           Wgt: 102 g (3.61 oz.)                Water:      84%  |
------------------------------------------------------------------
```

Calories	55.9		Vitamin C	13.7 mg
Protein	2.15 g		Vitamin D	0 mcg
Carbohydrates	12.3 g		Vit E-Alpha E	.235 mg
Fat - Total	.722 g		Vitamin K	mcg
Saturated Fat	.11 g		Biotin	mcg
Mono Fat	.195 g		Calcium	14 mg
Poly Fat	.335 g		Copper	.079 mg
Cholesterol	0 mg		Iodine	mcg
Dietary Fibre	2.34 g		Iron	.565 mg
Soluble Fibre	.376 g		Magnesium	25.2 mg
Total Vit A	41 RE		Manganese	.149 mg
Thiamin-B1	.126 mg		Phosphorus	56.5 mg
Riboflavin-B2	.046 mg		Potassium	246 mg
Niacin-B3	1.2 mg		Selenium	.548 mcg
Niacin Equiv.	1.2 mg		Sodium	162 mg
Vitamin B6	.083 mg		Zinc	.315 mg
Vitamin B12	0 mcg		Complex Carbs	5.36 g
Folate	28.8 mcg		Sugars	4.63 g
Pantothenic	.467 mg		Water	86.3 g

CALORIE BREAKDOWN		FAT		EXCHANGES	
Protein	13%	* Saturated:	1.5%	Bread	.555
Carbohydrates	77%	Mono Unsat:	2.7%	Vegetables	.458
Fat-Total *	10%	Poly Unsat:	4.7%		

EGGPLANT CREOLE (makes 10 servings)

375 mL	(1 1/2 cups)	minced onion
250 mL	(1 cup)	sliced celery
75 mL	(1/3 cup)	minced green pepper
5 mL	(1 tsp.)	olive oil
450 mL	(1 3/4 cups)	chopped tomatoes (may use canned)
1	(about 1 1/2 lbs.)	medium eggplant, cut into 1/2 inch cubes
10 mL	(2 tsp.)	salt
3 mL	(1/2 tsp.)	sweet basil
3 mL	(1/2 tsp.)	ground coriander
2	(2)	bay leaves, crushed (optional)
250 mL	(1 cup)	TASTY CRUMBS (see recipe below)

Tasty Crumbs (makes 1 cup)

250 mL	(1 cup)	dry, fine whole wheat bread crumbs
75 mL	(1/3 cup)	food yeast flakes
5 mL	(1 tsp.)	olive oil
2 mL	(1/4 tsp.) **EACH**	Italian seasoning, parsley flakes, **and** garlic powder

Method:

　　STEAM vegetables in the oil until crispy tender. **ADD** tomatoes and **BRING** to a boil. **ADD** eggplant and seasoning and **MIX** well. **PUT** into a casserole. **TOP** with TASTY CRUMBS. **BAKE** at 375°F for 30-45 minutes. **SERVE** hot. For the TASTY CRUMBS **MIX** all ingredients thoroughly.

Analysis: EGGPLANT CREOLE   Divided by: 10
          Wgt: 157 g (5.54 oz.)   Water: 84%

Calories	88.1		Vitamin C	12.2 mg
Protein	4.59 g		Vitamin D	.036 mcg
Carbohydrates	17.2 g		Vit E-Alpha E	.293 mg
Fat - Total	.812 g		Vitamin K	mcg
Saturated Fat	.164 g		Biotin	mcg
Mono Fat	.238 g		Calcium	89.6 mg
Poly Fat	.247 g		Copper	.157 mg
Cholesterol	0 mg		Iodine	mcg
Dietary Fibre	3.36 g		Iron	2.34 mg
Soluble Fibre	1.04 g		Magnesium	29.2 mg
Total Vit A	35.2 RE		Manganese	.277 mg
Thiamin-B1	.844 mg		Phosphorus	137 mg
Riboflavin-B2	.325 mg		Potassium	432 mg
Niacin-B3	3.62 mg		Selenium	4.03 mcg
Niacin Equiv.	1.49 mg		Sodium	595 mg
Vitamin B6	.292 mg		Zinc	.443 mg
Vitamin B12	.002 mcg		Complex Carbs	7.25 g
Folate	169 mcg		Sugars	4.95 g
Pantothenic	.725 mg		Water	131 g

CALORIE BREAKDOWN		FAT		EXCHANGES	
Protein	19%	Saturated :	1.6%	Bread	.48
Carbohydrates	73%	Mono Unsat:	2.3%	Vegetables	1.49
Fat - Total *	8%	Poly Unsat:	2.4%	Fat	.025

EGGPLANT EXCELLENT (makes 6 servings)

250 mL	(1 cup)	chopped onion
1	(1)	large garlic clove, minced
30 mL	(2 Tbsp.)	lemon juice
45 mL	(3 Tbsp.)	water
625 mL	(2 1/2 cups)	canned or fresh tomatoes
3 mL	(1/2 tsp.)	basil
3 mL	(1/2 tsp.)	paprika
3 mL	(1/2 tsp.)	salt
4	(4)	dates, minced
1 L	(4 cups)	diced, unpeeled eggplant

Method:

   STEAM first 4 ingredients in covered sauce pan until crispy tender. **ADD** remaining ingredients. **BRING** to boil. **SIMMER**, covered 15 minutes. May be topped with breadcrumbs and baked or served as is over brown rice. **ADD** SUNFLOWER-PIMENTO "CHEESE" (see recipe) for added flavour.

```
----------------------------------------------------------------------
| Analysis: EGGPLANT EXCELLENT                    Divided by: 6       |
|           Wgt: 180 g (6.36 oz.)                 Water:      90%      |
----------------------------------------------------------------------
```

Calories	58.2		Vitamin C	16.3 mg
Protein	1.87 g		Vitamin D	0 mcg
Carbohydrates	13.9 g		Vit E-Alpha E	.365 mg
Fat - Total	.361 g		Vitamin K	mcg
Saturated Fat	.063 g		Biotin	mcg
Mono Fat	.051 g		Calcium	52.2 mg
Poly Fat	.141 g		Copper	.188 mg
Cholesterol	0 mg		Iodine	mcg
Dietary Fibre	3.48 g		Iron	1.02 mg
Soluble Fibre	1.28 g		Magnesium	21.7 mg
Total Vit A	65 RE		Manganese	.246 mg
Thiamin-B1	.106 mg		Phosphorus	46.8 mg
Riboflavin-B2	.051 mg		Potassium	391 mg
Niacin-B3	1.13 mg		Selenium	1.66 mcg
Niacin Equiv.	1.13 mg		Sodium	135 mg
Vitamin B6	.173 mg		Zinc	.303 mg
Vitamin B12	0 mcg		Complex Carbs	.727 g
Folate	22.4 mcg		Sugars	9.68 g
Pantothenic	.257 mg		Water	163 g

CALORIE BREAKDOWN		FAT		EXCHANGES	
Protein	11%	*Saturated :	.9%	Bread	.007
Carbohydrates	84%	Mono Unsat:	.7%	Fruit	.27
Fat-Total *	5%	Poly Unsat:	1.9%	Vegetables	1.68

GREEN BEAN CASSEROLE (makes about 6 servings)

250 mL	(1 cup)	sliced onions
125 mL	(1/2 cup)	chopped green pepper
125 mL	(1/2 cup)	water
1	(1)	large clove of garlic, minced
3 mL	(1/2 tsp.)	salt
3 mL	(1/2 tsp.)	basil
3 mL	(1/2 tsp.)	oregano
500 mL	(2 cups)	green beans, cut diagonally 1" long
500 mL	(2 cups)	canned or stewed tomatoes

Method:

STEAM onions, peppers, and garlic in the water until limp. ADD remaining ingredients SIMMER until beans are done.

```
-------------------------------------------------------------------
| Analysis: GREEN BEAN CASSEROLE              Divided by: 6        |
|           Wgt: 181 g (6.38 oz.)             Water:     93%       |
-------------------------------------------------------------------
```

Calories	41.5		Vitamin C	25.2 mg
Protein	1.8 g		Vitamin D	0 mcg
Carbohydrates	9.35 g		Vit E-Alpha E	.459 mg
Fat - Total	.334 g		Vitamin K	mcg
Saturated Fat	.055 g		Biotin	mcg
Mono Fat	.04 g		Calcium	53.3 mg
Poly Fat	.143 g		Copper	.145 mg
Cholesterol	0 mg		Iodine	mcg
Dietary Fibre	3.11 g		Iron	1.07 mg
Soluble Fibre	1.24 g		Magnesium	23.9 mg
Total Vit A	79.2 RE		Manganese	.334 mg
Thiamin-B1	.076 mg		Phosphorus	38 mg
Riboflavin-B2	.067 mg		Potassium	292 mg
Niacin-B3	.876 mg		Selenium	1.49 mcg
Niacin Equiv.	.876 mg		Sodium	316 mg
Vitamin B6	.155 mg		Zinc	.494 mg
Vitamin B12	0 mcg		Complex Carbs	.906 g
Folate	16.8 mcg		Sugars	5.34 g
Pantothenic	.196 mg		Water	168 g

CALORIE BREAKDOWN		FAT		EXCHANGES	
Protein	15%	*Saturated :	1 %	Vegetables	1.76
Carbohydrates	79%	Mono Unsat:	.8%		
Fat-Total *	6%	Poly Unsat:	1.7%		

HARVARD BEETS (makes 4 servings)

500 mL	(2 cups)	sliced or diced cooked beets
125 mL	(1/2 cup)	beet liquid and water
75 mL	(1/3 cup)	fresh lemon juice
15 mL	(1 Tbsp.)	**EACH** honey **and** cornstarch
3 mL	(1/2 tsp.)	salt

Method:

HEAT the beets in the liquid. **MIX** cornstarch with lemon juice and **STIR** into the hot beets. **ADD** the remaining ingredients and **SIMMER** together for about five minutes.

```
-----------------------------------------------------------------------
| Analysis: HARVARD BEETS                        Divided by: 4        |
|           Wgt: 143 g (5.04 oz.)                Water:     86%       |
-----------------------------------------------------------------------
```

Calories	66.2		Vitamin C	12.4	mg
Protein	1.54	g	Vitamin D	0	mcg
Carbohydrates	16.4	g	Vit E-Alpha E	.273	mg
Fat - Total	.181	g	Vitamin K		mcg
Saturated Fat	.032	g	Biotin		mcg
Mono Fat	.032	g	Calcium	16.3	mg
Poly Fat	.072	g	Copper	.074	mg
Cholesterol	0	mg	Iodine		mcg
Dietary Fibre	2.12	g	Iron	.713	mg
Soluble Fibre	.709	g	Magnesium	21.5	mg
Total Vit A	3.81	RE	Manganese	.285	mg
Thiamin-B1	.029	mg	Phosphorus	34	mg
Riboflavin-B2	.038	mg	Potassium	287	mg
Niacin-B3	.308	mg	Selenium	.452	mcg
Niacin Equiv.	.308	mg	Sodium	333	mg
Vitamin B6	.069	mg	Zinc	.333	mg
Vitamin B12	0	mcg	Complex Carbs	2.06	g
Folate	70.7	mcg	Sugars	12.2	g
Pantothenic	.148	mg	Water	123	g

CALORIE BREAKDOWN		FAT		EXCHANGES	
Protein	8%	* Saturated :	.4%	Bread	.125
Carbohydrates	89%	Mono Unsat:	.4%	Fruit	.333
Fat-Total *	2%	Poly Unsat:	.9%	Vegetables 1.53	

RISK FACTORS OF HEART DISEASE:

Risks that cannot be changed:
   Heredity
   Male Sex
   Increasing age

Risks that can be changed:
   Cigarette smoking
   High blood pressure
   Stress
   Lack of exercise
   Obesity

POLYNESIAN VEGETABLES (4-6 servings)

250 mL	(1 cup)	chopped onion
125 mL	(1/2 cup)	water
180 mL	(3/4 cup)	green pepper, cut into 1 inch pieces
500 mL	(2 cups)	assorted vegetables, chopped
30 mL	(2 Tbsp.)	soy sauce
15 mL	(1 Tbsp.)	cornstarch or arrowroot powder
250 mL	(1 cup)	water chestnuts, drained
250 mL	(1 cup)	pineapple chunks

Method:

STEAM the onions in 1/4 cup of water about 5 minutes. DRAIN the pineapple, reserving the juice. SET aside the pineapple chunks and 1/4 cup of the juice. POUR the remainder of the juice into the saucepan. ADD the green pepper, vegetables, water, and soy sauce. BRING to a boil. REDUCE the heat, COVER and SIMMER about 10 minutes. MIX the cornstarch with the reserved pineapple juice and ADD to the saucepan. COOK and STIR until the mixture boils and thickens. ADD the water chestnuts and pineapple chunks. HEAT through. SERVE over rice or other whole grains.

```
Analysis: POLYNESIAN VEGETABLES (4 SERVINGS)     Divided by: 4
          Wgt: 288 g (10.2 oz.)                  Water:    86%
```

Calories	141	Vitamin C	28.6 mg
Protein	4.28 g	Vitamin D	0 mcg
Carbohydrates	33.3 g	Vit E-Alpha E	.746 mg
Fat - Total	.315 g	Vitamin K	mcg
Saturated Fat	.054 g	Biotin	mcg
Mono Fat	.032 g	Calcium	44.8 mg
Poly Fat	.142 g	Copper	.213 mg
Cholesterol	0 mg	Iodine	mcg
Dietary Fibre	5.63 g	Iron	1.59 mg
Soluble Fibre	1.77 g	Magnesium	39.8 mg
Total Vit A	404 RE	Manganese	1.22 mg
Thiamin-B1	.162 mg	Phosphorus	83.7 mg
Riboflavin-B2	.155 mg	Potassium	384 mg
Niacin-B3	1.54 mg	Selenium	3.16 mcg
Niacin Equiv.	1.54 mg	Sodium	551 mg
Vitamin B6	.278 mg	Zinc	.784 mg
Vitamin B12	0 mcg	Complex Carbs	8.47 g
Folate	35.5 mcg	Sugars	15.6 g
Pantothenic	.364 mg	Water	247 g

CALORIE BREAKDOWN		FAT		EXCHANGES	
Protein	11%	*Saturated :	.3%	Bread	.125
Carbohydrates	87%	Mono Unsat:	.2%	Fruit	.625
Fat-Total *	2%	Poly Unsat:	.8%	Vegetables	3.3

POTATO-CARROT SPECIAL (makes 6 servings)

750 mL	(3 cups)	carrots, cut into 1/2 inch slices
75 mL	(1/3 cup)	water (may need a little more)
1250 mL	(5 cups)	potatoes, peeled and cut into chunks
500 mL	(2 cups)	onions, sliced
2	(2)	large cloves of garlic, minced
5 mL	(1 tsp.)	salt
75 mL	(1/3 cup)	CASHEW CREAM (made from equal amounts of raw cashews and water well blended)
250 mL	(1 cup)	peas (optional)

Method:

PLACE water, salt and carrots in pan and cook partly before adding potatoes, onions, and garlic. COVER and SIMMER until vegetables are tender. STIR in CASHEW CREAM and SERVE immediately. GARNISH with freshly cooked peas.

```
| Analysis: POTATO-CARROT SPECIAL (6 SERVINGS)      Divided by: 6    |
|            Wgt: 186 g (6.56 oz.)                  Water:     80%   |
```

Calories	145		Vitamin C	13.6 mg
Protein	3.5 g		Vitamin D	0 mcg
Carbohydrates	27.9 g		Vit E-Alpha E	.364 mg
Fat - Total	2.88 g		Vitamin K	mcg
Saturated Fat	.569 g		Biotin	mcg
Mono Fat	1.57 g		Calcium	31.2 mg
Poly Fat	.547 g		Copper	.317 mg
Cholesterol	0 mg		Iodine	mcg
Dietary Fibre	3.58 g		Iron	.854 mg
Soluble Fibre	1.07 g		Magnesium	42.9 mg
Total Vit A	1012 RE		Manganese	.303 mg
Thiamin-B1	.163 mg		Phosphorus	94.6 mg
Riboflavin-B2	.06 mg		Potassium	525 mg
Niacin-B3	1.68 mg		Selenium	2.47 mcg
Niacin Equiv.	1.68 mg		Sodium	375 mg
Vitamin B6	.376 mg		Zinc	.701 mg
Vitamin B12	0 mcg		Complex Carbs	17.8 g
Folate	26.8 mcg		Sugars	6.46 g
Pantothenic	.653 mg		Water	150 g

CALORIE BREAKDOWN		FAT		EXCHANGES	
Protein	9%	*Saturated :	3.4%	Bread	1
Carbohydrates	74%	Mono Unsat:	9.3%	Vegetables	1.17
Fat-Total *	17%	Poly Unsat:	3.3%	Fat	.5

CARROTS:

Carrots are a member of the parsley family. They are high in water content and low in calories. However, they are the richest source of Beta-Carotene, the pre-cursor of Vitamin A. among the commonly-used vegetables. In half a cup of carrots there is more than twice the Canadian Recommended Nutrient Intake. Cooking does not destroy Beta-Carotene, so cooked carrots are also rich in it. Grated raw carrots are good in salads. When mixed with peanut butter they make a good sandwich filling.

AGAR CASHEW SLICING CHEESE (makes 2 cups)

375 mL	(1 1/2 cups)	water
52 mL	(3 1/2 Tbsp.)	agar flakes or Emes Kosher jel
125 mL	(1/2 cup)	raw cashew pieces (well washed)
2 mL	(1/4 tsp.)	garlic powder
8 mL	(1 1/2 tsp.)	onion powder
3 mL	(1/2 tsp.) **EACH**	salt **and** celery seed
125 mL	(1/2 cup)	pimento pieces or red pepper
60 mL	(1/4 cup) **EACH**	lemon juice **and** food yeast flakes

Method:

  SOAK the agar in 1 cup of the water for 5 minutes. **COOK** until clear over a medium heat. While the agar is simmering, **WHIZ** the other ingredients with the remaining 1/2 cup of water until creamy in the blender. **ADD** the cooked agar while still blending. **POUR** at once into a mould. **CHILL. SERVE** sliced in a sandwich with lettuce, or cubed in macaroni salad.

```
----------------------------------------------------------------------
| Analysis: AGAR CASHEW SLICING CHEESE (32 Tbsp)    Divided by: 32    |
|           Wgt: 21.2 g (.748 oz.)                  Water:      73%   |
----------------------------------------------------------------------
```

Calories	29	Vitamin C	4.12 mg
Protein	1.09 g	Vitamin D	0 mcg
Carbohydrates	2.19 g	Vit E-Alpha E	.041 mg
Fat - Total	2.01 g	Vitamin K	mcg
Saturated Fat	.398 g	Biotin	mcg
Mono Fat	1.18 g	Calcium	5.65 mg
Poly Fat	.339 g	Copper	.131 mg
Cholesterol	0 mg	Iodine	mcg
Dietary Fibre	.665 g	Iron	.463 mg
Soluble Fibre	.012 g	Magnesium	14.5 mg
Total Vit A	8.04 RE	Manganese	.042 mg
Thiamin-B1	.167 mg	Phosphorus	39.6 mg
Riboflavin-B2	.052 mg	Potassium	51.2 mg
Niacin-B3	.455 mg	Selenium	1.46 mcg
Niacin Equiv.	.455 mg	Sodium	36.1 mg
Vitamin B6	.073 mg	Zinc	.333 mg
Vitamin B12	0 mcg	Complex Carbs	.949 g
Folate	43.2 mcg	Sugars	.543 g
Pantothenic	.146 mg	Water	15.4 g

CALORIE BREAKDOWN		FAT		EXCHANGES	
Protein	14%	* Saturated :	11.5%	Bread	.031
Carbohydrates	28%	Mono Unsat:	33.9%	Lean Meat	.062
Fat-Total *	58%	Poly Unsat:	9.8%	Fruit	.008
		Fat .25 ---->		Vegetables	.037

KIND OF CHEESE	PROTEIN	FAT	CARBOHYDRATES
Cheddar	24.7%	73.9%	1.2%
Colby	23.9%	73.1%	2.5%
Cream Cheese	8.5%	90 %	3.2%

CASHEW SLICING "CHEESE" (makes 4 cups - 64 one Tbsp servings)

250 mL	(1 cup)	cold water
90 mL	(6 Tbsp.)	Emes Kosher jel
250 mL	(1 cup)	hot water
30 mL	(2 Tbsp.) **EACH**	food yeast flakes **and** onion powder
3 mL	(1/2 tsp.)	garlic powder
5 mL	(1 tsp.)	paprika
12 mL	(2 1/2 tsp.)	salt
125 mL	(1/2 cup)	well-washed raw cashew pieces
125 mL	(1/2 cup)	canned roasted pimentos
30 mL	(2 Tbsp.)	lemon juice

Method:

SOAK gelatin in one cup of cold water in blender. **ADD** 1 cup hot water and **BLEND** until smooth. **ADD** yeast, onion powder, garlic powder, paprika, and salt. **BLEND** well and **ADD** cashew pieces. **BLEND** until very smooth. **ADD** lemon juice and pimento and **BLEND** until smooth. **POUR** into loaf pan and **LET** set.

```
------------------------------------------------------------------------
| Analysis: CASHEW SLICING CHEESE              Divided by: 64          |
|           Wgt: 13.6 g (.478 oz.)             Water:     71%          |
------------------------------------------------------------------------
```

Calories	17.6		Vitamin C	1.68 mg
Protein	1.18 g		Vitamin D	0 mcg
Carbohydrates	1.25 g		Vit E-Alpha Eq	.02 mg
Fat - Total	1.01 g		Vitamin K	mcg
Saturated Fat	.198 g		Biotin	mcg
Mono Fat	.586 g		Calcium	5.2 mg
Poly Fat	.174 g		Copper	.064 mg
Cholesterol	0 mg		Iodine	mcg
Dietary Fibre	.26 g		Iron	.302 mg
Soluble Fibre	.001 g		Magnesium	7.35 mg
Total Vit A	6.9 RE		Manganese	.022 mg
Thiamin-B1	.094 mg		Phosphorus	22.7 mg
Riboflavin-B2	.04 mg		Potassium	31.3 mg
Niacin-B3	.327 mg		Selenium	.652 mcg
Niacin Equiv.	.05 mg		Sodium	99 mg
Vitamin B6	.036 mg		Zinc	.146 mg
Vitamin B12	0 mcg		Complex Carbs	.524 g
Folate	20.9 mcg		Sugars	.256 g
Pantothenic	.102 mg		Water	9.66 g

CALORIE BREAKDOWN		FAT	EXCHANGES	
Protein	25%	*Saturated : 9.4%	Bread	.001
Carbohydrates	27%	Mono Unsat: 27.9%	Lean Meat	.194
Fat-Total *	48%	Poly Unsat: 8.3%	Fruit	.049
		Fat .152---->	Vegetables	.016

1 CORINTHIANS 10:31

"Whether therefore ye eat, or drink, or whatsoever ye do, do all to the glory of God."

SUNFLOWER-PIMENTO "CHEESE" (Makes about 6 cups)

150 mL	(2/3 cup)	**RAW** sunflower seeds
350 mL	(11 oz.)	roasted pimentos -Primo brand (May use cooked red sweet pepper)
75 mL	(1/3 cup)	corn starch
150 mL	(2/3 cup)	rolled oats
125 mL	(1/2 cup)	flake food yeast (nutritional yeast)
60 mL	(1/4 cup)	lemon juice
15 mL	(1 Tbsp.)	salt
5 mL	(1 tsp.)	garlic powder
10 mL	(2 tsps.)	onion powder
1 L	(4 cups)	water (1 cold and 3 boiling)

Method:

WHIZ the sunflower seeds in blender until a smooth paste. **ADD** pimentos and **WHIZ** again. **ADD** all remaining ingredients except the water and **BLEND** thoroughly. **ADD** cold water and **BLEND** again. **ADD** part of the boiling water and **BLEND**. **POUR** entire mixture into a pot containing most of the hot water. **STIR** while mixture cooks. **RINSE** blender with remaining hot water and stir into mixture. **STIR** constantly until entire mixture boils and is thickened. **USE** as a cheese sauce, a sandwich spread, a dip, or **FREEZE, GRATE** and **USE** as a garnish.

```
------------------------------------------------------------------------
| Analysis: SUNFLOWER-PIMENTO CHEESE              Divided by:  24       |
|           Wgt: 65.4 g (2.31 oz.)                Water:       81%      |
------------------------------------------------------------------------
```

Calories	51.5		Vitamin C	10.1 mg
Protein	2.75 g		Vitamin D	0 mcg
Carbohydrates	6.07 g		Vit E-Alpha E	2.07 mg
Fat - Total	2.2 g		Vitamin K	mcg
Saturated Fat	.24 g		Biotin	mcg
Mono Fat	.426 g		Calcium	22.8 mg
Poly Fat	1.38 g		Copper	.088 mg
Cholesterol	0 mg		Iodine	mcg
Dietary Fibre	.982 g		Iron	1.22 mg
Soluble Fibre	.109 g		Magnesium	24.7 mg
Total Vit A	29.7 RE		Manganese	.176 mg
Thiamin-B1	.579 mg		Phosphorus	99.2 mg
Riboflavin-B2	.19 mg		Potassium	127 mg
Niacin-B3	1.75 mg		Selenium	3.58 mcg
Niacin Equiv.	.272 mg		Sodium	271 mg
Vitamin B6	.185 mg		Zinc	.38 mg
Vitamin B12	0 mcg		Complex Carbs	3.56 g
Folate	111 mcg		Sugars	.401 g
Pantothenic	.683 mg		Water	52.8 g

CALORIE BREAKDOWN		FAT	EXCHANGES	
Protein	20%	P:S (Poly/Saturated Fat) 5.76 : 1	Bread	.191
Carbohydrates	44%	Potassium : Sodium .469 : 1	Lean Meat	.148
Fat-Total *	36%	Calcium : Phosphorus .23 : 1	Fruit	.455
Alcohol	0%	* Saturated : 3.9%	Vegetables	.096
		Mono Unsat: 7%	Fat	.278
		Poly Unsat: 22.6%		

TOFU COTTAGE "CHEESE" (makes about 2 cups)

625 mL	(2 1/2 cups)	tofu (2 cups, mashed, 1/2 cup blended)
15 mL	(1 Tbsp.)	fresh parsley, minced
7 mL	(1 1/2 tsp.)	fresh chives (optional)
1 mL	(1/4 tsp.)	dill weed
3 mL	(1/2 tsp.)	garlic powder
5 mL	(1 tsp.)	onion powder
7 mL	(1 1/2 tsp.)	lemon juice
5 mL	(1 tsp.)	salt

Method:

   MIX the mashed tofu, parsley, chives, dill, garlic powder, and onion powder. **BLEND** the remaining tofu, lemon juice, and salt in food processor or blender until smooth. **ADD** blender mixture to first mixture. **MIX** well and **SERVE** as a sandwich spread, topping for baked potatoes or in lasagna.

```
Analysis: TOFU COTTAGE "CHEESE"                    Divided by: 12
          Wgt:48.9 g (1.72 oz)                     Water:      83%
```

Calories	36.9	Vitamin C	1.15 mg
Protein	3.81 g	Vitamin D	0 mcg
Carbohydrates	1.27 g	Vit E-Alpha E	.011 mg
Fat - Total	2.23 g	Vitamin K	mcg
Saturated Fat	.323 g	Biotin	mcg
Mono Fat	.493 g	Calcium	51.1 mg
Poly Fat	1.26 g	Copper	.091 mg
Cholesterol	0 mg	Iodine	mcg
Dietary Fibre	.617 g	Iron	2.54 mg
Soluble Fibre	.005 g	Magnesium	48.2 mg
Total Vit A	6.61 RE	Manganese	.286 mg
Thiamin-B1	.04 mg	Phosphorus	46.6 mg
Riboflavin-B2	.025 mg	Potassium	64.3 mg
Niacin-B3	.1 mg	Selenium	.764 mcg
Niacin Equiv.	.101 mg	Sodium	181 mg
Vitamin B6	.05 mg	Zinc	.387 mg
Vitamin B12	0 mcg	Complex Carbs	.271 g
Folate	7.94 mcg	Sugars	.377 g
Pantothenic	.049 mg	Water	40.8 g

CALORIE BREAKDOWN		FAT		EXCHANGES	
Protein	38%	* Saturated :	7.2%	Lean Meat	.375
Carbohydrates	13%	Mono Unsat:	11 %	Fruit	.005
Fat-Total	50%	Poly Unsat:	28 %	Vegetables	.192
				Fat	.187

BETTER BUTTER (makes 16 servings)

250 mL	(1 cup)	cooked cornmeal (1/4 cup cornmeal + 1 cup water)
60 mL	(1/4 cup)	unsweetened coconut
15 mL	(1 Tbsp.)	flake food yeast
3 mL	(1/2 tsp.)	salt
125 mL	(1/2 cup)	water

Method:

    COOK the cornmeal. While it is still warm **PLACE** in blender or food processor with remaining ingredients. **WHIZ** until very smooth. **POUR** into container and **CHILL**. It will become the consistency of soft butter. May use on baked potatoes, bread, and almost any other place you would use butter (not frying or baking).

```
------------------------------------------------------------------------
| Analysis: BETTER BUTTER                    Divided by: 16            |
|           Wgt: 25.3 g (.891 oz.)           Water:      47%           |
------------------------------------------------------------------------
```

Calories	22.8		Vitamin C	.018 mg
Protein	.628 g		Vitamin D	0 mcg
Carbohydrates	3.29 g		Vit E-Alpha E	.085 mg
Fat - Total	.852 g		Vitamin K	mcg
Saturated Fat	.705 g		Biotin	mcg
Mono Fat	.048 g		Calcium	6.94 mg
Poly Fat	.034 g		Copper	.014 mg
Cholesterol	0 mg		Iodine	mcg
Dietary Fibre	.435 g		Iron	.317 mg
Soluble Fibre	.01 g		Magnesium	6.23 mg
Total Vit A	1.46 RE		Manganese	.044 mg
Thiamin-B1	.107 mg		Phosphorus	16.2 mg
Riboflavin-B2	.046 mg		Potassium	25.8 mg
Niacin-B3	.436 mg		Selenium	.941 mcg
Niacin Equiv.	.007 mg		Sodium	3264 mg
Vitamin B6	.03 mg		Zinc	.095 mg
Vitamin B12	0 mcg		Complex Carbs	0 g
Folate	20.2 mcg		Sugars	.137 g
Pantothenic	.088 mg		Water	11.8 g

CALORIE BREAKDOWN		FAT		EXCHANGES	
Protein	11%	*Saturated :	27.2%	Fat	.125
Carbohydrates	56%	Mono Unsat:	1.9%		
Fat-Total *	33%	Poly Unsat:	1.3%		

MILLET BUTTER (makes 32 servings)

250 mL	(1 cup)	cooked hot millet (packed)

(Cook millet 1 part millet to 4 parts water 50 minutes)

15 mL	(1 Tbsp.)	unflavoured Emes Kosher Jel or agar flakes
375 mL	(1 1/2 cups)	cold water
60 mL	(1/4 cup)	raw cashews (washed thoroughly)
5 mL	(1 tsp.)	salt
30 mL	(2 Tbsp.)	cooked, peeled carrots

Method:

COOK the millet. **STIR** Kosher Jel into 1 1/2 cups of cold water in a saucepan. **LET** stand 5 minutes, **COOK** until gelatin is dissolved and liquid is clear. **PLACE** cashews in blender and **WHIZ** until smooth. **ADD** hot millet, salt, carrots and half of the gelatin mixture and **WHIZ** until super smooth. **BLEND** in remaining half of gelatin at low speed. **LET** stand a few minutes so air bubbles can escape. **POUR** into containers and **CHILL**. (Keeps about a week.)

```
-------------------------------------------------------------------
| Analysis: MILLET MARGARINE                    Divided by: 32    |
|           Wgt: 20.8 g (.734 oz.)              Water:      82%   |
-------------------------------------------------------------------
```

Calories	16.2	Vitamin C	.014 mg
Protein	.453 g	Vitamin D	0 mcg
Carbohydrates	2.44 g	Vit E-Alpha E	.039 mg
Fat - Total	.574 g	Vitamin K	mcg
Saturated Fat	.111 g	Biotin	mcg
Mono Fat	.306 g	Calcium	3.16 mg
Poly Fat	.123 g	Copper	.039 mg
Cholesterol	0 mg	Iodine	mcg
Dietary Fibre	.191 g	Iron	.183 mg
Soluble Fibre	.053 g	Magnesium	8.74 mg
Total Vit A	14.9 RE	Manganese	.048 mg
Thiamin-B1	.01 mg	Phosphorus	13.1 mg
Riboflavin-B2	.009 mg	Potassium	15.6 mg
Niacin-B3	.119 mg	Selenium	.264 mcg
Niacin Equiv.	.119 mg	Sodium	84.6 mg
Vitamin B6	.013 mg	Zinc	.152 mg
Vitamin B12	0 mcg	Complex Carbs	1.91 g
Folate	4.05 mcg	Sugars	.11 g
Pantothenic	.037 mg	Water	17 g

CALORIE BREAKDOWN		FAT		EXCHANGES	
Protein	11%	*Saturated :	6 %	Bread	.109
Carbohydrates	58%	Mono Unsat:	16.4%	Lean Meat	.016
Fat-Total *	31%	Poly Unsat:	6.6%	Vegetables	.046
				Fat	.062

BROWN GRAVY (makes 3 cups)

5 mL	(1 tsp.)	canola or olive oil
500 mL	(2 cups)	chopped onions
15 mL	(1 Tbsp.)	minced garlic
750 mL	(3 cups)	water (1 cold + 2 cups boiling)
75 mL	(1/3 cup)	unbleached all-purpose flour
5 mL	(1 tsp.)	Marmite, Savorex, or Vegex

Method:

STEAM onions and garlic in the oil with enough of the water to cover until soft.. ADD most of the hot water to the onions. STIR part of the cold water into the flour until a very smooth paste. ADD the remaining hot water to the flour paste and STIR into the onions. BRING to a boil and COOK until thickened. ADD marmite. This may be served as is or whizzed in blender until smooth. (Some people may want to add salt, but the Marmite is salty so it may not be necessary. If you want a thicker gravy use more flour.)

```
--------------------------------------------------------------------------------
| Analysis: BROWN GRAVY                        Divided by: 10                  |
|            Wgt: 108 g (3.82 oz.)             Water:      93%                 |
--------------------------------------------------------------------------------
```

Calories	30.4		Vitamin C	2.31 mg
Protein	1.05 g		Vitamin D	0 mcg
Carbohydrates	5.53 g		Vit E-Alpha E	.126 mg
Fat - Total	.54 g		Vitamin K	mcg
Saturated Fat	.047 g		Biotin	mcg
Mono Fat	.277 g		Calcium	13.8 mg
Poly Fat	.169 g		Copper	.03 mg
Cholesterol	0 mg		Iodine	mcg
Dietary Fibre	.653 g		Iron	.457 mg
Soluble Fibre	.189 g		Magnesium	4.81 mg
Total Vit A	0 RE		Manganese	.08 mg
Thiamin-B1	.049 mg		Phosphorus	15.2 mg
Riboflavin-B2	.066 mg		Potassium	56.9 mg
Niacin-B3	.538 mg		Selenium	1.67 mcg
Niacin Equiv.	.238 mg		Sodium	3.3 mg
Vitamin B6	.069 mg		Zinc	.119 mg
Vitamin B12	0 mcg		Complex Carbs	2.72 g
Folate	6.92 mcg		Sugars	2.06 g
Pantothenic	.093 mg		Water	101 g

CALORIE BREAKDOWN		FAT	EXCHANGES	
Protein	13%	*Saturated : 1.3%	Bread (starch)	.141
Carbohydrates	71%	Mono Unsat: 8 %	Vegetables	.4
Fat-Total *	16%	Poly Unsat: 4.9%	Fat	.089

CASHEW-RICE MILK (makes 5 cups)

75 mL	(1/3 cup)	raw cashews, washed
30 mL	(2 Tbsp.)	honey or 6 dates
375 mL	(1 1/2 cups)	well-cooked rice
1 mL	(1/4 tsp.)	salt
10 mL	(2 tsp.)	vanilla
1 L	(4 cups)	water
1 mL	(1/4 tsp.)	guar gum (optional to prevent settling)

Method:

BLEND cashews and rice in enough warm water to blend thick and smooth. ADD salt, vanilla, honey, and guar gum. ADD more water (about 4 cups) to bring to 5 cup mark. Dates may be used in place of honey, if you don't mind the colour. LEAVE out the honey and vanilla if you wish to use this in cream sauce or chowder. STRAIN in a fine sieve.

```
Analysis: CASHEW-RICE MILK                  Divided by: 5
          Wgt: 267 g (9.41 oz.)             Water:      88%
```

Calories	145	Vitamin C	.085	mg
Protein	2.93 g	Vitamin D	0	mcg
Carbohydrates	23.6 g	Vit E-Alpha E	.637	mg
Fat - Total	4.76 g	Vitamin K		mcg
Saturated Fat	.938 g	Biotin		mcg
Mono Fat	2.68 g	Calcium	14.4	mg
Poly Fat	.902 g	Copper	.275	mg
Cholesterol	0 mg	Iodine		mcg
Dietary Fibre	1.63 g	Iron	.848	mg
Soluble Fibre	.1 g	Magnesium	51	mg
Total Vit A	0 RE	Manganese	.612	mg
Thiamin-B1	.074 mg	Phosphorus	93.3	mg
Riboflavin-B2	.036 mg	Potassium	81.1	mg
Niacin-B3	1.03 mg	Selenium	9.98	mcg
Niacin Equiv.	1.03 mg	Sodium	117	mg
Vitamin B6	.11 mg	Zinc	.956	mg
Vitamin B12	0 mcg	Complex Carbs	13.9	g
Folate	8.82 mcg	Sugars	7.86	g
Pantothenic	.284 mg	Water	234	g

COMPARISON OF FAT IN VARIOUS MILKS

1 Cup	Whole	2%	1%	Skim	Cash-rice
Calories	149	121	102	85.5	145
Total fat	8.15 g	4.68 g	2.59 g	.441 g	4.76 g
Sat. fat	5.08 g	2.93 g	1.61 g	.287 g	.938 g
Mono unsat	2.35 g	1.35 g	.749 g	.115 g	2.68 g
Poly unsat	.303 g	.173 g	.095 g	.017 g	.902 g
Cholesterol	33.2 g	18.3 g	9.76 g	4.41 g	0
% of fat	49%	35%	23%	5%	29%

CHICKEN STYLE GRAVY (makes 2 cups)

250 mL	(1 cup)	finely chopped onions
5 mL	(1 tsp.)	olive or canola oil
60 mL	(1/4 cup)	flour
3 mL	(1/2 tsp.)	garlic powder
15 mL	(1 Tbsp.)	chicken style seasoning
500 mL	(2 cups)	water

Method:

SAUTE the onion in the oil until soft. STIR in flour and seasonings. ADD water slowly and COOK until thickened. SIMMER 5 minutes.

```
Analysis: CHICKEN STYLE GRAVY                    Divided by: 6
          Wgt: 113 g (3.99 oz.)                  Water:      91%
```

Calories	41	Vitamin C	1.7	mg
Protein	.871 g	Vitamin D	0	mcg
Carbohydrates	7.2 g	Vit E-Alpha E	.142	mg
Fat - Total	.902 g	Vitamin K		mcg
Saturated Fat	.117 g	Biotin		mcg
Mono Fat	.562 g	Calcium	7.82	mg
Poly Fat	.101 g	Copper	.028	mg
Cholesterol	0 mg	Iodine		mcg
Dietary Fibre	.565 g	Iron	.298	mg
Soluble Fibre	.178 g	Magnesium	4.65	mg
Total Vit A	0 RE	Manganese	.071	mg
Thiamin-B1	.042 mg	Phosphorus	14.9	mg
Riboflavin-B2	.027 mg	Potassium	49.5	mg
Niacin-B3	.296 mg	Selenium	2.03	mcg
Niacin Equiv.	.296 mg	Sodium	3.43	mg
Vitamin B6	.08 mg	Zinc	.114	mg
Vitamin B12	0 mcg	Complex Carbs	3.81	g
Folate	6.08 mcg	Sugars	1.75	g
Pantothenic	.068 mg	Water	103	g

CALORIE BREAKDOWN		FAT	EXCHANGES	
Protein	9%	*Saturated : 2.6%	Bread	.192
Carbohydrates	71%	Mono Unsat: 12.5%	Vegetables	.333
Fat-Total *	20%	Poly Unsat: 2.3%	Fat	.145

CHICKEN STYLE SEASONING (makes 1/3 cup)

75 mL	(1/3 cup)	flake food yeast
5 mL	(1 tsp.)	onion powder
5 mL	(1 tsp.)	turmeric
5 mL	(1 tsp.)	dried parsley
4 mL	(3/4 tsp.)	salt
3 mL	(1/2 tsp.)	sage
3 mL	(1/2 tsp.)	celery seed
3 mL	(1/2 tsp.)	thyme
3 mL	(1/2 tsp.)	garlic powder
3 mL	(1/2 tsp.)	savory
3 mL	(1/2 tsp.)	paprika (sweet Hungarian)
2 mL	(1/4 tsp.)	marjoram

Method:
BLEND all ingredients together in seed mill or food processor.

```
-----------------------------------------------------------------------
| Analysis: CHICKEN STYLE SEASONING           Divided by: 15          |
|           Wgt: 4.37 g (.154 oz.)            Water:        6%         |
-----------------------------------------------------------------------
```

Calories	11.6	Vitamin C	.135 mg
Protein	1.46 g	Vitamin D	0 mcg
Carbohydrates	1.67 g	Vit E-Alpha E	.002 mg
Fat - Total	.076 g	Vitamin K	mcg
Saturated Fat	.007 g	Biotin	mcg
Mono Fat	.013 g	Calcium	20 mg
Poly Fat	.012 g	Copper	.003 mg
Cholesterol	0 mg	Iodine	mcg
Dietary Fibre	.228 g	Iron	.86 mg
Soluble Fibre	.002 g	Magnesium	7.11 mg
Total Vit A	5.96 RE	Manganese	.018 mg
Thiamin-B1	.5 mg	Phosphorus	62.6 mg
Riboflavin-B2	.184 mg	Potassium	80.4 mg
Niacin-B3	1.6 mg	Selenium	.079 mcg
Niacin Equiv.	.025 mg	Sodium	108 mg
Vitamin B6	.128 mg	Zinc	.09 mg
Vitamin B12	0 mcg	Complex Carbs	.139 g
Folate	107 mcg	Sugars	.087 g
Pantothenic	.404 mg	Water	.252 g

CALORIE BREAKDOWN		FAT		EXCHANGES	
Protein	44%	*Saturated :	.5%	Bread	.005
Carbohydrates	51%	Mono Unsat:	.9%	Vegetables	.003
Fat-Total *	5%	Poly Unsat:	.8%		

DUMPLINGS (makes 16 one-tablespoon dumplings)

7 mL	(1 1/2 tsp.)	yeast
300 mL	(1 1/4 cups)	hard wheat whole wheat flour
15 mL	(1 Tbsp.)	cornmeal
15 mL	(1 Tbsp.)	low-fat soy flour
1 mL	(1/4 tsp.)	salt
125 mL	(1/2 cup)	warm water

Method:

MIX dry ingredients together. STIR in water. LET batter stand for 20 minutes. DROP by tablespoonsful into hot soup and COOK gently for 20 minutes, without removing the lid. (This should be eaten the next day reheated, because foods made with yeast digest more easily after standing 24 hours.)

```
-----------------------------------------------------------------
| Analysis: DUMPLINGS                      Divided by: 6        |
|           Wgt: 48 g (1.69 oz.)           Water:      47%      |
-----------------------------------------------------------------
```

Calories	95.1		Vitamin C	.002 mg
Protein	4.24 g		Vitamin D	0 mcg
Carbohydrates	19.8 g		Vit E-Alpha Eq	.31 mg
Fat - Total	.581 g		Vitamin K	mcg
Saturated Fat	.096 g		Biotin	mcg
Mono Fat	.093 g		Calcium	11.2 mg
Poly Fat	.24 g		Copper	.147 mg
Cholesterol	0 mg		Iodine	mcg
Dietary Fibre	3.43 g		Iron	1.19 mg
Soluble Fibre	.546 g		Magnesium	38.1 mg
Total Vit A	.626 RE		Manganese	.984 mg
Thiamin-B1	.14 mg		Phosphorus	101 mg
Riboflavin-B2	.096 mg		Potassium	140 mg
Niacin-B3	1.93 mg		Selenium	20.2 mcg
Niacin Equiv.	1.93 mg		Sodium	91.2 mg
Vitamin B6	.103 mg		Zinc	.801 mg
Vitamin B12	0 mcg		Complex Carbs	15.7 g
Folate	30.1 mcg		Sugars	.703 g
Pantothenic	.344 mg		Water	22.5 g

CALORIE BREAKDOWN		FAT		EXCHANGES	
Protein	17%	*Saturated :	.9%	Bread	.12
Carbohydrates	78%	Mono Unsat:	.8%	Lean Meat	.042
Fat-Total *	5%	Poly Unsat:	2.1%	Vegetables	.071

GOLDEN PUNCH (makes 15 eight-ounce servings)

341 mL	(12 oz.)	frozen orange juice concentrate
3	(3)	12 oz cans of water
1.36 L	(48 oz.)	pineapple juice
150 mL	(2/3 cup)	fresh lemon juice or less according to taste
3	(3)	large, very ripe bananas

Method:

 WHIZ the bananas in the blender or food processor with part of the juice.
COMBINE all ingredients.

```
------------------------------------------------------------------------
| Analysis: GOLDEN PUNCH                      Divided by: 15            |
|           Wgt: 232 g (8.19 oz.)             Water:         86%        |
------------------------------------------------------------------------
```

Calories	120		Vitamin C	55.3 mg
Protein	1.35 g		Vitamin D	0 mcg
Carbohydrates	29.5 g		Vit E-Alpha Eq	.17 mg
Fat - Total	.227 g		Vitamin K	mcg
Saturated Fat	.055 g		Biotin	mcg
Mono Fat	.024 g		Calcium	22.4 mg
Poly Fat	.05 g		Copper	.161 mg
Cholesterol	0 mg		Iodine	mcg
Dietary Fibre	.762 g		Iron	.483 mg
Soluble Fibre	.22 g		Magnesium	26.4 mg
Total Vit A	11 RE		Manganese	1.04 mg
Thiamin-B1	.163 mg		Phosphorus	29.4 mg
Riboflavin-B2	.062 mg		Potassium	425 mg
Niacin-B3	.544 mg		Selenium	.804 mcg
Niacin Equiv.	.544 mg		Sodium	4.27 mg
Vitamin B6	.254 mg		Zinc	.202 mg
Vitamin B12	0 mcg		Complex Carbs	.638 g
Folate	59.5 mcg		Sugars	28.1 g
Pantothenic	.35 mg		Water	200 g

CALORIE BREAKDOWN		FAT		EXCHANGES	
Protein	04%	*Saturated :	.4%	Fruit	1.99
Carbohydrates	94%	Mono Unsat:	.2%		
Fats-Total *	2%	Poly Unsat:	.4%		

GARBANZO DELIGHT (makes 4 servings)

473 mL	(16 oz.)	garbanzos, drained and rinsed
30 mL	(2 Tbsp.)	GARLIC-DILL DRESSING
1	(1)	small tomato, diced
1	(1)	clove of garlic, crushed
30 mL	(2 Tbsp.)	lemon juice
3 mL	(1/2 tsp.)	ground cumin
1 mL	(1/8 tsp.)	turmeric
10 mL	(2 tsp.)	fresh parsley, chopped
4	(4)	pita pockets or 8 slices of whole wheat bread

Method:

MASH garbanzos. **MIX** all ingredients together. **SERVE** with sliced tomato, onion, or cucumber.

```
Analysis: GARBANZO DELIGHT (4 servings)          Divided by: 4
          Wgt: 120 g (4.22 oz.)                  Water:    70%
```

Calories	147		Vitamin C	10.2 mg
Protein	7.98 g		Vitamin D	0 mcg
Carbohydrates	24.8 g		Vit E-Alpha E	.602 mg
Fat - Total	2.51 g		Vitamin K	mcg
Saturated Fat	.268 g		Biotin	mcg
Mono Fat	.542 g		Calcium	51.9 mg
Poly Fat	1.12 g		Copper	.323 mg
Cholesterol	0 mg		Iodine	mcg
Dietary Fibre	5.62 g		Iron	2.98 mg
Soluble Fibre	1.65 g		Magnesium	48.8 mg
Total Vit A	20.6 RE		Manganese	.897 mg
Thiamin-B1	.119 mg		Phosphorus	152 mg
Riboflavin-B2	.068 mg		Potassium	318 mg
Niacin-B3	.621 mg		Selenium	3.46 mcg
Niacin Equiv.	.61 mg		Sodium	31.6 mg
Vitamin B6	.149 mg		Zinc	1.35 mg
Vitamin B12	0 mcg		Complex Carbs	16.7 g
Folate	147 mcg		Sugars	2.35 g
Pantothenic	.309 mg		Water	83.3 g

CALORIE BREAKDOWN		FAT		EXCHANGES	
Protein	21%	*Saturated :	1.6%	Bread	1.45
Carbohydrates	65%	Mono Unsat:	3.2%	Lean Meat	.41
Fat-Total *	15%	Poly Unsat:	6.6%	Fruit	.031
				Vegetables	.192

GARBANZO SPREAD (makes 1 cup)

250 mL	(1 cup)	cooked garbanzos, drained and blended (save juice)
60 mL	(1/4 cup)	roasted pimento
60 mL	(1/4 cup)	finely chopped green onion
60 mL	(1/4 cup)	finely chopped sweet green pepper
60 mL	(1/4 cup)	finely sliced celery
5 mL	(1 tsp.)	parsley flakes
3 mL	(1/2 tsp.)	flake food yeast
3 mL	(1/2 tsp.)	basil
1 mL	(1/4 tsp.)	garlic powder

Method:

BLEND the garbanzos and pimento until smooth. REMOVE from blender and STIR in remaining ingredients. If mixture is too thick to spread easily ADD some of the liquid from the garbanzos. (USE as a sandwich spread or in pita bread with lettuce.)

```
Analysis: GARBANZO SPREAD (T)                   Divided by: 8
          Wgt: 36.9 g (1.3 oz.)                 Water:     74%
```

Calories	38.5	Vitamin C	9.13	mg
Protein	2.11 g	Vitamin D	0	mcg
Carbohydrates	6.71 g	Vit E-Alpha E	.151	mg
Fat - Total	.575 g	Vitamin K		mcg
Saturated Fat	.062 g	Biotin		mcg
Mono Fat	.123 g	Calcium	18.2	mg
Poly Fat	.257 g	Copper	.083	mg
Cholesterol	0 mg	Iodine		mcg
Dietary Fibre	1.7 g	Iron	.904	mg
Soluble Fibre	.437 g	Magnesium	12.5	mg
Total Vit A	22.4 RE	Manganese	.238	mg
Thiamin-B1	.06 mg	Phosphorus	42.8	mg
Riboflavin-B2	.033 mg	Potassium	105	mg
Niacin-B3	.293 mg	Selenium	.971	mcg
Niacin Equiv.	.201 mg	Sodium	6.43	mg
Vitamin B6	.079 mg	Zinc	.36	mg
Vitamin B12	0 mcg	Complex Carbs	4.45	g
Folate	46.4 mcg	Sugars	.486	g
Pantothenic	.104 mg	Water	27.2	g

CALORIE BREAKDOWN		FAT		EXCHANGES	
Protein	21%	*Saturated :	1.4%	Bread	.359
Carbohydrates	66%	Mono Unsat:	2.7%	Lean Meat	.103
Fat-Total *	13%	Poly Unsat:	5.7%	Vegetables	.152

KETCHUP (1 1/3 cups)

156 mL	(5 1/2 oz.)	tomato paste
15 mL	(1 Tbsp.)	fresh lemon juice
15 mL	(1 Tbsp.)	brown sugar **or** date butter
5 mL	(1 tsp.)	onion powder
3 mL	(1/2 tsp.)	garlic powder
3 mL	(1/2 tsp.)	salt
125 mL	(1/2 cup)	water

Method:

MIX all ingredients together with a spoon. **REFRIGERATE**, covered. (This will keep about a week in the refrigerator.) **SERVE** in place of regular ketchup.

```
-------------------------------------------------------------------
| Analysis: KETCHUP                             Divided by: 10     |
|           Wgt: 36.5 g (1.29 oz.)              Water:      82%    |
-------------------------------------------------------------------
```

Calories	20.6		Vitamin C	8.12 mg
Protein	.747 g		Vitamin D	0 mcg
Carbohydrates	4.84 g		Vit E-Alpha E	.295 mg
Fat - Total	.174 g		Vitamin K	mcg
Saturated Fat	.027 g		Biotin	mcg
Mono Fat	.026 g		Calcium	8.22 mg
Poly Fat	.068 g		Copper	.11 mg
Cholesterol	0 mg		Iodine	mcg
Dietary Fibre	.907 g		Iron	.554 mg
Soluble Fibre	.191 g		Magnesium	10.2 mg
Total Vit A	43.3 RE		Manganese	.093 mg
Thiamin-B1	.031 mg		Phosphorus	15.9 mg
Riboflavin-B2	.035 mg		Potassium	179 mg
Niacin-B3	.604 mg		Selenium	.224 mcg
Niacin Equiv.	.571 mg		Sodium	246 mg
Vitamin B6	.102 mg		Zinc	.16 mg
Vitamin B12	0 mcg		Complex Carbs	2.28 g
Folate	4.79 mcg		Sugars	.693 g
Pantothenic	.164 mg		Water	29.9 g

CALORIE BREAKDOWN		FAT		EXCHANGES	
Protein	12%	*Saturated :	1 %	Fruit	.146
Carbohydrates	81%	Mono Unsat:	1 %	Vegetables	.267
Fat-Total *	7%	Poly Unsat:	2.5%		

LENTIL PATE (makes about 3 cups)

250 mL	(1 cup)	cooked lentils
60 mL	(1/4 cup)	pecans or pecan meal
500 mL	(2 cups)	frozen green beans (cooked)
250 mL	(1 cup)	chopped onions, steamed until soft
1	(1)	large garlic clove, steamed with onions
15 mL	(1 Tbsp.)	soy sauce
5 mL	(1 tsp.)	chicken-style seasoning

Method:

WHIZ all ingredients in blender or food processor. MIX well and REFRIGERATE to blend in flavours. SERVE on crackers as hors d'oeuvres or in pita bread.

```
-----------------------------------------------------------------------
| Analysis:  LENTIL PATE                    Divided by: 16            |
|            Wgt: 52.5 g (1.85 oz.)         Water:       82%          |
-----------------------------------------------------------------------
```

Calories	39.2		Vitamin C	2.94 mg
Protein	1.79 g		Vitamin D	0 mcg
Carbohydrates	5.86 g		Vit E-Alpha E	.116 mg
Fat - Total	1.25 g		Vitamin K	mcg
Saturated Fat	.109 g		Biotin	mcg
Mono Fat	.725 g		Calcium	15.1 mg
Poly Fat	.329 g		Copper	.076 mg
Cholesterol	0 mg		Iodine	mcg
Dietary Fibre	1.59 g		Iron	.656 mg
Soluble Fibre	.606 g		Magnesium	12.6 mg
Total Vit A	9.29 RE		Manganese	.235 mg
Thiamin-B1	.053 mg		Phosphorus	39.3 mg
Riboflavin-B2	.029 mg		Potassium	105 mg
Niacin-B3	.285 mg		Selenium	1.16 mcg
Niacin Equiv.	.285 mg		Sodium	67.3 mg
Vitamin B6	.062 mg		Zinc	.398 mg
Vitamin B12	0 mcg		Complex Carbs	2.1 g
Folate	28.3 mcg		Sugars	2.03 g
Pantothenic	.143 mg		Water	43.1 g

CALORIE BREAKDOWN		FAT		EXCHANGES	
Protein	17%	* Saturated :	2.3%	Bread	.12
Carbohydrates	56%	Mono Unsat:	15.6%	Lean Meat	.077
Fat-Total *	27%	Poly Unsat:	7.1%	Fruit	.02
				Vegetables	.5
				Fat	.203

MARINARA SAUCE (makes about 3 1/4 cups)

796 mL	(28 oz can)	peeled Italian plum tomatoes
180 mL	(6 oz can)	tomato paste
5 mL	(1 tsp.)	olive oil
20 mL	(4 tsp.)	finely minced garlic
7 mL	(1 1/4 tsp.)	crumbled oregano
		salt (to taste or as allowed)
75 mL	(1/3 cup)	minced fresh parsley

Method:
PUREE the tomatoes in a blender or food processor. In a medium saucepan, HEAT the oil briefly, ADD garlic, stirring it for 15 seconds (do not let it brown) ADD pureed tomatoes, tomato paste, oregano, and salt. BRING the sauce to a boil, REDUCE heat, and SIMMER the sauce for 20 minutes. REMOVE from heat, and stir in the parsley.

```
Analysis: MARINARA SAUCE (12 SERVINGS)        Divided by: 12
          Wgt: 89.7 g (3.17 oz.)              Water:      89%
```

Calories	33.6		Vitamin C	20 mg
Protein	1.4 g		Vitamin D	0 mcg
Carbohydrates	6.6 g		Vit E-Alpha E	.615 mg
Fat - Total	.722 g		Vitamin K	mcg
Saturated Fat	.103 g		Biotin	mcg
Mono Fat	.33 g		Calcium	30.5 mg
Poly Fat	.173 g		Copper	.181 mg
Cholesterol	0 mg		Iodine	mcg
Dietary Fibre	1.79 g		Iron	1.1 mg
Soluble Fibre	.611 g		Magnesium	18.3 mg
Total Vit A	92.2 RE		Manganese	.2 mg
Thiamin-B1	.061 mg		Phosphorus	28.9 mg
Riboflavin-B2	.055 mg		Potassium	323 mg
Niacin-B3	1.08 mg		Selenium	.664 mcg
Niacin Equiv.	1.08 mg		Sodium	333 mg
Vitamin B6	.138 mg		Zinc	.28 mg
Vitamin B12	0 mcg		Complex Carbs	2.38 g
Folate	11.7 mcg		Sugars	2.43 g
Pantothenic	.252 mg		Water	79.8 g

CALORIE BREAKDOWN		FAT		EXCHANGES	
Protein	15%	* Saturated:	2.4%	Fruit	.125
Carbohydrates	69%	Mono Unsat:	7.7%	Vegetables	.858
Fat-Total *	17%	Poly Unsat:	4%	Fat	.073

SALSA, TOMATO SAUCE, (makes about 2 3/4 cups)

60 mL	(1/4 cup)	minced onion
1	(1)	clove of garlic, minced
15 mL	(1 Tbsp.)	olive oil
60 mL	(1/4 cup)	shredded raw carrot
250 mL	(1 cup)	minced celery
60 mL	(1/4 cup)	minced fresh sweet basil
		salt to taste
379 mL	(13 oz can)	tomato paste
400 mL	(1 2/3 cups)	water

Method:

    SAUTE onion and garlic in the oil until golden brown. **ADD** carrot, celery, basil, and salt. **CONTINUE** cooking until vegetables are wilted. **ADD** tomato paste and water and **SIMMER** for 45 minutes until tasty and thick. **SERVE** over your favourite cooked pasta.

```
Analysis: SALSA (8 SERVINGS)                     Divided by: 8
          Wgt: 123 g (4.32 oz.)                  Water:      87%
```

Calories	60.3		Vitamin C	21.4 mg
Protein	2 g		Vitamin D	0 mcg
Carbohydrates	10.2 g		Vit E-Alpha E	1.05 mg
Fat - Total	2.14 g		Vitamin K	mcg
Saturated Fat	.295 g		Biotin	mcg
Mono Fat	1.31 g		Calcium	27.8 mg
Poly Fat	.333 g		Copper	.291 mg
Cholesterol	0 mg		Iodine	mcg
Dietary Fibre	2.46 g		Iron	1.52 mg
Soluble Fibre	.578 g		Magnesium	27.8 mg
Total Vit A	217 RE		Manganese	.292 mg
Thiamin-B1	.085 mg		Phosphorus	44.6 mg
Riboflavin-B2	.099 mg		Potassium	499 mg
Niacin-B3	1.59 mg		Selenium	.806 mcg
Niacin Equiv.	1.59 mg		Sodium	446 mg
Vitamin B6	.205 mg		Zinc	.437 mg
Vitamin B12	0 mcg		Complex Carbs	5.88 g
Folate	16.8 mcg		Sugars	1.81 g
Pantothenic	.392 mg		Water	107 g

CALORIE BREAKDOWN		FAT		EXCHANGES	
Protein	12%	*Saturated :	3.9%	Fruit	.352
Carbohydrates	60%	Mono Unsat:	17.4%	Vegetables	.911
Fat-Total *	28%	Poly Unsat:	4.4%	Fat	.327

SPLIT PEA PUREE (6 half-cup servings)

500 mL	(2 cups)	yellow split peas
1 L	(4 cups)	water
250 mL	(1 cup)	chopped onion
1	(1)	clove of garlic, minced
7 mL	(1 1/2 tsp.)	salt
15 mL	(1 Tbsp.)	olive oil
1	(1)	lemon, cut into 6 wedges

Method:

WASH peas well and PLACE in a heavy-based saucepan. COVER with cold water and BRING to the boil. SKIM off froth. ADD chopped onion. COVER and SIMMER gently without stirring for 2 hours until very soft. STIR in salt and LADLE puree into deep plates. POUR 1/2 teaspoon olive oil on each serving. SERVE with lemon wedges. Crusty bread, finely chopped onion, sliced tomato and cucumber make a good accompaniment. It can also be served in pita bread with the above vegetables. (This is a favourite Greek dish, particularly during Lent.)

```
------------------------------------------------------------------
| Analysis: SPLIT PEA PUREE (12 x 1/4 cup)     Divided by: 12     |
|           Wgt: 132 g (4.66 oz.)              Water:      75%     |
------------------------------------------------------------------
```

Calories	129	Vitamin C	4.08	mg
Protein	8.31 g	Vitamin D	0	mcg
Carbohydrates	21.4 g	Vit E-Alpha E	.545	mg
Fat - Total	1.54 g	Vitamin K		mcg
Saturated Fat	.211 g	Biotin		mcg
Mono Fat	.911 g	Calcium	24.3	mg
Poly Fat	.272 g	Copper	.301	mg
Cholesterol	0 mg	Iodine		mcg
Dietary Fibre	5 g	Iron	1.53	mg
Soluble Fibre	1.68 g	Magnesium	40.6	mg
Total Vit A	5.08 RE	Manganese	.482	mg
Thiamin-B1	.246 mg	Phosphorus	126	mg
Riboflavin-B2	.075 mg	Potassium	351	mg
Niacin-B3	.975 mg	Selenium	9.88	mcg
Niacin Equiv.	.976 mg	Sodium	274	mg
Vitamin B6	.08 mg	Zinc	1.05	mg
Vitamin B12	0 mcg	Complex Carbs	12.6	g
Folate	93.1 mcg	Sugars	3.82	g
Pantothenic	.603 mg	Water	99.1	g

CALORIE BREAKDOWN		FAT	EXCHANGES	
Protein	25%	*Saturated : 1.4%	Bread	1.15
Carbohydrates	64%	Mono Unsat: 6.2%	Lean Meat	.41
Fat-Total *	10%	Poly Unsat: 1.8	Fruit	.056
			Vegetables	.167
			Fat	.218

TAHINI SAUCE (makes about 1 cup)

250 mL	(1 cup)	sesame seeds
125 mL	(1/2 cup)	water
3 mL	(1/2 tsp.)	salt (or to taste)
15 mL	(1 Tbsp.)	lemon juice (or to taste)

Method:

BLEND sesame seeds in food processor or blender until smooth. ADD remaining ingredients and BLEND until smooth. SERVE in pita with falafels and vegetables or on cooked vegetables.

```
-------------------------------------------------------------------------
| Analysis: TAHINI SAUCE                          Divided by: 16         |
|           Wgt: 17.9 g (.632 oz.)                Water:       49%       |
-------------------------------------------------------------------------
```

Calories	55.4		Vitamin C	.438 mg
Protein	2.48 g		Vitamin D	0 mcg
Carbohydrates	.964 g		Vit E-Alpha E	.235 mg
Fat - Total	5.14 g		Vitamin K	mcg
Saturated Fat	.719 g		Biotin	mcg
Mono Fat	1.94 g		Calcium	12.6 mg
Poly Fat	2.25 g		Copper	.138 mg
Cholesterol	0 mg		Iodine	mcg
Dietary Fibre	.647 g		Iron	.732 mg
Soluble Fibre	.001 g		Magnesium	32.7 mg
Total Vit A	.675 RE		Manganese	.135 mg
Thiamin-B1	.068 mg		Phosphorus	72.8 mg
Riboflavin-B2	.008 mg		Potassium	39.4 mg
Niacin-B3	.44 mg		Selenium	.757 mcg
Niacin Equiv.	.44 mg		Sodium	70.6 mg
Vitamin B6	.014 mg		Zinc	.972 mg
Vitamin B12	0 mcg		Complex Carbs	.134 g
Folate	9.12 mcg		Sugars	.183 g
Pantothenic	.065 mg		Water	8.72 g

CALORIE BREAKDOWN		FAT		EXCHANGES	
Protein	17%	*Saturated :	10.8%	Fruit	.004
Carbohydrates	6%	Mono Unsat:	29.1%	Fat	1.01
Fat-Total *	77%	Poly Unsat:	33.8%		

FOOD PROCESSING LEADS TO CALORIE CONCENTRATION

8 oz. potato	140 calories
8 oz. potato with sour cream and butter	420 calories
8 oz. potato made into hash browns	520 calories
8 oz. potato made into French fries	530 calories
8 oz. potato made into potato chips	870 calories
8 oz. potato made into "Pringles" potato chips	1,125 calories

SUGGESTED SEVEN DAY MENU:

	BREAKFAST	DINNER	SUPPER

D A Y 1	3/4 cup Spoon Size Shredded Wheat
	1 c Better than Milk (lite)
	1 pink grapefruit
	*1 sl BONNIE'S BREAD
	2 tsp Just Peanuts peanut butter
	*1 tsp BETTER BUTTER
		*1 c SAVORY LENTIL POTAGE
		3/4 c steamed broccoli
		1 large baked potato
		*1 Tbsp SUN-PIMENTO CHEESE
		*1 sl MULTIGRAIN BREAD
		1 c tossed green salad
		*1 Tbsp GARLIC-DILL
		    DRESSING
			*1 c QUINOA WITH SCRAMBLED
			    TOFU
			1/2 c green peas
			1/4 c cooked carrots
			*1 BANANA POPSICLE

D A Y 2	1/4 c Red River Cereal (dry)
	1/2 c Better than Milk
	1 Tbsp chopped dates
	1 banana
	2 sl MULTIGRAIN BREAD
	*2 Tbsp TOFU COTTAGE CHEESE
	*2 Tbsp STRAWBERRY-
	    PINEAPPLE JAM
		*1 1/2 C PUERTO RICAN RICE
		*1 c FIVE BEAN SALAD
		1 c Brussels sprouts
		1 c tossed green salad
		*1 Tbsp GARLIC-DILL
		    DRESSING
			*1 1/2 c NEWFOUNDLAND PEA
			    SOUP
			1 plain bagel
			*1 Tbsp SUNFLOWER-PIMENTO
			    CHEESE
			1 c seedless green grapes
			1 Tbsp whole almonds

D A Y 3	*1/2 c MALT GRANOLA 1 c Better than Milk 1 medium orange *2 sl BONNIE'S BREAD *2 Tbsp PINEAPPLE MARMALADE	*1 1/2 c SUPER SEA SHELL STEW 1/2 c green beans *15 CORN-OAT CRACKERS *1 c COLE SLAW	*1/2 c BREAKFAST FRUIT AND RICE 3 c air popped corn 1 medium Bartlett pear 2 Tbsp dry roasted unsalted peanuts 1/4 c dried apricots (cooked)

D A Y 4	1/2 cooked oat bran
	1 c Better than Milk
	*2 Tbsp STRAWBERRY-
	    PINEAPPLE JAM
	*2 sl MULTIGRAIN BREAD
	1 banana
	2 Tbsp whole almonds
		*2 BARLEY BALLS IN GRAVY
		1 c mashed potatoes
		1/2 c green beans
		1 c Romaine lettuce
		1 c zucchini
		*2 Tbsp GARLIC-DILL
		    DRESSING
			*1 1/3 c LIMA-TOMATO CASSEROLE
			1 sl rye bread
			*1 serving APPLE CRISP

D A Y 5	1/3 c rolled oats (dry)
	1 c Better than Milk
	*1/4 c PINEAPPLE MARMALADE
	*1 sl MULTIGRAIN BREAD
	*1 c BREAKFAST FRUIT AND
	    RICE
		*1 serving KASHA AND ONIONS
		*1 c HACIENDA CHILI BEANS
		*1/4 c BEET SALAD
		1 c cauliflower, cooked
			*1 serving "CHICKEN" NOODLE SOUP
			*8 CORN-OAT CRACKERS
			*1/4 c SUNFLOWER-PIMENTO
			    CHEESE
			*1/2 c RICE AMBROSIA

D A Y 6	1/4 c Red River Cereal (dry) 1 c Better than Milk 1 pink grapefruit *2 sl BONNIE'S BREAD *1 tsp BETTER BUTTER *1/4 c FRUIT MINCEMEAT 1 Tbsp Just Peanuts peanut butter	*1 serving TOFU FU YOUNG *1/2 c TABBULI 1 c cooked brown rice 1 c green peas 1/2 c cooked carrots	*1 c MILLET-VEGETABLE CHOWDER 1 c strawberries 2 brown rice cakes
D A Y 7	*1 c MILLET PUDDING 1 medium orange 1/2 cup mango slices 1 sl rye bread *3 Tbsp TOFU COTTAGE CHEESE	1 baked potato *1 c STROGANOFF *1 c COLE SLAW 1/2 c butternut squash	*1 sl BONNIE'S BREAD *1 tsp BETTER BUTTER *1 GORILLA MUNCHIE 1 c air popped corn 1 medium apple

*This recipe appears in this book.

EXPLANATION OF DATA:

The menus given in this section are **NOT** intended to be carefully followed. They were prepared as a result of the challenge of a group who thought it was impossible to get the recommended nutrients from a vegan diet. They were done to help people who have lactose intolerance etc. to be assured that it is possible to have a balanced diet without animal products. For 6 of the 7 days the protein content exceeded the Canadian Recommended Dietary Intake for a 130 pound 5'4" moderately active 40-year-old woman. Because protein needs are actually based on body weight, recommended protein may be different (usually less) than the 12% suggested in the dietary goals. The average for the 7 days was 55.8 g (120% of recommended allowances. Every day was short on calories, but that could easily be rectified by eating more of the items given, not by adding junk foods. As is, it could be a satisfactory weight-loss diet. Where there are blanks there is not an established recommended allowance. The only nutrient that is lacking is Vitamin B_{12} (See note on Vitamin B_{12} page 136) For most nutrients a wide enough margin is allowed that there is no reason to worry if you a little bit short on some. Note that the **CALCIUM** and **IRON** as well as protein exceed the recommended allowances. Another item worthy of note is that the fat averaged 15% of total calories which is closer to what many authorities are recommending rather than the 30% that the computer programme recommended, so although it appears that the fat intake is too low, it really is not.

The reason there seems to be far too much potassium and sodium is that they used minimum allowances as the amount needed for those two elements. A committee of the Food and Nutrition Board recommended that daily intake of sodium be about 2400 mg and potassium be about 2000 mg. In the nutrient breakdowns for each recipe and for the daily menus the Exchanges are for the benefit of those on a diabetic diet. The Canadian and American ways of calculating them vary slightly as follows:

American Exchange System	Canadian Choice System
1 Starch (bread)	1 Starch
1 Lean Meat	1 Protein
1 Medium Fat Meat	1 Protein and 1/2 Fat
1 High Fat Meat	1 Protein and 1 Fat
1 Vegetable	1/2 Fruits and Vegetable
(no Equivalent)	Extra Vegetables
1 Fruit	1 1/2 Fruits and Vegetables
1 Milk	2 Milk (Skim)
1 Fat	1 Fat

Source: American Diabetes Association, 1989
Prepared by: Debbie Towell R.P. Dt., Pediatric Diabetes Education Centre
Oshawa General Hospital,   June 1991

The recipe and menu analyses were done with the IBM compatible computer programme FOOD PROCESSOR PLUS   Phone: 503-585-6242
ESHA RESEARCH   Fax: 503-585-5543
Box 13028
Salem, OR 97309-1028

```
-----------------------------------------------------------------------
| Analysis: MENU DAY 1                    Wgt: 1767 g (62.3 oz.)       |
| % RNI:    AVERAGE LADY -                Water:         76%           |
|           40 yrs. old, 130 lb., 64", lightly active                 |
-----------------------------------------------------------------------
|   Amount        Item                                                |
-----------------------------------------------------------------------
```

Amount	Item
3/4 cup	Shredded Wheat Cereal-Small Biscuits
2 tbsp	BETTER THAN MILK-LT-DRY
1 each	Pink/Red Grapefruit
1 each	BONNIE'S BREAD
2 tsp	Chunky Peanut Butter-Unsalted
1 tsp	BETTER BUTTER (1/48 - 1 TSP SERVINGS)
1/2 cup	Applesauce-Unsweetened
1 cup	SAVORY LENTIL POTAGE
3/4 cup	Broccoli Pieces-Steamed
1/2 cup	Yellow Corn-Frozen-Boiled
1 each	Baked Potato w/Skin-Long
1 tbsp	SUNFLOWER-PIMENTO "CHEESE" .25 c serving
1 piece	MULTIGRAIN BREAD
1 cup	Tossed Green Salad
1 tbsp	GARLIC-DILL DRESSING
1 cup	QUINOA WITH SCRAMBLED TOFU
.5 cup	Green Peas-Frozen-Boiled
1/4 cup	Carrots-Raw Slices-Boiled
1 each	BANANA POPSICLES

Calories	1565	80%	Vitamin C	276 mg	921%
Protein	67.8 g	134%	Vitamin D	0 mcg	0%
Carbohydrates	282 g	100%	Vit E-Alpha E	7.58 mg	126%
Fat - Total	28.8 g	44%	Vitamin K	mcg	--
Saturated Fat	4.92 g	23%	Biotin	mcg	--
Mono Fat	8.99 g	41%	Calcium	982 mg	140%
Poly Fat	11.8 g	54%	Copper	2.89 mg	115%
Cholesterol	0 mg	0%	Iodine	mcg	%
Dietary Fibre	38.2 g	195%	Iron	29.4 mg	226%
Soluble Fibre	6.24 g	--	Magnesium	571 mg	285%
Total Vit A	1682 RE	210%	Manganese	5.05 mg	--
Thiamin-B1	1.81 mg	226%	Phosphorus	1293 mg	152%
Riboflavin-B2	1.24 mg	124%	Potassium	4233 mg	239%
Niacin-B3	19.4 mg	138%	Selenium	48.6 mcg	88%
Niacin Equiv.	12.5 mg	89%	Sodium	1552 mg	292%
Vitamin B6	2.9 mg	382%	Zinc	9.99 mg	111%
Vitamin B12	0 mcg	0%	Complex Carbs	86.3 g	--
Folate	546 mcg	299%	Sugars	45.5 g	--
Pantothenic	5.82 mg	83%	Water	1348 g	--

CALORIE BREAKDOWN		FAT		EXCHANGES	
Protein	16%	*Saturated :	2.7%	Bread	7.99
Carbohydrates	68%	Mono Unsat:	4.9%	Lean Meat	2.79
Fat-Total*	16%	Poly Unsat:	6.4	Fruit	3.24
		P : S (Poly/Sat. Fat)	2.4 : 1	Vegetables	2.59
		Potassium : Sodium	2.73 : 1	Milk	.25
		Calcium : Phosphorus	.759 : 1	Fat	.938

```
-------------------------------------------------------------------------
| MENU DAY 2                                                            |
-------------------------------------------------------------------------
| Amount           Item                                                 |
-------------------------------------------------------------------------
     1/4 cup        RED RIVER CEREAL (DRY MEASURE)
       1 tbsp       BETTER THAN MILK-LT-DRY
       1 tbsp       Dates-Chopped
       1 each       Banana
       2 piece      MULTIGRAIN BREAD
       2 tbsp       TOFU COTTAGE CHEESE (3 Tbsp servings)
       2 tbsp       STRAWBERRY-PINEAPPLE JAM
     1.5 cup        PUERTO RICAN RICE
       1 cup        FIVE BEAN SALAD
       1 cup        Brussels Sprouts-Cup Measure-Boiled
       1 cup        Tossed Green Salad
       1 tbsp       GARLIC-DILL DRESSING
     1.5 cup        NEWFOUNDLAND PEA SOUP
       1 each       Plain Bagel
       1 tbsp       SUNFLOWER-PIMENTO "CHEESE"
       1 cup        Thompson Seedless Grapes-Cup Measure
       1 tbsp       Dried Almonds-Whole
-------------------------------------------------------------------------
| Analysis:  MENU DAY 2                    Wgt: 1857 g (65.5 oz.)       |
| % RNI:     AVERAGE LADY -                Water:   78%                 |
-------------------------------------------------------------------------
```

Calories	1536	79%	Vitamin C	199	mg	663%
Protein	60.7 g	120%	Vitamin D	0	mcg	0%
Carbohydrates	297 g	105%	Vit E-Alpha E	8.99	mg	150%
Fat - Total	19.6 g	30%	Vitamin K		mcg	--
Saturated Fat	2.95 g	14%	Biotin		mcg	--
Mono Fat	7.67 g	35%	Calcium	698	mg	100%
Poly Fat	6.2 g	29%	Copper	2.28	mg	91%
Cholesterol	0 mg	0%	Iodine		mcg	%
Dietary Fibre	48 g	245%	Iron	19.6	mg	151%
Soluble Fibre	8.44 g	--	Magnesium	476	mg	238%
Total Vit A	1510 RE	189%	Manganese	4.62	mg	--
Thiamin-B1	2.39 mg	299%	Phosphorus	1102	mg	130%
Riboflavin-B2	1.32 mg	132%	Potassium	3819	mg	216%
Niacin-B3	16.8 mg	119%	Selenium	115	mcg	210%
Niacin Equiv.	11.3 mg	80%	Sodium	2870	mg	541%
Vitamin B6	2.41 mg	317%	Zinc	8.25	mg	92%
Vitamin B12	0 mcg	0%	Complex Carbs	96.4	g	--
Folate	686 mcg	376%	Sugars	77	g	--
Pantothenic	4.45 mg	64%	Water	1449	g	--

CALORIE BREAKDOWN		FAT		EXCHANGES	
Protein	15%	*Saturated:	1.7%	Bread	7.24
Carbohydrates	74%	Mono Unsat:	4.3%	Lean Meat	1.24
Fat-Total *	11%	Poly Unsat:	3.5%	Fruit	4.39
Alcohol	0%			Vegetables	5.47
				Milk	.125
				Fat	1.19

```
---------------------------------------------------------------------
| MENU DAY 3                                                         |
---------------------------------------------------------------------
| Amount          Item                                              |
---------------------------------------------------------------------
    1/2 cup        MALT GRANOLA
      2 tbsp       BETTER THAN MILK-LT-DRY
      1 each       Medium Orange
      2 each       BONNIE'S BREAD
      2 tbsp       PINEAPPLE MARMALADE (6 cups)
  1 1/2 cup        SUPER SEASHELL STEW
    1/2 cup        Green Snap/String Beans-Frozen-Boiled
     15 each       CORN-OAT CRACKERS
      1 each       COLE SLAW (1/4 RECIPE)
    1/4 cup        Dried Apricot Halves-Cooked
      3 cup        Air Popped Popcorn
      1 each       Medium Pear (Bartlett)
     .5 cup        BREAKFAST FRUIT AND RICE .5 cup servings
      2 tbsp       Dry Roasted Peanuts-Unsalted
```

```
---------------------------------------------------------------------
| Analysis:  MENU DAY 3               Wgt: 1482 g (52.3 oz.)        |
| % RNI:     AVERAGE LADY -           Water: 71%                    |
---------------------------------------------------------------------
```

Calories	1586	81%	Vitamin C	163	mg	543%
Protein	51.7 g	102%	Vitamin D	.03	mcg	1%
Carbohydrates	279 g	98%	Vit E-Alpha E	11.2	mg	187%
Fat - Total	36.9 g	57%	Vitamin K		mcg	--
Saturated Fat	6.89 g	32%	Biotin		mcg	--
Mono Fat	14.4 g	66%	Calcium	850	mg	121%
Poly Fat	11.8 g	54%	Copper	2.15	mg	86%
Cholesterol	0 mg	0%	Iodine		mcg	%
Dietary Fibre	41.8 g	214%	Iron	17.3	mg	133%
Soluble Fibre	8.88 g	--	Magnesium	473	mg	236%
Total Vit A	876 RE	110%	Manganese	4.93	mg	--
Thiamin-B1	1.83 mg	228%	Phosphorus	1103	mg	130%
Riboflavin-B2	.967 mg	97%	Potassium	2787	mg	158%
Niacin-B3	13.5 mg	96%	Selenium	85.8	mcg	156%
Niacin Equiv.	11 mg	78%	Sodium	2233	mg	421%
Vitamin B6	1.97 mg	259%	Zinc	9.38	mg	104%
Vitamin B12	.002 mcg	0%	Complex Carbs	80.1	g	--
Folate	384 mcg	210%	Sugars	82.4	g	--
Pantothenic	3.31 mg	47%	Water	1059	g	--

CALORIE BREAKDOWN		FAT		EXCHANGES	
Protein	12%	* Saturated	3.7%	Bread	6.09
Carbohydrates	67%	Mono Unsat:	7.9%	Lean Meat	1.22
Fat-Total *	20%	Poly Unsat:	6.4%	Fruit	5.59
				Vegetables	3.52
				Milk	.25
				Fat	2.75

```
-----------------------------------------------------------------------------
|    MENU DAY 4                                                              |
-----------------------------------------------------------------------------
|    Amount          Item                                                    |
-----------------------------------------------------------------------------
     1/2 cup         Oat Bran-Cooked
       2 tbsp        BETTER THAN MILK-LT-DRY
       2 tbsp        STRAWBERRY-PINEAPPLE JAM
       2 piece       MULTIGRAIN BREAD
       1 each        Banana
       2 tbsp        Blanched Almonds-Whole
       1 each        Baked Potato w/Skin-Long
       2 tsp         BETTER BUTTER (1/48 - 1 TSP SERVINGS)
     1/4 cup         Onion Gravy-Dry Mix + Water
       4 tbsp        BARLEY BALLS (46)
       1 cup         Mashed Potatoes
     1/2 cup         Green Snap/String Beans-Frozen-Boiled
       1 cup         Romaine Lettuce-Chopped
       1 cup         Zucchini Squash-Raw
       2 tbsp        GARLIC-DILL DRESSING
     1.3 cup         LIMA BEAN-TOMATO CASSEROLE
       2 piece       Rye Bread
       1 piece       APPLE CRISP
-----------------------------------------------------------------------------
| Analysis: MENU DAY 4                     Wgt: 1359 g (47.9 oz.)           |
| % RNI:    AVERAGE LADY -                 Water: 73%                        |
-----------------------------------------------------------------------------
```

Protein	50.7 g	100%	Vitamin D	.068 mcg	3%
Carbohydrates	267 g	94%	Vit E-Alpha E	5.59 mg	93%
Fat - Total	22.3 g	34%	Vitamin K		mcg	--
Saturated Fat	3.53 g	16%	Biotin		mcg	--
Mono Fat	10.2 g	47%	Calcium	863 mg	123%
Poly Fat	6.29 g	29%	Copper	2.45 mg	98%
Cholesterol	0 mg	0%	Iodine		mcg	%
Dietary Fibre	48.1 g	246%	Iron	18.2 mg	140%
Soluble Fibre	11.2 g	--	Magnesium	529 mg	265%
Total Vit A	293 RE	37%	Manganese	4.59 mg	--
Thiamin-B1	1.77 mg	221%	Phosphorus	1076 mg	127%
Riboflavin-B2	1.07 mg	107%	Potassium	4172 mg	236%
Niacin-B3	12.8 mg	91%	Selenium	64 mcg	116%
Niacin Equiv.	10.4 mg	74%	Sodium	1938 mg	365%
Vitamin B6	2.38 mg	313%	Zinc	7.55 mg	84%
Vitamin B12	.002 mcg	0%	Complex Carbs	96.8 g	--
Folate	518 mcg	283%	Sugars	46.5 g	--
Pantothenic	4.05 mg	58%	Water	998 g	--

CALORIE BREAKDOWN		FAT		EXCHANGES	
Protein	14%	* Saturated:	2.2%	Bread	8.63
Carbohydrate	73%	Mono Unsat:	6.3%	Lean Meat	.19
Fat-Total *	14%	Poly Unsat:	3.9%	Fruit	1.76
Alcohol	0%			Vegetables	3.58
				Milk	.25
				Fat	2.11

```
------------------------------------------------------------------------------
| MENU DAY 5                                                                 |
------------------------------------------------------------------------------
| Amount            Item                                                     |
------------------------------------------------------------------------------
        2 tbsp      BETTER THAN MILK-LT-DRY
      1/3 cup       Rolled Oats-Dry
      1/4 cup       PINEAPPLE MARMALADE (6 cups)
        1 piece     MULTIGRAIN BREAD
        1 cup       BREAKFAST FRUIT AND RICE .5 cup servings
        1 each      BASIC KASHA AND ONIONS
        1 cup       HACIENDA CHILI BEANS
      1/4 cup       BEET SALAD -2
        1 cup       Cauliflower-Cup Measure-Boiled
        1 each      "CHICKEN" NOODLE SOUP 1/12 OF RECIPE
        8 each      CORN-OAT CRACKERS
      1/4 cup       SUNFLOWER-PIMENTO "CHEESE" .25 c serving
       .5 cup       RICE AMBROSIA (1/8)
------------------------------------------------------------------------------
| Analysis:  MENU DAY 5                 Wgt: 1613 g (56.9 oz.)               |
| % RNI:     AVERAGE LADY -             Water:      78%                      |
------------------------------------------------------------------------------
```

Calories	1406		72%	Vitamin C	144 mg	479%
Protein	50.5 g		100%	Vitamin D	0 mcg	0%
Carbohydrates	260 g		92%	Vit E-Alpha E	6.78 mg	113%
Fat - Total	23.5 g		36%	Vitamin K	mcg	--
Saturated Fat	5.1 g		23%	Biotin	mcg	--
Mono Fat	7.73 g		36%	Calcium	846 mg	121%
Poly Fat	7.97 g		37%	Copper	1.96 mg	78%
Cholesterol	0 mg		0%	Iodine	mcg	%
Dietary Fibre	37 g		189%	Iron	18.7 mg	144%
Soluble Fibre	8.63 g		--	Magnesium	497 mg	248%
Total Vit A	1439 RE		180%	Manganese	6.18 mg	--
Thiamin-B1	2.09 mg		262%	Phosphorus	1071 mg	126%
Riboflavin-B2	.907 mg		91%	Potassium	2906 mg	164%
Niacin-B3	11.8 mg		84%	Selenium	68.4 mcg	124%
Niacin Equiv.	7.68 mg		55%	Sodium	1699 mg	320%
Vitamin B6	1.99 mg		262%	Zinc	7.5 mg	83%
Vitamin B12	0 mcg		0%	Complex Carbs	85.1 g	--
Folate	472 mcg		258%	Sugars	72.9 g	--
Pantothenic	4.16 mg		59%	Water	1257 g	--

CALORIE BREAKDOWN		FAT		EXCHANGES	
Protein	14%	* Saturated 3.2%		Bread	5.78
Carbohydrate	72%	Mono Unsat: 4.8%		Lean Meat	1.27
Fat-Total *	15%	Poly Unsat: 7.0%		Fruit	4.21
Alcohol	0%			Vegetables	5.52
				Milk	.25
				Fat	1.25

```
---------------------------------------------------------------------------
|   MENU DAY 6                                                            |
---------------------------------------------------------------------------
|   Amount         Item                                                   |
---------------------------------------------------------------------------
     1/4 cup       RED RIVER CEREAL (DRY MEASURE)
       2 tbsp      BETTER THAN MILK-LT-DRY
       1 each      Pink/Red Grapefruit
       2 each      BONNIE'S BREAD
       1 tsp       BETTER BUTTER (1/48 - 1 TSP SERVINGS)
     .25 cup       FRUIT MINCEMEAT
       1 tbsp      Natural Peanut Butter-Unsalted
       1 each      TOFU FU YOUNG (1/16)
      .5 cup       TABBULI
       1 cup       Long Grain Brown Rice-Cooked-Hot
       1 cup       Green Peas-Frozen-Boiled
      .5 cup       Carrots-Raw Slices-Boiled
       1 cup       MILLET-VEGETABLE CHOWDER
       1 cup       Fresh Strawberries-Slices-Cup
       2 each      Brown Rice Cake-Sesame Seed
---------------------------------------------------------------------------
|  Analysis:  MENU DAY 6                     Wgt:  1664 g (58.7 oz.)      |
|  % RNI:     AVERAGE LADY -                 Water:    76%                |
---------------------------------------------------------------------------
```

Calories	1400		72%	Vitamin C	262 mg	874%
Protein	47 g		93%	Vitamin D	0 mcg	0%
Carbohydrates	263 g		93%	Vit E-Alpha E	8.51 mg	142%
Fat - Total	24 g		37%	Vitamin K	mcg	--
Saturated Fat	3.32 g		15%	Biotin	mcg	--
Mono Fat	8.07 g		37%	Calcium	798 mg	114%
Poly Fat	9.63 g		44%	Copper	1.89 mg	76%
Cholesterol	0 mg		0%	Iodine	mcg	%
Dietary Fibre	38.3 g		196%	Iron	16.2 mg	124%
Soluble Fibre	6.37 g		--	Magnesium	431 mg	216%
Total Vit A	2291 RE		286%	Manganese	5.86 mg	--
Thiamin-B1	2.2 mg		275%	Phosphorus	1012 mg	119%
Riboflavin-B2	.967 mg		97%	Potassium	2570 mg	145%
Niacin-B3	17.5 mg		124%	Selenium	72.6 mcg	132%
Niacin Equiv.	13.3 mg		94%	Sodium	1529 mg	288%
Vitamin B6	2.4 mg		315%	Zinc	7.62 mg	85%
Vitamin B12	.001 mcg		0%	Complex Carbs	65.4 g	--
Folate	504 mcg		276%	Sugars	58 g	--
Pantothenic	4.51 mg		64%	Water	1268 g	--

CALORIE BREAKDOWN		FAT		EXCHANGES	
Protein	13%	* Saturated 2.1%		Bread	7.08
Carbohydrates	72%	Mono Unsat: 5%		Lean Meat	.75
Fat-Total *	15%	Poly Unsat: 6%		Fruit	4.16
Alcohol	0%			Vegetables	2.06
				Milk	.25
				Fat	1.59

```
-------------------------------------------------------------------------
|   MENU DAY 7                                                          |
-------------------------------------------------------------------------
|   Amount        Item                                                  |
-------------------------------------------------------------------------
      1 cup       MILLET PUDDING (2) 12 half-cup servings
      1 each      Medium Orange
      .5 cup      Mango Slices
      1 each      RYE BREAD (total recipe 58 slices)
      3 tbsp      TOFU COTTAGE CHEESE (3 Tbsp servings)
      1 each      Microwave Baked Potato w/Skin-Long
      1 cup       STROGANOFF (8 HALF-CUP SERVINGS)
      1 each      COLE SLAW (1/4 RECIPE)
      .5 cup      Butternut Squash-Baked Cubes
      1 each      BONNIE'S BREAD
      1 tsp       BETTER BUTTER (1/48 - 1 TSP SERVINGS)
      1 each      GORILLA MUNCHIES (EACH SERVING - 1/40)
      1 each      Medium Apple w/Peel
      1 cup       Air Popped Popcorn
-------------------------------------------------------------------------
| Analysis:  MENU DAY 7                  Wgt: 1766 g (62.3 oz.)         |
| % RNI: AVERAGE LADY -                  Water:    77%                  |
-------------------------------------------------------------------------
```

Calories	1512		77%	Vitamin C	209 mg	696%
Protein	61.9 g		122%	Vitamin D	.004 mcg	0%
Carbohydrates	272 g		96%	Vit E-Alpha E	8.72 mg	145%
Fat - Total	29 g		45%	Vitamin K	mcg	--
Saturated Fat	5.14 g		24%	Biotin	mcg	--
Mono Fat	7.53 g		35%	Calcium	570 mg	81%
Poly Fat	12.8 g		59%	Copper	2.5 mg	100%
Cholesterol	0 mg		0%	Iodine	mcg	%
Dietary Fibre	35 g		179%	Iron	23.2 mg	179%
Soluble Fibre	8.42 g		--	Magnesium	527 mg	263%
Total Vit A	1186 RE		148%	Manganese	5.14 mg	--
Thiamin-B1	2.09 mg		261%	Phosphorus	1229 mg	145%
Riboflavin-B2	1.16 mg		116%	Potassium	3642 mg	206%
Niacin-B3	17.1 mg		122%	Selenium	50.2 mcg	91%
Niacin Equiv.	13.8 mg		98%	Sodium	2370 mg	447%
Vitamin B6	2.61 mg		343%	Zinc	7.84 mg	87%
Vitamin B12	0 mcg		0%	Complex Carbs	129 g	--
Folate	471 mcg		258%	Sugars	86.3 g	--
Pantothenic	4.39 mg		63%	Water	1364 g	--

CALORIE BREAKDOWN		FAT		EXCHANGES	
Protein	16%	* Saturated:	2.9%	Bread	9.47
Carbohydrates	68%	Mono Unsat:	4.2%	Lean Meat	2.32
Fat-Total *	16%	Poly Unsat:	7.2%	Fruit	5.12
Alcohol	0%			Vegetables	3.57
				Milk	
				Fat	1.53

```
-----------------------------------------------------------------------
| Analysis: AVERAGE OF 7 DAYS' MENUS          Wgt.1644 g (58 oz.)      |
| % RNI:      AVERAGE LADY -                  Water:  76%              |
-----------------------------------------------------------------------
```

Calories	1485	76%	Vitamin C	193	mg	642%
Protein	55.8 g	110%	Vitamin D	.015	mcg	1%
Carbohydrates	274 g	97%	Vit E-Alpha E	8.17	mg	136%
Fat - Total	26.3 g	40%	Vitamin K		mcg	--
Saturated Fat	4.55 g	21%	Biotin		mcg	--
Mono Fat	9.24 g	42%	Calcium	801	mg	114%
Poly Fat	9.5 g	44%	Copper	2.3	mg	92%
Cholesterol	0 mg	0%	Iodine		mcg	%
Dietary Fibre	41 g	209%	Iron	20.4	mg	157%
Soluble Fibre	8.3 g	--	Magnesium	501	mg	250%
Total Vit A	1325 RE	166%	Manganese	5.19	mg	--
Thiamin-B1	2.02 mg	253%	Phosphorus	1126	mg	132%
Riboflavin-B2	1.09 mg	109%	Potassium	3446	mg	195%
Niacin-B3	15.5 mg	110%	Selenium	72.2	mcg	131%
Niacin Equiv.	11.4 mg	81%	Sodium	2175	mg	410%
Vitamin B6	2.38 mg	313%	Zinc	8.31	mg	92%
Vitamin B12	.001 mcg	0%	Complex Carbs	91.2	g	--
Folate	511 mcg	280%	Sugars	66.9	g	--
Pantothenic	4.38 mg	63%	Water	1249	g	--

CALORIE BREAKDOWN	FAT	EXCHANGES
Protein 14%	*Saturated : 2.6%	Bread 52.2 (7.46 per day)
Carbohydrates 70%	Mono Unsat: 5.3%	Lean Meat 9.59 (1.37 per day)
Fat-Total * 15%	Poly Unsat: 5.5%	Fruit 28.4 (4.06 per day)
	P : S (Poly/Sat Fat) 2.09 : 1	Vegetables 26.3 (3.76 per day)
	Potassium : Sodium 1.58 : 1	Milk 1.37 (.20 per day)
	Calcium : Phosphorus .711 : 1	Fat 11.3 (1.6 per day)

COMPARISON OF EGG, TOFU, AND GREEN PEAS

Nutrient	1 large egg (hard-cooked)	1/3 cup tofu	3/4 cup cooked green peas
Calories	82	121	86
Cholesterol (mg)	252	0	0
Fat (g)	6	7.33	less than 1
Protein (g)	6	13.3	6
Vitamin A (I.U.)	590	14.3 RE	645
Thiamine (mg)	0.04	.133	0.34
Riboflavin (mg)	0.14	.086	0.14
Niacin (mg)	trace	.32	2.8
Vitamin C (mg)	0	.168	24
Calcium (mg)	27	172	28
Iron (mg)	1.2	8.8	2.2
Phosphorus (mg)	103	159	118
Potassium (mg)	65	199	236

LEGUME COOKING GUIDE

KIND (1 cup)	WATER NEEDED	COOKING TIME	YIELD
Black Beans	3 cups	1 1/2 -2 hours	1 1/2 cups
Black-eyed Peas	2 1/2 cups	30 minutes	2 1/2 cups
Garbanzos (chickpeas)	4 cups	2 hours or more	2 1/2 cups
Kidney Beans	3 cups	about 2 hours	2 3/4 cups
Lentils (green) Don't Soak.	2 1/2 cups	30-45 minutes	2 1/2 cups
Lentils (red) Don't soak.	2 1/2 cups	7 minutes	2 cups
Lima Beans (large)	3 cups	about 1 hour	2 1/2 cups
Lima Beans (small)	2 1/2 cups	45 minutes	2 cups
Navy Beans (pea beans)	3 cups	1 1/2 to 2 hours	2 1/2 cups
Peas (split) Don't soak.	2 cups	30-40 minutes	2 1/2 cups
Pinto Beans	3 1/2 cups	1 1/2-2 hours	2 1/2 cups

GRAIN COOKING GUIDE

Grain 1 cup dry	Water	Cooking Times	Yield
Barley (Soak first)	3 cups	75 minutes	3 1/2 cups
Buckwheat (kasha)	2 cups	15-20 minutes	2 1/2 cups
Cornmeal	4 cups	25 minutes	3 cups
Millet	4 cups	40 minutes	4 cups
Quinoa	2 cups	15-20 minutes	4 cups
Rice (brown)	2 1/2 cups	25-45 minutes	3 cups
Whole Wheat (Soak first)	4 cups	6-8 hours	2 1/2 cups

TOFU:

What is it?

Tofu, a high protein, Oriental food, is a cheese made from soybeans. It is smooth, bland, and fragile, with a texture somewhat like firm custard. It is made by curdling the mild white "milk" of the soy bean. It is high in protein and low in calories, fats (by comparison with dairy cheese), and carbohydrates. Tofu is an economical source of protein and contains **NO** cholesterol.

How long will it keep?

It is usually water-packed in a sealed container and must be refrigerated. Fresh tofu may be kept over a week by changing the water every day. Tofu has been a protein staple in parts of Asia for over 2,000 years. It has become popular in N.A. only recently.

How can it be used?

Tofu can be prepared in a variety of main dishes, desserts, soups, salads, salad dressings, and dips for any meal. It has very little flavour and blends well with more flavourful foods.

Can you freeze it?

Yes, for some dishes it is preferable to freeze it because after freezing the texture is changed. It becomes more meaty and chewy than regular tofu and soaks up marinades and sauces more readily than the plain form.

Who should use it?

Anyone who has to cut down on or cut out cholesterol and those who cannot tolerate dairy products will find tofu an especially good addition to the food choices available. It is also a good choice for all who are health conscious. It should be remembered, however, that tofu is a very concentrated protein and so should be used in limited amounts.

KNOW YOUR CONDIMENTS:

Irritating, stimulating, harmful
cayenne pepper
chili powder
horse-radish
mustard
pepper (black or white)

Strongly aromatic, irritating
cloves
ginger
paprika (Hungarian)

Slightly irritating
allspice   cinnamon
anise   mace
cassia   nutmeg

Sweet Herbs, not irritating
basil	oregano
bay leaf	paprika (Spanish)
caraway seed	parsley
cardamon	peppermint
celery seed	saffron
chives	sage
cumin	savory
dill weed or seed	spearmint
fennel	tarragon
kitchen bouquet	thyme
marjoram	rosemary
mint	turmeric
onion powder	wintergreen

Ingredients of Mixed Spices

Poultry Seasoning	Curry, Foreign Type	Curry, American Type
allspice	black pepper	cinnamon
marjoram	cayenne pepper	cloves
nutmeg	cinnamon	coriander
sage	cloves	ginger
savory	nutmeg	mace
thyme		nutmeg
		pepper

ONION FAMILY:

Onions, garlic, leeks and shallots belong to the Allium family. There are over 120 different documented uses of the alliums.

Onions may provide mild protection against the growth of tumours, they may be natural anticlotting agents.

Recent studies have confirmed the value of garlic in reducing the risk of heart attacks and strokes. Garlic has been shown to lower both the total cholesterol and LDL cholesterol levels, raise HDL cholesterol levels, lower triglyceride levels as well as lower blood pressure levels. It appears that garlic is a dietary cancer-fighting substance and can reduce the incidence of certain spontaneously occurring tumours. It is reported to stimulate the immune system, enhance the activity of lymphocytes and macrophages to destroy cancer cells. Various studies show that garlic can reduce the development of bladder, skin, stomach, and colon cancer.

(Taken from *Nutrition for the Nineties* by Winston J Craig, Ph.D., R.D., Golden Harvest Books, Eau Claire, MI.)

WHY IT IS BEST NOT TO USE VINEGAR:

1.   Vinegar destroys Vitamin C. Vitamin C losses were studied in individual cabbage salads containing vinegar. (*Handbook No. 8*, U.S. Department of Agriculture.)

2.   Vinegar's acidity hinders digestion. Vinegar lengthens the time that vegetables remain in the stomach. By definition, vinegar is formed by the action of mycoderma aceti on an alcohol commonly obtained from fruit juices, wine, or other fermented liquids. Food and Drug regulations state that the word vinegar without an adjective means vinegar made from apple juice.

        In addition to the 4% acetic acid which by law it must contain, vinegar has in a variety of other substances such as malic acids, alcohol, glycerin, sugars, esters such as ethyl acetate, pentosans, artificial colouring, and inorganic salts. (Bronson: *Nutrition and Food Chemistry*.)

3.   Vinegar is naturally or artificially flavoured acetic acid, commonly ranging between 4 and 6 %. Mild gastritis or enteritis may be caused by it. (*The Journal of the American Medical Association.*)

4.   Ellen White wrote, "The salads are prepared with oil and vinegar, fermentation takes place in the stomach, and the food does not digest, but decays or putrefies; as a consequence, the blood is not nourished, but becomes filled with impurities, and liver and kidney difficulties appear." (*Counsels on Diet and Foods*, page 345.)

5.   Virtually all vinegar sold for food purposes is composed of waste products from bacterial decomposition of apples. Therefore, most vinegar is apple cider vinegar, and one brand is not better than another. The principle chemical giving the sour flavour is acetic acid.
        This acid, a waste product in the human body, is an irritant to both the stomach and the nerves. It is one of the three commonest dietary causes of gastritis in the United States today, along with aspirin and alcohol. All products made with vinegar are injurious to the stomach lining, causing loss of the protective mucus and changes in the lining cells "nuclear enlargement and coarsening of the chromatin and increased mitosis". (*Nutrition for Vegetarians*, page 81.)

6.   Many people drink apple cider vinegar straight from the bottle because they believe it has certain health-giving properties, but none of these claims has ever been substantiated.

        Vinegar is high in acid, and if you have some reason to want to balance your system with acidity this may be of value. But as far as curing arthritis goes, well that's more a matter of faith than fact. (*Discovering Natural Foods*, page 230.)

ADAPTING FAVOURITE FAMILY RECIPES TO MAKE THEM MORE HEALTHFUL

Although I don't believe in evolution as to the origin of the world, I have to admit that many of the recipes in this collection have "evolved". In some cases only minor changes in family favourites were made as I became more health conscious. Such changes as steaming vegetables rather than sauteeing them cuts down the total fat considerably. Another change that is easy to make is to cut down on the quantity of nuts and seeds. In some cases harmless seasonings have been substituted for the black pepper and other harmful spices. Dates have been used instead of sugar in many instances. Since there has been some question recently on the wisdom of using mushrooms because they are a fungus, eggplant has been used in many cases where mushrooms were used formerly. An example of a recipe that has been changed radically and still remains a favourite is "Oriental Vermicelli Delight" on page 34. The original recipe called for a quarter cup of margarine to saute the vegetables. Now they are steamed. It called for five large scrambled eggs. The cubed frozen tofu takes the place of the eggs. Eggplant has been substituted for the mushrooms called for in the original.

This revised recipe was used in a recent class and one of the class members could hardly wait to get back to class to report the following story. She has a very picky nineteen-year-old daughter who didn't even want to try the things her mother was making that she had learned in class. One day they went shopping and bought some chicken breasts that the daughter wanted to make some special dish. A day or so later her mother made the Oriental Vermicelli Delight. The daughter ate some and said, "Mother, you didn't use all those chicken breasts in this did you? I had something else planned." The mother answered, "No, there are still some left." The daughter was sure there was chicken in the casserole and she ate it every time her mother served it.

In the Breakfast Sweets section some of the recipes there could very easily be used for dessert for other meals. The cook's imagination is the only limiting factor. However, it is suggested that the recipe be carefully followed the first time it is used before making revisions.

If someone in the family does not like a certain kind of bean another kind can be substituted in many instances to it make it acceptable to that person.

If someone is allergic to nuts, sunflower seeds can often be substituted.

There has been an attempt in this book to answer the questions most commonly asked by people who may or may not be vegetarians when they first come to our Healthy Choices classes. Those that are not answered on the bottom of pages are in the miscellaneous section at the back of the book and they all can be located by looking in the index.

* * * * * * * * * * * * * *

Anyone wishing to contact me for information or classes can do so by calling or writing me as follows:

(Miss) Leona R. Alderson　　　　　　　or if I am not available ther contact:
389 Townline Road North　　　　　　　　**The Ontario Conference Office of SDA**
Courtice, ON, Canada L1E 2J4　　　　　　**Box 520, Oshawa, ON Canada L1H 7M1**

Telephone: (905) 404-0412   **Telephone: (905) 571-1022**

MENU PLANNING:

With the vegetarian natural foods diet, menu planning is very easy. Just follow these few simple principles:

1.   Prepare your own "fast foods" by cooking up a good supply of (several different kinds of legumes (beans, lentils, split peas, etc.) and freeze.

2   Make up one or two easy spreads for bread and one or two salad dressings (enough to last for a week).

3.   Use a crockpot to prepare cereal for breakfast. Start it at night and the next morning your meal is almost ready. Just add fruits, whole grain bread, and a spread. Use fruit or non-dairy milk on the cereal.

4.   For the main meal prepare baked or boiled potatoes, or a pasta, a legume (from the "fast food" preparation), and a raw vegetable or salad. A cooked vegetable can also be added if desired. Be sure to use a variety of green and yellow vegetables throughout the week.

5.   Soup, fruit, and whole grain bread with spread, or sandwiches can be served for a lunch or light supper.

6.   It is most desirable to have a hearty breakfast, followed by the main meal, with a light meal to finish the day. Families with children in school and working parents can accomplish this by taking suitable lunches (see "Lunch Box Ideas"), or by serving the main meal for breakfast which can easily be done by using the crockpot to prepare one-dish meals such as soups, stews, bean dishes, etc. in place of cereal, and adding whole grain bread and a raw vegetable or salad to complete the meal.

7.   More complex dishes such as patties, loaves, waffles, pancakes, etc. can be used as time and energy permit.

8.   Left-overs can be used in soups, and stews and small amounts can be blended up in making gravy.

9.   Meals can be kept very simple and yet be very satisfying. Three or four items is ample if there is sufficient quantity. This also promotes better digestion.

CANADA'S FOOD GUIDE TO HEALTHY EATING

Different people need different amounts of food. The amount of food you need every day from the 4 food groups and other foods depends on your age, body size, activity level, whether you are male or female and if you are pregnant or breast-feeding. That's why the food guide gives a lower and higher number of servings for each food group. For example, young children can choose the lower number of servings, while male teen-agers can go to the higher number. Most other people can choose servings somewhere in between.

GRAIN PRODUCTS	VEGETABLES AND FRUIT
5-12 servings per day Choose whole grain and enriched more often One serving would be 1 slice of bread 3/4 cup of hot cereal 30 gm of cold cereal 1/2 pita 1/2 bagel 1/2 cup cooked rice or pasta	5-10 servings per day Choose dark green and orange vegetables and orange fruit often One serving would be 1 medium size vegetable or fruit 1/2 cup of fresh, frozen or canned vegetables or fruit 1 cup salad vegetables 1/2 cup of juice
MILK PRODUCTS	MEAT AND ALTERNATIVES
Choose lower fat milk products more often One serving would be 1 cup of milk 2 cheese slices 3" x 1" x 1" piece of cheese 3/4 cup yoghurt Children 4-9 . . . . 2-3 Youth 10-16 . . . . 3-4 Adults . . . . 2-4 Pregnant and breast-feeding women 3-4	2-3 servings per day Choose leaner meats, poultry, and fish, as well as dried peas, beans, and lentils more often. 50-100 grams of meat, fish or poultry 1-2 eggs 1/2-1 cup of beans 1/3 cup of tofu 2 Tbsp. of peanut butter

NOTE: Canada's Food Guide was planned for the average person who uses the animal products, but the nutrient breakdown for the pure vegetarian menus shows the nutrients can be obtained on a pure vegetarian menu of grains, fruits, vegetables, and nuts. (See page 222)

For a vegan guide see The New Four Food Groups by The Physicians Committee for Responsible Medicine, on page 91.

STEPS IN BECOMING A VEGETARIAN

1. Make the transition gradually, possibly over a period of several weeks.
   Start by planning one meatless day a week. Then progress to two meatless days, etc., until meat is eliminated. Many find it easier to eliminate red meat first, then chicken, fish, and finally eggs and dairy products.
2. Include a variety of fresh fruits and vegetables, whole grains and legumes, seeds and nuts in your diet from day to day.
3. Alternate a dark green leafy vegetable with a deep yellow vegetable in the daily diet. For total vegetarians, 1 cup of dark green leafy vegetables daily, such as broccoli or collards, and 2 tablespoons of sesame seeds.
4. Include a Vitamin B_{12} supplement, fortified soy milk, or fortified food yeast in the diet if you are eliminating all dairy products.
5. Provide Vitamin D by spending a few minutes in the sunlight daily.
6. Grated raw potatoes, wheat germ, rice polishings, soy flour, gluten flour, and food yeast may be used as binders and protein supplements in place of eggs.

IMPORTANCE OF BREAKFAST AND SUGGESTIONS:

Breakfast means **BREAK FAST**. If you think you have no time for breakfast part of the preparation can be done the night before. If you don't have an appetite for breakfast it is often because there is still supper in the stomach. It is the most important meal of the day because there have been more hours since the last meal and it is important to have "fuel" for the day's activities. For those who need to watch their weight it is better to eat more earlier in the day. The advice to "Eat breakfast like a King, lunch like a Prince and supper like a Pauper" is good. A good breakfast should provide at least 1/3 of the recommended amount of protein and 1/3 of the daily calories. Breakfast skippers are more accident prone, less efficient, and may have nervous tremors. Children are more likely to be discipline problems and have lower scholastic records. The Iowa Breakfast Study of several years ago on hundreds of school children showed that children who ate a good breakfast were better in the following ways: fewer headaches, less fatigue, better manual and mental dexterity and better behaviour.

Breakfast does not have to be traditional cereal, juice, and toast. In the Breakfast Sweets section of this book are several suggestions for variety in whole grain cereals, many of which can be made ahead and reheated in the morning. The more preparation that can be done the night before the more likely a family is to have a hearty breakfast. Setting the table the night before saves time in the morning. Use a crockpot to prepare cereal for breakfast. Start it at night and the next morning your meal is almost ready. Just add fruits, whole grain bread, and a spread. Use fruit or a non-dairy milk on the cereal.

There are no rules about what to include in breakfast as long as there are sufficient foods with satiety value. it is important to have complex carbohydrates, not empty calorie foods. Some families like to have their "dinner" in the morning. This may be especially helpful for those needing to lose weight.

LUNCH BOX IDEAS
A PACKED LUNCH SHOULD:
1. Be a substantial, balanced meal with a significant part of the day's calories.
2. Be carefully planned and prepared so that it is a pleasure to eat.
3. Be varied from day to day so it will be something to look forward to.
4. NOT include "junk" and empty calories.

GOOD PLANNING WILL HELP YOU TO MAKE NICE LUNCHES.
I. Plan all meals a week ahead, including lunches, and make definite plans to have needed lunch supplies on hand.
II. Good equipment will help you. Keep it all together:
    1. A good quality lunch box, chosen to fit your luncher's personality.
    2. Thermos bottle
    3. Assorted plastic containers with tight-fitting lids or little jars.
    4. Waxed paper, sandwich bags, plastic wrap, foil
III. Working ahead pays off.
    1. Lettuce, celery, carrots, radishes, should be washed and stored in the crisper in plastic bags or containers, ready to use.
    2. Some sandwiches can be made ahead and frozen.

SUGGESTED SANDWICH FILLINGS
I. Peanut butter--creamy or chunky goes nicely with any of the following:
    1. Finely chopped apples, dates, crushed pineapple, golden raisins or bananas sliced in at the time of eating.
    2. Sliced tomato and lettuce added at the last minute.
II. Chopped nuts combined with Garlic-Dill Dressing to hold them together go nicely with:
    1. Celery
    2. Olives
    3. Grated carrots

VARIETY IN SANDWICHES
Be adventurous with bread:
    1. Raisin bread, banana bread go nicely with any of the fruit combinations or peanut butter.
    2. Oatmeal bread, rye bread, pumpernickel, onion bread, sandwich buns are all welcome changes.
    3. Pita bread--used as a sandwich or ready to stuff with salad or sprouts.
    4. Use whole grain crackers with stews or fruit salads instead of sandwiches.

TO CARRY IN A THERMOS BOTTLE
    1. Vegetable stews
    2. All soups and hot beverages
    3. Creamed vegetable or casserole dish
    4. "Chili" beans or other beans
    5. Hot fruit sauce such as apple sauce

DON'T OVERLOOK THE OBVIOUS
    1. Fresh fruit--lots of it. (Include a sharp knife if needed)
    2. All fresh, canned, frozen and dried fruits
    3. Vegetable sticks

LUNCH BOX MENU SUGGESTIONS:

These meals are planned for those who prefer to eat their heavy meal at noon to avoid eating a heavy supper. They can be altered to fit the needs of school children.

1.   Hot pinto beans seasoned with canned tomatoes or plain (in thermos)
      Rice cakes plain or with peanut butter or almond butter
      Fresh oranges and-or bananas
      Haystack cookies or simple dessert

2.   Hot mixed vegetables - thickened with soy cream (in thermos)
      Sandwiches - sunflower-pimento cheese, etc.
      Raw vegetables with dip such as Garlic-dill dressing (page 112) on carrots, celery, cauliflower, broccoli
      Mixed nuts for dessert

3.   Hot corn tomato chowder-page 119 (in thermos)
      Fruit salad in small container
      Corn-oat crackers with spread (page 76)
      Tofu cottage cheese (page 196)
      Cookies

4.   Hot lima bean chowder-page 127 (in thermos)
      Oatburger with tomatoes and sprouts and hummus on whole wheat bread
      Fresh fruit
      Simple dessert if needed

5.   Split pea soup (in thermos)
      Whole wheat crackers with garbanzo (page 111)
      Mixed nuts
      Polynesian Bar (page 156)

6.   Barley and Pinto Bean Soup (in thermos) - page 115
      Whole wheat bread with sunflower-pimento cheese
      Carrot and celery sticks
      Olives

7.   Hot creamed peas (in thermos)
      Rye bread to spread the peas on
      Sliced cucumber and tomatoes
      Mixed nuts
      Apple prune cookies

A cheery note in the lunch box can be a pleasant surprise for the lunch-carriers especially if they have to eat alone.

For children: Add a surprise from time to time (a little note, a small box of raisins) Pre-cut fruit for easy eating. Use pretty serviettes often.

VEGETARIAN RESOURCE MATERIALS:

Pure Vegetarian:

Beltz, Muriel, *Cooking with Natural Foods,* ($18.70), Black Hills Health and Education Center, Box 1, Hermosa, SD 57744, (highly recommended, has % of fat, protein, and carbohydrate in each recipe, also theropeutic recipes).

Beltz, Muriel, *Cooking with Natural Foods II,* ($18.70), Black Hills Health and Education Center, Box 1, Hermosa, SD 57744 (no refined fat or refined sugar, no cholesterol. Lists foods high in fibre, vitamins, and minerals).

Hullquist, Eriann and Timothy *Nutrition Workshop Guide,* TEACH Services, Inc., Donivan Rd, Route 1, Box 182, Brushton, New York 12916.

Lawson, Gloria, *Caring Kitchens,* ($12.95) Donivan Rd, Route 1, Box 182, Brushton, New York 12916 (uses some oil and sugar).

Nutrition Books

Barnard, Neal, M.D. *Food For Life,* Harmony Book, 201 East 50th Street, New York, New York 10022 (1993)

Beltz, Melvin, M.D. *Wellness to Fitness,* ($20.45) Black Hills Health and Education Center, Box 19, Hermosa, SD 57744 (20 chapters on various wellness topics with emphasis on nutrition).

Craig, Winston J., *Nutrition for the Nineties,* Golden Harvest Books, Eua Claire, MI, 49111, 1982 (excellent information, no index, good bibliography).

Diehl, Hans, *To Your Health,* ($13.25), The Quiet Hour, 630 Brookside Avenue, Redlands, CA 92373.

McDougall, John, M.D. *The McDougall Plan,* New Century Publishers, Inc.,1983.

McDougall, John, M.D. *McDougall's Medicine,* New Century Publishers, Inc., 220 Old New Brunswick Rd., Piscataway, NJ 08854, 1985.

Oski, Frank A., M.D., *Don't Drink Your Milk,* ISBN 0-945383-34-7, TEACH Services, Inc., Donivan Road, Route 1, Box 182, Brushton, NY 12916.

Pennington, Jean A. T., *Bowes and Church's Food Values of Portions Commonly Used, 15th Edition*, Harper and Rowe, New York, 1989.

Sorenson, Marc, ED.D. *Mega Health*, ISBN:0-87346-1002, Marc Sorenson, National Institute of Fitness 1992.

White, Ellen G., *Counsels on Diet and Food*, Review and Herald, (1938) A compilation of nutrition information written over a period of many years - each entry dated. Up-to date science verifies the concepts presented, much of it over a century ago.

White, Ellen G., *The Ministry of Healing*, Pacific Press Publishing Association, (1905) A general & health book with fairly extensive nutrition information.

CHECK UP ON YOUR EATING HABITS -

Be sure to check after several weeks to note improvement.

Score
Now

After
Several
Weeks

___ 1. I eat two or three regular meals a day, including breakfast -- nothing between meals.
       (10 points) . . . . _____

___ 2. I eat at least one serving of dark green or yellow vegetables every day.
       (5 points) . . . . _____

___ 3. I eat at least one large serving of food rich in Vitamin C every day.
       (5 points) . . . . _____

___ 4. I eat at least two servings of fruit each day.
       (5 points) . . . . _____

___ 5. I eat at least one raw vegetable each day.
       (5 points) . . . . _____

___ 6. I eat at least two other vegetables each day.
       (5 points) . . . . _____

___ 7. I eat a high-protein food each day such as soybeans, other legumes, tofu,
        or a prepared vegetable protein food.
       (10 points) . . . . _____

___ 8. I eat at least one food known to have calcium, such as lentils, garbanzos,
        or broccoli.
       (5 points) . . . . _____

___ 9. I eat whole grain or near whole grain in some form every day.
       (10 points --all whole grain) . . . .
       (5 points half whole grain) . . . . _____

___10. I eat only a small amount of sweets (no more than 6 teaspoons including what
        is in foods, for the entire day and that only at the close of meals.
       (10 points) . . . . _____

___11. I use only a small amount of fat, and that oil rather than hard fat.
       (5 points) . . . . _____

___12. My vegetables are cooked in as little water as possible and as quickly as
        possible.
       (5 points) . . . . _____

___13. I drink at least 8 cups of water daily.
       (5 points) . . . . _____

___14. I drink fruit juices, in limited amounts, rather than soft drinks.
       (5 points) . . . . _____

___15. I do not drink tea, coffee, or cola drinks containing caffeine.
       (5 points) . . . . _____

___16. I maintain a good emotional attitude at mealtime.
       (5 points) . . . . _____

       Excellent score . . . . 100 points   Fair score. . . . . .75 points
       Good score   . . . . 90 points   Poor score. . . . . 74 or below

ENTREES

Other books by TEACH Services, Inc.

Absolutely Vegetarian *Lorine Tadej* . . . . $ 8.95
A complete guide to maintaining a strict vegetarian lifestyle. A way to reach your ideal weight and maintain it, as long as you live.

Adam's Table *Reggi Burnett*. . . . . $ 8.95
A cookbook to help the user obtain optimum healthier and happier lifestyle through changes in their cooking style. Originated from Adam's Table Restaurant in Albuquerque, NM.

Angel At My Side *Bob Hoyt* . . . . $ 8.95
The author, a pastor, Bible worker, and Literature evangelists, tells of his experiences with angels, dogs, guns, horses, floods, skunks, life threatening hazards, and a heart-wrenching deathbed vigil.

The Antichrist 666 *William Josiah Sutton* . . . . $ 8.95
Positive proof for Bible Believing People: Who the beast is; Who his image is; What the mark of the beast is; How to count the number of the beast. Edited by Roy Allan Anderson, D.D.

The Anti-Christ Exposed *Dan Jarrard* . . . . $ 5.95
A biblical and historical study of the counterfeit religious system which is against God and His people.

The Art of Massage *J. H. Kellogg* $12.95
A practical manual for the student, the nurse and the practitioner.

Aunt Joanne's Plays *Joanne Johnson* . . . . $ 9.95
This collection gives alternative Christmas themes to work with rather than just the regular Joseph and Mary or Wise Men themes.

Aunt Joanne's Skits *Joanne Johnson*. . . . . $ 9.95
A collection of skits that children can act out, training them to not only hear, but see the results of Biblical morals.

Caring Kitchen Recipes *Gloria Lawson* $12.95
Specializes in recipes for better health that features: whole grains, vegetarian, dairy-free and nourishing dessert recipes.

The Celtic Church in Britain *Leslie Hardinge* . . . . $ 8.95
This is an authoritative study of the beliefs and practice of the Celtic Church which at the same time holds much interest for the non-specialist, containing as it does fascinating descriptions of the life of the early Celtic Christians in their monastic walled villages modelled on the Old Testament cities of refuge. Their clergy were permitted to be married and women were allowed to exercise the highest ecclesiastical function. Their elaborate penitential discipline was based on Old Testament compensatory regulations. Obedience to the Scriptures led them to establish a remarkable theocracy based on the laws of the Pentateuch and including the keeping of the Seventh-day Sabbath.

Children's Bible Lessons   *Bessie White* . . . . $ 3.95

These seven Children's Bible Lessons are prepared for use during Evangelistic Meetings, Bible seminars, Vacation Bible Schools, or at the Church's discretion.

Don't Drink Your Milk   *Frank Oski, MD* . . . . $ 7.95

Dr. Oski, the head of Pediatrics at Johns Hopkins University School of Medicine, gives the frightening new medical facts about the world's most overrated nutrient.

Earthly Life of Jesus   *Ken LeBrun* $19.95

Biblical accounts of each event in Christ's earthly life carefully arranged together from the KJV Bible. Words of Jesus in red with full index.

The Elijah People   *Ken LeBrun* . . . . $ 1.00

Those who, in the spirit and power of Elijah, take part in this final work of reform, will be those who, like Elijah, will be taken to heaven seeing death. Let us be among them.

Fire Bell in the Night   *Ralph Moss* . . . . $ 5.95

News items and stories from both the secular press and from religious newspapers, along with journals and articles by secular and religious authors will be linked with Bible prophecy to reveal a most startling scenario in just the last few years, and to lay a case to expose an undreamed of enemy who is rapidly winning the confidence of most of this world's inhabitants.

From Eden to Eden   *J. H. Waggoner* . . . . $ 9.95

A most interesting study of the more important historic and prophetic portions of the Scriptures.

God's DNA for Pure Religion   *Ernest H. J. Steed* . . . . $ 5.95

This book presents a key formula to measure truth and error, the genuine or the counterfeit, so essential in today's world of confusion.

Gospel In Creation   *E. J. Waggoner* . . . . $ 6.95

This book directs our wandering gaze to the open pages of God's created works as the expression of the gospel, the power of God to save from sin. Facsimile Reprint.

Happy Home Farm   *Reinhold R. Bietz* . . . . $ 6.95

A biography about life with Mom and Dad Bietz and their devotion and caring relationship with their nine children.

Healing By God's Natural Methods   *Al. Wolfsen* . . . . $ 4.95

Al. Wolfsen has taught hundreds of sick people how to use only simple, non-poisonous remedies.

Healthful Living   *Ellen G. White* $10.95

Wherever this book has been received, it has been recognized as a veritable storehouse of seed thoughts relating to the great practical themes with which it deals. Facsimile Reprint.

Holy Spirit Seminar   *Harold Penninger* . . . . $ 7.95

A collection of Holy Spirit Seminars for study, inspiration, etc.

Hoofbeats in Time   *W. G. Moore* . . . . $ 6.95

The title is an allusion to one of the 4 major prophecies of Revelation—*the Four Horsemen of Apocalypse*. These horsemen hold fascinating predictions concerning the world we live in, events both in the past and the future to come.

Hydrotherapy—Simple Treatments *Thomas/Dail* .... $ 8.95
   Help your body overcome common diseases using hydrotherapy and simple home treatments.

The Illuminati 666 *William Josiah Sutton* .... $ 8.95
   Find out about the Illuminati, its startling history, and how powerful it has become. Includes
   a study of the origins of false religions, and the forms they are taking today. Introduction by
   Roy Allan Anderson, D.D.

In Heavenly Places Now! *Richard Parent* .... $ 5.95
   A devotional study of the sanctuary service which seeks to focus our attention on our High
   Priest, Jesus Christ, who ever lives to make intercession for us.

Incredible Edibles *Eriann Hullquist* .... $ 7.95
   Some "health" meals taste bland, some are hard to make, others require strange or hard to find
   ingredients. Eriann has developed a simple method of meal preparation where each recipe
   looks good and tastes great.

Judgment?? Whose Judgment? *Robert Frazier* .... $ 6.95
   Is God really on trial and being judged? This book explores this question and others.

The Justified Walk *Frank Phillips* .... $ 8.95
   Before you can rightly tackle a problem, you must first be able to clearly understand its nature.
   Before you can discuss it with others, you must first clearly define your terms. In this book
   Elder Phillips makes clear how the plan of salvation works in our daily lives. Faith, Grace,
   Sin, Justification, Sanctification and Righteousness are made real and tangible.

Lessons On Faith *Jones & Waggoner* .... $ 6.95
   This is a compilation of articles and sermons given in the 1890's by Jones and Waggoner on
   Righteousness By Faith.

Let the Holy Spirit Speak *Garrie Fraser Williams* .... $ 4.95
   A remarkable new book that is not just a study guide but a unique resource of Bible study
   methods and small group information.

Living Fountains or Broken Cisterns *E. A. Sutherland* $12.95
   This book tells how we should set up our education systems to follow the heavenly blueprint.
   The goal is to have the best Christian schools in the world.

Nutrition Workshop Guide *Eriann Hullquist* .... 10 for $ 9.95
   Chock full of nutritional recipes, as well as lots of helpful nutritional tips for special situations,
   such as road trips, fast foods, etc.

Place of Herbs in Rational Therapy *D. E. Robinson* .... $ .90
   Quotations relative to the use of herbs in therapy from D. E. Robinson, who was the secretary
   to Mrs. White.

Power of Prayer *E. G. White* .... $ 7.95
   Prayer is our connection with God—our strength, our bridge to heaven! As we pray, the Holy
   Spirit Himself unites in our petitions and "maketh intercession for us." We are not alone in
   our battle of life; all heaven is on our side!

Preparation For Translation   *Milton Crane* . . . . $ 7.95
> This book is about YOUR preparation for translation. It is about YOUR plans to live without
> a mediator after probation closes. It is about God's plans for YOUR overcoming temptation
> NOW in anticipation of those events. It is about His plans for the renewing of YOUR mind
> through the final atonement ministry of Jesus. *English and Spanish editions.*

Principles To Live By   *Mel Rees* . . . . $ 4.95
> Dominion calls for individual decision and action—therefore, God gave man guiding princi-
> ples to live by.

Protect Your Family Against AIDS   *J. & M. Wehr* . . . . $ 7.95
> This book provides a detailed program used by those who have experienced good success
> against this deadly virus.

Quick-n-Easy Natural Recipes   *Lorrie Knutsen* . . . . $ 2.95
> Every recipe has five or fewer ingredients and most take only minutes to prepare. Now you
> can enjoy simple, natural recipes without the drudgery!

Returning Back To Eden   *Betty-Ann Peters* . . . . $ 9.95
> These recipes have been taste-tested by the world-wide travelers that have visited the Back to
> Eden Restaurant & Bakery in Minocqua, WI.

Right of the People   *A. T. Jones* $11.95
> This work, first printed in 1895, showed the relation that should exist between the church and
> state at the present time, as proved by Holy Writ and the historical evidence of twenty-five
> centuries

Rural Economy   *Ken LeBrun* . . . . $ 2.50
> "All that God's Word commands, we are to obey. All that it promises, we may claim. The life
> which it enjoins is the life that, through its power, we are to live."—Education, p. 188, 189.

The Sanctuary and the 2300 Days   *J. N. Andrews* . . . . $ 4.95
> What happened in 1844? Is there an Investigative judgment? This book will answer your
> questions in regard to these and many more controversies. Facsimile Reprint.

Simple Remedies for the Home   *Dail & Thomas* $11.95
> This book is intended to teach instructors in simple remedies and treatments that can be used
> in the home.

Sin Shall Not Have Dominion Over You   Charles Fitch . . . . $ 6.95
> Fitch clarifies his position on sanctification and holiness by answering three questions: 1) Has
> God made provisions to save His people from their sins? 2) If so, can Christians avail
> themselves of it in this life? and 3) In what way may this provision become available? He uses
> the Bible as his only source to answer these questions.

Spurious Books of the Bible   *Gar Baybrook* . . . . $ 9.95
> Compare the so-called Lost Books of the Bible with proven Scripture. Most have flagrant
> errors, some are tainted with pagan beliefs, while others are quite subtle in their claims.

Steps To Christ Study Guide   *Gail Bremner* . . . . $ 2.95
> This study guide is designed to encourage the youth, and the young at heart, to understand and
> experience more fully a living relationship with Jesus.

Story of Daniel the Prophet   *S. N. Haskell* $11.95

    This book especially applicable to our day: points out the immediate future and in its simplicity will attract many who might not be inclined to read deep, argumentative works. Facsimile Reprint.

Story of the Seer of Patmos   *S. N. Haskell* $12.95

    The Book of Revelation pronounces a blessing upon everyone who reads it or hears it. This books gives the historic SDA view. Facsimile Reprint.

Stress: Taming the Tyrant   *Richard Neil* . . . . $ 8.95

    Stress is an inevitable part of our 20th century lifestyle. Under the proper circumstances stress can be uplifting as well as depressing. It can either help us grow our hasten or death. Find out how to control, manage and modify stress.

Studies in Daniel and Revelation   *Kraid Ashbaugh* . . . . $ 4.95

    A convenient handbook containing paraphrases of EG White's comments after each verse in the books of Daniel & Revelation.

Studies in the Book of Hebrews   *E. J. Waggoner* . . . . $ 6.95

    A series of studies given at the General Conference of 1897. The Bible studies that Elder Waggoner gave each day, are presented as live and full of hope for each Bible student today.

Subtle Challenge to God's Authority   *Milton Crane* . . . . $ 5.50

    Satan's deceptions are many and subtle. He has concentrated his attack on God's authority.

Such A Cloud of Witnesses   *Milton Crane* . . . . $ 1.95

    You are called to be a witness for or against the government of God. Will your testimony help God or aid His enemy?

375 Meatless Recipes–CENTURY 21   *Ethel Nelson, MD* . . . . $ 7.95

    This book will help you learn how to feed your family in such a way that they will enjoy eating the foods that nutritionists tell us are an absolute must if we are going to make it into the twenty-first century.

The Truth About Sunday Laws   *Susan Johnson* . . . . $ 1.95

    Comparing Sunday laws in Fiji and Puerto Rico and Constantine's first Sunday laws.

Truth Triumphant   *B. G. Wilkinson* $12.95

    The history of God's true Church from Ireland, to the Waldenses, the struggle to preserve the Bible and the pure doctrine of the apostles is disclosed. Facsimile Reprint.

Understanding the Body Organs   *Celeste Lee* . . . . $ 7.95

    Simply and concisely explains how the body organs function and how they relate to one another. Also includes the eight laws of health, explaining each one and sharing many benefits that will be derived from following the entire plan.

Victory and Self-Mastery   *J. N. Tindall* . . . . $ 5.95

    How Christ maintained a sinless character in a fallen, sinful, human nature. Facsimile Reprint.

Warning in Daniel 12   *Marian Berry* $14.95

    A study of the twelfth chapter of Daniel. It is warning we shall all need to understand before the end of time.

Who Killed Candida? *Vicki Glassburn* $17.95

> Although diet is an important part of getting well, even the best food and supplements are undermined if you continue to unknowingly support yeast growth! The author will show you how making simple lifestyle choices can actually STOP THE YEAST SUPPORT CYCLE that other Candida programs do not address.

Whole Foods For Whole People *Lucy Fuller* $10.95

> Whole Foods For Whole People is not just a cookbook, but a manual to teach people how they can live a longer, healthier lifestyle by using the natural resources which surround us.

To order any of the above titles, see your local bookstore.

However, if you are unable to locate any title,
call 518/358-3652.